REFORM IN TSARIST RUSSIA

NEIL B. WEISSMAN

REFORM IN TSARIST RUSSIA

THE STATE BUREAUCRACY AND

LOCAL GOVERNMENT, 1900–1914

Rutgers University Press
New Brunswick, New Jersey

Publication of this book has been aided by a grant from the
National Endowment for the Humanities.

Library of Congress Cataloging in Publication Data

Weissman, Neil B.
    Reform in Tsarist Russia.

    Bibliography: p.
    Includes index.
    1. Local government—Soviet Union. 2. Soviet Union—
Politics and government—1894-1917. I. Title.
JS6061.W44   320.8′0947   81-1049
ISBN 0-8135-0926-2   AACR2

To my wife Joanne

my daughter Sarah

my teacher Douglas K. Reading

CONTENTS

CONTENTS

ACKNOWLEDGMENTS

This work reflects the contributions of many colleagues and friends. I would like to thank the Danforth Foundation, the International Research and Exchanges Board, the Fulbright-Hayes Program, the Department of History at Princeton University, and Dickinson College for funding parts of my work. Many archivists and librarians have assisted in the collection of materials, including the staffs of the Central State Historical Archive in Leningrad, the Princeton University Library, and the Dickinson College Library, and Lev Magerovsky of the Archive of Russian and East European History and Culture at Columbia University. Professors James H. Billington, Jerome Blum, E. D. Chermenskii, Arno Mayer, S. Frederick Starr, George L. Yaney, and Stephen Weinberger have contributed in a variety of different ways ranging from specific criticism of earlier drafts of this study and archival direction to general questioning of my view of history. I owe a special debt to Cyril E. Black, who not only provided constructive advice but also was wise enough to force a struggling graduate student to stand on his own two feet. Gladys Cashman has my particular gratitude for her uncanny ability to produce accurate typescript from illegible rough drafts and for her unfailing optimism and encouragement. Willa Speiser contributed a careful and intelligent editorial review of the manuscript. Herbert Mann and the staff of Rutgers University Press demonstrated a professionalism and sensitivity to Russian history that made this author's first experience with a publisher a thoroughly positive one.

Three others made contributions that were sometimes indirect, but all the more important for that reason. Douglas K. Reading, my first Russian history teacher, gave me an excitement for the study of the past that I continue to carry with me in my research and in the classroom. My wife Joanne made constructive criticism of style and substance in seemingly endless trial drafts of this work. Together with our daughter Sarah she bore the brunt of the sacrifices and absences imposed by the project. The dedication of this book to them is a small indication of my gratitude and affection.

RUSSIAN TERMS

chinovnik	civil servant
desiatina	2.7 acres
desiatskii	tener (village policeman)
gorodovoi	patrolman
gradonachal'nik	city chief
guberniia	province
gubernskii sovet	provincial council
gubernskoe pravlenie	provincial board
gubernskoe prisutstvie	provincial bureau
ispravnik	police chief
mir	commune
pisar'	clerk
poselok	settlement
predvoditel' dvorianstva	gentry marshal
sel'skoe obshchestvo	village community
skhod	assembly
soslovie	estate, corporation
sotskii	hundreder (village policeman)
Sovet po delam mestnago khoziaistva	Council on Local Affairs
stanovoi pristav	constable
starosta	elder
starshina	headman
strazha	guard
strazhnik	guardsman
uezd	district
uezd nachal'nik	district commander
uprava	board
uriadnik	sergeant
zemskii nachal'nik	land captain

REFORM IN TSARIST RUSSIA

INTRODUCTION

It has been a commonplace to associate Tsarist Russia, particularly in its last decades, with conservatism and even stagnation. Yet at that very time, and largely at the instigation of its own autocratic government, the empire was beginning a period of rapid and fundamental change. State-sponsored industrialization combined with other forces, including the impact of Western ideas and war, to initiate a transformation of Russian social, political, and economic life. While this transformation had many ramifications, one of its most immediate results was to create a political crisis for the government. The empire's rulers were compelled to alter traditional policies and institutions to meet new conditions—in a word, to reform.

The tsarist government's efforts to manage change through reform, efforts both shared and contested by the parties and factions of the politically active public, were interrupted prematurely by the outbreak of war in 1914. As a result, the capacity of tsarist society for evolutionary change has become the subject of sustained historical controversy. In the Soviet Union discussion has focused around the ability of tsarist absolutism "to accomplish the objective tasks of the bourgeois revolution."[1] In the West argument continues between those "optimists" who see prewar Russia as avoiding social upheaval through gradual reform and "pessimists" who maintain that the accumulating obstacles to peaceful evolution were insurmountable.[2] Yet despite the intensity of the debate, the precise nature of the reform process in the last decades of the pre-Revolutionary period remains unclear. This work is an attempt to examine the tsarist political system's potential for innovation through a case study of the single issue of local government.

The importance of local administrative reform for the regime should be obvious. No society can function without at least a minimum of governance, and as social change accelerates, this minimum grows apace. In a sense the requirements of political modernization are threefold. First, government must be sufficiently centralized. The national authorities must be able to enlist the loyalty of the mass of the populace by at least partially overcoming narrow particularist interests. Simultaneously. however, the state must also

[3]

develop effective institutions on the local level. Centralization must be matched by appropriate decentralization of administrative authority and activity. Finally, and perhaps most important, the political system must provide avenues for popular participation. Methods must be found to mobilize the citizenry for active involvement in administrative affairs and to bring various elements of the populace together for constructive cooperation.

By 1900 the tsarist government had clearly completed the first of these tasks. Over the course of the preceding century various ministries had emerged as effective instruments of central power, and tsarist autocracy had established itself as an all but exclusive focal point of political activity. Yet perhaps as a result of its very success in centralization, the tsarist state lagged seriously in the other areas. The administrative apparatus in the provinces was weakly developed, and the populace was largely denied a decisive role. There existed a wide, unbridged gap between the educated classes and the worker-peasant mass. Although this state of affairs had been acceptable earlier, by the beginning of the twentieth century it was no longer so. Industrialization and urbanization placed unprecedented demands on government. Similarly, the continuing stagnation of agriculture necessitated the creation of institutions able to undertake a program of agrarian renewal. Moreover, the educated public was increasingly shaking off its traditional passivity and vocally insisting upon a larger role in decision making. In order to meet these challenges, the local administrative system required substantive reform.

While effective administration in the provinces was, therefore, of central concern to Tsarist Russia from a functional viewpoint, there was a further, more pressing, reason for its consideration. As the problem of participation suggests, local government was not merely a technical question but a highly political one. Count Sergei Iu. Witte, a leading imperial bureaucrat, once commented, "He who is the ruler in a country must also be master of its administration."[3] One might well reverse the point and argue that he who controls a nation's administration will also be its ruler. Tsarist officials and the citizenry were well aware of this and consequently debated the issues of local governance with great vigor. Although attention also focused heavily on agrarian reform and a national constitution, the question of administration at the grass roots remained a burning one throughout the late history of the tsarist regime. Indeed, in addressing this particular concern, both government leaders and spokesmen for the educated public made more explicit than in any other context their views on the nature and future of Russian society. They clearly articulated their basic beliefs about such fundamental questions as the nature of political authority, the role of the citizen in government, and the mutual relations that ought to exist among the empire's social groups or classes. In this sense, one can argue that while local administrative reform was but one of many problems debated in the late tsarist period, it is among the most revealing. It serves as a barometer for measuring the broad philosophies of the empire's various groups and their relative strength in the political struggle.

When viewed through the lens of local reform, much of the prewar political process comes into clearer focus. Traditionally, for example, opposition to change in the old regime has been described largely in terms of the activity of the tsar, Nicholas II, and his court camarilla. Yet as discussion of rural governance indicates, the defense of the existing order had broad support among the gentry estate. More importantly, the struggle for local reform indicates the crucial role of the state bureaucracy in Imperial Russia. There has been a growing recognition of late of the centrality of tsarist officialdom. In the Soviet Union historians have introduced the concepts of *absolutism* and *Bonapartism* in a major attempt to adapt Marxist-Leninist analysis to deal with this group. In this interpretation a temporary equilibrium between feudal and bourgeois classes, or camps, allowed the state and its servitors to achieve a certain freedom of action politically. As A. Ia. Avrekh, the most outspoken supporter of this approach, has put it, the state bureaucracy can "maneuver" (*lavirovat'*) between the dominant social classes.[4] Some recent Western students of the tsarist polity have adopted an opposite perspective.[5] Here, government leaders are seen increasingly as almost independent directors or managers of Russian social development. Consciously or not, they serve as the largely disinterested, apolitical "modernizers" of Russian society.

Each of these approaches is instructive but also seriously flawed. In the Soviet case there remains a continuing inclination to define the state bureaucracy in class terms, to force perception of the state into traditional class molds. In the modernization perspective, on the other hand, the central authorities are all but divorced from their surroundings, standing above conflicting particular interests. What is required is neither a reduction of the state bureaucracy to dependence upon outside social groups nor its complete emancipation. Rather a determination must be made of its place within the political process as a separate force, yet one continually interacting and contending with others. The debate over local reform provides a useful tool for making just such a determination.

Admittedly, the present study is limited in several respects. Geographically, it is generally restricted to the European core of the Russian Empire. Within this core the focus is primarily on rural affairs, a reflection of the overwhelmingly agrarian orientation of most reformers in and out of the government. Ideologically, the study emphasizes the nonrevolutionary public, those who sought to work within the broad context of the existing order, not to overthrow it. Finally, commentary concentrates on those social groups who took an active part in the debate itself. The masses of peasants and workers, except as they were represented by their elected delegates, do not play a central role. These limitations sacrifice much in breadth and detail, but they do make it possible to deal more squarely with what was a central issue for the old regime, the ways in which Tsarist Russia's social and political elites responded to the challenge of change.

CHAPTER I

TSARIST LOCAL GOVERNMENT
IN A NEW CENTURY

One of the most frequently repeated generalizations about tsarist government is that it was highly centralized. The history of the Russian Empire is commonly described in terms of an autocratic state directing or controlling nearly every aspect of national development. As the liberal politician and historian P. N. Miliukov put it, the tsarist government represented "a state stronger than society." At the same time, however, students of Russian administration have been quick to point out its superficiality, the degree to which the state's institutional structure failed to reach the local level. In the words of one official commission of the 1880s reporting on the problems of provincial administration, "In the place of real authority there remains only its weak spectre."[1]

These contradictory observations are both correct. The tsarist state did claim and, in fact, exert autocratic control over the empire.[2] Yet simultaneously it failed to develop effective local administrative machinery. The key to the resolution of this paradox is in understanding that through much of the nineteenth century Russian society was essentially traditional. The basically agricultural, stable nature of the existing order meant that relatively few claims were made on the state's administrative apparatus. In addition there existed in the provinces traditional institutions, especially those of the empire's estates, upon which the power of the autocratic government could rest.

By the start of the twentieth century this was no longer the case. As Russia began the transition from a traditional agrarian order to a modern industrialized one, pressing new demands were made of its administration. The various estate institutions that had previously provided a local foundation for central authority eroded. And the processes of change galvanized groups among the populace to demand more active participation in government for themselves. The resulting vigorous debate over administrative reform involved not merely technicalities of local governance but the basic principles of the tsarist polity.

[7]

REFORM IN TSARIST RUSSIA

The Elements of Local Administration

Any attempt to evaluate the impact of change on tsarist local government requires a prior understanding of the system as it existed in the closing decades of the 1800s. This is no easy task, for above all, Russian administration in the provinces was characterized by diversity and complexity. Tsarist administration, wrote the French visitor Leroy-Beaulieu, "resembles those castles, constructed at different epochs, where the most discordant styles are seen side by side, or else those houses, built piecemeal and at intervals, which never have either the unity or convenience of dwellings erected on one plan and at one rush."[3] A. D. Gradovskii, perhaps the leading nineteenth-century student of Russian law, frankly admitted, "We lack a unified system of local governance, [one] imbued in all its parts with a single idea."[4]

This absence of unity or common principle makes it possible to analyze the administrative system in a number of ways. Perhaps the most fruitful of these was suggested by Gradovskii himself: tsarist local government can be seen as a synthesis of three elements—state bureaucracy, estate institutions, and organs of self-government.

Unquestionably, the dominant role in tsarist politics, both in the capital and in the provinces, was played by the state bureaucracy.[5] There has been a tendency in the West to minimize the role of the state and its agents, to view the state apparatus as a passive instrument employed by various social forces. Yet as one scholar has argued recently, the state must be treated as "an autonomous structure—a structure with a logic and interests of its own not necessarily equivalent to, or fused with, the interests of the dominant class in society or the full set of member groups in the polity."[6] This is certainly so in regard to Tsarist Russia, where the consciousness of the state as a separate entity was highly developed, particularly among its own servitors. The independent outlook of the state bureaucracy had many sources. In their social origins and economic position tsarist officials were a relatively distinct group, often dependent upon their posts for status and material support. One Soviet scholar has calculated that more than two-thirds of the 3,420 ranking state servants in 1901 held no lands or estates smaller than one hundred desiatinas.[7] Moreover, their legal power rested not upon the consent of the governed but upon the autocratic authority of the tsar. Most significantly, however, the inclination toward a distinctive bureaucratic perspective was rooted in the functional role of the civil service. Tsarist administrators performed tasks that could easily be seen as representing the vital interests of society as a whole. In international relations, the state bureaucracy was the primary vehicle for the development of imperial power, as a means both of national defense and of projecting Russian influence and prestige outward. Domestically, the officials were responsible for maintaining order and for the general well-being of the populace. Whether the central authorities actually did rule in the objective interests of all classes is, of course, open to serious question. The important point is their subjective conviction that they did so.

The particular self-perception of many tsarist bureaucrats is evident in numerous writings of the period. One excellent example is Minister of Finance Witte's *Autocracy and the Zemstvo* [Samoderzhavie i zemstvo], a treatise written in 1899 on the nature of political authority in Russia.[8] Witte based his comments on an affirmation of the concept of autocracy, the unlimited power of the monarch. The tsarist autocracy, he argued, standing as it did above the narrow interests of individual citizens, groups, and classes, ruled benevolently and paternally for the general good of all. Yet it is clear from Witte's comments that the primary instrument of autocratic authority, its "necessary center" as he put it, was not the ruler himself, but rather the state bureaucracy.[9]

Although Witte did not overlook the shortcomings of the bureaucracy, his text was a strong defense of the civil service. The empire's officials were characterized as an "aristocracy of labor and education." Their accomplishments included the unification of the Russian state, its elevation to the status of a great power, and—in a reference to Peter the Great's policy of westernization—the introduction of its very culture. Indeed, so expansive was Witte's conception of the paternalistic relationship of the state bureaucracy to Russian society that the most suitable parallel he found was the colonial rule of the British civil service over India.[10]

Witte's view of the tsarist bureaucracy, characterized appropriately by one colleague as a form of "rational absolutism," was of course idealized. The author himself acknowledged that officials were guilty of a multitude of sins, including venality, formalism, and arbitrary behavior. And he was certainly aware of other major shortcomings, which he chose not to admit in his treatise. Witte realized that the state bureaucracy hardly ruled with complete impartiality, but rather displayed considerable favoritism toward the interests of the gentry estate. Nevertheless, his remarks were accurate in two senses. They represented the degree to which leading administrators perceived themselves as guardians of Russian society. And they were correct in emphasizing the state and its officials as the prime movers, whether for better or worse, in Russian history. Even the bureaucracy's staunchest opponents were prepared to concede this point. As one later put it, although the tsarist government ruled oppressively, it did represent "the only organized force" in Russian society.[11]

The power and authority of the civil service was naturally most evident in Saint Petersburg, where it literally monopolized the operation of the central government. But its voice was also theoretically paramount on the local level. Each of the ministries and major departments in the capital possessed subordinate agents in the provinces, and through them the central authorities exerted their influence over local affairs.[12] Of the ministerial hierarchies, the most extensive and the most representative of the potential power of the state bureaucracy beyond the capital was unquestionably that of the Ministry of Internal Affairs (*Ministerstvo vnutrennikh del,* or MVD for short).

The MVD's sphere of activity was broad—overall concern for the internal "well-being and security" of the empire, as one leading administrative expert put it.[13] This wide jurisdiction was reflected in the responsibilities and prerogatives of the ministry's chief local subordinate, the provincial governor. As part of the MVD hierarchy, the provincial governor and his staff were held accountable for such matters as public order, law enforcement, health and sanitation, food relief in time of famine, fire protection, economic prosperity, and local charities and welfare. Furthermore, beyond his capacity as MVD subordinate the governor was considered to be the local agent of the tsar's personal authority. As such he bore generalized responsibility for supervising the entire local governmental system, including not only the organs of all ministries but also the estate institutions and self-government.[14]

The provinces were subdivided into districts (*uezdy*); in each the MVD was represented by the police chief (*ispravnik*). As a police official his jurisdiction was less expansive than that of his superior, the governor, but it was still wide enough. Unlike many Western states, where the police function had been specialized to focus on law and order, the Russian Empire retained the earlier and broader understanding of policemen as general administrators. Hence, while the central concern of the police chief was law enforcement, his duties also included such tasks as participation in tax collection, statistical work, registration of internal passports, rehabilitation of prostitutes, temperance measures, and care of orphans.[15] In performing these functions the chief relied primarily upon the aid of his subordinates, the bottom links in the MVD chain of command, the constables (*stanovye pristavy*) and police sergeants (*uriadniki*).

Even this cursory description of the MVD local hierarchy reveals an essential point. Although its sphere of authority embraced almost every aspect of local life, the interior ministry lacked the means to realize this authority. There was a marked discrepancy between the MVD's formal power and its institutionalization. In the countryside, for example, the ministry depended upon a force of 1,582 constables and 6,874 sergeants to administer a rural population that by the close of the century was approaching ninety million.[16] What was true of the MVD applied even more emphatically to the other branches of the central government. The Ministry of Finance was alone among them in having effective subordinates below the district level.

Indeed, the aggregate size of the tsarist state bureaucracy was not impressive, particularly given the huge expanse of the empire it ruled. Whereas the number of administrators per thousand inhabitants was 17.6 in France and 12.6 in Germany, in Russia it was 6.2.[17] Similarly, the resources devoted by the government to its own machinery were far below European standards. One expert estimated, for instance, that Russian per capita expenditures on police were less than half those of Austria, Italy, and France; one-quarter those of Prussia; and one-sixth those of Great Britain.[18] Obviously, in order to rule the country effectively, it was necessary for the state bureaucracy to depend upon other, nonbureaucratic, organs. Of these, the most important traditionally were the empire's estate institutions.

Russian estates (*sosloviia*) resembled to some degree those of the *ancien régime* in western Europe. The leading estates—gentry, clergy, merchantry, and peasantry—all had their western analogues.[19] Beneath the superficial similarities, however, lay fundamental differences between the two sets of institutions. Where the western European estates had emerged as corporate bodies, each with a strong sense of autonomy, the Russian estates had been created directly and explicitly by the central authorities. Where the western European estates were defined primarily in terms of heredity and relationship to property, particularly land, their tsarist counterparts were organized in terms of state service. The unique quality of the Russian corporate bodies was evident in their role as the second element in local administration.

Just as Witte had spoken for the state bureaucracy, so too did the estates have their ideologues. Among the most prominent was A. D. Pazukhin, a member of the landed gentry and author of an influential treatise on the estate idea published in 1885.[20] Like Witte, Pazukhin began with an affirmation of autocracy. Yet where Witte had identified the development of autocratic power with the activity of its bureaucracy, Pazukhin emphasized the empire's estates. Reviewing

European history, he argued that in the West the decline of traditional corporate institutions had been paralleled by a decline in morality and order. A negative, "mechanistic" society had arisen in which individuals and classes were driven by greed and competition for power. Russia's history had been the opposite. Here, a moral, "organic" order had been maintained through the cooperation of tsarism and the estates. As he wrote at one point, "Unlike the western European polities, which developed under the influence of internal struggle of social groups, Russia emerged as a powerful state through struggle with external enemies . . . . Under these conditions the autocratic authority of the Muscovite ruler originated and expanded, and side by side with it emerged the Russian estates."[21] In keeping with this interpretation, Pazukhin insisted that the government, in its administration of the empire, "cannot be satisfied with the instrument of bureaucracy alone, but must also rely on public elements."[22] Chief among these was the first, or gentry, estate.

Pazukhin's characterization of the ideal member of the gentry was even more flattering than Witte's of the civil servant.[23] From the start he took pains to argue that the Russian gentry were not aristocrats like the nobles of western Europe, but loyal servants of the tsar. For example, while admitting that the gentry often had landholdings like the European notables, Pazukhin insisted that the significance of ownership was quite different in the Russian case. In Russia land was neither a means of self-aggrandizement nor a mark of status, but an important instrument in performing the service role. Proprietorship guaranteed the material support of the gentry while they served and also insured that they would retain contact with the rest of the local citizenry. He argued that "being at one with the state through service and retaining a close tie with the populace through land ownership, . . . gentry have been the connecting link between the Supreme Authority and the people." The gentry role of mediating between tsar and people applied particularly to the peasantry. "The hereditary gentryman possesses among the peasants full confidence and deep sympathy," Pazukhin asserted. "He is their petitioner before the authorities, their defender from the oppression of kulaks and usurers."[24]

The peasant estate was thus assigned a rather passive role in Pazukhin's scheme of things, but it was not unimportant. The muzhiks were not only the primary producers in the countryside but also an "inexhaustible storehouse of good sense and true patriotism."[25] In order to protect this precious storehouse, Pazukhin argued, it was necessary to prevent the peasantry from being exposed to corrupting influences. Socially and economically, this could be achieved by maintaining the traditional family structure and communal landholding of the peasants. Administratively, it required leaving village governance in the hands of the villagers themselves.

Like Witte's work, as Pazukhin himself must have known, this paean to the estates was idealized, particularly in respect to the gentry. For one thing, far from all gentry actually served. Though service had once been required, after 1762 it had ceased to be so. Of the empire's almost two million gentry a large number were willing to remain on their estates or pursue private professions without participating in local or central administration.[26] Furthermore, a substantial segment of the first estate failed to meet Pazukhin's second requirement for true nobility—ownership of land. Even among the landed, holdings varied in size from thousands of acres to tens. If the characterization of the gentry as a landed, serving estate was thus wide of the mark, so too was the portrayal of gentry attitudes. Nobles' treatment of their "little brothers" the peasants often fell far short of the benevolent paternalism described by the author. Certainly the peasants themselves considered members of the first estate more exploiters and enemies than guardians; peasant hatred for their noble neighbors was to be one of the most disruptive forces in the late tsarist era. Nevertheless, just as Witte's treatise contained a large kernel of truth, so too did Pazukhin's. Pazukhin romanticized the role of the estates but was still accurate in describing them as the foundation of the tsarist system.

The Russian gentry did indeed play a significant part in government. Many officials, particularly those in such leadership positions as provincial governor, were of gentry origin. Further, the gentry estate dominated the rural institutions of self-government. Beyond these indirect modes of participation, the gentry also possessed a direct avenue for engagement in local administration through their own corporate organization. Within each province and district of the empire the nobility had been granted the right to form assemblies and to elect gentry marshals as their representatives. While these dignitaries initially concerned themselves primarily with internal estate affairs, they gradually came to have various functions in the general administrative structure as well. On the provincial level the marshals served not only as spokesmen for gentry interests but also as key participants on numerous state boards and councils. In their districts, their role was more important. Since the government lacked any district agent comparable to the provincial governor, the gentry marshal was legally considered the leading functionary in district affairs. To this general responsibility were added specific duties such as chairmanship of the district board and school council.

Although the gentry thus maintained an active presence in local administration, peasant estate institutions were even more fundamental. For reasons that only partly coincided with those suggested by Pazukhin, the tsarist government had decided after emancipating the Russian serfs in 1861 to retain the peasantry's special, separate position. The peasants were placed not under the jurisdiction of the empire's regular civil and criminal codes but under the authority of traditional law. Peasant landholdings were not converted to private property but remained collective, with ownership vested in the commune (*mir*).

The administrative separation of the peasantry was equally rigorous. The peasants were governed by their own corporate organs—the village community (*sel'skoe obshchestvo*) and, uniting several village communities above, the volost (*volost'*).[27] Each of these possessed its own council and selected a chief executive officer, an elder (*starosta*) in the case of the former and a headman (*starshina*) for the latter. The jurisdiction of the peasant institutions was broadly defined, covering almost the entire range of village affairs. In fact, beyond caring for the needs of their constituents, the peasant bodies were required to assist the representatives of the central authorities in the general operation of local administration. The way this system functioned is clearest in relation to police affairs. Formal responsibility for patrolling the countryside rested with the state bureaucracy's constables and sergeants, but in actuality their role was supervisory. Most law enforcement in the village was performed by the peasants themselves through their elders and headmen. In their police function these officials were assisted by special peasant patrolmen called "hundreders" (*sotskie*) and "teners" (*desiatskie*), after the number of households at one time responsible for their election.

The realities of grass-roots police work illustrate the estate institutions' basic role in tsarist local governance. By the early twentieth century the apparatus of the state bureaucracy had scarcely penetrated below the district level. This was because the vast majority of the empire's inhabitants, especially the peasantry, administered themselves through their own corporations.

Reliance upon the estate institutions as a means of enlisting the aid of the populace had proven a satisfactory participatory system through much of Russian history. By the middle of the nineteenth century, however, change within the empire made it clear that the burden of local administration could no longer be borne by the state bureaucracy and estates alone. Stimulated by the atmosphere of crisis brought on by Russia's defeat in the Crimean War, tsarist statesmen, as part of a series of measures known as the Great Reforms of the 1860s, sought to resolve the problem by adding a third element to the local administrative system—self-government.[28] The key act was the promulgation of an edict on 1 January 1864 that introduced rural self-governing bodies (*zemstvos*), on both the provincial and district levels. Each zemstvo consisted of an elected assembly and an executive board (*uprava*) chosen by the assembly. The functions of the new institutions were never made very precise, overlapping in part with those of the state bureaucracy and estates. Broadly speaking, the jurisdiction of the zemstvos, and of the town councils introduced soon after, included socio-economic matters pertaining to local welfare, such as elementary education, public health, and charity.

The officials who created the self-governing bodies did not intend to revolutionize tsarist administration, and they therefore sought to integrate the zemstvos and town councils into the existing order. Certainly the new institutions were in no way to infringe upon the autocratic authority of the tsar or the state bureaucracy that ruled in his name. This is amply demonstrated by the evolution of Russian attitudes on the definition of the term *self-government* itself. Initially, thinking on this issue was dominated by the "socio-economic" (*khoziaistvennyi*) and "societal" (*obshchestvennyi*) schools.[29] Though differing in detail, both were rooted in the earlier German concept of a "free community" (*freie Gemeinde*). According to this notion, there existed a fundamental distinction between general state concerns like defense and local affairs like fire prevention or sanitation. Each of the two spheres—state and local—was separate, and each required its own form of administration. For the latter, this could only be elective self-government, and the tasks to be assigned to this self-government could only be local ones having no direct connection with the wider concerns of the state bureaucracy. Hence, self-government would be autonomous, but its independence depended upon the drastic narrowing of its jurisdiction and the abandonment of any broader political aspirations.

By the end of the century this outlook had given way to a second, the "state" (*gosudarstvennyi*) theory. Unlike its predecessors, the state approach was based upon the explicit denial of any distinction between state and local functions. The institutions of self-government were assigned certain administrative tasks not by virtue of their peculiarly local nature but solely because they could handle them more efficiently than the state bureaucracy. Hence, the zemstvos and councils were considered an integral part of the state structure, unique only in that their personnel were selected differently than regular civil servants. The elective character of self-government was essentially a pragmatic device for recruiting participation. It did not provide an independent, popular basis for zemstvo authority. As N. I. Lazarevskii, a prominent professor of administrative law and strong supporter of self-government, put it, "Since elective organs of self-government are undoubtedly state bodies and cannot be seen juridically as representatives of the local populace, . . . an interpretation of self-government as the autonomous activity of local society is scientifically inadmissable." The zemstvos and town councils, he continued, "have no rights against the state and can have none such."[30]

Just as the new element of local administration did not in theory contradict the claims of autocracy and the state bureaucracy, so too was it formally compatible with the estate principle, especially in the countryside. While "all-estate" in nature in that inhabitants from each corporation participated in elections, the zemstvos operated with a strong gentry presence. The ex officio chairman of the zemstvo assembly, for instance, was the gentry marshal. Moreover, throughout the entire history of the rural bodies the large majority of assembly delegates were noble.[31] At the same time, the new institutions of self-government presented no challenge to the estate administration of the peasantry. The zemstvos did not extend below the district level and relied on the volosts and village communities in their dealings with the peasantry.

Despite this formal harmony with the other elements of local governance, from the start the new institutions of self-government represented a potentially discordant note. Theories to the contrary, certain basic ideas associated with the zemstvos and town councils lent themselves to a challenge to tsarist autocracy and the power of its bureaucracy. One such idea was autonomy. Although the self-governing bodies were admittedly part of the state mechanism, their supporters insisted that they be granted a significant degree of independence to guarantee their success. At the same time that Lazarevskii maintained that the zemstvo could have no rights against the state, for instance, he urged that its autonomy be assured by judicial guarantees.[32] Of course, the idea of judicial guarantee was not far from that of rights, and the notion of rights was not far from the notions of constitutionalism and limitation of autocracy.

This also applied to the electoral principle. Juridically, the delegates to the zemstvo assemblies were not representatives of the populace but state officials who happened to be selected by local residents. In fact, however, the fine legal distinction between elected delegates who did not represent and ones who did was difficult to maintain. The implications of parliamentarianism and popular sovereignty inherent in zemstvo elections were noted by many, including Witte. As he wrote in *Autocracy and the Zemstvo,* "The source of the authority of these new organs is the confidence not of the Supreme Ruler but of the local populace. . . . The name of this populace is substituted for that of the Supreme Authority."[33]

If self-government was thus at least potentially incompatible with the continued predominance of the tsar and the state bureaucracy, it was no more fully in accord with the estate concept. Despite some concessions to the corporate idea, such as the gentry marshal's zemstvo chairmanship, most active supporters of self-government insisted upon its all-estate nature. Zemstvos in particular were seen as places where all rural inhabitants—gentry, peasants, merchants, and clergy—met to work for the general good. As one publicist put it, "Estate divisions . . . are not in keeping with the character of the zemstvo institutions, which in principle represent not the estate but the common material interests of a given area."[34]

As the ambiguous status of the zemstvo indicates, the Great Reforms of the 1860s gave Russian local administration an essentially tripartite division into state bureaucratic, estate, and self-governmental elements. But Alexander II and his ministers did not establish guidelines for interaction among the three branches. This problem was not merely a technical matter of clarifying jurisdictions. It raised fundamental questions of principle. What was the precise relationship between the state and the populace? Were the empire's inhabitants no longer to be viewed solely as subjects, but now also as active citizens? What was the proper ordering of the various social groups within the public? Would estate divisions remain, or would they be replaced by class distinctions or civil equality? Indeed, the task of synthesizing the basic elements of administration in the provinces involved defining both the structure of the imperial polity and the nature of tsarist society generally.

Not surprisingly, given the magnitude of the issues involved, most statesmen chose to avoid the difficulty by shrinking from the more radical implications of the reforms. The second half of Alexander II's reign was largely a period of caution, consolidation, and even limitation of reform. The real retreat, however, occurred after the Tsar Liberator's assassination in 1881 and the accession to the throne of his conservative son, Alexander III. True, the new ruler was initially persuaded to create a special commission chaired by M. S. Kakhanov to consider basic changes in local institutions. As the decree that established the commission read, despite the accomplishments of the Great Reforms, the basic assignment of "a fundamental and systematic restructuring of the entire provincial and district administrative apparatus remains unfulfilled."[35] Yet by the time Kakhanov and his colleagues presented their recommendations in 1884, the tsar had turned against further innovation. The task of synthesizing the elements of local administration was left in the hands of a man whose appointment as minister of internal affairs in 1882 had brought dismay to Russian progressives, Count Dmitrii A. Tolstoi.

Tolstoi's activity as minister directly reflected his own life experience. He had held a remarkable number of prominent positions within the official apparatus, including chancellery director of the Naval Ministry, senator, head of the Holy Synod, minister of education, state councillor, and finally minister of internal affairs. He was indeed, in the words of a prominent colleague, "the typical Petersburg bureaucrat."[36] Accordingly, Tolstoi predicated all his efforts at provincial reform upon the continued predominance of the tsarist state bureaucracy. Generally speaking, he rejected the elective principle in local affairs on the assumption that officials chosen by the populace, unlike civil servants, were little inclined to support the autocratic authority of the tsar. Conversely, he placed great emphasis on the local role of centrally appointed agents, particularly the subordinates of his own ministry.[37]

Tolstoi did, of course, recognize that provincial administration could not be run by the civil service alone. As he wrote in an 1886 report to Alexander III, he was "far from the thought" of transferring all local tasks to the "bureaucratic organs" and considered the participation of the populace "unconditionally necessary."[38] The minister did not, however, follow the precedent of the Great Reforms of the 1860s in focusing on self-government as a vehicle for public participation. He turned instead to the empire's estates, particularly the gentry. Drawing inhabitants into service was no problem, he wrote at one point, for the "landed gentry, who are the best educated estate [and] who possess the confidence of the local population, faithfully retain a consciousness of duty to the state."[39] This language clearly reflected that used by Pazukhin in his idealized description of the nobility. The similarity was no coincidence, for Tolstoi, in an act of considerable political and symbolic import, had chosen Pazukhin to head the MVD chancellery.

Tolstoi based his program on the first and second elements of local administration, the state bureaucracy and estates. The combination of these themes is readily apparent in the two most important acts of his ministry, an 1889 law creating the institution of "land captain" (*zemskii nachal'nik*) and a revision of the zemstvo code enacted in 1890.[40] From the beginning of his tenure in office, Tolstoi was particularly concerned with the deficiencies of peasant administration, which he attributed to a lack of supervision. In keeping with this view he sought not fundamental restructuring of the corporate organizations of the peasantry but the provision of guidance and direction through the creation of the land captain post. The land captain would, Tolstoi hoped, fill the gap between the state bureaucracy's district apparatus and the village. The new functionary was supplied with wide discretionary authority in the inspection of both peasant administrative bodies and village courts.

The land captain was legally considered part of the civil service. He was to be appointed "bureaucratically" by the governor and placed under the general supervision of the MVD.[41] Yet simultaneously the land captain was envisioned as a representative of the first estate. According to the 1889 legislation, he was to be chosen from among the gentry of his given locality when possible, and his work was to be coordinated by the gentry marshal. Ideally, therefore, the land captaincy was to have a dual nature, joining the authority and power of the state bureaucracy with the virtue of the landed nobility.

The same combination of bureaucratic and estate principles also informed Tolstoi's revision of the legislation on self-government, although here the results were mediated by the minister's death in April 1889, a year before the measure could be enacted. In Tolstoi's conception, self-government suffered from two fundamental flaws—"the separation of zemstvo institutions from those of the government and the incorrect organization of zemstvo representation."[42] In other words, Tolstoi saw the independence of self-government as introducing a dangerous element of conflict and disunity into local administration, and he viewed the zemstvo electoral law as opening the door to the participation of political unreliables.

Tolstoi and his successor, I. N. Durnovo, invoked the state principle to deal with the problem of zemstvo autonomy. By tightening the state bureaucracy's control they hoped to integrate self-government more completely into the local apparatus. According to the zemstvo code of 1864, for instance, the governor had been given the right to challenge zemstvo acts only on the grounds of their illegality. The revised code of 1890 gave the provincial chief the additional prerogative of halting measures he considered "not corresponding to the general welfare and needs of the state," or "inexpedient."[43] The ministers invoked the estate principle to rectify the second flaw in self-government, its faulty electoral law. Specifically, suffrage rules were rewritten to contract the electorate and to give an even more advantageous position to the local gentry. The nobles were separated into a special and heavily favored first curia from which to choose their zemstvo deputies.[44]

Tolstoi's efforts have been harshly criticized by historians as a form of class legislation. Soviet scholars especially have denounced the statesman himself as an "evil genius" and the measures of 1889 and 1890 as maintaining an essentially feudal system of gentry exploitation of the peasantry.[45] Indeed, the first estate was well served by the new legislation. The land captaincy, for instance, was often used by the local nobility in such matters as compelling peasant laborers to fulfill contractual obligations to estate owners or pressing village officials to prevent peasants from illegally grazing cattle on gentry land.[46] Yet at the same time, it would be inaccurate to characterize Tolstoi's primary intent as that of strengthening gentry privilege. In his view the first estate was not a ruling class but a pool of potential servitors from which the authorities could draw. One observer aptly noted, "Tolstoi's policy is not 'aristocratic,' but 'gentry.'"[47] Hence the minister staunchly refused to allow gentry marshals to discuss questions of political policy, and he attempted to insure the state bureaucracy's control over the land captains.[48] As he wrote on one occasion regarding rules for entering the nobility, "The Russian *dvorianstvo* is not of feudal origin and as a service estate it cannot have the right of self-determination without changing its historical significance."[49] The corporate principle, in Tolstoi's conception, remained a tool of the state, a device for enlisting public participation in local affairs while retaining the hegemony of the central authorities.

Tolstoi's vision of a powerful civil service ruling in the provinces with the aid of dedicated gentry had roots deep in the empire's past. It represented an attempt to synthesize local government by focusing on the two older elements of state bureaucracy and estate. This, combined with a firm reassertion of the tsar's autocratic national authority, would, it was hoped, resolve administrative difficulties and avoid the democratizing and egalitarian implications of the Great Reforms. Yet the appeal to the ideas and institutions of an earlier era was futile. At the very time that Tolstoi was turning to the basic traditions of Tsarist Russia, a fundamental social transformation was undermining those traditions. Ironically, this transformation was partially produced by the government's own policy of industrialization.

Administration and Social Change

Tsarist authorities had for some time been moving toward encouraging economic development. Motives varied, but prominent among them was concern for the Russian Empire's position in a rapidly industrializing Europe. With Witte's accession to the Ministry of Finance in 1892, the policy of stimulating manufacture and commerce became explicit, indeed, emphatic.[50] Through such measures as the introduction of protective tariffs and the adoption of the gold standard, the government successfully initiated steady growth in industry. The decade following Witte's appointment saw output in this sector of the economy increase at an annual rate of over 8 percent and the total length of railway track in the empire almost double.

Economic growth was naturally accompanied by social change. Industrialization, combined with factors like rural overpopulation, brought rapid migration to cities. Where the number of urban inhabitants had been a mere seven million at the time of the emancipation, by the first decade of the twentieth century it had almost tripled.[51] Between 1886 and 1896 alone, the population of Ekaterinoslav rose from 47,000 to 120,000, and the population of Odessa from 200,000 to 350,000. The expansion of the empire's municipalities not only drastically increased the aggregate level of demands on tsarist administrators but also created new social groups to be dealt with. A large and volatile working class emerged, and in a more indirect way, commercial and industrial progress contributed to the growth of the empire's middle classes. For example, there were only 1,800 students in the nation's law faculties in 1880, but by the turn of the century there were over 7,000.[52] Not surprisingly, both elements—the proletarian and the professional—were to make active political as well as administrative claims on the old order.

Social change extended beyond the city to the countryside. For one thing, the forces of urbanization penetrated formerly agrarian areas as the spread of the railroad network and the construction of factories in rural settlements transformed many villages into small towns. According to the census of 1897, over half of the empire's industry and sixty percent of its workers were located in the country.[53] The Ministry of Internal Affairs admitted at one point, for instance, that in the province of Moscow alone some two hundred villages had become commercial and industrial in nature.[54] The results of this change were, again, to increase the demands on the local administrative system and, simultaneously, to blur distinctions between the lower estates. Peasants entered the urban labor force and were gradually, though not completely, transformed into industrial workers. Workers and merchants moved to newly commercialized villages. In general, the old estate separation of town and country eroded.

The economic and social strains created by industrial expansion in this period were exacerbated by the relative stagnation of Russian agriculture. Though there has been debate of late on the precise nature of the "crisis" in the agrarian sector of the economy, it seems clear that large segments of the rural populace were in difficult straits.[55] Among the gentry this was reflected in the flight of individual nobles from the countryside. Between 1877 and 1902 the number of estates owned by middle gentry, supposedly the prime category of service candidates, fell by almost 24 percent. Only one-third of all gentry lived in cities in 1858; by the end of the century more than half did.[56] Many peasants, too, joined the urban migration, though their plight in the cities was much harsher than that of the nobles who relocated. Most villagers, however, remained in their communes, attempting to maintain an agricultural system whose weakness was graphically revealed when a massive famine swept the empire in 1891 and 1892.[57]

The conjuncture of industrial growth and agrarian difficulties had many ramifications for local administration. The chief impact was to seriously undermine the two basic pillars of the Tolstoi synthesis, the institutions of the state bureaucracy and those of the social estates. Though the state apparatus was beset by many troubles, most revolved around the long-established problem of excessive centralization. The administrative reforms of the 1860s had largely been directed at the resolution of this problem, though no definitive answer was found. The issue surfaced again in the 1880s in the work of the Kakhanov Commission. As one of its main tasks, the commission was instructed to find means of expanding the decision-making authority of local institutions; in reference to the issue of supervision, it recommended immediate decentralization of the administrative structure.[58] The measures of Tolstoi and his successor Durnovo did not achieve this. The editors of the conservative periodical *New Times* reviewed the status of the imperial bureaucracy in 1902, for example, and concluded that among its basic shortcomings was "unwarranted centralization."[59] One civil servant who contributed a letter to the paper's columns summarized contemporary opinion succinctly, commenting that from the beginning of civilization there had been neither an administrative mechanism larger than Russia's nor one "so centralized and bureaucratic."[60]

The problem of excessive centralization can be illustrated by envisioning the institutional structure of the tsarist civil service as a huge inverted pyramid. At the top was a welter of ministries, departments, and councils, all well staffed and well organized. On the bottom, however, were only a handful of thinly spread subordinates, usually poorly paid and poorly trained. Among the various ministerial hierarchies, only that of the MVD reached much below the district level at the turn of the century, and even its presence in the village was extremely superficial. A police constable might find himself responsible for an area of up to eighteen hundred square miles and a population averaging between fifty thousand and one hundred thousand. Normal workload could reach six thousand cases a year, many requiring extensive investigation and all involving written reports.[61] There were police sergeants to aid the constables, but low salaries and lack of education—most sergeants were ex-soldiers who had not reached officer rank—hampered their effectiveness. Even capable sergeants could find themselves swamped with assignments. As one reported somewhat later, over the course of a decade of service there had never been a year in which he had handled fewer than fifteen hundred cases of illegality, a figure that presumably did not include other administrative functions.[62] The situation of urban law enforcement agencies was not much better.

Since the policeman was almost the sole representative of the state outside district capitals, his plight did not escape official notice. Even before Tolstoi's ministry the Kakhanov Commission had vigorously criticized the overburdening of the police that resulted from the lack of a more effective local administrative apparatus. Although the creation of the land captaincy had helped somewhat, peace officers remained overtaxed after Tolstoi's death.[63] A government commission created in 1905 to study the empire's system of emergency laws found in terms almost literally the same as those used by the Kakhanov group twenty years before that one "major obstacle" to the proper functioning of the police was their responsibility for "the most numerous obligations, distracting them from their direct task [of maintaining order]."[64] Among these tasks were delivering subpoenas, reporting lost goods, handling passports, registering the local population, and collecting taxes. The commission might well have added such duties as checking building codes, enforcing sanitation regulations, caring for orphans and—a very important one—carrying out measures of the zemstvos and town councils. In June of 1900 the Council of Ministers indicated that the state police were having difficulty meeting their central responsibility for order by easing the procedure by which individual settlements and private citizens could petition to establish additional police posts (under state control) at their own expense.[65]

While the local police were probably the most overloaded, other bureaucratic institutions were only marginally better off. Matters submitted to district or provincial boards, for example, often required four or five years to be resolved. Land captains, who were expected by Tolstoi to correct some of these administrative shortcomings, soon found themselves caught up in the same syndrome. The piling on of petty tasks made it increasingly difficult for the new functionaries to fulfill their primary duty of supervising peasant affairs.[66]

Of course, overburdening was not the only cause for the slowness with which the administrative machine sometimes operated. In a letter printed by the editors of *New Times* as part of their series on bureaucracy, one official attributed the delays to what he termed the civil servant's "ten commandments." Among them were "Hurry and you will become a laughing stock" and "Business should first be left to ripen well."[67] The primary reason for this lack of initiative was the concentration of decision-making authority, like institutional resources, in Saint Petersburg. Administrative practice required approval from the capital for even the smallest matter; the lower ranks were almost completely dependent upon their superiors. One result was to sap the energy of local officials. This point was also emphasized by the sharp-tongued civil servant in his commandments, which included "Don't serve, but fawn" and "Two times two is not four, but what his excellency orders." The extreme servility of many bureaucrats was well recorded in contemporary literature. In Chekhov's "Death of a Clerk" the protagonist Cherviakov ("Wormish") is so distraught at sneezing over a prominent dignitary that he simply expires. In "The Chameleon," by the same author, Police Inspector Ochumelov ("Crazed") threatens to have a stray puppy killed until news that it belongs to a high-ranking official makes the inspector himself whimper.

Excessive centralization contributed to other serious deficiencies in the quality of state service. The style of official behavior can vary sharply from nation to nation. In the tsarist empire the predominant attitude of civil servants toward the populace seems to have been arbitrary and violent. Police, for example, often resorted to "the law of the fist," a practice that official commentators themselves admitted alienated both the masses and the educated public.[68] Even Witte, the staunch defender of the state bureaucracy, agreed in *Autocracy and the Zemstvo* that administrators were inclined to be highhanded. In a subsequent report to the tsar, he put the matter even more sharply. Noting the rise of popular unrest in 1901 and 1902, Witte wrote, "Arbitrary action by officials is everywhere, [and] the populace is responding with force."[69] Hand in hand with capriciousness went corruption. Indeed, this form of malfeasance was long considered the cardinal sin of imperial officialdom. "Ignorance, indolence, routine are only faults," commented Leroy-Beaulieu, "but the great vice of Russian bureaucracy is its venality."[70]

This pattern of misbehavior had many roots. Poor pay and a general lack of training were certainly important, especially (though not exclusively) in the lower ranks of the civil service. Consider the characterization of the average tsarist peace officer given by L. Kosunovich, the leading columnist of the semiofficial *Police Messenger*. "Men drawn primarily from the poorest and least influential strata of local society, crushed from childhood by severe poverty, lacking any education or breeding, coming to police service almost entirely without professional preparation . . . are given very extensive powers over the populace with little precise regulation."[71] Yet as Kosunovich's comment indicates, official malfeasance was also greatly facilitated by a lack of control over the administrative apparatus. This in turn was attributable to the fact that of all the functions of the tsarist state, that of supervision was most centralized.[72] In the West systems of administrative justice based largely upon either public or judicial review of bureaucratic activity had long since emerged. For its entire history, however, the Russian state had rejected both notions. No representative institutions had been created to give the populace a role in the supervision of administration, and the empire's legal codes made it difficult, if not impossible, for the courts to exert on behalf of individual citizens any serious restraint on the behavior of officials. Under the practice of "administrative guarantee," for example, no civil servant could be brought to trial without the approval of his administrative superior.

The tsarist regime's refusal to view inspection as a public or judicial task meant that this function would have to be undertaken by the state bureaucracy itself. The central authorities in Saint Petersburg sought to control administrative operations through a constant flow of detailed directives and circulars. Even the most routine decision, such as the granting of hunting licenses, the registration of salt works, or the opening of a theater, had to be duly registered and reported back to the ministries in the capital for final approval. Further, the government took added steps lest this "paper type" of supervision, as one MVD subordinate termed it, fail.[73] The chief figure in local affairs, the governor, was charged with full responsibility for inspecting literally all administration in the province.

There is no doubt that by the end of the nineteenth century this system of control, relying so heavily upon the upper echelons of the bureaucratic hierarchy, was not working effectively. The Kakhanov commissioners, for instance, reported "an almost complete lack of real responsibility for violation of the law, inactivity, and tolerance of malfeasance."[74] The first mechanism of supervision, circulars from the capital, did little more than contribute to the already mammoth sea of red tape in which the administration operated. This "formal" control from the center achieved an equally "formal" acquiescence from below, as individual bureaucrats grew adept at writing impressive reports to cover their less laudable behavior. The *New Times* correspondent noted in yet another insightful commandment, "Never write seriously, write for form only."[75]

The shortcomings of inspection from Saint Petersburg were hardly remedied by gubernatorial supervision. The provincial chiefs, with their limited staffs, lacked the capacity to inspect the entire local administrative apparatus, which by the end of the century included almost half a million public employees.[76] The problems were clearly indicated by Governor S. D. Urusov in a description of his own efforts in this direction. Upon his appointment Urusov tried strenuously to replace corrupt officials and to inspect all major administrative institutions within his province. In short order, however, he discovered "that the task of halting illegal extortion was beyond me." The position of the governor, he concluded, was "a complete sham."[77] Urusov's experience was verified by others. Unable to oversee the entire provincial network, or even part of it, personally, governors too were forced to join in the "paper type" of inspection.[78]

The new institution introduced by Tolstoi to improve supervision over village governance, the land captaincy, soon fell victim to the same shortcoming. For years after the creation of the office the MVD struggled ineffectually to develop detailed circulars or codes to regulate land captain operations. Attempts to encourage governors, gentry marshals, and other local authorities to exert more direct control were no more successful. The district conference charged with immediate supervision of land captains—itself including the land captains as members—was, in the words of MVD Land Section Director V. I. Gurko, merely a "company of conniving colleagues."[79] Beyond individual complaints, Gurko argued, there was "virtually no supervision" over land captain activity.[80]

Excessive centralization, then, was a many-headed evil which contributed directly to the fundamental irony of tsarist local government. In theory, the state bureaucracy remained all-powerful, sharing in the autocratic authority of the monarch. But as social change progressed, it was increasingly limited in its ability to operate effectively. As Witte described it, by the turn of the century the civil service was "omnipotent in the extent of its authority, but through its own organization incapable of any vital activity."[81] Of course, no one expected the state bureaucracy to carry the burden of administration alone. Even Tolstoi anticipated that the central government would require popular assistance, primarily through the empire's estate institutions. Yet by the beginning of the twentieth century this traditional mechanism for mobilizing popular participation was rapidly becoming obsolete.

The effects of change on the first estate were obvious in the contraction of gentry landholding and in the progressive urbanization of the nobility. The disinclination of individual nobles to remain on the land adversely affected the quality of gentry administrative service. As the prominent student of administrative law Baron S. A. Korf wrote in comparing the situation with that of the 1840s:

> The provinces are again deserted, there exists an even more chronic shortage of qualified men locally; gentry are either living in the capitals immersed in financial speculation, sojourning abroad on the remains of their inheritances or expending their last breaths of life in the stuffy chancelleries of the central government, instead of serving in the vital area of local administration; young people upon graduating from the university are not drawn to life in the provinces, but remain in the capital day-dreaming of their future careers.[82]

The negative effects of the pull of urban life were evident in the activity of the gentry marshals. Particularly in the districts, the marshals' performance of their extensive duties was marked by growing absenteeism. Moreover, their competence declined steadily. Korf, for example, noted the growing practice of electing younger, inexperienced gentry, including many who had barely completed their education.[83]

The situation was even more serious in relation to the land captaincy. After the initial excitement that accompanied the introduction of the office had waned, it became difficult for the government to find qualified members of the first estate to fill the captains' ranks. As Land Section Director V. I. Gurko explained, "The level of the zemskie nachalniki personnel fell noticeably, and it was very difficult to entice into the rural wilderness for a small salary a man who had a chance of making a livelihood in more or less cultured urban surroundings."[84] The Ministry of Internal Affairs reported to the State Council in 1902 that of twenty-three hundred land captains, only about one-fifth met the MVD's optimal requirements of owning a local estate and having previously served in local administration. Moreover, the MVD staff commented on the captains' poor training, noting that only 32 percent had higher education, while 19 percent had not even entered middle school. Less than half of the land captains, the report concluded, had sufficient experience or preparation to hold their posts successfully.[85]

In order to cope with these shortcomings, the interior ministry resorted to two measures. In cases where no suitable local candidate could be found, nonlocals, often from the civil service, were appointed captains. Moreover, an attempt was made to develop detailed instructions and regulations to guide their activity. This process of what might be called the bureaucratization of the land captaincy, its subordination to more thorough central control, was far from a complete success. Nevertheless, it did indicate that the gentry as an estate were finding it difficult to fulfill the key administrative role Tolstoi had assigned to them.

Equally serious were the inadequacies of peasant estate institutions. In the face of the relative stagnation of peasant agriculture and the simultaneous commercialization of the countryside, the all-peasant volost and village community became increasingly unsatisfactory as governing organs. Like the local agencies of the state bureaucracy, the peasant bodies were badly overburdened by the 1890s. In the first half of the decade alone, the government assigned the volost new obligations regarding conscription, postal service, tax collection, building inspection, factory registration, passports, supervision of handicrafts, and notarial services.[86] Beyond their sheer weight, such new assignments contributed to a change in the nature of the peasant institutions. As they had emerged from the Great Reforms, the village organs were expected to perform a dual function. Being corporate bodies, the volost and village community were responsible for the immediate welfare of their constituents, the peasantry. Simultaneously, they served as units of "general administration," charged with assisting the state bureaucracy and zemstvos. By the turn of the century, the latter, more general, function had come to far outweigh the corporate. The village units were increasingly drawn into the operations of outside institutions and were increasingly subject to outside control. Originally, the peasant assemblies elected headmen and elders. After 1889, it was the land captain who made the final selection for both offices, choosing between two candidates for each post presented by the assemblies. Moreover, land captains held the authority to fine, arrest, and even suspend village officials for malfeasance. Indeed, in 1893 the government gave the district conference the power to set salaries for the peasant functionaries.[87] As a result of such measures, and as the MVD itself admitted in relation to the volost headman, the typical village official was transformed from "the representative and guardian of the public interests of the peasant population" to "the executive organ of all authorities in the district."[88]

The negative effects of new duties and outside control on the peasant institutions were evident in their budgets. In 1894, for instance, well over 80 percent of all volost expenditures was devoted to administrative costs, while only 12 percent went for public health and charity, and a shocking 3 percent to improving the lamentable state of peasant agriculture.[89] The situation of individual settlements could be even worse. A government study of the village of Pavlovo in the province of Nizhnii Novgorod found that administrative expenses absorbed 90 percent of the budget, leaving only 10 percent for education and health and absolutely nothing for economic improvement. In fact, the local volost and village community suffered from chronic deficits.[90]

The problems of peasant administration were also reflected in the poor quality of officials. Volost headmen and village elders were supposed to be prominent members of the local community, but this was often not so. Prince V. N. Tenishev, for example, in an empire-wide survey of rural governance, found that most able peasants actively avoided election. Indeed, neither Tenishev nor any of his many correspondents could discover a significant number of cases in which the elder was actually an undisputed leader of the village.[91] This applied even more sharply to the village police, who were clearly the least competent functionaries in the entire administrative system. Police service was sometimes considered a duty in kind that peasants were to perform without compensation. Moreover, election took a peasant from pursuing his own agricultural interests and substituted the onerous task of patrolling fellow villagers. As a result, communes tended to choose their poorest and least productive members to serve. Election of criminals as a form of punishment was a not uncommon practice, as was the hiring of drifters from outside the village.[92] So undependable were many peasant police that constables in many areas virtually ignored their services, assigning them menial tasks like carrying messages or guarding the police station.

As the case of law enforcement suggests, the reluctance of peasants to serve in village administration had many sources, including poor pay and lack of free time. Among the most important was the problem of the relationship of the peasant institutions to the central state bureaucracy, a relationship characterized by growing subservience. As the peasantry's administrative burden expanded, the budgets and energy of the village institutions turned steadily to the service of non-peasant functionaries. Among these were the gentry land captains, whom the peasants often feared or resented, and the rough and arbitrary police sergeants, whom the peasants commonly detested. The muzhiks responded to the bureaucratization of their estate institutions in two basic ways, both destructive from the standpoint of effective administration. On the one hand, many peasants became progressively more alienated from their own corporate bodies. Able candidates refused to serve as officials. Village assemblies sometimes ceased to meet more than once or twice a year, leaving administrative responsibility in the hands of the elder and headman, or even the village clerk (*pisar'*).[93] On the other hand, many peasant functionaries, perhaps as a result of closer attentiveness to the sentiments of their constituents, became unreliable as instruments of general administration. As the minister of internal affairs reported in 1902 in regard to village police, "The close ties of economic interest between the elected and the commune, familial relations to fellow villagers, and material dependence on the commune have caused them to shrink from various types of prosecution, fail to execute orders of the authorities, hide crimes, and not uncommonly participate in mass disorders."[94]

The troubles of the gentry and peasant institutions strongly suggest that Tolstoi's view of the potential role of the estates as pillars of administration was chimerical. The deterioration of the corporate organs provided firm evidence that a new, more dynamic relationship between the government and public had become a necessity. This conclusion was reinforced by another phenomenon of the period, the participation of at least some estate officials in political opposition. In the case of the nobility this meant individual marshals joining the empire's burgeoning progressive movement. Among those active in agitating for liberal reform, for example, were such prominent gentry officials as Provincial Marshals M. A. Stakhovich of Orel, Prince P. N. Trubetskoi of Moscow, and Count V. V. Gudovich of Saint Petersburg.[95] With the peasantry, dissatisfaction took the more direct form of deviance. Though hard data on rural criminality is difficult to come by, there was a definite perception among the landed elite that villagers were stepping up crimes like theft and illegal pasturing. In any case, by 1902 and 1903 open peasant rebellion had reemerged after more than a century of passivity.[96] And, as the minister of internal affairs noted, not only did village officials fail to combat unrest, they often joined it.

In sum, it is fair to argue that the Tolstoi synthesis of the elements of local government was not viable. Change was remolding Russian society and calling into question the very principles upon which tsarist administration was based. Of course, many of the problems described here existed earlier. Many had figured prominently in the work of the Kakhanov Commission in the 1880s and, indeed, in the proceedings of government committees created by Alexander II, and Nicholas I before him. Yet by the end of the nineteenth century a traditional approach to these difficulties was no longer sufficient. This was underscored by the development among the educated citizenry of a broadly based consensus on the need for reform.

The Public and Reform

In the decades or, one could argue, centuries before 1900 the attitude of the Russian populace toward government had been relatively passive. Both as a cause and a result of the state's monopolization of the political process, the empire's citizenry had been active neither in decision making nor in the implementation of policy through administration. This was evident in the sluggish popular reaction to the creation of self-government once the novelty of the reforms of the 1860s had faded. One foreign observer described the failure of the zemstvos and town councils to take a more vigorous role in provincial affairs:

After working so hard to put out every spark of local life, the government found it could not kindle it again at a moment's notice, just because it chose to. The crease of administrative discipline had been pressed down hard into the country at large as well as into the official world, and neither of the two— neither society nor the agents of the supreme power—could cast off the old slough. . . . If the tsar's subjects cannot walk better alone, it is because they have been too long kept in leading-strings.[97]

Whether responsibility for public lethargy rested with the government or the citizenry itself, there is no doubt that by the end of the nineteenth century the situation was changing drastically. The expansion of the middle classes produced by industrialization and urbanization, rising dissatisfaction with the authorities' inability to aid agriculture, and continued exposure to progressive Western ideas all encouraged the mobilization of popular opinion, especially among the educated. First small groups and then ever larger segments of the public conspired to throw off the "leading-strings" of state paternalism.

In the provinces, the new attitude was evident in the rejuvenation of self-government. For a variety of reasons, including shock at the massive famine of 1891 and 1892, the closing decade of the century was a time of rapid expansion in the work of zemstvos and town councils. Between 1880 and 1890 zemstvo budgets had only grown from a total of thirty-six million rubles to forty-seven million, with annual increases never over 5.1 percent. In the following ten years, however, the sum expanded from forty-seven to eighty-eight million, with annual increases of up to 18 percent.[98] The leap in zemstvo expenditures was accompanied by a proliferation of personnel—the "third element," as zemstvo employees were called. In 1890, for example, the entire agronomical staff of the empire's self-governing bodies numbered 29; by 1904 the total was over 400. In the veterinary field, the corresponding figures were 459 and 837. As far as education was concerned, zemstvo activity had always been well developed, and by the end of the century the self-governing bodies were supporting almost twenty thousand elementary schools.[99]

Beyond its direct administrative effects, the activation of the zemstvo had profound political implications. Zemstvos, like universities, became focal points for the empire's growing liberal movement. The reasons for this are worth noting. First, a large number of individual zemstvo figures, such as the Moscow board chairman D. N. Shipov or Kursk's Dolgorukov brothers, assumed leadership roles in progressive circles. Further, zemstvo boards often served as organizational centers for the progressive movement, and professional congresses of the zemstvo's third element served as surrogates for the open national political meetings otherwise prohibited by the authorities.[100] Finally, the organs of self-government were an inspiration for what one historian has aptly characterized as a "zemstvo ideology."[101] Out of this set of views, many of which had been articulated at the time of the Great Reforms or before, there emerged a radical liberal critique of tsarist government.

The basic assumptions of the zemstvo outlook, particularly in reference to the issue of administration, were expounded in many works of the period. One was an article written in 1903 by V. V. Ivanovskii on the subject "Bureaucracy as an Independent Social Class" [Biurokratiia, kak samostoiatel'nyi obshchestvennyi klass].[102] Ivanovskii's analysis centered on a rather straightforward scheme of historical development. He contended that initially bureaucracy arose as an instrument of absolute monarchy, inspired by the ideal of achieving the common good through the exercise of unlimited royal power. While bureaucracy in its early phases was in certain senses "progressive," it eventually ceased to be so. Instead, it became a brake on growth, primarily by undermining the citizens' sense of worth and inculcating a spirit of "obsequiousness" and "self-abasement." As society developed, Ivanovskii continued, public organizations arose to participate in administration. Being closer to the populace, these societal bodies gradually began to displace the bureaucracy. As self-government and decentralization advanced, Ivanovskii concluded, bureaucracy would retreat until administration was entirely in the hands of "society itself."[103]

Though his argument was brief and simplistic, Ivanovskii's article contained all the key elements of the zemstvo outlook. A clear distinction was drawn between the state, which was identified with its officials, and "society" (*obshchestvo*). In this scheme, the civil service, or bureaucracy, was understood to be an independent and isolated class or category, divorced from society. Precisely because it was alienated from society, bureaucracy was doomed. As society progressed and developed its own governing bodies, the state bureaucracy would, to borrow a term, wither away. Ivanovskii indicated precisely the mechanism by which this withering away would occur: through the decentralization of the administrative structure and the expansion of public institutions, officialdom would eventually disappear as a ruling stratum. In the Russian case the primary societal bodies were the zemstvo and the town council.

The points presented in Ivanovskii's short essay were developed by others, usually with considerable vehemence. For example, progressive spokesmen initiated a vigorous polemical assault on the state bureaucracy, characterizing it as bloodless, inhuman, even antihuman. V. M. Gessen, the foremost liberal legal expert of the period, prefaced his study of local administration with a biting attack on the civil service. "Bureaucracy," he argued, "fears life, movement, change; the noise of the street interferes with office work. Professional routine is an impenetrable wall separating the paper world of the chancellery from the living world of reality. Beyond the walls of the chancellery people live, within its walls people write."[104] Boris Chicherin argued similarly in response to Witte's *Autocracy and the Zemstvo*. "The power-hungry bureaucracy," he wrote, "desires to direct all of Russian social life, to guide it according to its own discretion, to ensnarl it in a network of agents, to suffocate it, in a word to destroy in it any independence or spontaneous activity."[105] Echoing Ivanovskii, both men went on to insist that the state bureaucracy's ignorance of the public's needs and its jealous defense of its privileges disqualified it for leadership. "Given its absence of principles and weakness of ethical impulses," Gessen concluded, the bureaucracy was "incapable of serving social needs."[106]

Ivanovskii's fellow liberals also joined him in seeing decentralization as a cure for the empire's political problems. Before 1905, many progressives defined reform not so much in terms of limiting the tsar's autocracy as in transferring administrative activity from the chancelleries of the state bureaucracy to the public itself, from the "dead hand" of officialdom to the zemstvo or town council. D. M. Shipov, for example, was a vocal supporter of the monarchic idea. Yet in a memorandum to the tsar written in 1901, he decried the civil service's apparent goal of "centralization in all the branches of local administration and . . . tutelage over all aspects of social life."[107] M. A. Stakhovich made essentially the same point in arguing, "Only progressive struggle with bureaucracy in the name of the preservation of autocracy is admissible."[108]

Of course, the idea of decentralization is ambiguous, open to at least two very different definitions. On the one hand, it can be understood in terms of *deconcentration,* the transfer of authority from the higher rungs of the administrative ladder to the lower. It was this process of deconcentration within the state bureaucracy that Witte had in mind when he recommended in *Autocracy and the Zemstvo* "bureaucratic decentralization." Borrowing a quote from a French statesman, the minister of finance aptly characterized such a policy as a "domestic arrangement between the Minister of Internal Affairs and the Prefects."[109] On the other hand, decentralization could be interpreted as a process of *devolution,* the transfer of duties from the state bureaucracy entirely to nonbureaucratic outside agencies.

There is no doubt that Russian liberals had this second definition in mind. Hence Lazarevskii distinguished between "fictional" decentralization, which he associated with deconcentration, and "real" decentralization, which meant devolution, hence self-government. In his view the former could never resolve the shortcomings of tsarist local government, because "decentralized organs of state administration are always passive, obedient subordinates of the ministers and eager executors of all commands from the center." The only effective remedy, he concluded, was decentralization through expanded jurisdictions for the zemstvo and town council.[110] The editors of the journal *Law* put the issue even more sharply, arguing, "The idea of decentralization in application to local affairs can have normal expression in one form alone: the replacement of the bureaucrat with administration by self-government."[111]

In keeping with this view, liberals made many recommendations for strengthening the zemstvos and town councils; by the turn of the century two were particularly important. The first of these involved the independence of self-government. As Gessen, Lazarevskii, and others insisted, the self-governing organs could not operate properly if left under the control of the civil service. In order to provide the necessary autonomy, liberals turned to the Western principle of "legality" (*zakonnost'*). They proposed that firm laws be drafted and enforced by the empire's independent judiciary to guard the zemstvos and town councils from outside interference. In particular, they demanded that the governor's power to rule on the "expediency" of local actions, a power granted by Tolstoi and Durnovo in 1890, be removed in favor of the original legislation of 1864.[112] The initial goal of the liberal movement was thus protection of self-government from the central authorities above; the second was its extension below through the creation of a local zemstvo (*melkaia zemskaia edinitsa*).[113] Aware of the shortcomings of the corporate volost and village community, progressive zemstvo activists urged that these institutions be abolished and the peasantry integrated with the rest of the rural population in all-estate zemstvos at the grass roots. It was hoped that participation in the new bodies might provide a mechanism for raising the "low cultural level" of the muzhiks and begin to bridge the gap between Russia's elites and the masses. The establishment of local zemstvos did indeed strike at both pillars of Tolstoi's synthesis of provincial government. The traditional participatory device of estates would be replaced by more egalitarian modern forms. Moreover, a unified local populace, no longer divided by corporate distinctions, would be better able to resist the encroachment of the state and its agents.

During the Tolstoi ministry, both the specifics of the liberal program and the general attitudes that supported it were advocated by only a small part of the Russian public. Yet by the beginning of the new century these attitudes were spreading rapidly through the educated classes. One testimony to this was the growing frequency with which individual zemstvos, particularly on the provincial level, passed resolutions supporting segments of the liberal platform.[114] Another was the great attention stimulated by various congresses of the zemstvo third element. In February of 1901, for instance, an all-Russian congress of agronomists in Moscow attracted considerable notoriety by adopting a resolution in favor of local zemstvos. More evidence in this direction is provided by the public's response to an initiative from the government itself, Witte's creation of the Special Conference on the Needs of Agriculture.

In the face of the steady deterioration of Russian agriculture, the minister of finance had in 1902 persuaded Nicholas II to convene in Saint Petersburg a special conference on rural productivity and related questions. Moreover, prompted by Witte, the tsar took the additional step of inviting members of the public to participate in local committees sponsored by the conference.[115] By the end of the year, 618 committees with over fourteen thousand participants had been organized. The local bodies were anything but radical. Most public representatives were chosen either by governors or district marshals, and the overwhelming majority of participants were either gentry landowners or civil servants.[116] Nevertheless, this rudimentary opinion poll of the rural-official elite indicated surprising sympathy for liberal goals. The question of the zemstvo was not included in the agenda prepared for the committees by the central authorities, but many managed to debate it. Of these, a significant number spoke out in favor of strengthening the independence of self-government, particularly by repealing that article of the 1890 zemstvo code which gave governors the right to rule on the expediency of zemstvo measures. More important, the introduction of an all-estate zemstvo below the district level was among the issues most extensively discussed by the committees. A majority of those expressing an opinion were in favor. Indeed, some committees simply repeated the resolution in favor of local zemstvos that had been passed by the agronomists in Moscow in 1901.[117] Clearly, a substantial segment of the educated public, including significant numbers of landed gentry, was moving rapidly in a liberal direction.

The diffusion of liberal, antibureaucratic attitudes among the empire's elites would have been enough to cause a sense of crisis in Russian society; the development was reinforced by the emergence of parallel sentiments among many conservatives. Tolstoi's program had been based, as the editors of one progressive periodical put it, "on an optimistic belief in the fraternal solidarity of the bureaucracy and gentry."[118] While it was true that through the nineteenth century the vast majority of the first estate had remained fully loyal to the regime, there had existed a certain tension between the two elements of Tolstoi's synthesis. Conservative Slavophil ideologues, for example, had since the reign of Nicholas I viewed the state bureaucracy with considerable reserve, considering it an obstacle to the true union of the holy tsar and his people. "A self-governing rural community with the Autocratic Tsar at its head—this is the Russian political ideal," wrote Slavophil I. S. Aksakov on one occasion, presenting a scheme in which there was very little room for officialdom.[119] Certainly during the 1860s there had been conservative opposition to the emancipation and other state-sponsored reforms, though not enough to seriously jeopardize implementation of the measures.[120]

During the 1890s the tension between the conservative gentry and governing officials was seriously exacerbated. In part this reflected the state bureaucracy's tendency to encroach upon what the nobility perceived as their role in local affairs. MVD attempts to regulate the activity of the land captains, for instance, were often interpreted in this light. More fundamentally, hostility toward the government was incited by Witte's program of rapid industrialization, which many gentry saw—quite accurately—as being implemented at the expense of all Russian agriculture, including their own. A series of government meetings to discuss measures to aid the nobility, at which Witte was a prominent stumbling block, did little to help.[121] The emergence of student and worker unrest in the first years of the new century strengthened gentry concern over the course of state policy. The reappearance of large-scale peasant disorder in 1902 ratified it.

Conservative alienation from government was reflected in the thinking of many influential nobles, such as State Councillor A. A. Polovtsov. In his diary for 12 June 1901, for instance, Polovtsov denounced the policy followed by the government since the reign of Alexander II as resulting in the "subversion of the landowning class." The primary outcome of this approach, he argued, had been the transfer of influence over the peasantry from the hands of the gentry to those of "people foreign to the land." Among these he significantly included "bureaucrats, sent from all sorts of back streets, [who] irresponsibly squeeze and insult the population, all under the guise of devotion to the tsar." The consequences of this policy of "social bureaucratism" were to be seen in the spread of student demonstrations and workers' strikes in the empire's cities. The only cure was action to strengthen the landed classes and narrow the authority of the civil service. Indeed, Polovtsov returned to these themes many times, each time more bitterly than before. After four weeks in Saint Petersburg in the summer of 1902, he travelled south to recover from a cold brought on by the capital's windy, rainy weather. "I carry away with me profoundly melancholic impressions of the times," he wrote on 22 August. "Thanks to limitless official caprice, to senseless bureaucratic fantasies, there is no healthy discussion of policy.

... The young tsar, who is told by all that salvation is in autocracy, has misunderstood this profound truth and gives Russia not the tsar's, but the bureaucrat's autocracy."[122]

Polovtsov's sentiments were echoed by other prominent conservatives. Muscovite Slavophil F. D. Samarin was no liberal. In a letter to Shipov in April 1900, for instance, he denounced the third element for their "alienation from the moral, practical and historical foundations of the ... surroundings in which our *intelligents* live and work."[123] Yet later, in a letter to the same Shipov, he also denounced the government's aspiration to "eliminate society from any, even the most modest, participation in state affairs." The officials, he argued, must recognize that "to administer Russia through the instrument of bureaucracy alone without any public participation is in present times impossible."[124]

The conservative critique of bureaucracy grew out of a perspective quite different than that of liberals. Where the latter argued for the equalization of all estates in law, the former insisted upon the preservation of corporate distinctions, particularly as they applied to gentry privilege. Moreover, where liberals were increasingly uneasy with the ideal of autocracy, the conservative gentry remained firm in their faith in the tsar's personal authority. These basic differences became quite apparent when individuals from the two camps attempted to join together for common action. Samarin, for example, participated in the discussions of progressive circles for some time but ultimately found himself unable to cooperate with even the moderate Shipov.[125] Normally, however, in the period before 1905, conservatives and liberals did not work together or engage in thorough debate. As a result, the very real dichotomy between their positions was not clearly articulated. Instead, conservative criticism of the empire's ruling bureaucracy reinforced liberal criticism, creating among the public a generalized sense of alienation from the common enemy, officialdom. In the eyes of the educated citizenry, a growing gap appeared between state and society that could only be rectified by increasing the populace's role in administrative affairs.

Students of development and revolution have argued that one of the most disruptive consequences of modernization for a traditional regime is the mobilization of public groups around demands for broader political participation. By the opening of the twentieth century such mobilization was occurring among Russian social elites. Both liberals and conservatives began to call for administrative reform based on an end to excessive centralization and the development of new, freer avenues of public involvement. The situation in the empire was caricatured by the editors of *New Times,* who noted that extreme centralization had led to a state of affairs in which the question of roads in N district was discussed in Saint Petersburg, while the citizens of N itself were busy debating national issues of political reform.[126] Only one important element was omitted from the characterization. At the same time that reform was being considered locally, it was also being debated in the capital by the very officials who were under attack. Over the course of the next ten years the empire's leading statesmen were to attempt to construct an approach to local governance that would answer the call for decentralization and broader participation yet retain the essential principles of tsarism.

CHAPTER II

PLEVE AND THE STATE BUREAUCRACY, 1902–1904

By 1902 it was clear that Tsarist Russia was entering a period of marked instability. Worker strikes and demonstrations had been growing at an alarming rate for almost a decade, there were ominous signs of peasant dissatisfaction in the countryside, and radical students were conducting a campaign of terror against the government. In 1901 a revolutionary killed the minister of education, and in April of the following year a young man disguised as an army officer shot to death Minister of Internal Affairs D. S. Sipiagin. Sipiagin's assassination, the first of an interior minister in the empire's history, had two immediate effects on Russian politics. It confirmed in the minds of many a sense of real crisis, and it brought to the leadership of the MVD Viacheslav Konstantinovich von Pleve. Pleve was to shake the ministry from the somnambulant attitude that had more or less characterized it since Tolstoi's death. In the process he supervised the articulation of a general attitude toward reform of local administration that would dominate the tsarist government's efforts for the next decade.

Despite Pleve's central role, few major figures have attracted as little study as he. This lack of historical attention reflects an almost universal distaste for a man at least partially responsible for the Kishinev pogrom, Russia's entry into the Russo-Japanese War, and the wave of police measures that helped provoke the Revolution of 1905. Even his personal character offers little appeal. Cold, suspicious, and secretive, he seemed to embody the contemporary liberal caricature of the antisocial, moribund civil service. Consequently, both Western and Soviet historians have been satisfied to dismiss Pleve as, in the words of one scholar, a "'scoundrel' and a 'yes-man,' i.e., a bureaucrat who had no convictions of his own."[1]

While much of the opprobrium attached to Pleve is well deserved, it has hampered serious evaluation of his ministry. Historical consensus to the contrary, Pleve was aware of the broad nature of the changes affecting Russian society and of the consequent need for some adjustment of the state's administrative structure. As he pointed out in a letter to A. A. Kireev on 31 August 1903, opposition to the government among educated society was the result not of recent events but of "several phenomena of our civil development over the last half-century." "The growth of social consciousness," he explained, "has coincided with profound changes in living conditions and a fundamental disruption of the socio-economic order." The only way to calm unrest, Pleve argued, was to "take away from the oppositional elements their reason for existence by basic work directed at the common benefit and good." He concluded specifically that "the means of administration themselves have decayed and are in need of significant improvement."[2]

Pleve's outlook on reform, especially administrative reform, was conditioned by his own background. Unlike his predecessor Sipiagin, who had at least some experience in the zemstvos and gentry organizations, Pleve made his career entirely within the state bureaucracy. After receiving a degree in law from Saint Petersburg University, he joined the staff of the Ministry of Justice, where he served for the next thirteen years. By 1881 he had risen to the position of public prosecutor of the Saint Petersburg court. That year, on the recommendation of "dictator of the heart" Count M. T. Loris-Melikov, Pleve was appointed director of the Department of Police.[3] In this position he gained the familiarity and public identification with police measures that was to mark his subsequent career. Pleve's abilities as a policeman were rewarded in 1884 by appointment as assistant to the minister of internal affairs and as senator. Over the next decade he sat as a member of government commissions on a broad range of issues, including factory legislation, agricultural prices, the peasant land fund, resettlement, peasant courts, the Jewish question, and famine relief. Most important, he served as one of Tolstoi's staunchest supporters in implementing the reorganization of rural administration and self-government in 1889 and 1890. Indeed, at least one prominent official maintained that it was Pleve, not Tolstoi, who actually directed the routine operations of the ministry in this period.[4]

Pleve's rapid advancement was due in part to his ability to please his superiors. Like most of his fellow bureaucrats, he developed a reputation for opportunism. Yet unlike many others in the state service he also became known for his outstanding ability and intelligence. Both characteristics were attested to rather unflatteringly by Prince

V. P. Meshcherskii, editor of the reactionary journal the *Citizen* and an influential court figure. In a successful attempt to block Pleve's appointment as minister of internal affairs in 1891, Meshcherskii described him as an "unreliable and even dangerous person, . . . bright and clever, like Beelzebub."[5]

Unable to win the minister's portfolio directly through service in the MVD itself, Pleve chose another path. In 1894 he was appointed government secretary and head of the Codification Department of the State Council. From this position, to which he added in 1898 that of state secretary and minister for Finnish affairs, Pleve was able to exert an important influence on all major legislation. He developed a particular reputation for the defense of gentry interests, usually against the antiagrarian programs of Finance Minister Witte. This attitude, adopted in part for careerist reasons, kept Pleve in the forefront of conservative attention. In 1902, with Sipiagin's assassination, he was, in the words of one commentator, the "natural candidate" for the internal affairs post.[6]

While Pleve's activities in the 1890s led many to consider him merely a spokesman for the nobility, it was clear even then that his primary loyalty was not to the gentry but to the tsarist state. In his concern for the nobility he consistently stressed its role not as a privileged stratum but as a group of state servants. Hence he championed not the interests of the large landholders but those of the middle range. "For local service," he maintained, "it is primarily the gentry of average holdings [who] are suitable; the rich will not serve in the countryside, sacrificing the comforts and advantages of life in the capitals."[7]

Yet not even the middle gentry were the primary bearers of the state interest in Pleve's eyes. This position was reserved for the tsarist civil service itself. Despite the opprobrium attached to the very term bureaucrat by the public, Pleve retained his faith in his colleagues and in their paternal guidance over Russian society. He stated his views frankly in a 1902 conversation with Witte on the subject of a constitution limiting the autocracy and its officials. Echoing sentiments Witte himself had expressed earlier in *Autocracy and the Zemstvo*, Pleve argued:

The Tsarist Government, whatever may be said, has experience, tradition, the habit of administering. Take note that all our most useful, most liberal reforms have been implemented exclusively on the government's authority, on its initiative, and usually without even the sympathy of the public. You yourself, Sergei Iul'evich, are a clear example of what a talented and energetic Russian minister can do for his homeland without a constitution.[8]

For Pleve the state administration was not only the chief guardian of order in the empire but also the prime mover in its development. Consequently, no administrative reform that failed to assign the leading role to the state bureaucracy could be permitted. As one of his MVD colleagues later commented, "Being a firm believer in the absolute monarchy, Pleve was of the opinion that neither the Russian people in general nor the educated circles in particular were sufficiently well trained to be allowed to govern their country."[9] This attitude was, of course, the opposite of the increasingly popular zemstvo ideology, which emphasized the maturity of the public and the importance of "local men" who were independent of the central authorities. Nevertheless, it was to serve as the guiding principle of Pleve's ministry.

While Pleve disagreed with zemstvo liberals on this basic question of policy, there was one issue upon which they were in full agreement: too much official business was being conducted in the capital. Any reorganization of the empire's administrative system would have to be based upon the transfer of authority to the provincial and district levels. As Pleve himself told one zemstvo official in 1902, "It is impossible to manage everything from Saint Petersburg, far away from local conditions."[10] Indeed, it was around the idea of decentralization that the Ministry of Internal Affairs fashioned its program of governmental reform.

Provincial Reform: Model for Decentralization

Pleve never presented his personal ideas on local administration, or on any other major issue of state policy, in any systematic way. Not given to theory, and accustomed to a degree of secrecy by his years as head of the police, he left no real summary of his views in the form of written reports, letters, or a diary. "This was a man," recalled one of his subordinates, "who did not communicate his thoughts."[11] Nevertheless, the main outlines of Pleve's approach can be discerned in the specific projects drafted during his ministry. Chief among these was a proposal for the reorganization of provincial administration. Both as an example of the basic presuppositions of Pleve's political philosophy and as an important precedent for almost all later MVD work, it merits detailed consideration.

The sorry state of administration at the provincial level had been a recurrent theme of Russian life at least since the reign of Nicholas I. Although the Great Reforms of the 1860s had brought some improvement, their salutary effect had been negated by the steady growth in size and complexity of the provincial apparatus over the following decades. As early as 1882, for example, the Kakhanov Commission concluded that the existing provincial structure "can in no case be seen as satisfying the most modest demands of unity, simplicity and strength."[12]

The multifold shortcomings of provincial administration are perhaps best captured by the situation of its nominal head, the governor. Clearly, the tsarist governor was badly overburdened. In addition to being the senior official of the interior ministry and thus in charge of the MVD's local operations, the governor also served as "representative of the supreme state authority," or personal agent of the tsar. In this capacity he was responsible for the supervision and coordination of practically all institutions in the province, including the organs of other ministries, self-government, the estate bodies, and even private societies. On any given day his attention might be devoted to matters ranging in importance from planning efforts to prevent a famine to granting approval for a charitable ball or replacement of a peasant's lost passport.

In addition to overworking him, the exalted legal position of the governor brought him into conflict with other institutions. By and large, the empire's provincial administration was organized on a linear system. Each Saint Petersburg ministry maintained a local office in the provincial capital to handle its affairs. As chief of the police apparatus the governor fitted neatly into this system as the subordinate of the minister of internal affairs. However, the governor was also the tsar's agent, charged with the unification of all provincial administration regardless of ministerial jurisdiction. This "territorial" responsibility conflicted directly with the linear order, and it was not surprising that other ministries resented the interference of the governor, whom they rightly regarded as a representative of the MVD. In particular, provincial administration tended to become another arena for a growing conflict between the Ministry of Internal Affairs and the Ministry of Finance.[13]

The ministries responded in various ways to the threat to their jurisdiction posed by the governor. They tried to exclude him from their local activity wherever possible. Failing this they sought to narrow the range for his incursions by concentrating authority for even the most inconsequential decisions in their Saint Petersburg offices.[14] As a last measure aimed at controlling the local situation, ministerial heads flooded both the governor and their own provincial subordinates with what one bureaucrat called "a continuous paper downpour" of circulars and directives detailing their views.[15] Ironically, they were joined in this by the governor's own superiors in the MVD, who also sought to control the activity of their powerful provincial agent.

The friction that often characterized the governor's relations with other ministries was a prominent feature in his dealings with the organs of self-government as well. By law the governor had extensive powers of supervision over the self-governing bodies, including in particular the notorious suspensive veto, the right to stop implementation of any resolution he considered either illegal or inexpedient. Even under normal conditions the granting of such powers to one institution over another would be cause for tension between them; in the case of the governor and self-government, discord was magnified by the absence of any real consensus on the role of the zemstvos and town councils in local administration. The jurisdictions of the state bureaucracy and self-government overlapped, and where the precise boundaries were located was a matter of interpretation. To make things worse, liberal publicists made good polemical use of every case of gubernatorial intervention in the affairs of the public organizations. While claims of administrative tampering were sometimes exaggerated, they undoubtedly helped deepen the psychological climate of hostility that existed between the state bureaucracy and much of the local citizenry.[16]

These difficulties in the governor's position were counterbalanced by his very considerable powers. Yet, paradoxically, even his prerogatives weakened him by undermining those institutions which were to aid him, especially the collegial institutions of provincial administration. Over the course of the nineteenth century there had developed in the provinces a large network of committees made up of representatives of the various ministries, the zemstvos and town councils, and the gentry estate. Taken as a whole these collegial bodies were intended to perform three basic functions.[17] First, some of them were to give rulings on important questions of provincial policy. In some cases these rulings were to have the weight of a final decision; in others they were only recommendations to the governor. Second, the collegial bodies were to provide a forum in which spokesmen of different institutions could discuss and coordinate their activities. For example, the forest protection committee was to unify efforts to develop and conserve woodlands; more important, the bureau for zemstvo and municipal affairs was supposed to bring together representatives of the state bureaucracy and of self-government in order to resolve conflicts between them. Third, the collegial units played an important role as courts of administrative justice. They shared with the governor responsibility for ruling on the legality of administrative acts, for disciplining officials, and for deciding whether those accused of malfeasance should be turned over to the regular courts for trial.

This collegial system of administration was characterized by a number of defects, many arising from the way the system had originated. Rather than being created simultaneously as part of a coherent whole, the various boards and committees had been formed on an ad hoc basis. No attempt was made to regularize or standardize procedure, coordinate the activities of the collegial institutions, or sort out overlapping jurisdictions. A more serious problem was the governor's extensive powers over the collegial bodies. He usually chaired meetings, and among those present were always representatives of the MVD staff who could be counted upon to support their superior's viewpoint. Moreover, collegial decisions were usually only consultative. Even in those cases when the vote of a collegial unit was considered binding, the governor retained ample powers of appeal to Saint Petersburg. As if this were not enough, certain emergency clauses in the administrative statutes allowed the governor to take into his own hands all measures he considered too urgent to delay.

The effect of these gubernatorial prerogatives was to deaden the collegial institutions. This was particularly true in the case of the very college that was meant to crown the entire network, the provincial board (*gubernskoe pravlenie*). In theory the board was to serve as "the highest office in the province."[18] In practice it had become, in the words of one governor, "completely obsolete and superfluous."[19] But the governor's domination of the collegial units, while sapping their vitality, did not mean that he himself would exercise their functions. The sheer volume of the work of the collegial institutions, which by 1902 numbered over twenty, was far beyond the capacity of the local chief and his chancellery to handle. Many collegial coordinating and supervising functions went largely unfulfilled.

As the situation of the governor suggests, the empire's provincial administration suffered from a host of imperfections. Some were essentially technical defects, like the lack of uniformity in the procedures of the various collegial institutions. Others were more basic, such as a serious lack of coordination among tsarist ministries. Beyond these deficiencies lay the fundamental flaw of excessive centralization. Within the hierarchy of the state bureaucracy, overcentralization was manifest in the accumulation in Saint Petersburg of power that could better be exercised in the provinces and in the similar concentration in the provinces of authority that could better be assigned to district institutions. More important, centralization also characterized the relationship of the state's civil service to the rest of Russian society. Hence a continued reluctance to allow broader participation by the populace through self-government, and the refusal to permit either the judiciary or the public to take an active part in policing administrative operations. The work of the Kakhanov Commission in the 1880s amply demonstrated that government leaders, like many among the educated citizenry, had been aware of all these problems for some time.

Pleve's concern with provincial reform is underlined by the speed with which his staff proceeded on the question. Upon assuming office in April 1902, Pleve instructed that material on the issue be transferred to his personal chancellery, and by 20 May the MVD's Department of General Affairs had completed a memorandum summarizing a projected provincial reorganization.[20] No further action was taken on the proposals raised in the 20 May document until 23 October, when the ministry produced a second memorandum very similar in content to the first. This time the results were more impressive. Within five days Nicholas II approved the memorandum in principle, and three months later, on 30 January 1903, he gave his assent to the formation within the MVD of a commission to prepare a detailed blueprint for provincial reform.[21] By 27 February the commission was ready to begin work, and the ministry's staff had prepared yet another memorandum to guide its deliberations.[22]

Although the three documents on provincial administration differed in details, they were based on a common idea that was to play a prominent part in almost all subsequent local reform efforts. This was an attack on the principle of collegiality in favor of "one-man" (*edinolichnoe*) administration. The authors of the first memorandum, for instance, opened their commentary by pointing to a sharp contradiction between state policy and the actual evolution of provincial institutions over the course of fifty years. They argued that although formal policy had been based upon a preference for individual officials, conditions had forced the government to create one collegial body after another, particularly during the 1890s, which had seen the appearance of the port committee, iron mine board, committee on public temperance, and factory and industrial boards. The MVD staff considered this proliferation of collegial institutions a negative phenomenon. Basing their argument particularly on the example of the provincial board, they described at some length the obvious "unsuitability of colleges." Thus, for instance, they noted that provincial committees and boards often failed to meet, leaving decision making to

[47]

the secretaries who drew up the reports of their findings. Even when the members did bother to hold sessions, they rarely overturned the recommendations of their secretaries.[23]

The MVD remedy for this chaotic state of provincial administration was to be found not in collective organization but in one-man administration, with the primary instrument being, of course, the governor. "History has established that the responsible director of the province should be the governor," the memorandum's authors maintained, "and once responsibility for provincial affairs is demanded of him it is impossible to deny him the means of fulfilling it."[24] The method proposed for making the governor's authority more effective was simple—an expansion of his powers in the areas of active administration and inspection. Formally, this would be achieved by granting him a new title, that of "master" (*khoziain*) of the province.[25] Practically, it would be accomplished by extending his control over almost all other institutions in the province.

The governor was to be given broad rights of inspection and interference over the local offices of the Saint Petersburg ministries. For example, he was to be empowered to review the appointment and transfer of officials and to veto them if necessary on grounds of "unreliability."[26] More important, he was to be given authority to issue offices of other ministries direct instructions on any matter "relating to general measures." Even more striking were the proposals for increasing the governor's influence over self-government. Almost all the existing gubernatorial controls, already widely resented by zemstvo activists, were to be reinforced. Whereas the governor had previously been limited to the "passive" role of vetoing resolutions he found inexpedient, he was now to have the "active" right to demand that a zemstvo or town council take indicated measures within a given period of time.[27]

In the same vein, concern over growing political unrest within the empire motivated the Ministry of Internal Affairs to propose special measures enlarging the gubernatorial hold over two other institutions, the provincial gendarmes administration and the school council. The gendarmes corps had been created under Nicholas I as a special political police force directly subordinate to the tsar—"Third Section" of his own chancellery. Although transferred from the Imperial Chancellery to the Ministry of Internal Affairs in 1880, the corps retained much of its independence both in the capital and in the provinces. Hoping to unify the counterrevolutionary work of the regular police, who were subordinate to the governor, and of the gendarmes, who were ultimately answerable only to their general staff and to the Department of Police in Saint Petersburg, the MVD now suggested that the governor be empowered to give the corps' local representatives "proposals, assignments and instructions."[28] This decision to seek gubernatorial direction over the gendarmes underlines the importance of one-man authority to Pleve, for it directly antagonized a powerful interest group with close ties to the tsar.

The same can be said of the interior ministry's recommendation that the governor be made chairman of the provincial school council. In essence, this measure was intended to improve the state's ability to control the seditious activities of schoolteachers, many of whom were suspected of revolutionary sympathies. However, it also challenged the estate interests of local gentry, for it was the gentry marshal who would be replaced as council chairman. MVD plans for extending the governor's prerogatives over the zemstvo had made it clear that the leading role in the reformed province would belong not to self-government but to the state bureaucracy. The change in the chairmanship of the school council conveyed a similar message to the first estate. This attitude on the respective standing of the civil service, personified by the governor, and of the gentry, represented by their marshal, was made even more explicit in the ministry's proposal for an editorial change in Article 303 of the existing Provincial Statute. In the past the governor was required "on demand" of the marshal to supply clerical aid to the noble assemblies. Now such aid would be extended only "on request." As the authors of the memoranda frankly stated, the old wording provided an erroneous conception of the "inordinate significance" of the gentry estate and its marshal.[29]

Finally, despite their low regard for the collegial institutions, the drafters of the MVD provincial reform realized they could not simply abolish them. Rather, they proposed measures that would better adapt the collegial network to their plans. Chief among these was the creation of a new institution, the provincial council (*gubernskii sovet*), at the top of the collegial system. The council was to serve the dual purpose of uniting all the boards and committees under one leadership and providing the governor with a forum for the discussion of important matters. The first goal was to be achieved by creating under the council a number of divisions, each of which would replace one or more of the hitherto independent collegial bodies. The second would be accomplished by limiting the composition of the council to six: the governor (as chairman), vice-governor, chief finance officer, chairman of the provincial zemstvo board, mayor of the provincial capital, and permanent member. Naturally, the governor was to retain broad powers of direction over the new body. This, coupled with the presence of two of his subordinates (the vice-governor and the permanent member), guaranteed his hegemony.[30]

In its new form the provincial collegial system would not violate the basic principle of one-man authority and would, in fact, become an important vehicle for its operation. Through the provincial council and its subordinate branches the governor and MVD could now reach out more effectively. The aggressive function of the revised structure was indicated by one participant in the MVD work who described its intent as "to include within the jurisdiction of the supreme provincial authority [governor] . . . those matters which had been the exclusive monopoly of local ministerial institutions."[31] This last comment is particularly helpful in clarifying the basic concept behind the three memoranda, all of which were formally submitted to the MVD commission on provincial administration on 27 February 1903. Although most of their commentary was directed specifically at the collegial units, their real target was the wider problem of administrative disunity. In this sense the dysfunctions of the collegial system were seen merely as reflections of the general shortcomings of a provincial apparatus in which organs of the various ministries and of self-government all operated without strong coherence or harmony. Through the imposition of gubernatorial authority the MVD now sought to end disunity by harnessing all provincial institutions essentially under its own direction.

Pleve and his subordinates were clearly following closely in Tolstoi's footsteps. The emphasis on single administrators and the MVD were continuations of the earlier approach. Pleve, like his predecessor and former chief, insisted absolutely upon the hegemony of the state bureaucracy in local affairs. Yet there was at least one fundamental innovation in the 1902–1903 program. Although Tolstoi's methods and assumptions were retained, Pleve and his staff applied them to a new goal. The attack on administrative disunity now became a first step toward a solution of the larger problem of excessive centralization. Although the MVD memoranda said little on this issue, Pleve and his staff were well aware of the need for decentralization. In fact, their intention to proceed in this direction was confirmed just one day before the MVD commission opened its deliberations.

Up to this point work on provincial reorganization had proceeded confidentially. On 26 February, however, the outlines of the government's program were made public, for on that day the tsar issued a manifesto listing all the measures deemed necessary by the central authorities to quell unrest. Considering the fact that Pleve personally directed the drafting of the manifesto, it is not surprising that a prominent place was given to administrative reform. Among the important matters requiring attention Nicholas II noted the need to "reorganize provincial and district administration by improving the means for the local populace to satisfy their diverse needs directly through their own labors, guided by a firm and lawful government strictly responsible to me."[32]

The 26 February Manifesto, and this passage in particular, obviously reaffirmed the tsar's support for Pleve's reform initiative. It also put the ministry's proposals in broader perspective. For instance, the MVD memoranda had already made it clear that the provincial apparatus would be unified by a "strong authority." The manifesto noted that similar measures would eventually be applied in the district. More important, the tsar's reference to direct satisfaction of local needs indicated that the government's program would include a large dose of decentralization. Of course, this left open the question of the form it would take. Yet in mentioning the need to enlist the local populace in administration, the manifesto strongly suggested that decentralization would include not only the transfer of authority down the state administrative hierarchy but the expansion of self-government activity.

What was implicit in the tsar's edict was made explicit in the work of the MVD commission, which Pleve inaugurated personally the following day. The group's composition insured approval of the ministry's program: its membership consisted of the chiefs of the various MVD departments and nine governors specially invited to attend.[33] Nevertheless, among the governors were several active opponents of Pleve's ideas, and their criticism at least provoked a debate that clarified the nature of the ministry's proposals.

The commission's first conclusion was agreement on the need for a major program of administrative reorganization, now officially described as "decentralization." Provincial reform, the commission's journal read, was to be only a first step in a full review of all legislation on local governance. Paraphrasing the 26 February Manifesto, the commission declared the ministry's goal to be "strengthening the means of satisfying local needs directly without turning to the central authorities." This was to be accomplished "both by broadening the competence of public organizations, and by decentralizing authority generally in the sense that questions of local requirements and needs, insofar as possible, be decided in the province itself and even in the district."[34] In other words, the reformers planned to combine the deconcentration of authority from Saint Petersburg with the devolution of activity to the zemstvos and town councils.

The unanimous approval of decentralization did not extend to the main principle of the ministry's proposed provincial reorganization, emphasis on the governor. Prince B. A. Vasil'chikov of Pskov, for one, argued that it would be sufficient to increase the governor's powers of inspection over the civil service. No expansion either of his role in routine administration or his control over the self-governing bodies was necessary.[35] This proposal presented a dual threat to the ministry's plans. It undercut the projected status of the governor as the director and unifier of all provincial institutions, and, since the governor's function as general inspector stemmed from his position as the tsar's agent rather than as an MVD subordinate, it undermined the ministry's command over him. As Vasil'chikov argued, "One musn't forget that the governor, in the eyes of Catherine [II] and the program of Speranskii, is supradepartmental, he is not an official of the Ministry of Internal Affairs." An even more radical proposal in this direction was offered by F. E. Keller of Ekaterinoslav who argued, "The governor needs no new rights, he needs to be freed from the constant tutelage of almost all the departmental directors of the Ministry of Internal Affairs, which binds him hand and foot."[36] Keller's proposal was supported in debate by Assistant Minister P. N. Durnovo. Nevertheless, with the backing of the MVD department chiefs (except probably Durnovo) and most of the governors present, Pleve overruled his opponents. Significantly, both Keller and Vasil'chikov soon left their positions as governors.

The second half of the provincial reform program, the reorganization of the collegial system, raised fewer questions of principle. Perhaps for this reason it underwent more changes in the commission. In its third memorandum the MVD staff had proposed organizing the collegial institutions in twelve branches under a new provincial council that would replace the old provincial board. The commission altered this plan by transferring the branches, reduced in number to nine, to the board, which would continue to exist alongside the new council. Apparently the decision was intended to separate the task of unifying the collegial bodies, to be accomplished by the board, from that of providing a convenient forum for the discussion of important matters of policy, i.e., the council.[37] Finally, the government's growing interest in agrarian reform was reflected in the decision to set up a special directorate to concentrate the handling of peasant affairs.

With the completion of the commission's work in June 1903, the basic features of the intended local reform were clear. Administration would be unified and decentralized under the guidance and supervision of the MVD's own hierarchy. Through the instrumentality of the newly strengthened governorship, the Ministry of Internal Affairs would be able to monitor and control the process by which activity was transferred down the administrative ladder and to the public. This program was not original to Pleve. Domination of the local administrative apparatus had been a goal of the Ministry of Internal Affairs for almost half a century, and, as the ministry itself was willing to admit in 1902, much of its proposed reorganization was inspired by the earlier work of Tolstoi. As for decentralization, no educated Russian who regularly read the periodical press could be unaware either of the concept or of the pressing need to apply it to the country. Moreover, outside the empire the nations of western Europe provided many models of decentralized administration with which the new minister and his staff were well acquainted.[38] Pleve's role was not to develop a new theory of local reform but to tie many elements together in a relatively coherent whole. By mid-1903 this had been achieved. The next task was to see to the program's enactment.

Decentralization: A Question of Definition

The first constituency to which the ministry turned for approval of its proposals was its own body of "local experts," the governors. On 15 July 1903, the MVD staff submitted the commission's work to the provincial chiefs in the form of a series of questions. By autumn, forty-six governors had sent their replies to Saint Petersburg.[39]

As Pleve must have foreseen, the large majority of the governors enthusiastically welcomed the plans to increase their powers. The doubts expressed by Vasil'chikov and Keller found little support among their fellows. For example, a clear majority approved of a proposal that all ministries be required to send directives to their provincial branches through the office of the governor. Only seven objected to the intention to grant the governor the extraordinary right to force the organs of self-government to take measures he considered necessary.[40] If anything, many of the respondents went further than the ministry in their demands for gubernatorial power, particularly over the local agencies of the Ministry of Finance.[41]

The governors' receptivity to an increase in their authority was only natural. Rather surprisingly, they did not couple this with a demand for more autonomy. In the MVD commission both Vasil'chikov and Keller had sought to free the governors of ministerial control by emphasizing their status as supradepartmental agents of the tsar. In their responses to the MVD inquiry, however, almost all the governors were quite willing to accept their place as subordinates. Only three suggested that the governors be removed from the MVD hierarchy and made representatives of the Committee of Ministers.[42] Whether from conviction or simply from a desire to please their superiors, the majority of the local dignitaries sought to improve their standing through the ministry rather than independently of it.

Gubernatorial allegiance to the MVD was a testimony to the development of the linear system in tsarist local administration. Yet while this helped the MVD win the support of its provincial experts, it could only hinder Pleve's effort to gain approval for his plans from the other Saint Petersburg departments. That the Ministry of Finance would oppose the program was a foregone conclusion. In the preceding three decades the MVD and the finance ministry had disagreed over practically every major issue of internal policy. Where the former stressed the need for stability and the defense of order, the latter emphasized highly destabilizing programs of industrialization and development. Pleve's appointment added the dimension of personal animosity to this broad variance over policy, for he and Witte had long considered each other archenemies.[43]

Many of the same factors strained relations between the MVD and the Ministry of Justice. Where concern for order had brought the interior ministry into conflict with finance over industrialization, it caused friction with the justice ministry over the question of legality. Seeking to keep the peace through vigorous repression of political crimes and mass unrest, local police often collided with judicial officials trying to preserve at least a pretense of law and due process in administration.[44] In fact, distrust of the judiciary and a desire to exclude it from peasant affairs had served as one of the MVD's major motivations in introducing the land captaincy in 1889. Moreover, personal rivalries were present here too. Minister of Justice N. V. Murav'ev had been widely considered a promising candidate for the interior post after Sipiagin's assassination, and he bitterly resented Pleve's appointment.[45]

Such frictions between the MVD and other branches of the tsarist government could only be exacerbated by the proposed provincial reform, based as it was upon the hegemony of the MVD's local representatives over the rest of the administrative apparatus. For this reason Pleve's staff carefully kept the drafting process entirely within its own offices, rejecting any preliminary debate of the proposals as "premature."[46] After receiving imperial approval for the plan in the 26 February Manifesto, however, the MVD bureaucrats did seek to press their initiative further. The most important effort in this direction was the convocation on 13 May 1903 of a special conference of ministers chaired by the tsar himself.

The 13 May conference was formally devoted to the question of decentralization, i.e., the transfer of decision-making power from Saint Petersburg to the provinces. Yet it is clear from the conference's official journal that both Pleve and his opponents used the meeting as a forum to debate the issue of provincial reform. It is also apparent that the victor was the minister of internal affairs. Referring to the work of the MVD commission, Pleve directly announced that the projected reorganization would be based upon the unification of all local administrative institutions in a council "under the leadership of the governor, who will be restored to the earlier status of 'master' of the province." Any objections by the other participants were over-ruled by the tsar, who expressed the wish (or de facto command) that "the office of governor be constructed precisely in this fashion."[47] Having lost for the moment the battle to limit the governorship, the best the rival ministers could do was to attempt to weaken the MVD's control over it. On Witte's recommendation, Nicholas II and the ministers agreed that the governor should be not merely a subordinate of the Ministry of Internal Affairs but also the "true representative" of the tsar.

On the official topic of the conference—decentralization—Pleve was also able to have his way. Wary of the precise form future provincial administration might take and generally suspicious of the MVD's intentions, the other ministers sought to postpone the transfer of any effective power from Saint Petersburg until after the reorganization had been completed. As Witte argued, under present circumstances only "relatively few matters" that were "essentially of little import and little value" could be deconcentrated. The minister of finance was supported by Minister of Agriculture A. S. Ermolov, who pointed out that the transfer of more significant activities would require sections of the empire's law codes to be redrafted. Nevertheless, the tsar directed that lists of tasks that could be decentralized be drawn up by all the ministries "immediately." These lists were to include items that could be transferred right away and those that would be so treated following the provincial reorganization. In other words, the ministries were to be coerced to commit themselves to decentralization before the provincial reform had been completed. The lists were to be submitted to a commission chaired by State Councillor S. Platonov by 1 August.[48]

The tsar's attitude at the 13 May conference indicated that a direct assault on the MVD's proposals was, for the time being at least, pointless. This conclusion was reinforced in the following months by Pleve's growing stature within the government; his increased influence was most strikingly demonstrated in August with Witte's ouster as minister of finance.[49] Since active opposition to the MVD was apparently futile, the other ministries chose the path of passive resistance. They refused to work seriously with the commission chaired by Platonov. This lack of cooperation was clearly reflected in the commission's results, which were meager in the extreme. First, the ministries prevented the commission from submitting to the State Council any but the most innocuous matters for immediate transfer to the provinces. With the exception of a few important recommendations from the MVD, the list debated by the council early in 1904 was limited to such questions as the approval of salt works and the granting of hunting licenses.[50] Equally modest were the ministries' lists of matters to be decentralized after provincial reform.[51] Only the Ministry of Justice made major suggestions, and these were predicated upon the weakening of the governor's role and the strengthening of the Supreme Senate's supervision of local administration. In short, unlike the governors, the leaders of other departments of the tsarist government refused to accept the conditions for decentralization laid down by the MVD. While they were unable to defeat Pleve's program outright, they were successful in slowing its implementation until other circumstances ended his initiative altogether.

The tsar's support for Pleve muted criticism of his provincial reorganization within the government. Ignorance of the MVD's intentions prevented any extensive debate outside the state offices. The three relevant memoranda were not made public, and the journal of the MVD commission was published only after Pleve's death. Nevertheless, the citizenry did get a notion of the government's intentions from the 26 February Manifesto. At least some sense of public attitudes on the question can be extrapolated from comments in the press on the imperial document. The various socialist parties, for example, roundly condemned the tsar's ideas. This was, of course, consistent with their general view that the empire was ultimately in need not of reform but of political and social revolution. Lenin, for one, denounced what he called the "cat and mouse game" the government was playing with the public. Rather than discuss individual improvements in local governance, or indeed the issue of local government at all, he demanded the convocation of a popularly elected national assembly and called upon the proletariat to continue its revolutionary struggle against autocracy.[52]

The liberal press was also predictably cool in its reception of the manifesto's promise of decentralization. Editors of the emigré *Liberation*, who were radically constitutionalist in their orientation, simply rejected the government's program as a false "masquerade" of reform.[53] Others did not go this far, but they did make it clear that their support would depend on the way the government defined decentralization. To the editors of the *European Herald*, for instance, the main fault of tsarist administration was not centralization per se, but "bureaucratism." Decentralization would not automatically cure this evil, for even in a decentralized state it was possible to have matters settled on "the discretion of the authorities without consideration of the wishes of the population." Turning to recent European history for an illustration, they maintained that Napoleon III's deconcentration of power from the Parisian ministries to the prefects had brought some increased efficiency to French administration but had not weakened that nation's tradition of bureaucratism.[54]

Liberals continued to insist that decentralization must be envisioned in terms of strengthening self-government in order to be meaningful. As the editors of the *European Herald* stated some months later in commenting on the work of Platonov's commission, "Decentralization is fruitful only when it broadens the sphere of self-government and autonomy and is not limited to increasing the prerogatives of the local administrative authorities."[55] The process, therefore, was to contribute not only to wider public participation in governance but to a change in the quality of that participation. Movement must be away from state bureaucratic direction and toward the spontaneous activity of the citizenry. When applied to administration, this interpretation of decentralization gave results directly opposite to the programs of the MVD. The *European Herald*'s writers again strikingly illustrated the difference by arguing that activation of the zemstvos and town councils would make it possible not to enhance the power of the governor but rather to remove him from participation in direct administration altogether.[56]

The moderate journal *New Times* greeted the tsar's manifesto with much more enthusiasm. Yet its commentary strongly suggested that conservatives would not accept the ministry's project wholeheartedly either. The editors did applaud the manifesto's emphasis on decentralization, and they argued that it should include not only the strengthening of self-government but the extension of gubernatorial powers. This was a direct echo of the interior ministry's conviction that a "strong authority" in the person of the governor was a prerequisite of provincial reform. However, the editors differed from the MVD in emphasizing that this authority must be not only strong but "law-abiding" and "strictly responsible" to the tsar.[57]

New Times columnists considered one of the most serious results of overcentralization to be the constant violation of the law by the representatives of the state bureaucracy. The concentration of decision-making power in Saint Petersburg, they argued, meant that the civil service had "become accustomed to executing only the orders of superiors and to hiding behind them. The entire art of bureaucracy consists solely of the ability to hit the right tone with superiors" and not in observing the law.[58] In order to restore legal norms to imperial administration, the journal's staff suggested two measures. First, both civil servants and representatives of self-government should be united locally in a provincial council that would have "broad competence in the decision of all local questions." The MVD had of course also suggested such a body, but its proposal was much different from that presented in *New Times*. The latter not only included more delegates from the public, it was specifically intended to occupy a position superior to that of the governor. The key "strong law-abiding authority" guiding local administration would be not the governor but the council.[59]

The second idea for guarding legality could no more please the Ministry of Internal Affairs than the first. One basic question of decentralization was who would oversee the operations of the newly reorganized administration. For the MVD reformers the answer was simply the ministry itself. For the editors of *New Times*, however, the chief supervisor could only be the ranking judicial body in the empire, the Supreme Senate. The ministry's memoranda included no mention of the senate; in *New Times* its revitalization was a fundamental prerequisite of reform. As one *New Times* columnist insisted, "The entire reorganization will not be assured of success if the senate is left incapable of insuring the precise execution by local authorities of all their obligations, is not empowered to immediately restore the law in cases of its violation, is deprived of the possibility of holding responsible those guilty of exceeding or of not fulfilling their role."[60]

Neither this concern for legality nor the liberals' emphasis on self-government was shared by the *Citizen* or the *Moscow News*, periodicals of the far right. These two papers wholeheartedly welcomed the 26 February Manifesto and vigorously recommended elevation of the governor as the primary means of battling unrest and rectifying shortcomings of local administration. Yet even their views differed from those of Pleve in fundamental respects. For one thing, some contributors argued that conflict between the state bureaucracy and self-government should be resolved simply by abolishing the provincial zemstvo, a course Pleve never seriously considered. Moreover, they cast the new governor in a way quite different from that of the Ministry of Internal Affairs. For Pleve and his staff the governor was simply the key link in a bureaucratic hierarchy stretching from Saint Petersburg (or, more precisely, from the MVD offices) to the village. To the columnists of these two archconservative journals, however, the most important feature of the reorganized governorship would be its very freedom from the MVD's "bureaucratic" control. The governor was not just to occupy another rung in the administrative ladder, but to be the true personal agent of the tsar. As Prince Meshcherskii wrote in the *Citizen*, local administration should be accomplished by local people working "under the protection of the strength not of a civil servant, but of a representative of the Tsar's authority."[61]

The programs presented by the various periodicals differed widely on points both general and specific. Yet they all shared one very important feature—hostility to what they called "bureaucratism." In the liberal journals this animosity stemmed from the zemstvo ideology and from Western, particularly English, concepts of legality and democracy. In the more conservative papers it had its roots both in the Slavophil distrust of the state bureaucracy as an obstacle to the mystical union of tsar and people and, as will be seen, in the defense of gentry privilege against Saint Petersburg officialdom. This shared hostility was directed primarily at the ministries in the capital, at excessive centralization. But it extended to the local representatives of those ministries as well. This aversion for the civil servant was indicated, for instance, in the reaction of the press to the false rumor that a new vice-governor might be created to replace the gentry marshal as the formal head of district administration. Prince Meshcherskii bluntly rejected the "fabrication of a new bureaucrat-commander in the district," and K. F. Golovin of *New Times* went even further. Arguing that the healthiest administrative structures of Europe, i.e., the English and the Prussian, placed elective officials in control at the grass roots, he insisted that the marshal's prerogatives be increased.[62] Even the *European Herald,* an ardent advocate of civil equality and an opponent of gentry privilege, came to the marshal's defense on the grounds that the status quo would be preferable to the appointment of a bureaucrat.[63] This issue was to play a crucial role in the reform debate much later.

The discussion of provincial and district reform in the periodical press was, of course, only a limited expression of public opinion. Still, it strongly suggested that socialists who looked forward to a radically egalitarian order, liberals with their ideal of a free individualistic citizenry, and conservatives concerned for the monarch's personal authority and the place of the gentry estate all viewed decentralization quite differently from the MVD. This difference in definition was basic, much broader than that separating Pleve from his fellow ministers. Since the MVD never reached the point of opening its proposed provincial reorganization to general debate, there was no direct attack on the ministry's projects. However, the contradiction between state policy and popular views was to be a fateful one. It not only severely hampered Pleve's activities in other areas but continued to thwart reform efforts of tsarist ministers until the downfall of the regime.

Rural Police: The State Reaches the Village

Pleve's plans for the reform of provincial administration were cut short by his death, but he was able to implement one significant change in the empire's administrative machinery—the extension of the central apparatus to the village level through the introduction of a new police guard. Although the measure affected the opposite end of the local government hierarchy from provincial reform, it too directly reflected Pleve's views on the relationship of the state bureaucracy to the populace.

In the decades preceding Pleve's appointment, numerical reinforcement of the police force had been one of the most constant concerns of the Ministry of Internal Affairs. This policy had been applied to all areas of the empire, but its focus in the last quarter of the nineteenth century had been distinctly urban. Although the overwhelming majority of the population remained in the countryside, large increases in police commands were limited primarily to major cities and factory towns.[64] There were several reasons for this urban orientation in an essentially rural society. First, at least from the 1860s, municipal population had been growing much more rapidly than village population, and it was only natural that the urban police force be expanded accordingly. Furthermore, the city police possessed the support of a lobby that not only pressed the Ministry of Internal Affairs for staff increases but was willing to foot the bill for them. Outside the government this lobby consisted of factory owners and businessmen who were willing to take advantage of provisions in the empire's law codes that allowed private citizens to pay the authorities to appoint new policemen. Of the 732 police posts established by private means between 1880 and 1899, some 572 were funded by industrialists.[65] Within official circles, the urban police enjoyed the support of the powerful Ministry of Finance. While that ministry often rejected plans for the reorganization of rural law enforcement agencies as burdening the state budget, it readily approved measures to insure order in the factories. Thus in 1899 it cosponsored with the MVD a proposal to appoint over 2,400 new factory police at an expense to the state of some five hundred thousand rubles.[66]

The basic cause of the government's urban orientation in police affairs, however, most likely lay in the attitude of the MVD. In part the ministry was influenced by the very size and complexity of the task of reforming the rural force. A serious reorganization would not only demand far more money and personnel than would be needed for improving the urban police, it would also touch upon general questions of the village administrative structure. Probably equally important in determining the ministry's attitude was the different degree of perceived danger in rural and urban areas. The threat to stability posed by neglect of the village police was seen as less serious than that posed by a weak urban force. The cities were the home of the government itself and of the majority of the empire's educated classes. It would be there that any breakdown of order, particularly if political in nature, would be most directly felt. This was reinforced by the fact that with the emergence of a large and volatile working class in the 1880s and 1890s, urban violations seemed much more likely to take on a mass and political character.[67]

The relative neglect of the rural police force, which in a sense dated back almost to the emancipation of 1861, could not be maintained forever. Although its rate of increase was somewhat slower than its city counterpart, the empire's rural population was also expanding steadily throughout this period. Furthermore, the same processes of industrialization and commercialization that were creating large urban centers in the empire were also disrupting traditional village society. The movement of rural crime rates is very difficult to determine, particularly since few reliable records are available for volost courts. It is true, though, that the percentage of peasants sentenced in the regular courts rose steadily in the last quarter of the nineteenth century.[68] Moreover, there is solid evidence of growing concern over deviance among the rural elites. Many of the local committees organized under the sponsorship of Witte's Special Conference complained of widespread criminality, which was in part related to the shortcomings of law enforcement. As one group put it, "At present one especially grave evil in the countryside is the weakness of police surveillance and the resulting absence of any punishment for various types of violations."[69] A majority of the local committees demanded reorganization of the village police.

By 1901 it was evident that the MVD was responding to such worries. In answer to an inquiry by the tsar in that year, Sipiagin informed the Council of Ministers that the question of district law enforcement had become a "subject of serious concern."[70] Pointing to the fact that neither police pay nor numbers had changed significantly in the last thirty-eight years, he maintained that "it is absolutely impossible to leave this question in its present form; a fundamental review of the existing police establishments is urgently necessary." Furthermore, he reported that the ministry had already initiated an investigation of the situation of the rural police by asking the governors for their recommendations. Sipiagin's assassination did not slow the progress of the MVD work; rather, it hastened it by bringing to the head of the ministry Pleve, a man with extensive experience in the police bureaucracy and strong views on the role and structure of the force. Any further hesitations were swept away by a wave of peasant disorder in the provinces of Poltava and Kharkov in the spring of 1902. By summer a legislative project for the reorganization of the village police was ready for the State Council's consideration.

The shortcomings of the existing law enforcement apparatus in the countryside were definitely substantive. The most obvious was the small size of the state's rural force and the magnitude of the populace and territory under patrol. Outside the cities the central authorities relied essentially upon a mere 1,582 constables and 6,874 sergeants to control a village population of ninety million.[71] Qualitatively, the situation was hardly better. Low pay and the formidable list of police duties often prevented the central authorities from recruiting capable candidates for service, particularly as sergeants. One columnist for the semiofficial weekly *Police Messenger* characterized sergeants as half-literate reservists, unacceptable in high society, and "completely incapable of any conscientious, tactful, or prudent execution of their authority."[72] Certainly they were widely resented by many local inhabitants. Tenishev and the hundred correspondents who aided him in his 1898 survey of peasant attitudes found overwhelming hostility to the sergeants, who "boast of their commanding superiority and almost always treat the peasants haughtily and coarsely."[73]

Government leaders had long been aware of these deficiencies, but they had assumed that the existence of an elective peasant force within the village would compensate for the weaknesses of the state police. The teners and hundreders were expected to bear primary responsibility for handling small crimes, executing lesser administrative tasks, and gathering information, leaving only major problems to the constables and sergeants. This system of essentially allowing the villagers to patrol themselves within limits set by the occasional presence of the state police dated back to the emancipation of 1861 and was not untypical of traditional agrarian societies. But by the end of the century it was evident that the system was no longer satisfactory in Tsarist Russia. For one thing, as has been noted, the quality of the village police was uncommonly low, as most able peasants actively avoided enrollment. Service was often poorly paid (or performed without renumeration as a corvée-like duty in kind), and it was not unusual for villagers to use election as a form of punishment. Moreover, there always remained the fact that even a conscientious peasant policeman remained much more a peasant than an agent of the law. He was very likely to retain the common attitude of hostility toward nonvillagers, including his own police superiors and the land captains, and as a result frequently ignored his duties. What tener, for example, would turn down a glass of vodka or a few eggs from a neighbor in exchange for failing to report a violation? Indeed, as a peasant, he normally shared the muzhiks' typical understanding of the nature of crime, an understanding often at variance with the empire's law code. The widespread peasant conviction that noble landholdings in fairness belonged to the villagers led peasant policemen to overlook such formally criminal acts as trespass on gentry property, illegal pasturing, and theft of firewood. It was this as much as anything else that gave rise to gentry complaints over the "absence of police" in the countryside.[74]

Of all the problems of the rural police force, it was the reliance upon the villagers that most concerned the Ministry of Internal Affairs in 1902. Consequently, the MVD project submitted to the State Council in that year was based on an old idea, the replacement of the village patrolmen with a new force of state police, the guard (*strazha*).[75] The reasons for the change were explained by Pleve himself in his formal presentation to the council. Referring to the pre-emancipation period when police chiefs were selected by the local gentry, Pleve admitted that the elective principle of service had deep roots in Russian tradition. Nevertheless, he argued, the reforms of the 1860s destroyed the conditions that had justified this elective principle and compelled the state to adopt the policy of appointment instead. The government had taken the first step in this direction in

1862 when it replaced gentry-chosen police officers with civil servants. Now, forty years later, the time had come to extend this approach to the peasant police.[76]

Basing his comments on gubernatorial reports collected by the ministry in 1901 and 1902, Pleve catalogued the deficiencies of the village force. Illiterate, untrained, poorly disciplined, and unaccustomed to their duties, the muzhik patrolmen, in Pleve's view, lacked all the qualifications for proper service. Most important, however, he maintained that the close ties of the peasant police to fellow villagers and their material dependence on the commune had "caused them to shirk from various types of prosecution, fail to execute orders of the authorities, hide crimes, and not uncommonly participate in mass disorders."[77] This unreliability now motivated the ministry to propose that all important duties be assumed by a different body, the guard. This new complement was to be made up of forty thousand recruits, appointed and fully funded by the state and directly subordinate to the state's police sergeants. The force of sixty-seven thousand hundreders would be disbanded. Teners would be retained, since a larger guard was beyond the treasury's financial means, but they were only to perform minor tasks at the command of village elders.

The project received a cool reception in the State Council. Some members objected that the forty-thousand-man guard, although almost equal in size to the entire existing tsarist state police, would not be sufficient to replace the more numerous force of hundreders. Others pointed to the excessive cost of the project—9,700,000 rubles—and suggested that instead half the sum be devoted to improving the village police. Finally, some criticized the project as pursuing two goals simultaneously without accomplishing either. On the one hand, the guard was intended to give the state a reliable force for handling agrarian disorders. On the other, it was to perform routine duties, patrolling the villages on a day-to-day basis. The guard was too small to accomplish the first purpose, the critics argued, and the need to concentrate the guardsmen in squadrons in anticipation of unrest would prevent it from achieving the second. Better to simply introduce additional troopers in troubled areas and postpone the reorganization of the rural police until the broader question of village administration had been settled, they suggested.[78]

Pleve's response was an impressive testimony to the deficiencies of the peasant police. It was impossible, he argued, to maintain the village patrolmen, and he insisted that a necessary condition of any new rural force was the "organization of its entire body, from the highest ranks to the lowest, with men appointed by the government." Pleve admitted that the guard was partially intended to halt agrarian disorders, but he contended that its primary task was the policing of the villages under normal circumstances. "The project does not have in view either a popular upheaval or exceptional conditions threatening the entire state order," he maintained. "This is not the present situation and, apparently, there is no reason to fear it in the future." That the minister of internal affairs sincerely believed this massive miscalculation of the state of affairs in the countryside in 1902 is proven by the one major concession he was willing to allow. Acknowledging the heavy cost of the guard to the treasury, Pleve suggested that it be introduced in stages over the next four years.[79]

Pleve's arguments convinced a majority of the council, which voted to accept the MVD project with only minor changes. This decision to almost double the state police force at a time when the treasury was in a highly unsettled condition was strong evidence of Pleve's increasing influence in Saint Petersburg. More important, it reflected a growing consensus in official circles that the protection of order was a task that could be fulfilled only by agents of the central government. That this consensus in favor of the "statization" of rural police was a matter of principle and not simply of immediate concern for the peasant risings of 1902 is clear in the council's decision to extend the introduction of the guard over not four but six years.

It cannot be denied that the police guard was very much a direct product of the conditions of order in rural Russia at the turn of the century. Those conditions did not, in fact, allow its introduction in the form envisioned by the empire's legislators. The upheaval that Pleve saw no reason to fear in 1902 occurred only three years later and drastically changed the nature of the force. Nevertheless, as originally conceived, the guard reflected several important aspects of MVD thinking on local administration. The project was based upon Pleve's belief in the central role of the Ministry of Internal Affairs as the supervisor of the empire's internal life. Throughout the debates in the State Council he constantly reiterated the need to provide the ministry with forces it could rely upon in the village. More broadly, the plan was inspired by Pleve's conviction of the importance of state bureaucratic tutelage over society. The guard was explicitly intended to improve the government's capacity for performing the most basic aspect of this tutelage, the maintenance of order. The corollary of this confidence in the civil service was, of course, a lack of trust in the populace. As Pleve himself pointed out, the assumption of full responsibility for order by the central authorities was an open rejection of the popular conviction that "the protection of local peace is among the duties of the inhabitants themselves."[80] Or, as Pleve's own chief of police, A. A. Lopukhin, rather pejoratively put it later, the government substituted the guard for the village police "as if from fear of leaving the external signs of authority in the hands of a social group."[81]

The ministry's work on police reform, then, was consistent with its efforts in the area of provincial administration. In both cases, the guiding principles were faith in the MVD apparatus and a converse suspicion of the citizenry. This attitude was the mirror opposite of the zemstvo ideology, which deprecated the "bureaucratism" of civil servants and extolled independent popular initiative. In the case of reorganization of the rural police, the essentially centralizing views of Pleve and his colleagues were no problem. In 1903 most of the educated public was willing to cede the task of law enforcement to the state bureaucracy.[82] For provincial reform the issue also was not crucial, since the entire program was developed within government offices without open debate. In one area, however, the contradiction between the MVD approach and that championed by zemstvo activists did threaten to cause a direct confrontation between Pleve and his staff and educated society. When the ministry turned its attention from the reorganization of the state bureaucracy to the reordering of the public's "own" institutions, the organs of self-government and estate, the question of the extent and nature of the citizenry's participation in administration had to be faced squarely.

CHAPTER III

PLEVE AND THE PUBLIC, 1902–1904

In his two years as minister of internal affairs, Pleve acted vigorously to press forward his plans for reordering the state bureaucracy. By the end of 1903 his ministry had definitely established decentralization as its guiding principle, drafted plans for the reorganization of provincial administration, and sponsored the introduction of a new state police force in the countryside. Yet in terms of the MVD's own program of decentralization, the repair of the state bureaucratic apparatus was only the first prerequisite of an effective reform of local government. The crucial task of "improving the means for the local populace to satisfy their diverse needs directly through their own labors," as the 26 February Manifesto put it, remained. The ultimate success of the decentralization program required the widening of popular participation in administration through the estate and self-governmental institutions. Yet in his attempts to grapple with the issue of participation, Pleve displayed not the decisiveness that characterized his approach to the civil service, but clumsiness and caution. The results were best summarized by V. I. Gurko, who wrote retrospectively of his MVD superior that Pleve "assumed the office of Minister of the Interior with great plans, but these dwindled to pettiness or evaporated into thin air. The mountain brought forth nothing but mice."[1]

This failure partially reflected the minister's lack of previous working contact with the populace, save in the role of a police chief combating sedition. Certainly Pleve's term in office was a period of severe repression of dissidence, a bitterly cold time in the recurrent Russian pattern of freeze and thaw. As Gurko admitted, in dealing with the public Pleve "manifested a faultfinding, hypercritical attitude toward everything and everybody," failing especially to distinguish between revolutionaries and loyal critics of policy.[2] Yet the difficulties with the citizenry were not entirely caused by Pleve's personal shortcomings—they were rooted in the nature of the MVD program. The debate over the role of the estate and self-governmental institutions made the contradictions between the government's statist outlook and the growing popular hostility to "bureaucratism" starkly manifest. The result was a conflict that alienated the educated classes from the government and contributed directly to the revolutionary upheaval of 1905.

The Corporate Institutions: State and Estate

Emphasis on the estate principle as a means of defining the nature of public participation in local affairs had been a cornerstone of MVD policy since Tolstoi. Yet by the time Pleve took office, this approach was under severe criticism. Concern over the condition of Russian agriculture had been mounting since the famine of 1891; calls for the reorganization of village administration were one way of expressing this concern. Zemstvo activists, for example, urged the extension of all-estate governance in the countryside through the introduction of a local zemstvo below the district level. Uneasiness with the present state of rural administration was shared by the government. In January 1902 Sipiagin announced the creation of a special Ministry of Internal Affairs commission to review existing peasant legislation. Simultaneously, Minister of Finance Witte initiated his own Special Conference on the Needs of Agriculture.[3] Moreover, beyond creating this competing body within the government, Witte took the unusual step of formally opening the doors to public debate of the agrarian question by establishing provincial and district committees of his conference and inviting fourteen thousand local officials and citizens to take part. The resulting grass-roots demands for action redoubled the pressure on the MVD to bring forth its own proposals.

Pleve was not pleased with public discussion of the state of the rural economy, but he did not repudiate Sipiagin's intention of having the MVD view the situation with an eye to change. Several times during his first months in office he expressed his interest in peasant reform and continued the preparations for the MVD's commission on the subject.[4] However, he lacked any firm notion of the direction in which reform should proceed. Initially, this absence of a set idea allowed a certain flexibility in his approach and permitted sections of the ministry staff to work toward far-reaching change. Ultimately, though, it gave rise to a belief in the need for caution that led to a narrowing of the ministry's program.

Pleve's ambivalence is clearly evident in his attitude on the most fundamental aspect of village life, landholding. During 1902, pressure for a change in the official policy of supporting the peasants' communal ownership grew both within the government and among the politically active public. Yet unlike Witte, who had concluded that individual landholding should be encouraged at the expense of the commune (*mir*), Pleve had "no definite opinion on the subject." As he informed State Councillor A. A. Polovtsov, "I am no sectarian in theories of landholding."[5] On the one hand, he understood the weaknesses of the commune and was attracted by the argument that respect for private property (and order) could be inculcated in the peasantry only by introducing individual ownership. Moreover, he was naturally suspicious of an institution that by virtue of its collective aspects bore the approval of agrarian radicals like the Socialist Revolutionary party. On the other hand, Pleve recognized that the commune was the traditional basis of peasant agriculture and understood the magnitude of any reform aimed at altering it. Furthermore, he feared that the breakup of the mir would facilitate the creation of a rural proletariat, a definite threat to order.

Pleve's indecision was reflected in his actions. He took pains to point out that he was no firm supporter of the commune, and in the summer of 1902 he appointed an open enemy of the mir in the person of Gurko to be head of the MVD's Land Section. At the same time, however, he retained Sipiagin's appointee, the conservative A. S. Stishinskii, as chairman of the MVD commission preparing the projects for peasant reform.[6] In a speech given during the celebration of the centennial of the ministerial system in February 1903, Pleve maintained that "the highest of all the tasks of our time is the task . . . of putting peasant affairs in good order," but he presented no specific program. Very uncharacteristically, he limited himself to stating that the solution of the peasant question could not be found by the Ministry of Internal Affairs alone, but would require the work of "all the creative spiritual forces of the country."[7]

The MVD's new direction—more precisely, its lack of direction— received formal approval in the 26 February Manifesto. In addition to noting the need for decentralization in administration, the manifesto directed that peasant legislation be revised. This revision was to be based, in the tsar's words, upon "the inviolability of the communal structure of peasant landholding, having simultaneously found means to ease exit from the commune by individual peasants."[8] Of course, the two recommendations of retaining the inviolability of the mir while at the same time weakening it by allowing peasants to leave were in opposition to each other. Nevertheless, this contradictory approach was to remain state policy until after Pleve's death. It was explicitly the basis of the Stishinskii Commission's recommendations, which were presented later in the year.[9]

The policy announced in the manifesto represented something of a compromise between two conflicting views in the government. Supporters of the commune remained influential in Saint Petersburg, particularly since Nicholas II himself favored the traditional order. Opponents, however, were able to compensate for royal disapproval by holding strategic positions within the state apparatus, particularly within the Land Section of the MVD. The interaction of these two camps was demonstrated in the drafting of the manifesto itself. Most of the basic points to be covered in the document, including the inviolability of the commune, were indicated by the tsar beforehand.[10] Yet the actual composition of the section dealing with peasant affairs was assigned to Gurko as head of the Land Section. In an instructive demonstration of the limits that bureaucracy can place on autocracy, Gurko was able to insert the provision on peasant exit from the commune into the manifesto and thus achieve official sanction for his own activities.

The basic factor producing the compromise, however, was not the existence of opposing views but equivocation in the mind of the man most responsible for the formation of policy. Still lacking strong convictions for or against the mir, Pleve allowed himself to be swayed by the tsar's inclinations and by the obvious difficulties of a more radical course in a period of growing disorder. Yet simultaneously he refused to halt the efforts of part of his own staff, led by Gurko, to work toward change. As Gurko himself concluded, "Pleve was totally incapable of taking a decisive step in either direction, both because he was insufficiently acquainted with the question and because he was not a reformer by nature."[11]

The handling of the issue of village governance, not surprisingly, closely paralleled that of land. For one thing, the rationale for separate, all-peasant administrative units was not greatly different from the justification for special communal forms of landholding. Indeed, volosts and village communities, the corporate administrative bodies of the peasantry, could be coextensive with the commune, especially in the empire's central provinces. Consequently, demands for reform of village government, like landholding, typically focused on the integration of the peasants with other classes. Here the issue was not the extension of private property to the muzhiks, but rather the extension of all-estate zemstvos. Furthermore, the same interplay of interests that had determined the debate over the land question existed in the discussion of village administration. For example, one of the most active proponents of reorganization of the corporate units was the same Gurko who had pressed hard for agrarian reform. And the thinking of the most important figure in the determination of policy, Pleve, was again characterized by ambivalence and caution.

Shortly after his appointment, Pleve showed signs of a willingness to consider major reorganization of rural government. Under Sipiagin the MVD policy had been one of firm support for the traditional peasant institutions.[12] For instance, in keeping with Witte's growing interest in encouraging individualism among the peasantry, the Ministry of Finance had proposed abolition of the joint legal responsibility of peasants of a commune for paying their taxes (*krugovaia poruka*). Sipiagin, who realized that the removal of collective responsibility would seriously undermine the justification for keeping the peasantry isolated from other estates administratively, strenuously opposed the change.[13] His assassination brought an abrupt shift in the MVD stance. On 25 April, three weeks after Pleve's appointment, the proposal for tax reform was passed in the State Council without any serious opposition. Furthermore, Pleve, through his subordinate Stishinskii, informed the council that he agreed with Witte that the step should be announced in an imperial manifesto.[14]

A second measure introduced in 1902, this time by the MVD itself, further weakened the case for a separate peasant administration. The creation of the state guard meant the rejection in theory of the policy of relying upon the peasantry to shoulder most of the burden for routine policing of the countryside. Instead, order in the rural areas would be protected by a force open to recruits from all social strata and supported financially by the tsarist treasury through general taxes on all estates. In his presentation to the State Council on the guard, Pleve himself acknowledged this implication when he maintained, "The charging of this estate [the peasantry] with a special obligation in the interests of the entire government cannot be justified from the standpoint of simple fairness."[15] It was only logical to argue further that charging the peasant institutions alone with other administrative tasks that redounded to the benefit of the whole populace was also unjust.

More explicit evidence of Pleve's willingness to consider reorganization of the peasant institutions was his appointment of Gurko to a leading post in the MVD. Gurko, who believed that separation of the peasantry insulated it from the beneficial effect of contact with the more cultured gentry, was a strong supporter of the idea of an all-estate volost. Early in Pleve's ministry he had made his views known by presenting to the Stishinskii Commission a draft plan aimed, although in a moderate way, at ending the peasantry's administrative isolation. Much to Gurko's surprise Pleve expressed approval of the draft and agreed to appoint him head of the Land Section.[16]

Despite these initial indications of flexibility, Pleve was unable to commit himself fully to reform. As with the land question, he remained undecided for some time. And again his indecision was reflected in the 26 February Manifesto. After listing all the government's other intended measures, the tsar concluded by proposing in reference to the volost "the combination of public administration with the parish organizations of the Orthodox church, where this seems possible."[17] Yet the idea of a parish body was a vague one, open to liberal and conservative interpretations. For the rightist Prince Meshcherskii it meant the continued separation of the peasantry under the supervision of the clergy, while to the editors of *New Times* it signified the inclusion of all estates in a new administrative unit coterminous with the parishes.[18] Moreover, as the codrafter of the manifesto, Gurko, has testified, neither Pleve nor his subordinates ever had any plans for implementing the parish scheme in any case.[19]

What Pleve was prepared to allow in regard to village reform was revealed in October 1903 in the recommendations of the Stishinskii Commission. It was obvious from the commission's report that the estate idea would not be abandoned as the defining principle of peasant administration. The first of the three major premises upon which the commission based its findings was the "separation of the peasant estate and a special form of peasant administration established accordingly."[20]

The reasons for the refusal to drop the corporate idea were various. There was, of course, the magnitude of the task of more radical reform, and pressure from the conservative supporters of the existing system. It can be argued, however, that the central factor in Pleve's decision to retain the administrative isolation of the peasantry was a perceived threat to order. In the case of land reform a concession to private ownership was expected to bring large dividends in terms of internal security by strengthening the peasants' sense of private property. The opposite seemed true of combining the peasantry with other estates in local government. Pleve, like his predecessor Sipiagin, realized that the judicial and administrative equalization of the muzhiks with other citizens would mean an end to special restrictions on peasant mobility and contribute directly to the creation of urban and rural proletariats.[21] Moreover, the inclusion of the villagers in all-estate institutions would mean exposing them to the influence of those Pleve considered the archenemies of order—the rural intelligentsia. From the very beginning of his tenure as minister, Pleve had been actively concerned about the zemstvo third element. For example, the government assigned to them much of the responsibility for the peasant disorders of spring 1902. As Pleve confided to zemstvo leader D. N. Shipov, the third element workers "pursue primarily political goals—the destruction of the entire existing social structure."[22]

The importance of internal stability as a factor in the ministry's thinking was clear in the report of Stishinskii's group. Among the justifications for the continued separation of the peasant estate the commission included what it described as the indelible impression left by agriculture on the peasants' world view.

> Raised in ceaseless, persistent labor, accustomed to an age-old, uniform condition of life, schooled by the varying success of agricultural labors to a consciousness of their dependence on the external forces of nature and consequently on principles of the highest order, the peasantry more than any other part of the population has always stood and does now stand behind the constructive and positive ideals of community and state.[23]

In order to maintain this special outlook, the members of the commission insisted upon the retention of the peasant administrative institutions, the volost and village community. No mention was made of either the local zemstvo or the parish idea.

Despite these generally conservative findings, the commission's work did differ from the existing legislation on the peasantry in two noteworthy ways. First, as with land, the report combined a reaffirmation of the old system with some concessions to a new one. The most important of these was the decision to separate the peasant landholding unit, the commune, from the basic peasant administrative unit, the village community. Despite its name, the latter was not necessarily made up of all the peasant inhabitants of a particular settlement. Rather, its membership was based upon the membership of the communes it represented. Since communes could hold land in several settlements, the village community sometimes covered more than one population center. Conversely, because communes might also hold only part of the land attached to any given settlement, it was quite possible for neighbors to belong to different village communities. All this led to considerable jurisdictional confusion. Who, for instance, was responsible for sanitation measures in a single settlement divided among several village communities?

Recognizing that interest in such matters as health, fire prevention, and schools was determined more by place of residence than membership in a commune, the Stishinskii Commission recommended reorganizing the village communities to correspond with the territorial boundaries of individual settlements.[24] Although the old corporate basis of the village community was retained in that only the peasant inhabitants of a given settlement were to be members, the measure was an important step toward an all-estate administrative unit. Once the boundaries of the village community actually corresponded to the territorial limits of a population center, it would be simple to make all residents members regardless of social status. This tendency in the commission's work was reinforced by the decision to allow the village community to tax certain nonpeasants living within its boundaries. As soon as artisans and petty merchants began to be assessed to support the local administrative unit it was only natural that they should expect the right of participation. Gurko, the man most responsible for the innovations, later reflected, "I tried to introduce the idea of an all-class volost and to build my project of village and volost public organization in such a way that it might be turned, by a few easy editorial changes, into a project for organizing an all-class village or volost society."[25]

The second change proposed by the Stishinskii Commission affected not the peasantry so much as the gentry. It was in essence a subtle but significant shift in the first estate's role in governance. As defined after the emancipation of 1861 and particularly as restructured by Tolstoi, the corporate principle in administrative affairs represented a combination of state interest and noble privilege. The mutually beneficial nature of the system was most clearly reflected, of course, in the combination of civil service and gentry supervision over the peasantry in the person of the land captain. Although the Stishinskii Commission's report suggested no major innovations in this supervision, its wording made it evident that emphasis was on the central government and not the gentry. For example, in a frank expression of the state principle, the commission contended that the right of the authorities to separate the peasantry "under the close supervision of special governmental organs" was "a logical result of the very serious sacrifices borne by the state for the insurance of the peasant mode of life."[26] In other words, having implemented the emancipation and restructured village administration in the 1860s, the government retained the power to oversee the course of peasant development. The implications of the commission's report were noted by one perceptive noble, who wrote, "It is peculiar to see that the rural population's need for direction and defense by the landed gentry—without which the authorities' concerns for the welfare of the peasant masses would remain, according to the drafters of the 1889 legislation, unfulfilled—is not noted in the observations of the ministerial commission; the principle of official-bureaucratic guardianship over the peasants appears in all its nakedness."[27]

The shift of emphasis was characteristic of other measures prepared by the ministry at this time. The insistence upon the primacy of the governor over the gentry marshal in the projected provincial reform, for instance, has already been discussed. Equally revealing was some minor legislation dealing directly with the land captaincy. Although the office had been created with great expectations, it rapidly became clear that there were serious difficulties. Soon after 1889 various officials began to complain about the inefficiency and poor quality of the new functionaries, and the MVD began to take remedial measures. During the 1890s, for example, an effort was initiated to draft regulations to control land-captain activity. Moreover, the ministry had increasingly resorted to the appointment of its own candidates when the local gentry were unable to provide satisfactory ones. The nobility and many land captains themselves resented such measures. They decried the practice of appointing nonlocals, whom they regarded as "common bureaucrats" or, in a reference to Norse invaders who ruled the ancient Kievan state, "Varangians."[28]

Hoping to improve the situation, Pleve and his subordinates now introduced in the State Council a project recommending changes in the method of recruiting land captains.[29] Outlining in some detail the local gentry's failure to provide a sufficient group of competent candidates, the MVD proposed a number of essentially palliative steps. Like the Stishinskii Commission findings, these all pointed to the further assimilation of the land captaincy into the state bureaucracy. The governor's influence over the selection of candidates was to be increased. Larger salaries were to be paid, thus encouraging service by men who lacked private income. Possibilities of advancement in the MVD hierarchy, which would increase the incentive to identify with the ministry in the hopes of promotion, were to be opened. Finally, the MVD Land Section was to be allowed to train candidates who could be substituted for local gentry in filling vacancies. In other words, the system of Varangians was to be formalized. Despite some objections in the State Council, the ministry's proposals were approved.

The Stishinskii Commission's report and the measures on the land captaincy indicated the essentials of Pleve's attitude toward the estate principle in administration. Movement was cautiously away from the estates, not toward them as under Tolstoi. In the case of the peasants, the village police force was partially disbanded and the commune itself weakened. In the case of the gentry, the already mixed nature of the land captaincy was compromised still further by continued bureaucratization of the office. Nevertheless, despite these indications of an interest in abandoning the estate principle, Pleve and the MVD shrank from the decision for radical change. The traditional foundations of rural government were questioned but ultimately left intact.

This approach was not calculated to win broad public support. Progressive critics of the existing situation found it halfhearted and timid, and conservatives were displeased with its statist character and consequent slighting of the gentry. However, Pleve's hopes for enlisting cooperation with the government were not pinned to his recommendations for the estate institutions. Rather, they rode on his plans for the other popular component of local administration—self-government.

Pleve and Self-Government: State and Society

The decade preceding Pleve's appointment had been characterized by the growing alienation of large segments of the educated citizenry from the tsarist government. As the development of the zemstvo ideology demonstrated, this alienation was expressed by many in terms of a gap between "state" and "society," or, as one prominent liberal later put it, between "authority" (*vlast'*) and "public" (*obshchestvennost'*).[30] Although this attitude was reflected in criticism of various aspects of state policy, it was especially obvious in widespread hostility toward the civil service and in friction between the organs of self-government and the local representatives of the state bureaucracy. To put the matter in wider perspective, the root of the difficulty lay in the increasing political activism of elements of the populace, an activism that transcended the traditional limits of public participation in government. By 1902 it was clear to many officials that the authorities would have to make a serious effort to win back support, at least in part by drawing the empire's inhabitants more effectively into administration at the local level.[31]

Pleve was not by nature inclined to let his actions be dictated by public opinion. As he had commented in his conversation with Witte at Yalta in 1902, in his conception the primary role in the direction of state policy belonged not to the public but to the state bureaucracy. This attitude was, of course, directly reflected in the MVD work on provincial reform, with its emphasis on state control. Pleve realized, however, that the civil service was not capable of shouldering the entire burden of local administration alone. Moreover, he recognized that some steps would have to be taken to restore shaken confidence in the government. Both factors necessitated measures to strengthen self-government and to improve cooperation between the zemstvos and the town councils on the one hand and the state bureaucracy on the other.

Historians have traditionally depicted Pleve strictly as an ardent opponent of self-government, but there is considerable evidence that the minister of internal affairs did intend to better relations with the public organizations, partially by expanding their activity. In July 1902 zemstvo activist D. N. Shipov was summoned to Saint Petersburg to be reprimanded by Pleve for his role in an illegal liberal gathering held the preceding spring. To Shipov's surprise, however, in their conversation Pleve stressed not the formal reprimand but his own interest in restoring harmony with the zemstvos. Describing himself as a supporter of zemstvo institutions, Pleve asserted that "no state structure is imaginable without the participation of society in local self-government." Denying the possibility of administering the country "by means of an army of bureaucrats," Pleve maintained that "under an autocracy the broad development of local self-government is necessary."[32] Although he later reversed his opinion, Shipov was convinced by Pleve's remarks and by a similar conversation with Witte that the government recognized the need to strengthen the zemstvo. So, too, were the moderate progressives N. N. L'vov and D. I. Shakhovskoi.[33]

Pleve reiterated the main points of his discussion with Shipov on a number of subsequent occasions. While accompanying the tsar on maneuvers in Kursk in August 1902, he made a special visit to the offices of the provincial zemstvo board, where he expressed his interest in and support of its work. And in a speech to the chairmen of the area's district zemstvo boards written with Pleve's aid, Nicholas II noted, "The rural economy is of the utmost importance and I hope that you will apply all of your energies to it. I shall be glad to assist you for I desire to unify the activity of all local authorities."[34] Several months later Pleve again met with zemstvo leaders, this time the chairman and a member of the board of the Nizhnii Novgorod provincial zemstvo. Once more he described himself as a "sincere defender of the zemstvo," reaffirmed his conviction that "it is impossible to administer everything from Petersburg, far from local conditions," and promised that soon self-government would be given very important new tasks to fulfill.[35] Indeed, Kharkov zemstvo delegate Prince A. D. Golitsyn was so impressed with his talk with Pleve in February 1903 that he sent a circular letter to colleagues arguing that law-abiding zemstvos could "count on full support and confidence from the minister, who is very interested in developing the independence and widening the rights and functions of district zemstvos."[36]

Although these remarks have been dismissed as mere public-relations statements, even lies, other evidence corroborates their sincerity. In the confidential memorandum to the MVD commission on provincial reform, Pleve's staff indicated an intention to review the legislation on self-government "with the goal of clarifying the question of decentralization, i.e., the possibility of the removal of certain duties from the state organs and their transfer to the zemstvo and public organs."[37] That is, the commitment to decentralization meant not only the deconcentration of authority within the state bureaucracy but the devolution of activity from the civil service to self-government. As Gurko described it, one of the main goals of the reform of the local administrative apparatus was to place it in "direct contact and cooperation" with self-government.[38]

Indeed, Pleve did not limit himself to expressions of goodwill for the zemstvos and town councils; he took steps to transform that goodwill into action. Before assessing his attempts to implement his views on self-government, it is necessary to determine precisely the nature of those views. If Pleve was no enemy of the public organizations, then what kind of friend was he?

Throughout the history of the zemstvo and town council there had been two dominant schools of thought on their significance. The first, or "societal" school, focused on the notion that self-government should operate autonomously within the limited sphere of strictly "local" concerns. The second, or "state" school, emphasized the integration of the elective bodies within the general state apparatus. That Pleve's attitude would heavily reflect the state interpretation was a foregone conclusion. This point of view had been predominant in Russia since the 1880s and had served as the cornerstone of the reorganization of self-government carried out by Tolstoi and Durnovo. The continuing predominance of a statist perspective in Pleve's ministry was amply demonstrated in the MVD work on provincial reform, with its generous provisions for bureaucratic control of the public organizations. The decision to grant the governor "active" authority to insist that the organs of self-government take necessary measures, to cite the most notorious example, was a logical supplement to Tolstoi's strengthening of the governor's "passive" power to veto inexpedient resolutions of the zemstvos and town councils. Primacy was naturally to remain with the civil service.

Pleve's approach reflected the societal theory in one important respect, however—the very sticky issue of jurisdiction. In the past, some liberals had espoused the state outlook partly in the hope that once the zemstvo was considered a state institution its activity could be extended into new areas. It was this interpretation of the state view that the Ministry of Internal Affairs explicitly rejected. The MVD considered the institutions of self-government to be government institutions in regard to control, but their functions were still to be limited strictly to local, socio-economic questions. As the tsar, on Pleve's prompting, informed the Kursk zemstvo employees, "Remember that your main task is to attend to immediate socio-economic needs. If you fulfill this obligation you may be assured of my heartfelt favor."[39] The minister himself made the point more bluntly to the leaders of the Nizhnii Novgorod zemstvo. "I am a sincere defender of the zemstvo and in me you will always find support," he said, "but I ask you, gentlemen, do not cross the demarcation line."[40]

Pleve's emphasis on central supervision and on a strict definition of the functions of self-government was sobering, but it did have a positive side. Just as unity through the governor's power was designed to allow decentralization within the state bureaucracy, so too would a firm delineation of the role of the zemstvo and town council permit them improved activity and increased state financial support within their own sphere. These benefits to self-government were, in the ministry's view, no small matter. In fact, they were the key to Pleve's attempt to reconcile the zemstvos—and the educated public in general—to the state bureaucracy. Central control and direction, a prerequisite for any reform in Pleve's eyes, were to be made palatable to the citizenry by financial aid and better working conditions locally. As one zemstvo constitutionalist perceptively, although very pejoratively, described it, the Ministry of Internal Affairs was attempting to buy the support of self-government.

The same bribery that is being applied to individual citizens will be applied on a large scale to the public institutions. . . . The distribution of subsidies to the zemstvos, sham favor for zemstvo activity as needed, but of course all within the sphere of bridge repair, the purchase of hospital linen, the sale of plows and roofing metal—here is the demarcation line to which Pleve refers.[41]

The regime's radical opponent Lenin put the point even more sharply by describing the plan as a "Zubatovshchina" for the zemstvos, an attempt to enlist zemstvo cooperation through state sponsorship in the same way that Okhrana chief Sergei Zubatov had tried to win worker loyalty through police trade unions.[42]

This program in which self-government essentially sacrificed its independence and broader political aspirations for expanded activity in fields like health and agronomy was not solely of Pleve's creation. In fact, its implementation in the financial sphere had been one of the primary concerns of Finance Minister Witte since the late 1890s. Through an 1898 law on land assessment and the 12 June 1900 regulations on zemstvo budgets, which made government approval mandatory for any increase of more than 3 percent, Witte gained effective control over zemstvo finances.[43] Yet this control was not used to restrict the rural bodies; instead, the central authorities readily approved substantial increases in zemstvo taxes, and expenditures rose by over 8 percent in 1902 and more than 9 percent the following year. In fact, the budgetary expansion was in large part attributable to a marked increase in direct subsidies from the state treasury.[44] Witte had not sought to stultify self-government, simply to direct it. What Witte had achieved in the specific field of finance Pleve now hoped to accomplish for government-zemstvo relations generally.

The most immediate attempt to implement this new policy was a series of conferences with zemstvo leaders organized by the MVD early in 1903. The first, held in late January, was devoted to a reconsideration of a 12 June 1902 law on veterinary inspection. The measure, which had been drafted by the ministry under Sipiagin, placed significant restrictions on the zemstvos in this area and had evoked a vigorous protest.[45] Seeing an opportunity for constructive work with the representatives of self-government within the socio-economic sphere, Pleve invited eight zemstvo board chairmen, three board members, and three zemstvo veterinarians to a meeting in Saint Petersburg. Following a review of the law with these local specialists, the MVD staff drafted new proposals, which when implemented later in the year created considerably more favorable conditions for zemstvo veterinary activity.[46]

The January conference was followed by others. In March, shortly after the promulgation of the 26 February Manifesto, five gentry marshals and eight zemstvo board leaders were summoned to the capital to investigate another sore point in zemstvo-government relations, a supply law passed in 1900. In addition to discussing the supply situation in the empire in depth, this group also exchanged opinions with Pleve on such issues as local schools, zemstvo taxes, and creation of a volost zemstvo.[47] A month later, at the end of April, yet another conference was convened, this time to work out measures for coordinating fire insurance. In eight days of deliberation held under the auspices of the MVD's insurance committee the representatives of twenty-three provincial zemstvo boards adopted a program for rural fire insurance presented by Shipov.[48] Finally, MVD subordinates and zemstvo activists were brought together once more in August for a session on country roads. Among the recommendations worked out by the participants were the transfer of upkeep on certain types of thoroughfares to the zemstvos and permission for the bodies to levy a tax for communications work. Further, a special fund was established to provide financial assistance to self-government in carrying out such new tasks.[49]

Beyond drafting individual measures for expanding zemstvo operations, the conferences had the second, more general, goal of improving relations between the central authorities and the public organizations. As Pleve informed those attending the April insurance meeting, "Your conferences in the ministry on practical subjects draw you together with representatives of the ministry, [and] facilitate common work and mutual interaction."[50] In order to achieve this goal on a more permanent basis, the MVD presented another major proposal to the State Council, a plan for the creation of a Council on Local Affairs (*Sovet po delam mestnago khoziaistva*).

Until 1903 relations between the interior ministry and self-government had been handled primarily by the MVD's Economic Department. Now the ministry leadership recommended that the department be reorganized into a Main Administration for Local Affairs. This measure was primarily technical, aimed at increasing efficiency in supervising and directing expanding zemstvo and municipal activity. But to it was added another idea, the organization of a council to work with the new administration. This body, to be chaired by the minister of internal affairs himself, was to consist of representatives of the various central departments that had dealings with self-government plus twelve to fifteen local men specially invited by the MVD. Its purpose, as described in the ministry's memorandum to the State Council, was to "create a procedure in which the drafting of important measures and legislative projects occurs by means of a lively intercourse and direct exchange of ideas between representatives of the central institutions on the one hand and people closely informed of local conditions and needs on the other."[51] The proposal was approved by the State Council on 22 March 1904.

The MVD also sought to secure zemstvo support in other ways. For instance, tax arrears laws were revised in order to make the state treasury responsible for the proper collection of zemstvo levies.[52] Furthermore, the practice of appointing officials of self-government to administrative positions, which had lapsed in the 1890s and been revived by Sipiagin, was pressed with vigor. This was particularly the case with the new Main Administration for Local Affairs. The logical candidate for its chairmanship was N. A. Zinov'ev, head of the MVD department in charge of self-government. However, Zinov'ev was widely reputed to be no friend of self-government, and he was passed over for the post in favor of S. N. Gerbel, former chairman of the Kherson zemstvo board.[53] To help develop a still more sympathetic attitude toward self-government, M. V. Islavin was appointed as the administration's permanent member. Islavin had at one time been chairman of the Tver zemstvo board and was known for his great personal tact.[54] Also joining the staff were another former zemstvo chairman, A. F. Nemirovskii, and a one-time provincial mayor, N. L. Psheradskii.

Finally, though the attention of the MVD focused essentially on the countryside, Pleve and his subordinates did take one urban initiative. In 1903 the ministry brought before the State Council a project for improving self-government in the city of Saint Petersburg. Admittedly, the imperial capital was a special case, as the MVD staff took care to note in the bill's presentation. But a number of principles involved had direct implications for more general urban reform. In regard to the franchise, under the provisions of the 1890 statute only forty-four hundred of Saint Petersburg's million inhabitants were allowed to participate in municipal elections. All were wealthy proprietors. Now, the MVD proposed a modest broadening of the electorate by including renters of apartments valued at approximately a thousand rubles per year. Restrictive though the annual rent figure was, the notion of extending suffrage in self-government to residents not owning substantial amounts of real estate was radical as indicated by the opposition of the capital's conservative Mayor Lelianov.[55]

Simultaneously, however, the interior staff combined this first innovation with a second directly in keeping with Pleve's conception of the role of the state bureaucracy. According to the draft regulations, the Saint Petersburg city chief (*gradonachal'nik*)—the urban equivalent of a governor—was to have the authority to fulfill certain obligations at the expense of the town council should the latter default in its duties. Moreover, the MVD was to be empowered not only to halt the implementation of council measures but to substitute ones of its own subject to approval by the Committee of Ministers.[56] As with the zemstvo, Pleve was consistent in arguing that any democratization of urban self-government or any broadening of its jurisdiction would require a corresponding strengthening of the state bureaucracy's ability to exert ultimate control and direction.

In sum, the MVD activity, rural and urban, indicated quite clearly that Pleve did intend to develop self-government and meet the public outcry for decentralization. Yet the form of decentralization that he had in mind was quite different from that of the zemstvo activists. In their view expanded public participation in administration could be meaningful only if based upon a presumption of independence and autonomy. For Pleve the opposite was the case. Devolution of tasks from the state bureaucracy to the self-governing institutions was possible only if accompanied by continued, even heightened, supervision. In this way Pleve and the MVD staff hoped to accommodate the demand for broader citizen involvement without abandoning support for the dominant position of the state bureaucracy.

Pleve and Public Opinion: State versus Society

Despite Pleve's intentions, his tenure as minister was characterized not by the restoration of harmony between government and public but by growing conflict. As one leading MVD official later commented, by 1904 Pleve had "aroused the indignation of nearly all public circles, even the most moderate and those most devoted to the existing order. It seemed that the government was suspended in mid-air and that its sole support was the administrative and police apparatus—an apparatus which seemed to function without spirit."[57] What were the reasons for the abject failure to reconcile the politically active citizenry to the regime?

The first and most obvious problem was the minister's own personality. Both by background and temperament Pleve was particularly unsuited to the role of winning popular support. Having spent his entire career in the state apparatus he had little effective experience in dealing with public leaders and lacked confidence in their abilities and devotion to the throne. This was strikingly illustrated in his conversation with Witte at Yalta in October 1902, when he turned to the subject of liberals among the members of the local committees sponsored by the Conference on the Needs of Agriculture. Rejecting the possibility of working with these very moderate dissidents, Pleve contended that the "so-called educated classes" had but one aim—revolution. "At present," he argued, "the campaign of public elements against bureaucracy is a battle cry hiding another goal—the destruction of Autocracy."[58] Having served as director of the Department of Police during an earlier period of unrest, Pleve was familiar with police methods and willing to use them against all elements he considered enemies of the state. As he frankly informed one local figure, the zemstvos might discuss economic policy as they wished, but once discussion touched upon the subject of autocracy, "I stop being the Minister of Internal Affairs and become only the Chief of the Gendarmes."[59] And, indeed, Pleve's ministry was one of stepped-up police activity in almost every area of Russian life.

Beyond the questions of repression and the attitude with which Pleve implemented his program was the problem of the program itself. In the first place, as Pleve's comments made clear, reform was to be strictly limited to local administration. Absolutely no debate of broader issues that might carry implications of constitutionalism or the weakening of autocracy would be permitted. Even within the restricted sphere of government in the provinces Pleve's program was based upon a principle that was increasingly rejected both by liberal and conservative elements of the public, the joining of decentralization with the continued hegemony of the state bureaucracy. In theory the citizenry was to be reconciled to this principle by expanded participation in local, material affairs through the organs of self-government. Yet as one zemstvo progressive repeated in 1903, "Man lives not by bread alone." The government had overlooked one simple truth, he argued. "No matter how wide the limits of the socio-economic activity of the zemstvo institutions, so long as the administrative authorities retain their exceptional and unlimited prerogatives . . . between government and zemstvo there can be no discussion of peaceful coexistence."[60] As time passed, this view, albeit in a more moderate form, became increasingly widespread among the populace. The development of public opinion was to show that the government's promises of subsidies and more scope for initiative in local questions were insufficient to satisfy growing demands for autonomy. A bureaucratic form of decentralization would not suffice.

Pleve initiated his ministry inauspiciously, at least in terms of winning public confidence, by attacking one part of the educated public, the zemstvo third element. He had long suspected these employees of political unreliability, and these suspicions were confirmed by the peasant disorders in Poltava and Kharkov in the spring of 1902, which local authorities attributed largely to the revolutionary propaganda of the rural intelligentsia.[61] Focusing on statisticians as especially responsible for sedition, Pleve ordered zemstvo statistical work halted in eighteen provinces and initiated a campaign of heightened police supervision of all zemstvo employees.

The fight against opposition soon spread from the zemstvo's third element to its "second," those gentry who supported the employees in expanding the scope of self-governmental activity. In June the government expressed its dissatisfaction with the behavior of the zemstvo activists by issuing an imperial reprimand to the fifty-two participants in an unofficial congress which had been held the preceding month.[62] In the fall the ministry initiated a more energetic effort against the zemstvo liberals, focusing particularly on their participation in the local committees of Witte's Special Conference on the Needs of Agriculture. In widely publicized acts, the central authorities reprimanded gentry marshal A. V. Evreinov and zemstvo board chairman Prince P. D. Dolgorukov for their role in the Sudzha district committee, and banished N. F. Bunakov, S. V. Martynov and F. A. Shcherbin from Voronezh for their activities there. Governors were directed to pressure the committees to limit their discussion to local issues and to take measures to exclude oppositional figures from attendance.[63]

Pleve's campaign against the local committees destroyed what little hope there was for cooperation between zemstvo liberals and the government. The emigré constitutionalist journal *Liberation* had, since its initiation in June 1902, mounted an increasingly vigorous assault on the government in the name of the "progressive elements" of the zemstvo. It denounced the promise of expanded opportunity for popular participation in local administration as a "fig leaf" hiding the MVD's real intention of subjugating self-government to the state bureaucracy.[64] The hostility of contributors to *Liberation,* if not their constitutionalism, now came to be shared by even the most moderate zemstvo activists. Shipov, for example, had initially believed Pleve was sincere in wishing to improve relations with the zemstvo. By early 1903 he had changed his opinion and concluded that the minister of internal affairs "is a man without conscience and a sense of honor," who "believes it is possible to deal with everyone through lies and hypocrisy."[65]

The growing gap between the MVD and the leaders of self-government was evident in heated disagreement over the question of zemstvo participation in drafting legislation on local affairs. For Pleve this involvement was permissible only if zemstvo activists were invited to take part in MVD conferences or in the deliberations of the Council on Local Affairs. Any other solution would carry implications of popular representation and constitutionalism. The liberals, however, rejected this limited role; they proposed that all public figures attending be elected by zemstvo assemblies rather than chosen by the ministry, and they argued that all measures prepared at the conferences be submitted to the organs of self-government for preliminary deliberation before going to the State Council. This divergence of opinion was amply demonstrated at the MVD's insurance conference in April 1903. Meeting with zemstvo leaders who had been invited to attend, Pleve expressed his satisfaction with such gatherings as a forum for the consideration of local problems. He noted that they allowed the zemstvo men not only to interact with the ministry's staff but to carry on discussions among themselves. Referring to Russian liberals' illegal practice of holding private congresses without official permission, he noted that the present conference was better than "secret meetings."[66] Yet only three days earlier, twenty-eight zemstvo activists had gathered at just such a "secret meeting" to condemn the MVD. On Shipov's initiative they adopted two resolutions: that self-governmental participants in future MVD bodies be elected and that all legislation on local needs be submitted to the zemstvos. Moreover, those present decided to press their demands by asking individual zemstvos to petition the government accordingly.[67]

Given Pleve's measures against the zemstvo liberals it is no surprise that they became his staunch opponents. Yet by spring 1903 it was evident that the central authorities were alienating many moderate and conservative gentry as well. The reasons for such dissatisfaction were various. For one thing, as the debates in the local committees and the provincial zemstvos demonstrated, increasing numbers of nobles had begun to sympathize with such individual elements of the liberal program as autonomy for the zemstvo and even equal rights for the peasantry. Evreinov's claims that a majority of his estate supported constitutionalism were exaggerated, but it was clear that a substantial minority of the gentry had come to advocate what one prominent young noble described as "our 'local,' 'loyal' liberalism."[68] Furthermore, those who had no inclination to such views were repelled by the methods employed by the government in its campaign to defeat opposition. Progressives like Shipov, the Dolgorukovs, Trubetskoi, or Stakhovich all came from the privileged estate and bore the names of its most venerated families. Even conservative gentry were appalled at the police measures being used. For example, D. N. Liubimov, the director of the MVD chancellery and Pleve's close supporter, was clearly disconcerted by the treatment accorded his brother-in-law, the "legal Marxist" Tugan-Baranovskii, and his childhood friends P. D. Dolgorukov, D. A. Pereleshin, and F. A. Golovin.[69]

Beyond repression of individuals, conservative nobles also became increasingly concerned over what appeared to be an assault on their estate officials. For instance, Pleve's attempt to force Evreinov to resign his post as district marshal embroiled the government in a conflict with the Kursk gentry, who saw the action as encroaching on the rights bestowed on the nobility by Catherine the Great.[70] When Pleve tried to instruct the marshals to use their authority as chairmen of the zemstvo assemblies to halt discussion of liberal proposals, he immediately received a hostile response. In a widely publicized letter to the local governor, the prominent Orel provincial marshal M. A. Stakhovich described the measure as "violating the legal rights of the Marshals and infringing upon their dignity." No marshal, he insisted, could accept the proposition that "he is the obedient executor of the illegal demands of the Minister, rather than the independent representative of the highest estate."[71] The impact of these events was reinforced later by the tsar's failure to approve the first candidate of the Chernigov gentry as their provincial marshal.[72]

As the marshal issue suggests, behind the discomfiture with the ministry's methods was a broader clash of outlook between Pleve and many conservative members of the first estate. In his reorganization of local governance two decades earlier, Tolstoi had tried to unify the divergent elements of the administrative system: the state bureaucracy, self-government, and the gentry estate. Self-government was tied more closely to the central apparatus and the gentry were integrated into the system in the role of land captains. But Tolstoi's synthesis was a fragile one, rapidly undermined by the great demands put upon it in the 1890s. Among the results were growing friction between the state bureaucracy and self-government on the one hand and a less noticeable but very real friction between the civil service and the gentry on the other. In dealing with the zemstvos and town councils Pleve sought to end discord by introducing a bureaucratic form of decentralization. The most direct outcome of this effort, however, was to give a tremendous impetus to the liberal opposition movement. Similarly, Pleve sought to resolve the problem of the gentry role in administration through the further bureaucratization of the land captaincy and marshaldom. And in a parallel fashion, the most significant result of his activity in this direction was to heighten conservative alienation. Of course Pleve's steps in relation to the first estate were much more cautious than those used in the case of the zemstvo. Consequently, noble discontent was less acute than its liberal counterpart and certainly less clearly articulated. Nevertheless, it was an important factor in a growing crisis of confidence among the tsarist social elite which contributed to the empire's movement toward a revolutionary breakdown.

Growing conservative dissatisfaction with state policy was evident at various points in the debate over local administration. For example, proposals for reform stressing the role of gentry institutions in the countryside proliferated. The prominent editor of *New Times*, K. F. Golovin, presented one such program in response to the 26 February Manifesto. Golovin's insistence upon steps to check the arbitrary behavior of governors and other civil servants has already been noted. To these he added plans for expanding the noble presence on the local scene. In reference to the provincial apparatus he proposed that a congress of district marshals be created to advise the governor. In the district itself gentry influence would be exerted more directly, for in Golovin's scheme district administration was to be concentrated in the hands of the marshal. As in the preemancipation period, even the police were to be his subordinates. Finally, on the village level, Golovin recommended that all estates be unified in a local zemstvo. But here too gentry interests would predominate, for representation in the body would be weighted according to landownership.[73]

The editor's preference for his own estate over the state bureaucracy was shared by others. An even franker expression of this sentiment was made by the Smolensk gentry in an address to the tsar dated 18 December 1903. Significantly, the nobility of Smolensk Province had been among the regime's most loyal followers since the 1860s. They had reaffirmed their long-standing immunity to liberalism in 1903 by rejecting both the idea of a local zemstvo and any democratization of the electoral laws for self-government. Yet by the end of that year they felt it necessary to appeal to the throne for a change in the course of government policy. In their address they complained that the authorities "through an entire series of measures taken without consulting the voice of the Gentry" was undermining the role of the nobility as "leaders of local life." They particularly decried the marshal's declining influence in comparison with that of the Saint Petersburg ministries' representatives. Peasant affairs, they claimed, were now handled by land captains who had been turned into appointed state officials and were no longer under the effective control of the marshal. Financial matters had been concentrated in the hands of the finance ministry's tax inspectors. Education was also slipping away from gentry supervision. Such a trend of events, the Smolensk notables concluded, could only be reversed by a reorganization of local governance that gave the leading role not to the state bureaucracy but to the gentry.[74]

With liberals, then, conservatives shared hostility toward the civil service, a common division, as Gurko put it, between "we" and "they."[75] Yet the impetus behind gentry conservatism was different from that of the liberal zemstvo movement. Whereas the latter was increasingly inspired by Western ideas of participatory democracy, the former was more rooted in traditional Slavophil concepts of "tsar and people." Where the liberals increasingly viewed their goal as progress toward a constitutional order, conservatives preferred to stress the real or imagined values and institutional arrangements of the past. Moreover, while the liberal movement steadily diversified its social base to include especially middle-class elements, conservatives continued to remain primarily noble by origin. Under the pressures of the Revolution of 1905 these differences were to be accentuated and the viewpoints radically polarized. In 1903 and 1904, however, they blended together to create a general feeling of public alienation from the government.

By spring 1903, then, Pleve was faced not only with the open opposition of socialists and liberals but the growing animosity of the conservative gentry. Both increased during the following months.[76] As before, the left was most outspoken. In July 1903 constitutionalists and more radical elements joined in a secret Union of Liberation. By fall, branches of the union had proliferated, and it had been joined by a union of "zemstvo constitutionalists." The depth of liberal sentiment was reflected in the debates of zemstvo assemblies. As planned at the April meeting of zemstvo activists, liberals in the assemblies had raised the demands that all legislation on local matters be submitted to self-government for preliminary debate and that all popular representatives at MVD conferences be chosen by the public bodies themselves. Despite government attempts to halt discussion of the proposals, by the end of the year over half of the provincial and many district zemstvos had expressed their support for them.[77] Although instigated by liberals, this insistence upon a broader role for self-government in the legislative process was also in part an indication of conservative discontent. Specifically, some of the zemstvo resolutions in favor had been made possible by the decision of a fall congress of gentry marshals not to block debate on these questions in the various assemblies.[78] Moreover, a number of prominent gentry hostile to liberalism had actively advocated the demands locally. The Saratov zemstvo's petition, for instance, was proposed by conservative leader Count A. A. Uvarov.

Pleve's response to the mounting criticism was to continue his efforts to strike down his opponents. In September 1903 he achieved one of his most conspicuous successes, with the resignation of Witte, his most formidable adversary within the government, as finance minister. Yet his rival's fall was a Pyrrhic victory. Now Pleve could no longer claim to be champion of agrarian interests against Witte's program of industrialization. Increasingly he himself came to occupy the role of representative of the state's attack on the interests of the gentry and peasantry. Equally counterproductive were Pleve's efforts against the zemstvo movement. Attempts to control the zemstvos culminated in January 1904 with the extraordinary and possibly illegal step of suspending self-government in Tver, whose zemstvo unquestionably possessed the most formidable liberal tradition in the empire. In the 1860s its leaders had been vocal spokesmen for the emancipation of the peasantry and the establishment of self-government. More recently, upon the accession of Nicholas II to the throne in 1894, Tver delegates had presented the new sovereign with the petition calling for political reform that provoked his famous denunciation of any "senseless dreams" of a limitation of autocracy. Pleve now formally accused the provincial and district boards of malfeasance and sedition. Government-appointed boards were created to replace the existing elective ones. Large numbers of progressives, including the prominent liberal I. I. Petrunkevich, were banished from the province. These actions were apparently intended to encourage gentry and clergy who supported the government to express their loyalty, but no outpouring of conservative support was forthcoming.[79] The only result was the further alienation of public opinion. A similar effect was achieved one month later by Pleve's decision to block reelection of the loyal monarchist Shipov as chairman of the Moscow provincial zemstvo. The outbreak of war with Japan in the same month temporarily restored some public solidarity with the government, but any improvement in this respect was soon dissipated by the failure of Russian arms on the battlefield and by a fruitless conflict with self-government over the issue of organizing aid for the sick and wounded.[80]

In the midst of this growing crisis, Pleve's ministry ended as it had begun—with an act of violence. On 15 July, the Socialist Revolutionary Sazonov threw a bomb into the carriage in which the minister was riding. The bomb exploded, tearing the carriage apart and killing Pleve instantly. As news of the assassination spread through the empire there was no great expression of grief for the fallen statesman. The prevailing sentiment was summarized by L. A. Tikhomirov, rightist editor of the *Moscow News*, in his diary. The

journalist was traveling to Moscow by steamship on the Volga when
word of the killing arrived.

In sixteen days on the same steamer I became acquainted with a great
number of passengers, who in general gladdened me with their patriotism
and good political spirit. And so? The news of the murder of Pleve, of course,
stunned everyone, the murderer was cursed. But for Pleve himself I did not
hear one word of sympathy.
I arrived here. I inquired, what was the reaction to the murder here? It
turned out exactly the same. Nowhere sorrow, nowhere a show of sympathy.
The poor devil—I pitied him above all because he died on absolutely cold
terms with all of Russia.

The lack of real sympathy, so much in contrast to the response to
Sipiagin's assassination, was ample evidence of the degree to which
Pleve had alienated the entire public. Although the reasons for this
animosity were many, the basic cause was unquestionably public hostility toward the one principle the deceased minister had held most
dear—bureaucratic rule. As Tikhomirov wrote in summarizing
Pleve's efforts:

A strange person. Everything was present: intelligence, character, honor,
efficiency, experience.... Many people expected much from him, many
people devoted to the ruler, Russia, and order offered him their powers, their
aid.... Gradually [he] eliminated all honest people, and himself only re-
pressed and nothing more. Who would argue? Of course, revolutionaries
should be halted. But you know Russia herself is not a revolutionary, and she
truly is in need of deep improvements. He wanted to do nothing. Why?
Indeed probably for the same reason all ministers do: they don't wish to stop
being lords over tsar and people. Pleve was fundamentally, to his marrow, a
civil servant, [he] carried in his soul and heart that great evil from which
Russia is perishing.[81]

Despite the general accuracy of his description, Tikhomirov was
wrong in insisting that nothing had been attempted. Pleve had perceived the need for change and had tried to implement a program for
dealing with the empire's growing difficulties. But unlike liberals, who
placed their faith in self-government and public initiative, and conservatives, who saw Russia's salvation in the role of the gentry, Pleve
chose another path. He turned to the idea that had been dominant
both in his own life and in the history of the empire for centuries, the
idea of bureaucratic absolutism. He believed the growing demand for
decentralization and broader citizen participation in governmental
affairs could be met only within this framework. By mid-1904 it was

evident that this approach had failed. Yet it was far from dead. Even during the turmoil of 1905, when reformers in the government were seeking to halt revolution by appeasing the public, it retained a strong hold on official thinking. With the restoration of order in 1906 it was to reemerge as the guiding principle of another, greater, tsarist statesman, Peter A. Stolypin.

CHAPTER IV

REVOLUTION AND REFORM, 1905-1906

The months following Pleve's assassination were ones of almost unprecedented violence in Tsarist Russia; the empire was gripped by what is called the Revolution of 1905. Although the unrest included several attempts to overthrow the existing order, use of the term *revolution* to describe it implies far more unity and direction within the opposition than in fact existed. The regime was assaulted not by a single revolutionary movement but by many, each with its own ends, direction, and dynamic. In the countryside, peasant rebellion aimed at the expropriation of noble landholdings. In the cities, urban workers sought goals ranging from pay increases to a socialist utopia. Middle-class liberals demanded a constitution. On the peripheries of the empire the same forces operated, but with the addition of movements for autonomy and national self-determination. Together these various currents created chaos as the central authorities rapidly lost control. The revolutionaries could not, however, sustain their attack, and by the following year the government was able to restore stability.

Although the revolution failed, it had significant consequences for tsarist society. In October 1905, for instance, the separate streams of opposition did flow together momentarily to win an important victory. Against his will Nicholas II issued an October Manifesto promising fundamental reforms, including the granting of civil rights and the creation of a representative assembly. To carry out these promises the tsar appointed a new cabinet under Witte, once a supporter of bureaucratic absolutism but now a proponent of limited monarchy. As part of his overall program Witte undertook a reorganization of local government based not upon the statist tradition of Pleve but rather upon an attempt to redefine that tradition in essentially liberal terms.

Beyond forcing the authorities to experiment with a new approach to reform, the revolution had a further result. The upheaval of 1905 served as a catalyst for the public. Under the pressure of crisis, political activists outside the government developed much more sharply and explicitly ideas and proposals that had been gestating for years. Assumptions of the earlier period were now carried to their logical conclusion. Moreover, the revolution proved to be a catalyst not only for ideology but also for organization. The October Manifesto allowed private citizens to create formal political parties for the first time in the empire's history. Indeed, in the weeks following the promulgation of the manifesto, the populace was showered with leaflets, pamphlets, and proclamations bearing the programs of freshly organized political groupings.

The revolution's catalytic effect was clearly evidenced in relation to the question of local government. In all the publications of the new parties, the issue of administration in the provinces occupied a prominent place. The left liberal party of Freethinkers, for example, demanded the abolition of estate privileges and the "widest possible application" of the principle of self-government. The business-dominated Progressive Economic party urged the "broad development of self-government in the interests of decentralization." The viciously right-wing Union of the Russian People called for laws protecting the individual from the arbitrary actions of petty officials. Even the Social Democrats, while retaining their ultimate goal of social revolution, claimed the achievement of a fully democratized local government to be one of their "immediate tasks."[1]

It would be an exaggeration to claim that local government was the most pressing issue of 1905. The need to define precisely the role of the new representative assembly, the State Duma, and to answer the demands of the rebellious peasantry for land were too urgent to allow that. Nevertheless, despite the attention devoted to these other questions, both the political parties and the government went to great pains to make their views on local administration explicit. In the process they articulated very clearly their newly crystallizing beliefs on the proper ordering of their society. As earlier, the issue of local government remained a basic guide to the ways the various segments of the empire's educated elite viewed Tsarist Russia's present and future.

Bureaucracy and Liberal Reform

Although discontent was general throughout Russian society, the radical wing of the empire's liberal movement set the tone of opposition to the government in the fall and winter of 1904.[2] Constitutionalists had certainly been active earlier, but in the wake of

Pleve's death they became far more vocal, attracting ever broader segments of the public to their ideas. New points were added to the liberal program to meet changing conditions, but at its heart was a simple extension of the zemstvo ideology that had emerged during the preceding decade. This relationship was evident, for instance, in an exposition of the constitutionalist position published about this time by the progressive professor of law, N. I. Lazarevskii, under the indicative title, "Bureaucracy and Society" (Biurokratiia i obshchest-vo).[3]

Like zemstvo moderates before him, Lazarevskii drew a sharp distinction between the state bureaucracy and the rest of society, and he adopted a traditionally liberal historical perspective. Bureaucracy, he argued, rules in the common good in the early stages of social development under the slogan "everything for the people, nothing by the people" (tout pour le peuple, rien par le peuple). But as the complexity of social tasks increases and the public outgrows "egotistical and antisocial" behavior, officialdom turns to society for aid. Eventually, he concluded, the bureaucracy retires altogether, transferring its authority to independent organizations of the citizenry. Of course, none of this was particularly new. Where Lazarevskii was innovative was not in his basic scheme of history but in his placement of Tsarist Russia in that scheme. Rather than argue that the time had come for the populace to share power with the ruling bureaucracy, the progressive professor insisted that the people should replace it altogether. For him the civil service had become simply an obstacle, a tenacious anachronism in the face of the "logical and historically inevitable" demand for popular sovereignty. Indeed, Lazarevskii went so far as to imply that the state bureaucracy would have to be overthrown by force, for it would "never voluntarily agree" to a constitutional order.[4]

Armed with such ideas, Russian liberals engaged in a campaign of agitation that was impressive by tsarist standards. During November 1904, in an event likened to the French Estates General of 1789 or the storming of the Bastille, zemstvo activists met illegally in Saint Petersburg to draft a program and plan strategy.[5] Although a moderate minority led by Shipov demurred, the congress approved a demand for civil rights and popular participation in the legislative process. The delegates then called upon individual zemstvos to petition the tsar accordingly. By early 1905 twenty-eight provincial zemstvos had passed appropriate motions. Eleven gentry assemblies had even joined in the movement for reform.[6] Simultaneous with these efforts by zemstvo progressives, the radically constitutionalist Union of Liberation initiated a series of public banquets in the empire's major cities as another forum for antigovernment speeches and resolutions.

Even before this unprecedented outburst of popular political activity it was evident that the authorities would have to choose between policies of concession and repression. For a government unused to responding to or even consulting public opinion, the choice was painful. The post of minister of internal affairs remained open for a month after Pleve's assassination as Nicholas II wavered. Though apparently inclined to appoint the archconservative B. V. Stürmer, the tsar finally allowed himself to be persuaded toward conciliation. On 25 August the ministry was offered to Prince P. D. Sviatopolk-Mirskii, a former officer and MVD bureaucrat who had left Saint Petersburg to become governor general of Vilna as a result of friction with Pleve.[7]

From the moment of his appointment the new minister made it clear that he intended to follow an approach radically different from that of his fallen predecessor. "You know me but little," he informed the ruler in his first audience, "and perhaps you consider me of like mind with the two previous ministers, but I am of completely opposite opinions." Describing himself as a "zemstvo man," Sviatopolk-Mirskii went on to outline a policy aimed at winning public confidence through essentially liberal reforms.[8] This determination to shift course politically was immediately reflected in the make-up of MVD personnel, as Pleve's associates Zinov'ev, Stishinskii, and Stürmer were all purged from the staff. Simultaneously, a large number of the zemstvo activists who had been either forbidden access to public service or exiled from their places of residence by Pleve regained full rights. The veteran progressive I. I. Petrunkevich, for example, was allowed to live in the capital after a two-decade absence.

The self-avowed reformer Sviatopolk-Mirskii announced publicly in August his general decision to proceed "with an attitude of sincere trust in the self-governing and estate institutions and the people." What this meant in terms of specific legislation was not clear until three months later. In November the minister ordered his staff, and S. E. Kryzhanovskii in particular, to draft proposals to be presented to the tsar. Chief among these was a recommendation to include elected representatives of the citizenry in the State Council. In addition, the MVD called for what amounted to a major restructuring of local government. The activity of the civil service was to be placed firmly within the limits of the law, partially by limiting the use of emergency legislation and also by improving senatorial supervision. The institutions of self-government were to have "the widest possible participation in the handling of local services" and the independence to make that participation effective. Finally, the peasantry, long isolated under its own customary laws and administrative apparatus, was to be given full civil equality with other estates.[9]

These were broad ideas. In December the ministry gave a specific indication of what this represented in regard to one arena of local administration, the village. Reporting for Sviatopolk-Mirskii to Witte's Special Conference on the Needs of Agriculture, Assistant Minister N. N. Kutler outlined the following plan.[10] The existing peasant volost and village community would be abolished, and in their place would be created a volost zemstvo. In large villages approaching urban status a special settlement (*poselok*) administration would be established below the new zemstvo. Both bodies, the volost zemstvo and the settlement, would be all-estate in nature, though the interests of large landholders were to be protected by direct participation without election in their assemblies. "The task of the law," Kutler argued, "is to transfer the handling of affairs touching the whole local populace from the hands of the peasants alone to those of the entire citizenry."[11] Finally, in order to guarantee the independence of village self-government, the MVD proposed an unusual step. For those matters "in which the local interest definitely takes precedence over the central" the state police—sergeants and guardsmen—were to be placed under the direction of the volost zemstvo.

The overall program presented by Sviatopolk-Mirskii for royal approval has been criticized as timid and halfhearted, largely as a result of its caution in opening avenues for popular participation in central government. Be this as it may, in local affairs the approach was a bold one. The MVD openly rejected the policy, championed by Tolstoi and accepted by Pleve, of relying upon the estate principle in administration. Equally important was a new attitude toward the state bureaucracy itself. The MVD now emphasized not the power and prerogatives of the civil servants, but their restraint. Moreover, as the admittedly modest plan for partial subordination of the rural police to the volost zemstvo suggests, there was an implicit recognition of the citizenry's predominance in its own local concerns. In other words, the MVD was turning its back on the statist perspective on provincial affairs in favor of one predicated upon local autonomy. Although couched in terms of autocracy, which Sviatopolk-Mirskii never disavowed, an attempt was being made at liberal reform. The significance of the program was grasped by at least one leading official, Police Director A. A. Lopukhin. While convinced that tsarist bureaucrats, "nurtured in arbitrary behavior," would never enforce such measures, Lopukhin underlined their importance. They represented, he argued, the first appearance within the government itself of a fundamental critique of the existing order.[12]

Lopukhin's pessimism on the possibilities for change reflected reality, for Sviatopolk-Mirskii's reform initiative soon ran aground. Narrowly speaking, the difficulty stemmed from the minister's own character, principled but indecisive and passive. In the case of the November zemstvo congress, for example, Sviatopolk-Mirskii was at first persuaded to give the meeting official sanction. Only belatedly did he realize its potential for subversion, and even then his attempts to control it were ineffectual. So great was confusion over the congress's status that several MVD bureaucrats innocently attended the oppositional gathering.[13] Indeed, serious work on the MVD's own proposals began only in November, by which time reform efforts were already being outrun by the leftward drift of public opinion. Beyond his personal shortcomings, Sviatopolk-Mirskii was caught in a more basic dilemma. His program represented a search for compromise in times of political polarization, an effort to bend existing traditions of government without breaking them. Because he was unwilling to abandon autocracy and become "a popular tribune," as he once put it, he disappointed the liberal opposition.[14] Because he was committed to altering the ruling state of affairs, he alienated conservatives, including the tsar.

The dynamics of Sviatopolk-Mirskii's fall were evident in the fate of his local reform. In December the MVD plans in this and other areas were submitted to a special council of dignitaries chaired by Nicholas II.[15] On the urging of Witte, whose presence Sviatopolk-Mirskii had naively insisted upon, the tsar decided to drop the crucial recommendation for popular participation in the State Council. Although other measures ranging from local government to religious toleration and workers' insurance were approved, implementation was taken out of MVD hands and transferred to Witte's Committee of Ministers. Sviatopolk-Mirskii left the conference in disgust, announcing, "Everything has failed. Let us build jails."[16] Defeated in the bureaucratic struggle and lacking the confidence of the tsar, he submitted his resignation on 13 December, ironically only one day after the formal announcement of the remains of his reform program in a special imperial edict (*ukaz*).[17] Some steps were subsequently taken to realize at least part of the promises enunciated in the 12 December Ukaz, but little was accomplished. In the case of self-government, for example, the Committee of Ministers voted for the creation of a special commission replete with public representation. The body, however, never convened.[18]

While the government toyed with reform, unrest within the empire broadened drastically. On 9 January 1905, a day known thereafter as Bloody Sunday, Saint Petersburg police fired on a procession of factory workers loyal to the tsar and killed or wounded more than four hundred. The event galvanized workers nationally, provoking strikes, demonstrations, and sporadic street fighting that continued with increasing violence throughout the year. By fall workers and socialist leaders were organizing local councils, or soviets, to direct strike activity in individual cities, and in December open rebellion broke out in factory districts of Moscow. Urban disorder found an even more violent echo in the countryside, where in the spring peasants in numerous villages began assaults—generally spontaneous—on neighboring gentry landholdings and on police. The wave of rural unrest rapidly gathered momentum, involving over seven thousand separate incidents before it was finally brought to a halt in 1907. Even the military, a traditional support of the regime, was shaken with revolutionary outbursts including strikes and open mutiny. And, of course, the liberal opposition continued its activity. All-Russian zemstvo congresses were convened in April, May, and November 1905, and national organizations or "unions" of middle-class professionals were formed to press for political change. Though essentially disunified in organization and aims, revolutionary forces did roughly coalesce for one joint action. In October 1905 a strike initiated by Moscow railwaymen for local reasons spread unplanned through the empire. Drawing support particularly in urban centers, the October General Strike took on enormous proportions and paralyzed the government for six days.

The response of the central authorities to the growing crisis was sluggish at best, a combination of halting concessions and largely unsuccessful attempts at repression. In February the tsar announced his intention to create a consultative national assembly, and Sviatopolk-Mirskii's successor, A. G. Bulygin, was put to work drafting appropriate legislation. The plan, however, fell far short of the escalating demands of the liberal and socialist opposition. Delegates to the April zemstvo congress, for example, though drawn from among the most restrained of the government's critics, explicitly rejected the "Bulygin duma." They voted instead for an assembly elected through universal suffrage to participate in reordering the political structure of the empire.[19] Only the October General Strike galvanized the government to action. Much against his will, Nicholas II accepted the need for basic reform. On 17 October he issued a manifesto granting civil rights and creating a representative assembly, or State Duma, with authority to rule on legislation. Simultaneously, he appointed Sergei Witte, chief sponsor of the manifesto (and someone Nicholas had recently said he "completely mistrusted" and suspected of "masonic" ties), as chairman of the Council of Ministers.[20]

Not surprisingly, Witte's primary attention in office was devoted to questions of national politics. He had been charged expressly with the weighty task of introducing the new constitutional order in the empire and beyond that bore responsibility for the even more formidable duty of bringing a halt to unrest. Yet despite his preoccupation with the twin issues of constitution and order, Witte did concern himself with local affairs. There was a pressing need to keep the administrative apparatus intact under conditions of revolutionary stress. This meant not only halting police desertions and the defection of officials, primarily of the judiciary, to the side of the opposition, but also combating the more sinister inclination of local police to engage in unauthorized counterrevolutionary violence, including pogroms. As the new chairman wrote in January 1906 while pressing for punitive legislation against all forms of official malfeasance, "I, for my part, am sure that a failure to take decisive measures against the mass of civil servants who act beyond the bounds of duty and loyalty will leave the governors largely *paralyzed in the struggle with revolution.*[21]

In addition to emergency measures aimed at strengthening the tsarist administration against revolution, such as an increase in urban police wages and accelerated introduction of the rural guard, the Witte cabinet did turn to general issues of local governance. In part, this was but a logical extension of the broader political reforms promised in the October Manifesto. Although the document itself spoke mainly of the State Duma, it also included references to "civic freedom" and habeas corpus. The idea here was expressed by Witte himself in a report to the tsar which helped bring about the promulgation of the manifesto. In what must have been an agonizing admission for the one-time idealizer of autocracy, Witte concluded, "Russia has outgrown the existing political framework and is striving for a legal order based on civil liberty."[22] This applied, naturally, not only to Saint Petersburg, but also to the empire's provinces, districts, villages, and towns.

While government efforts must thus be placed within the framework of the October Manifesto, it should also be recognized that Witte had been considering the issue of local reform long before the

Revolution of 1905, albeit in a context other than constitutionalism. As tsarist finance minister he had been concerned over the state of Russian agriculture as well as industry and commerce. In the face of the continued poor showing of the agrarian sector he had become convinced of the need for a broad reordering of the social and economic structure of village life. As early as 1898 this concern prompted a lengthy letter to the tsar. Significantly, although the problem discussed was an economic one—low productivity of the rural masses—the implied solution was essentially political-administrative. Everywhere, Witte argued, the initiative of the peasant was being crushed by the capricious authority of "masters" (*bariny*): the police constable and sergeant, the zemstvo employee, the local doctor and teacher, and indeed even the peasant's own chosen representatives, the volost headman and the village judges. "Therefore," he concluded, "it is impossible to aid [the peasant] through material measures alone, even though extensive ones. First and foremost it is necessary to raise the spirit of the peasantry, to make them truly your free and loyal sons."[23] In other words, the creation of a productive, capitalist populace in the countryside could only be achieved by liberating the peasants from the arbitrary imposition of outside authority.

Witte's thoughts were more fully formed by 1904, largely as a result of the work of the Special Conference on the Needs of Agriculture he had initiated two years before. He presented his ideas in a *Memorandum on Peasant Affairs* (*Zapiska po krest'ianskomu delu*).[24] The report, apparently authored by civil servant A. A. Rittikh under Witte's direction, was ostensibly a summary of the findings of the Special Conference's local committees. In reality it was a straightforward expression of Witte's position. The stated goal of rural reform was simply the equalization of the peasantry with other estates. In one respect this was an economic task, to be resolved by allowing individual peasants to leave the commune and claim their land as private property. More significantly, however, it was for Witte a political question, as reflected in the fact that the bulk of the memorandum was devoted to local governance. In this sphere, equalization of the peasantry would require a restructuring of rural administrative institutions. The volost and village community would be replaced respectively by two all-estate bodies "of the zemstvo type." These would be responsible both for social welfare measures normally handled by self-government and the administrative duties previously performed by volost officials. Therefore, they would be assigned their own police force. Conversely, the land captains, bêtes noires of liberals and peasants alike, would be restricted in activity to directing the state police and monitoring the legality of local governmental operations.

Throughout the evolution of his views on rural affairs Witte remained fully loyal to autocracy. This commitment was expressed, for example, in 1899 in his *Autocracy and the Zemstvo* or, as late as December 1904, in his opposition to Sviatopolk-Mirskii's plans for popular representation in national government. Nevertheless, Witte's original concern for the material welfare of the empire and his basic commitment to capitalist enterprise led him to conceive of a program of local governmental reform that admirably suited the constitutionalism of the October Manifesto. Ironically, the responsibility of the state bureaucracy's chief financier for a centrally directed program of industrial development interested him in the limitation of that bureaucracy's own tutelage over rural inhabitants.

Theoretically, as chairman of the Council of Ministers Witte was well placed to implement his ideas. The office was intended to provide a unifying focus for government activity in the dawning constitutional era. In point of fact, though, Witte's very elevation to the post left him with a serious difficulty in obtaining the bureaucratic instruments he required. The chairman's actual authority over the various ministries was not clearly defined, and the retention of practices like direct consultation between individual ministers and the tsar made that authority questionable at best. By tradition, initiative in local matters was the prerogative of the Ministry of Internal Affairs, which also possessed the personnel and experience necessary for drafting appropriate legislation. This institutional problem was compounded by a personal one. Political considerations had seriously constrained Witte in his selection of ministers, and his choice for the MVD, P. N. Durnovo, was far more concerned with repression than reform. Relations between the two strong-willed men were strained throughout much of their incumbencies, a tension reflected in Witte's subsequent judgment that Durnovo's appointment had been among his most serious errors.[25]

To deal with this situation Witte apparently followed the rather unorthodox procedure of relying in matters of reform upon his own choice as assistant interior minister, S. D. Urusov.[26] Urusov was undoubtedly well suited for the role. His career spanned both the zemstvos and civil service and included the difficult assignment of taking over the governorship of Bessarabia in the wake of the Kishinev pogrom. His reputation among progressives was quite positive for an MVD official, so good in fact that a number of leading liberals had actively supported his candidacy for the post of minister. In December 1905, then, it was Urusov who was made chairman of a six-man MVD commission on local governance.[27] Also serving were MVD staff members Lopukhin, I. Ia. Gurliand, Liubimov, Gerbel, and Gurko. Lopukhin had been police chief under Pleve, but by 1905 his convictions were moving rapidly to the left. Further, he was well-disposed toward Urusov, who was his wife's brother. Liubimov and Gurliand, though also Pleve appointees, appear to have been willing to cooperate with Urusov in reform. Significantly, the most vocal opposition in the commission was provided by the two men who had been among the MVD's leading reformers under Pleve, Gerbel and Gurko.

As one might expect, the findings of the Urusov group heavily reflected the liberal ideas championed by Sviatopolk-Mirskii and now Witte. First, there was a clear consensus on the need to reject the estate principle in local government. Specifically, the commission repeated the already familiar plan of abolishing the peasant volost and village community in favor of local zemstvo and settlement administrations. Participation in both new institutions was to be open to all estates, though there was disagreement in the commission on the terms of that participation. Lopukhin and Gurliand argued against any property qualification in order to insure inclusion of merchants and zemstvo employees. Gurko, Gerbel, and Liubimov, conversely, pressed for a relatively stiff property qualification precisely to prevent subversive "politicking" by the third element. In the end the chairman struck a compromise. The idea of a high qualification was rejected. However, suffrage would be granted only to those who paid zemstvo taxes, i.e., owned at least some property, and elections would be based on the Prussian three-class system.[28]

At the same time that they turned their backs on the corporate ideal in village administration, the commission majority also recommended what amounted to a weakening of the hegemony of the state bureaucracy in the countryside. The key measure in this regard was the transfer of all administrative functions of the volost and land captaincy, except those of the state police, to the elected chairman of the new zemstvo. Local voters would be constrained in their choice by educational and property qualifications for the office, but of more consequence was the fact that the successful candidate would not be subject to any form of confirmation by the central authorities. The significance of this proposal as a break with the MVD statist approach of Tolstoi and Pleve was evident in the opposition it aroused. Gurko in particular energetically criticized such a broad devolution of administrative activity to a public figure and insisted upon the creation of a new office of the state bureaucracy to parallel the volost-level zemstvo, in essence a revitalized land captaincy stripped of its gentry trappings. Gurko and the tradition he represented were overruled in favor of self-government.[29]

Finally, the commission called for the unification of district administration in the hands of a commander (*uezd nachal'nik*) appointed by the central authorities and possessing powers of coordination and supervision mirroring those of the provincial governor. MVD adviser N. L. Psheradskii raised the possibility of an elected representative as head of district affairs, but the idea was categorically rejected. In part this decision for an appointed district chief contradicted the earlier movement in the commission away from the state bureaucracy. Still, for all his prerogatives, the commander was expected to work in conjunction with a special district board on which self-government and the judiciary would be well represented.[30] Moreover, Urusov's group was explicit that the new functionary would not be free of more general outside control. The commission's comments here deserve quotation in full:

It should not be forgotten that with the reorganization of our entire system on the basis of the 17 October Manifesto the exercise of administrative authority inevitably acquires a completely different character. If earlier it was necessary to be cautious in defining the boundaries of official authority so as not to encourage caprice, under the new conditions—freedom of the press, inquiries in the State Duma, etc.—it is conversely desirable to give officials the widest possible powers, since there is no doubt that [they] . . . will employ them with proper circumspection.[31]

As the reference to free press and representative assembly made evident, even in this essentially "bureaucratic" proposal the Urusov Commission worked under the influence of ideas championed by the liberal movement. True, the MVD reformers did not in their work adopt the opposition's perspective in full. Universal suffrage in zemstvo elections was rejected in favor of a property-oriented system. The district commander remained a civil servant. Nevertheless, taken as a whole, the group's program for local government represented a definite if perhaps cautious step away from the old conceptions of estate administration and of state bureaucratic control.

The Witte cabinet was not unproductive. In regard to its basic task of simultaneously defending and remodelling the state structure, much was achieved. Urban revolution was defeated, the first national elections in the history of the empire were held successfully, and plans were laid for the convocation of the first State Duma in April 1906. On the crucial land question, Witte helped set in motion machinery for a fundamental transformation of peasant agriculture. Under the pressure of mounting violence in the countryside, the government had initially considered a plan developed by Kutler, former assistant to Sviatopolk-Mirskii and now minister of agriculture, which included provisions for the compulsory sale of tracts of gentry-held and other land to the peasants. The very notion, however, provoked a storm of protest from the nobility and court and was quickly disavowed. In the wake of this fiasco the government turned to the idea of an agrarian reform based upon the breakup of communal landholding among the peasantry in favor of individual private farms. By spring, work on appropriate legislation was well advanced.[32]

Despite these successes very little was accomplished in the area of local government. The MVD did in fact complete a bill based on the deliberations of the Urusov Commission and duly submit it to the Duma.[33] But the legislation was never debated, and it simply dropped into obscurity. This quiet death resulted largely from the fate of the bill's sponsors. In April, shortly before the Duma he had created opened its sessions, Witte was relieved of his post. He had asked the tsar to free him from duty, but his request came in the face of general opposition from left and right. Witte left office bitterly, denouncing Russia as "one vast madhouse."[34] Urusov had abandoned the government earlier. Disgusted at the discovery of a printing press turning out pogrom literature in the Department of Police, the assistant minister joined the liberal opposition in time to be elected as a representative to the First Duma. Here he distinguished himself with biting and knowledgeable attacks on the authorities. Lopukhin followed a similar path. During the revolution he ended official service and turned to publicistic activity against the government. In 1908 the ex-police chief was arrested for disclosing secret information on agents provocateurs to representatives of the Socialist Revolutionary party. A tsarist court sentenced him to exile for this indiscretion; an amnesty in 1912 restored his full freedom.

Reform of local government was undoubtedly an indirect victim of the politics of revolution in 1905 and 1906. In a period of chaos and anarchy such reform could only be overshadowed by the issues of a national constitution and order. Hence the most important concrete step taken by the MVD in the local arena was the rapid introduction of Pleve's police guard in those provinces where it did not exist. Yet the work toward liberalization of district and village administration also suffered from the nature of the undertaking itself. Redefinition of a tradition of centralized authority as deeply rooted as that of the tsarist bureaucracy is not an easy matter. Certainly both Witte and Sviatopolk-Mirskii operated in an atmosphere of hostility from their Saint Petersburg colleagues, who considered the two overly influenced by "irresponsible" advice from outside the government.[35] Witte, for instance, had been forced to place both the ministries of Internal Affairs and Justice in the hands of "safe" men unsympathetic to liberal reform. Within the Urusov Commission itself only two members were strongly committed to liberalization, and both were ultimately driven from official circles as pariahs.

Indeed, even the leading advocates of reform were themselves restrained by the pull of old patterns of behavior. Sviatopolk-Mirskii refused to break openly with Nicholas II and go into opposition. For Witte the tension was more severe. Despite concessions to revolutionary conditions, he remained in part the man who had extolled the state bureaucracy in *Autocracy and the Zemstvo* and idolized the dictatorial Alexander III. At the same time that he worked toward constitutional reform, Witte showed an inclination to engage in punitive repression so arbitrary and violent that Nicholas II himself was forced to complain that his chief official wanted "to hang and shoot everybody."[36] Moderate liberals who were invited to join Witte's cabinet in October declined, citing among other factors what Shipov described as the chairman's "organic incapacity to free himself from the accepted habits and methods of the bureaucratic regime."[37] Perhaps the difficulty was best captured in a later conversation between Witte and the Englishman Bernard Pares. When Witte was questioned on the issue of popular participation through constitutionalism, Pares recorded, "He replied: 'I have a constitution in my head; but as to my heart'—and he spat on the floor."[38]

The Cadets: Imperatives of Constitutionalism

At the same time that the Russian government wrestled with the complex issues of reform, so too did the Russian public. Violence in urban centers and in the countryside, the government's inability to quiet criticism, and the October Manifesto's legalization of political expression all encouraged the articulation of programs for change in national and local affairs. Admittedly, for much of the left the problem of local government was peripheral. The Social Democrats and Socialist Revolutionaries called for estate equality, universal suffrage, and the election of all officials, but their primary concern remained the creation of a democratic republic nationally, and, beyond that, social revolution.[39] Workers did during 1905 create an embryonic form of self-government in the soviets, but these institutions were ephemeral, tied closely to the strike movement. Their reality as an alternative structure for local administration emerged only in 1917.[40] The peasantry, too, concentrated on other questions, chiefly that of land. In regard to administration the peasants simply drove off any outsiders who might restrain them or levy duties on them. Village affairs were left in the hands of peasant officials or, should they be too closely identified with land captain or noble, in the care of the village council.[41] The task of developing detailed projects for legislation to reform local governance was taken up primarily by the empire's liberal movement.

It came as no surprise that liberals were among the first to take advantage of the new opportunities for political organization. Zemstvo progressives and constitutionalists, together with the socialist parties, had pioneered in the organization of illegal opposition before the revolution, and they had continued their activity during the upheaval. This reached a new level in the summer of 1905, when two of the most important liberal groupings, the Union of Liberation and the Union of Zemstvo Constitutionalists, decided to create an "open political party in the European sense of the term." By 12 October, five days before the promulgation of the tsar's manifesto, a congress convened to formally initiate what popular usage had already christened the Constitutional Democratic party, or *Cadets* for short. The new group grew rapidly, drawing support particularly from among the middle classes. As one leader put it, the party was intentionally designed to stand midway between conservative agrarians and industrialists on the one hand and the proletariat on the other.[42] At the fourth zemstvo congress in November 1905, the Cadets formed a distinct majority and were able to pass a series of resolutions consonant with their party position. By the end of November they had established forty-four local branches, and by late January 1906 the tally had risen to eighty.[43]

As the name of the party indicated, the heart of the Cadet program was the long-sought goal of an effective constitution. In the party's view, this constitution was to be modelled closely on that of England, with popular sovereignty guaranteed by universal suffrage and a cabinet responsible only to the new national assembly. In keeping with their essentially middle-class roots the Cadets were much less radical in dealing with social, as opposed to political, issues. On the pressing question of agrarian reform, for instance, they were willing to endorse compulsory alienation of noble land. However, they insisted that compensation be offered and that the principle of private property be firmly protected.[44]

Although the primary attention of the Cadets was fixed on the twin issues of the constitution and agrarian reform, it was inevitable that they would have strong convictions on the question of provincial administration. For one thing, most of the party's leadership had long been connected in one way or another with the cause of self-government. More important, the Cadets realized that a successful transformation of the empire's political system would require fundamental change at the grass roots as well as at the top. Rights granted in a constitution would be meaningless if petty civil servants were exempted from the control of the new constitutional authority in Saint Petersburg. Popular sovereignty would be a farce if it applied only to national and not to local affairs. Therefore, both by their origins and by the logic of their constitutionalism the Cadets were fully committed to the basic reform of local government.

The Cadets sought to restructure administration in the provinces through the application of three principles, all deeply rooted in the pre-revolutionary zemstvo outlook.[45] The first of these was estate equality. In the opening point of their party program the Cadets maintained that all Russian citizens were equal before the law and demanded that "all corporate distinctions" be abolished.[46] For example, they insisted upon reworking the zemstvo and municipal electoral laws on an estateless basis. The old curial system was to be scrapped in favor of the Cadet "four tail" formula of direct, equal, secret, and universal suffrage. In the same vein, they called for the abolition of the peasant estate institutions, the volost and village community. Both were to be replaced by local zemstvos.[47] With electoral reform and the creation of these new self-governmental units, the Cadets would achieve the cherished liberal goal of uniting the entire populace equally in a hierarchical chain of democratized zemstvos stretching from the provincial capital to the village. Finally, in keeping with the new all-estate approach, the Cadets insisted that the gentry be deprived of their special governing privileges. The land captaincy, that hated embodiment of the principle of noble "tutelage" over the peasantry, was to be destroyed.

The Cadets added to the principle of civil equality yet another concept well developed in the movement's past—legality (*zakonnost'*). Liberals had always viewed the establishment of rigorous juridical norms as the best way to curb the arbitrary power of the state bureaucracy. "Legality," the party maintained in its program, "is a necessary condition for the proper operation of all organs of adminis-tration and self-government."[48] Yet the Cadets realized that the impo-sition of strict legal control upon the civil service would be difficult. "The entire preceding history of our law," they admitted, "has been characterized by the overdevelopment of the principle of unlimited administrative authority and by the corresponding diminution of the natural and inalienable rights of the citizen."[49] The violent repression of revolution in 1905 through mass arrests, field courts-martial, and even police-sponsored pogroms was, in the liberal view, ample tes-timony to this legacy.

Nevertheless, the Cadets believed that the history of tsarist official behavior could be reversed through a single mechanism—the time-honored Western practice of judicial review of administrative acts. As the Cadets stated in the explanatory note to their draft project on civil rights, the party's program in this area was founded upon "one gen-eral demand: the constant and unfailing supervision of the courts over the administration."[50] In order to implement this "general de-mand" the Cadets undertook a broad campaign to bring officialdom under control. Shocked by the ferocity of the government's repressive activity, they demanded the repeal of the empire's emergency regu-lations and an immediate halt to the use of field courts-martial against suspected rebels. Realizing that despotic behavior by civil servants was not limited to exceptional times, they drafted a bill guaranteeing the inviolability of the individual under all circumstances.[51] Most impor-tant, the Cadets launched a direct assault on the primary bulwark of the state administration's independence, the tsarist system of adminis-trative justice.

As has been noted, until 1905 the task of policing the civil service had been left essentially to the state bureaucracy itself. Complaints against officials were resolved either by their own chiefs or by collegial boards made up of fellow bureaucrats. Under the practice of adminis-trative guarantee no official could be brought before the courts for violating the law in the exercise of his duties without the approval of his superior. The Cadets now demanded that this entire system be dismantled and both administrative guarantee and the collegial in-stitutions abolished. In their place was to be substituted a special de-partment of the district court. This new body, as part of the indepen-dent judiciary, would be free of any state interference and, therefore, fully able to perform its function of ending official injustice. In this way the Cadets believed it possible to achieve their goal that "every administrative act directed against individuals inevitably and automat-ically, by virtue of firm laws, be verified by the courts."[52]

The final and most important principle in the Cadet program for the provinces was self-government. The zemstvo and town council, the heart of the liberal program for local government before 1905, remained so in the post-revolutionary years. Indeed, the first two points of the Cadet program, equality and legality, could be interpreted essentially as prerequisites for the third. Estate equality would, in the Cadet conception, democratize the conditions of public participation in local affairs. Legality would guarantee the freedom of public participation from arbitrary interference. Yet it was self-government that would provide the primary vehicle for that participation. Just as the new State Duma was to be the expression of popular sovereignty at the national level, to the Cadets the zemstvos and town councils were to be its embodiment locally.

In keeping with their exalted conception of the role of self-government, the Cadets proposed a dual plan. First, it would be necessary to "decentralize authority from Saint Petersburg to the local level." Then, "the largest possible amount" of this authority could be transferred to the public institutions.[53] Of course, this combination of deconcentration and devolution was no novelty. Even Pleve's program of decentralization had included the transfer of some activity to the zemstvos and town councils. What distinguished the Cadet proposals from others, beyond the emphasis on autonomy, was their radical extent. Not just some authority was to devolve upon self-government; almost all of it was. As the party argued in its official program, the sphere of the self-governing bodies was to include "the entire area of local administration," excluding only those very few functions which "under the contemporary conditions of political life" required handling by the central authorities, such as defense and the imperial budget.[54]

That the Cadets were serious in their intention to guarantee the independence of self-government and to extend its jurisdiction to the "entire area" of governance was evident in their suggestions for the reorganization of the state bureaucratic apparatus. The governors, to this point the linchpins of the entire provincial administration, were to be stripped of all direct participation. The various collegial bodies were to be abolished. Literally every active function performed by these organs would be reassigned to the zemstvos and town councils. These included not only such matters as taxation, education, health, and welfare, but also control of the police.[55] All that would be left to the civil service was the modest role of seeing that self-government acted legally, and even in this the formerly all-powerful bureaucrats would be under the watchful eye of the courts.

The transfer of police affairs to the institutions of self-government emphatically demonstrated the radical nature of the Cadet proposals. The tsarist police had been the backbone of the state administration's control over local life, the ultimate coercive foundation of its power. As police chief-turned-liberal Lopukhin bluntly stated in 1907, the empire's law enforcement system—like the entire polity—had been based on a conception of the state as "something divorced from the people," something standing above the citizenry. In keeping with this notion, he argued, the police force operated first and foremost to guarantee the state protection from its own populace. Therefore, it had to be "in opposition to the population and could not be in any way dependent upon it."[56] Removing the police function from the control of the central authorities and putting it in the hands of self-government would, therefore, fundamentally reverse this old relationship. The police, and indeed the entire administrative apparatus, would become the instrument of the populace, not its overseers.

In sum, the Cadet party, through its plans for police reform, the broadening of self-government, estate equality, and legality, proposed nothing less than standing the administrative and political structure of the empire on its head. Authority and sovereignty were not to flow from the top down, but rather from the bottom up. The people, or "society" as Russian liberals were wont to put it, would rule the state.

Local Government and Gentry Reaction

The alacrity with which liberals made use of the new opportunities for political organization in 1905 and 1906 was in keeping with their past behavior. Far more unexpected was the speed and vigor with which their staunchest opponents among the educated public, the gentry right, did the same. For decades before the revolution, conservatives among the nobility had not normally felt the need for formal organization to press their views. Subtler private ties in court and throughout Saint Petersburg officialdom had seemed to offer ample opportunity for influence. The events of 1905 drastically altered the situation, again serving as a catalyst for change.

The single most important force mobilizing gentry activity was the massive wave of peasant violence against gentry estates. In autumn of 1905 alone almost thirty million rubles of property damage was registered in nineteen central provinces.[57] Saratov led the way with almost ten million rubles, Simbirsk with four million, and Kursk and

Chernigov with three million each. The impact of peasant unrest on the majority of nobles was twofold. It drove them to the right politically, away from any liberal sentiments, and it created a sense of near panic among them. Many would agree with the prominent Moscow noble who predicted, "Alas, it is all too clear that satan has begun his rule on earth. One can see his time approaches!"[58]

The direct local assault on gentry life and property, unequalled since the great Pugachev rising during the reign of Catherine the Great, would have been sufficient of itself to galvanize the gentry, but it was reinforced by national events. For one thing, the tsarist regime was now a constitutional monarchy with a popular assembly. The creation of a State Duma with a broad suffrage threatened to take power out of the hands of the tsar and his ministers and vest it in those of radical delegates. Worse yet, the ministers themselves seemed to be turning a deaf ear to gentry demands, and even supporting the revolutionary cause. The clearest demonstration of noble concern over the policies of the government came in the strong reaction against the Kutler plan for land redistribution. Gentry sentiment was captured by one noble petition to the tsar which complained that "over our country is arising a new danger, not from among the revolutionary parties, . . . but from the omnipotent representatives of state authority, [who] are drafting legislative projects and issuing directives and circulars which have all the destructive force of false sociological teachings [i.e., socialism]."[59] In the face of peasant violence and what appeared to be government treachery, the first estate could no longer remain satisfied with traditional methods of influencing policy. For the first time in decades many of the Russian gentry felt the need for formal organization to defend their interests.

The dynamics of conservative noble activity are most clearly discerned at the local level. The institutions of self-government, hitherto more or less dominated by liberals, were now in the grips of what was commonly referred to as a mounting "zemstvo reaction." The Kursk zemstvo, for instance, had been a leader in the progressive movement before 1905. Its third element was among the most active in the empire in areas like education and agronomic aid, and its leadership included such prominent liberals as A. V. Evreinov and the Dolgorukov brothers. Yet the progressives' work had been consistently opposed by a small but vocal rightist minority led by Prince N. F. Kasatkin-Rostovskii, Count V. F. Dorrer, and M. Ia. Govorukho-Otrok. During the Revolution of 1905, which struck Kursk Province with particular fury, control of the zemstvo passed into the hands of this former minority. Kasatkin-Rostovskii was elected to represent the zemstvo in the reorganized State Council, and Govorukho-Otrok was chosen to replace the well-known educator N. V. Raevskii as zemstvo board chairman.[60]

Like its Kursk counterpart, the Saratov provincial zemstvo had taken a leading role in the pre-Revolutionary zemstvo movement. After election as chairman of the Saratov board in 1900, N. N. L'vov had initiated a vigorous campaign to expand self-governmental activity, a campaign that among other things established the *Saratov Zemstvo Weekly* as one of the most respected official periodicals in the empire. The local elections of 1906, which followed in the wake of widespread peasant disorder in the province, sharply altered the zemstvo's direction. The conservative K. N. Grimm became chairman, and the "rightist" Count D. A. Olsuf'ev won election as Saratov's representative to the State Council. The events in Kursk and Saratov were mirrored in a majority of the other provincial zemstvos. Of fifteen Cadets who held positions as board chairmen at the outset of 1906, only one, Ufa's P. F. Koropachinskii, retained his seat through 1907.[61]

Conservative gentry did not limit themselves to asserting control over the zemstvos and over their own noble associations. At a time when peasants were applying the torch, or "red rooster," to estates across the land and when liberals and other "subversive" elements were rushing to form political parties, local forums of activity seemed clearly inadequate. By the beginning of 1906 various nobles, particularly in Tambov and the rightist bulwark of Kursk, were expressing interest in unification. The old method of articulating gentry views through congresses of gentry marshals was rejected, primarily for fear of the great influence of the liberal marshals of Saint Petersburg and Moscow. Instead the conservatives sought to establish a broader union of the nobility, and in the spring they formed a commission, eventually under the chairmanship of Kasatkin-Rostovskii, to prepare for a national congress of gentry representatives. By May the commission had completed a draft statute and agenda for the new body. On 22 May 1906 the first Congress of the Representatives of Noble Associations opened its deliberations in Saint Petersburg.[62]

Ostensibly the new congress was intended to defend the interests of the entire nobility, but its composition was hardly representative. Delegates were drawn almost exclusively from among the largest gentry proprietors. Moreover, it was soon evident that there would be little role in the organization for liberals. At its April meetings, for instance, the preparatory commission established the rule (later approved by the full congress) that voting would be by province, thus guaranteeing that the more cosmopolitan gentry of Saint Petersburg and Moscow could not override their more conservative rural brethren.[63] Six of the most progressive gentry associations, including those of Saint Petersburg, Voronezh, and Chernigov, simply chose to boycott the first congress. And those liberals who did attend were not well received. When a number of centrist marshals, including Prince P. N. Trubetskoi and M. A. Stakhovich, expressed reservations about the goals of the organization they were rudely overridden. In an act of considerable symbolic value, Trubetskoi and twenty-one others quit the sessions.[64] The Permanent Council chosen to represent the congress when it was not in session was dominated by rightists.

The two issues that captured gentry attention, both in the zemstvos and in their national organization, were agrarian reform and the Duma suffrage. The Kutler proposal, with its threat of compulsory alienation of noble land, had terrified much of the first estate. The existence of a legislature elected primarily by the land-hungry peasant masses only made this threat more starkly real. Therefore, the gentry right lobbied intensively to force the government to protect their estates and to impose strict limitations on the franchise. Despite this primary involvement in the struggle to defend their property, however, the conservative nobility very early also gave clear indications of their views on the question of local government. They made it plain that they would have no part of the zemstvo progressives with their plans for broadening zemstvo activity and democratizing self-government. Until 1905 the differences between Russian liberals and conservatives had been partially masked by a common animosity to "bureaucratism." With the revolution, the fundamental opposition between Slavophil conservatism and Western-oriented liberalism was brought into sharp relief. Cooperation between the two camps was no longer possible.

This hostility was evident in the wave of reaction that swept the zemstvos after 1905, a wave aimed essentially at washing away all that the liberals had achieved. Gentry fury was directed particularly at the third element, which was held responsible (in part justifiably) for encouraging peasant unrest. As Kasatkin-Rostovskii declared in reference to the Kursk zemstvo employees, "For some time the [zemstvo] board has been a hotbed of the revolutionary movement; that is, among the employees has been organized a party that secretly and openly effectively furthered the spread of revolutionary propaganda." In Simbirsk accusatory speeches were so bitter that, in the words of the assembly's secretary, "even the paper blushed."[65]

Not satisfied with firing employees considered politically unreliable—an operation that they engaged in with unbridled enthusiasm—conservative gentry turned also to the liquidation of many branches of self-governmental activity. Spurred on by the drop in revenue caused by the 1905 disorders, new conservative majorities in the zemstvo assemblies voted to abolish sanitary bureaus, shut down statistical offices, and close schools. In Saratov, for example, agronomic work, legal aid, sanitation efforts, provision of cattle insurance, and publication of the *Saratov Zemstvo Weekly* all were terminated. Zemstvo finances were definitely in disarray in 1906 and 1907, largely as a result of citizens' refusal to pay taxes. In Voronezh, for instance, arrears on 1905 levies reached 25 percent of the total, and in Saratov 35 percent. Nevertheless, financial difficulties were not the primary reason for retrenchment. Many of the zemstvo budgetary cuts were made on explicitly political grounds, and there is a very high correlation between "liquidations" and liberal associations. The Saratov zemstvo, for example, did find funds for a twelve-thousand-ruble subsidy for the newly founded conservative periodical *Volga*.[66] Through their purge of the third element the landed gentry strikingly asserted their determination to resist the democratization and liberalization of local government and to make the local institutions proof against progressive influence.

If the zemstvo employees were not to predominate in local affairs, who was? Perhaps the official defenders of the existing order, the state's civil servants? On the face of it, relations between the gentry and government in 1906 and 1907 were very cordial. The central authorities had strongly supported gentry efforts to cleanse self-government of "subversive" influences. In Saint Petersburg, Ministers of Internal Affairs Durnovo and Peter A. Stolypin had both issued circulars warning administrators to keep close surveillance over oppositional elements, and in the provinces many governors had initiated action against suspect zemstvo boards and their employees.[67] In addition, a number of ranking bureaucrats had actively encouraged the creation of the United Nobility. For example, when gentry marshals expressed concern that their semiofficial status might rule out participation in the new organization, the minister of internal affairs sent his approval. A. S. Stishinskii, head of the main administration of agriculture, went further, offering his home as a meeting place for the first congress.[68] Most important of all, however, the government began to demonstrate what seemed to be a renewed concern for gentry interests. In the fall of 1906 Stolypin initiated land reform without compulsory alienation, and on 3 June of the following year he drastically limited the Duma suffrage.[69]

Some have interpreted these actions as evidence that conservative nobles and the central authorities were in close alliance, or even that the former actually dictated state policy, particularly that the members of the United Nobility were the prime movers in both the Stolypin agrarian reform and the revision of the Duma electoral law.[70] It is true that on these important issues the government's policy and that of the United Nobility were almost identical, but there is incontrovertible evidence that the administration's plans evolved largely independently of pressure from the first estate. In reference to the land question, for example, both Stolypin and his primary adviser in this field, Gurko, had been opponents of communal agriculture long before 1905.[71] Much the same can be said of the government's views on the Duma electoral law. Rather than draw any causal connection between state policy and gentry demands on agrarian and suffrage reform, it is more accurate to speak of a convergence of opinion in these two areas. Violent disagreement could and did exist between the two parties elsewhere. No issue demonstrates this more clearly than that of local governance.

Throughout 1906 and 1907, conservative gentry were quite careful not to identify themselves with the government. In a sense, the very creation of the United Nobility was proof that the old confidence in the state administration's attentiveness to the gentry had been broken. The sharp distinction that the agrarian nobles drew between themselves and landless officialdom was voiced by V. N. Snezhkov in a report to the United Nobility's first session. "The task of our congress is terribly weighty and significant," he wrote. "We are not sly courtiers, We are not civil servants under Pleve tracking down 'harmful modes of thought' or under Witte demanding a constituent assembly in response to political strikes; We are, after all is said and done, gentry." During the Kursk purge N. E. Markov argued similarly. "We are proprietors here, and we wish to manage our own affairs! I am for the peasant and estate owner, I am for proprietors and not intelligents, even if they hold a general's rank."[72]

As Snezhkov's comment indicates, gentry distrust of the state bureaucracy dated back at least to Pleve's ministry and peaked during Witte's, with the October Manifesto and the Kutler project. This suspicion of the bureaucratic world extended beyond leaders like Witte and Pleve to the entire civil service. In fact, in the gentry view the local officials had committed the most reprehensible transgression of all. They had failed in their sacred duty to protect noble life and property. "Confidence in authority is shaken," the gentry marshals reported in a January 1906 address to the tsar, and "cannot exist as long as the government does nothing in the face of the development of the revolutionary movement."[73]

Much hostility was directed at the judiciary, which, it was felt, had shown a distinct lack of vigor in employing the empire's legal apparatus for repression. Yet the staff of the MVD, from governor to village policeman, also stood accused. G. A. Shechkov, for one, believed that only by making the administration financially liable for revolutionary acts would the government "show more energy" and "watch more strictly for disorders."[74] The majority attending the third congress of the United Nobility hit upon another remedy. Special senatorial investigations should be undertaken to review the behavior of all officials so as to "put an end to the weakness of the government."[75] Whatever their solution, the conservative gentry agreed on one thing. The civil service could not be relied upon to direct local affairs.

If both the third element and the state officials were unacceptable, who was to assume the role of leadership in local administration? The answer is to be found in gentry opinions as to who was primarily responsible for the suppression of revolution in 1905. Illusory though their conception may have been, by 1906 conservative nobles had come increasingly to believe that they themselves, and not the empire's police force or army, had led in the restoration of order. In particular, it was the officials of the first estate—marshals and land captains—who had rallied the forces of stability in the face of chaos. It is true that as late as April 1906 many conservatives among the gentry were quite hostile toward their liberal marshals. Yet as the year progressed the composition of the marshaldom shifted to the right. In Moscow, for instance, the liberal Trubetskoi was unseated, eventually to be replaced by the Slavophil A. D. Samarin. As the political complexion of the body of marshals was transformed, their constituents came increasingly to see them retrospectively as the heroes of 1905. Many wholeheartedly agreed with E. A. Iseev's later claim that when the police captains and constables were nowhere to be found it had been the marshals with their comrades the land captains who had stood as the bulwark against peasant anarchy.[76]

In keeping with this belief, or myth, the rightist gentry insisted that hegemony in local affairs be reserved for their own officials. Where the Cadets prescribed the democratization of self-government, the gentry looked to the revitalization of their corporate institutions as a means of local administrative reform. They turned to the estate principle, back to the measures of Tolstoi in 1889, and further. This unwillingness to relinquish their traditional role in the management of provincial matters was clearly reflected in the address to the tsar adopted by the first congress of the United Nobility. It concluded: "We firmly believe that the extensive efforts of the state to rejuvenate the Russian regime will result in renewed vigor for the nobility rather than its extinction and will lead to permanent cooperation with you, sire, and with the whole Russian nation, in accordance with the new principles of national life."[77] This insistence upon the renewal of the estate ideal not only brought the gentry into conflict with their traditional antagonists, the liberal Cadets, it also embroiled them in bitter conflict with the government. As will be seen, the estate principle and the gentry institutions that were its embodiment were the primary target of the Stolypin ministry in its work toward local reform.

The Pragmatism of the Octobrists

The organization of the United Nobility demonstrated that the revolution had activated not only the empire's liberal and socialist left, but also the right. Polarization of public opinion, which reflected the deep social and class tensions within tsarist society, was the dominant theme of the hour. Yet not everyone was content with the options offered at the political extremes. A significant minority primarily among the upper classes preferred to seek a middle way, a moderate program that would be at once progressive and conservative. The search for moderation in an extremely immoderate time, for a conservatism that would preserve through limited change, took many forms, including above all the organization of the Octobrist Union.

Octobrism was born out of the collapse of the united zemstvo movement. From its beginning, zemstvo progressivism had been an extremely loose amalgam of various approaches. On the one hand, it included the constitutionalism and even socialism of the third element, and, on the other, the mild reformism of gentry Slavophils of Shipov's persuasion. In the chaotic months of revolution, differences in outlook increased. With the formal organization of the zemstvo left into the Cadet party, they could no longer be contained.

The degree of discord was decisively demonstrated at the November 1905 zemstvo congress, which ended in a full split. Unhappy with the perceived radicalism of the Cadet majority, a significant minority of those present, including Shipov and M. A. Stakhovich, resolved to follow Moscow industrialist A. I. Guchkov's recommendation to organize a "new political group."[78] Even before the congress adjourned an appeal appeared in Moscow and Saint Petersburg calling for support in the formation of a "Union of the 17th of October." Among the document's signatories were Shipov, Stakhovich, Guchkov, Saint Petersburg Mayor N. A. Reztsov, and a number of other prominent figures from the ranks of self-government.[79] Work on the establishment of the union continued through the winter. Forty-two local branches had been opened by the end of January. Broadening its base beyond the zemstvos and municipalities, the union established important contacts with groups representing commercial and industrial interests, such as the All-Russian Commerical and Industrial Union and the Progessive-Economic Party. The new party also attracted a growing following among petty officials and the more conservative members of the free professions.[80] By 8 February the union was ready to hold its first "All-Russian" congress at the hunting club in the Moscow home of the Sheremetev family.

Although the Octobrists were later to play a crucial role in the Third State Duma, their importance as a national organization before the 3 June 1907 revision of the suffrage was very limited. More impressive initially was their strength locally, particularly in the institutions of self-government. From the outset the Octobrists possessed influential adherents in the town councils, among them Guchkov of Moscow and Reztsov of Saint Petersburg, and they soon achieved this in the zemstvos as well. The wave of rural "reaction" that contributed so essentially to the emergence of the gentry right also boosted Octobrism. Even before the 1906–1907 zemstvo elections thirteen provincial board chairmen were identified as Octobrists, and after the elections the total had increased to nineteen.[81]

Indicative of the shift in zemstvo opinion was the case of Moscow. Under Shipov's guidance the Moscow zemstvo had developed a reputation as one of the most progressive in the empire. When the government had refused to approve Shipov's reelection as board chairman in 1903, the assembly responded by choosing the outspoken liberal F. A. Golovin. During the summer of 1905 Golovin took an active part in the organization of the Cadet party, and he was later to be chairman of the Second Duma. But his views were not compatible with those of the zemstvo majority led by Guchkov. In a bitterly contested election in 1906, Golovin was unseated by the Octobrist N. F. Rikhter.[82] Rikhter himself had earlier been of more liberal views, but by 1906 he had, in Shipov's words, "reversed his political physiognomy" to suit the views of conservatives.[83] He proved his newly adopted conservatism the following year by leading an attack on Golovin's former administration that resulted in a suit against the old board.

An even more graphic demonstration of the dynamics of Octobrism in the zemstvos was offered by the Kharkov Provincial Zemstvo. From 1903, oppositional sentiment here had grown steadily among the third element employees, and relations between the zemstvo board and the local governor became increasingly strained. However, a series of strikes in the provincial capital early in 1905 alarmed a majority of the zemstvo assembly and led to the cashiering of Board Chairman V. F. Kolokol'tsev. His place was taken by Prince A. D. Golitsyn. Golitsyn had entered self-government earlier to oppose liberals in the Kharkov District Zemstvo. As its chairman he had devoted himself to the task of turning the district body away from its commitment to popular education toward the more practical tasks of agronomy, road building, and the development of a telephone network. In 1905, fearing that the provincial board was becoming a "new revolutionary center with clearly political tendencies," he became the successful conservative candidate for its chairmanship. Golitsyn attended the November zemstvo congress, but left in discouragement at the Cadet predominance. Worried lest the Cadets also dominate Kharkov's elections to the Duma, he set about organizing "zemstvo men of a liberal-progressive inclination" into a more moderate party. He successfully enlisted a majority of the local assembly members to his cause and founded a newspaper, characteristically named *The Center*. Following the electoral reform of 3 June 1907, Golitsyn won election to the Third Duma. There he immediately affiliated with the Octobrists and was chosen to the party's Duma bureau.[84]

Given the prominent place of men like Golitsyn and Rikhter in the union's development, it is not surprising that local government occupied an important place in the party program. Unlike the Cadets, who now called for the radical restructuring of all administration on the basis of popular sovereignty, the Octobrists contented themselves with the modest proposals the zemstvo movement had advanced in 1902 and 1903. In its initial platform the union called for the strengthening of self-government by broadening jurisdiction, guaranteeing independence from "administrative tutelage," and supplying the long-expected local zemstvo unit.[85] Although they proclaimed the need for including the "widest possible circle of people" in the zemstvos and municipalities, the Octobrists did not follow the Cadets in insisting on universal suffrage. For the moment the limits of this "widest circle" were left undefined. In time, however, the union was

to circumscribe it closely through the application of a property qualification for suffrage.

Just as the Octobrists would not go along with the Cadets in their
demand for universal suffrage, so too did they refuse to support the
more extreme liberal plans for drastic limitations on the role of the
state bureaucracy. No mention was made in the union's program of
such Cadet measures as transfer of the local police to self-government
or weakening of the office of governor. The Octobrists simply insisted
that all officials be held "strictly responsible" for violations of the law.
And they recommended the "general simplification" of the local administrative apparatus.[86]

While the members of the moderate union were thus at odds with
the Cadets over the suffrage and other questions, they were no more
in agreement with the gentry right. In fact, they were in full opposition to the main pillar of the gentry program, the estate principle.
The Octobrists frankly insisted that all privileges and restrictions of
estate be removed from the structure of self-government. Indeed,
they argued that the peasantry should be given "full civil rights equal
with other citizens."[87] As has been noted, the Octobrists had a new
discriminatory principle of their own to replace that of traditional
corporations. This was to be the "progressive" principle of property
or wealth. In 1906, however, the precise nature of the union's intentions in this respect had still to be developed. Nothing was said of it in
the party program.

The appearance of Octobrism was a welcome phenomenon for the
government. In the first place, this party had been organized for the
explicit purpose of cooperation with the central authorities. As the
future Octobrist Prince N. S. Volkonskii had argued at the November
zemstvo congress, "It is time to clasp the government's outstretched
hand."[88] Accordingly, the party's initial platform called upon the
populace to "harmoniously unite around those principles proclaimed
in the Manifesto of 17 October" and to "aid the government" in its
work of reform.[89] In fact, the warmth with which most Octobrists, led
by Guchkov, welcomed such measures as the establishment of field
courts-martial to battle unrest quickly caused a split in the union.
Fearful of official brutality, Shipov and Stakhovich withdrew to form
a new political group of their own.

Even more important than any particular programmatic statement
was the basic nature of Octobrism. The members of the party, like
many in the government, considered themselves to be both reformers
and conservatives. To use a word they might well have chosen, they
considered themselves pragmatists. Their basic commitment was to

cautious and gradual change aimed at meeting specific practical needs, needs "arising directly out of life," as some Octobrists were wont to put it. Again the careers of Golitsyn and Rikhter are illustrative. As chairman of the Kharkov district zemstvo Golitsyn's primary efforts were in the unspectacular fields of road repair and telephone installation. Even during the tumultuous year of 1905 his greatest excitement was reserved for the inheritance of full title to his maternal estate, an inheritance that enabled him to realize his "cherished dream" of building a distillery and dairy farming.[90] In all his endeavors, both official and private, he was pleased to work hand in hand with civil servants, and he developed close ties with the Ministry of Agriculture and the Resettlement Administration. The same flavor characterized Rikhter's activity in Moscow. After the bitterness that followed his election and his early measures against the liberals who had formerly dominated the zemstvo, he proved a capable manager of zemstvo affairs. Significantly, Rikhter was well respected by the Moscow governor, avoiding the clashes that characterized the tenure of his predecessors Shipov and Golovin.[91]

Octobrism, therefore, held great potential for the central authorities. Yet in 1906 it was far from clear that any of this potential could be realized. The dominant theme remained divisive polarization, not constructive consensus. Sharp cleavages existed not only between the government and the educated public but also within the public itself. Before the revolution the fundamental ideological differences that characterized various social and political groups had been muted by a general shared hostility to the state bureaucracy. Now the distinctions between such organizations as the Cadets and United Nobility were glaringly clear.

Indeed, the Revolution of 1905 crystallized the basic dilemma facing the tsarist system at the beginning of the twentieth century. Rapid social change within the empire and an ever closer relationship with western Europe created a need for more effective administrative institutions capable of dealing more efficiently and creatively with new tasks. Yet at the same time these developments heightened citizen attitudes that made the establishment of such governmental institutions very difficult. Political and social tensions within the populace made the achievement of any broad agreement on the direction of reform problematic. Moreover, insistence upon the limitation of the state bureaucracy and upon greater public participation made the tsarist government's traditional, centralist method of imposing solutions to social problems all but impossible. As one historian noted in reference to Witte's failure to overcome these difficulties, "A revolution from below was not the time for a revolution from above."[92]

It can of course be argued that conditions in 1905 and 1906 were exceptional. The polarization and hardening of outlook that accompany revolution might be expected to moderate after mass unrest had been brought under control, but this did not happen. Overt violence did decline drastically after 1906, yet just as the deeper problems of tsarist society predated the revolution, they persisted unresolved thereafter. In order to overcome them, the tsarist government was to commit itself to one last great effort at reform.

CHAPTER V

THE STOLYPIN REFORM PROGRAM, 1906–1907

There is no question that Peter A. Stolypin and V. I. Lenin are the two dominant figures in the political history of late Tsarist Russia. The reasons for their prominence, however, are quite different. Lenin's is rooted essentially in his later success, not in the influence he exerted before 1917. His rival, by contrast, was the leading actor on the political stage before World War I, occupying a position reminiscent of Bismarck's in Imperial Germany. It is not that Stolypin was exceptionally profound—he certainly lacked the insight and adroitness of his Prussian counterpart. Rather, Stolypin appeared upon the national scene at a crucial moment. Although the Fundamental Laws approved by the government in 1906 laid down the legal structure of the empire's nascent constitution, the State Duma had not yet met. As Witte's successor, Stolypin still had to oversee the actual implementation of the October Manifesto's formal principles. More broadly, Stolypin was forced to confront the ways in which change, ratified violently by the Revolution of 1905, had upset the traditional social order. Old elites were seeking to reassert their influence, new groups ranging from businessmen to radical socialists were claiming a place of power, and the masses were demanding redress of basic grievances. It was up to Stolypin to find a balance among the conflicting elements of tsarist society. He attacked the task with relish. Indeed, his ministry constituted one of the most important attempts by the state bureaucracy to manage change through reform and achieve a conservative modernization of the empire.

Stolypin's program was multifaceted. It covered the fields of agriculture, the constitution, education and, most importantly here, local administration. Indeed, Stolypin himself on several occasions described his plans for reorganizing the governmental apparatus in the provinces as second only to agrarian reform in importance.[1] As an indicator of the general nature of Stolypin's activity it might well rank first. The package of reform bills drafted by the staff of the Ministry of Internal Affairs in this area fully embodied the basic elements of Stolypin's vision of the empire's future.

Stolypin and the MVD

Stolypin's emergence as a national political figure in the spring of 1906 caused a major shift in the balance of power within the empire. This was not so much a matter of the relationship of the government to the newly organized political parties as of a change within the chancelleries of the state bureaucracy. Following Pleve's assassination in 1904 the Ministry of Internal Affairs had lost the initiative in attempts to reorganize the state structure. Its successive heads— Sviatopolk-Mirskii, Bulygin, and Durnovo—all failed to attain even a fraction of the influence over policy held by their fallen predecessor. Instead, leadership of the government during the Revolution of 1905 had been assumed by Pleve's archenemy, Witte. Long hostile to the MVD in any case, Witte had become convinced of the need to abandon the highly statist approach to administration that had been personified by Pleve. Both Witte's distaste for the interior ministry and his interest in a new and more liberal attitude toward reform were underlined by his appointment as chairman of the Council of Ministers, an office that was distinctly outside the MVD and smacked of western European notions of a cabinet and constitution. The MVD was definitely in eclipse.

All this changed dramatically with Witte's involuntary resignation in April of 1906. In his place as chairman the tsar selected I. L. Goremykin, a colorless and indolent bureaucrat who had been largely responsible for the MVD's inactivity through much of the 1890s. The real driving force in the government was to be not Goremykin, but a relative newcomer to the capital, the dynamic young governor of Saratov who was now appointed minister of internal affairs, Stolypin. Appearing, in the words of one admirer, like a "lonely rocket" against the "dull and dark background" of Petersburg officialdom, Stolypin was in the following months able to restore a large measure of public confidence in the authorities' ability to deal with the revolutionary crisis. In the process he returned the MVD to a level of influence equal to that it had possessed before Pleve's death. Though later appointed chairman of the Council of Ministers in place of Goremykin, he retained his ministry and continued to rely heavily upon its support. The combination of these two factors—the personality of Stolypin and the reemergence of the MVD staff as the dominant force in policy formulation—led to the resurrection of Pleve's approach to administrative reform.

On the face of it Stolypin was an unlikely successor to the arch-bureaucrat Pleve. As a student at Saint Petersburg University Stolypin had chosen to study in the natural sciences (doing his thesis on tobacco cultivation) rather than in the more political legal faculty. A disinclination for political theory, relative financial security, and an early marriage all insulated him from student activism at the university.[2] Following graduation he entered service in the Ministry of Agriculture. Yet unlike Pleve, who made his career in the chancelleries of Saint Petersburg, Stolypin tired of the life of a civil servant and retired to the earthier pursuit of husbandry at his family estate in the western province of Kovno. He returned to formal state service with an appointment as district gentry marshal, a nonelective position in the empire's western provinces. In this modest position he began to build a reputation for ability and pragmatism that thrust him, half unwillingly it seems, up the hierarchical ladder of the state bureaucracy. Success in the district brought promotion to the office of provincial marshal and then in 1902 appointment as governor of Grodno. Despite his relative youth Stolypin must have made an immediate impression on his superiors (including Pleve), for within a year he was transferred to Saratov, perhaps the most volatile and difficult province in the empire. The outburst of revolutionary disorder that swept the province from 1904 to 1906 presented him not only with a grave challenge but with an opportunity to demonstrate his mettle. His ability to hold the provincial administrative apparatus together, plus a talent for dramatic displays of personal courage in the face of physical danger, brought him to the tsar's attention and resulted in his appointment as Durnovo's successor in April 1906.[3]

Stolypin arrived in the capital to take his post with relatively little experience in Saint Petersburg politics. Even the servants at his new official residence were astonished by his lack of ribbons and medals. Unlike Pleve and many of his colleagues, Stolypin drew his attitudes on matters of policy from personal experience in the provinces rather than more abstract notions or principles. For example, direct observation of the success of individual farming in East Prussia and Kovno and of the failure of communal cultivation in Saratov had made him an ardent opponent of the mir. Similarly, his work as a district and provincial administrator had attuned him to the importance of developing positive working relationships with the citizenry, especially local notables. He brought this determination to reach out to "society" with him to Saint Petersburg. As one MVD staffer put it, Stolypin was not a minister of the old bureaucratic type, but rather the first to seek a firm base of popular support by offering "a new heroic form of leadership."[4] Yet, paradoxically, Stolypin's experience with the public outside the capital had led him to the same conclusion on local administration that Pleve had reached in Saint Petersburg—the need to retain the predominant position of the state bureaucracy.

In Kovno, where Lithuanians, Jews, and Poles together outnumbered the Russian population by better than ten to one, and in Grodno, where Great Russians were also a minority, Stolypin learned the importance of the tsarist administrative apparatus in holding the multinational empire together. This lesson was reinforced by his stormy years in Saratov, although nationality was not the dominant issue there. Instead, order was threatened not only by rebellious peasants and the radical intelligentsia but by conservative landowners and other supporters of tradition who sought to answer revolutionary violence with violence of their own.[5] Stolypin's response to the situation was evident in his 1904 report to Nicholas II. Referring to the banquet campaign organized by the liberal opposition in the province, the governor echoed other officials in decrying the political tendentiousness of the zemstvo and its employees. Yet he did not find a counterweight to sedition in the landed gentry who, he wrote, "might have a great restraining influence in the area, [but] do not live on their estates and often even fear to appear in them." Instead he argued, "The only obstacle in the path of the 'third element' is the administration."[6] In keeping with this view, and despite the beseeching of many Saratov notables, Stolypin frequently declined to send troops on risky expeditions into the countryside to protect gentry estates, preferring to retain firm control of the provincial and district capitals. "The strength of Russia is not in her landowners," he told his daughter on one occasion. "The salvation of Russia is not with them, but with the tsar."[7] And, after all, it was the governor and his subordinates in the state bureaucracy who were by law the direct representatives of the tsar's authority. They would form the cornerstone in Stolypin's program of local reform.

As it happened, the new minister's convictions on this issue were reinforced by those of his staff. Given his inexperience in the task of drafting legislation Stolypin was unusually dependent on the personnel of the Ministry of Internal Affairs. Moreover, his lack of familiarity with the inhabitants of Saint Petersburg's bureaucratic world inclined him to leave the MVD staff largely as he found it.[8] With the exit of liberals like Urusov and Lopukhin this staff, particularly in the area of local governance, was dominated by men who had been protégés of Pleve.

The Main Administration for Local Affairs, for example, was still controlled by Pleve appointees. Its director, Gerbel, urban affairs specialist N. L. Psheradskii, and executive officer M. V. Islavin had all been selected by Pleve and were all to play major roles in the Stolypin ministry. Similarly, the Land Section, automatically a key institution in work on local matters, was still directed by Gurko. Another Pleve appointee, who was to be most influential of all in the drafting of Stolypin's program, was Gurliand. A convert to Russian Orthodoxy but of Jewish extraction, he had initially achieved a brilliant career in the field of administrative law. As a professor at the Demidov Lycée he had authored a study of Tsar Aleksei Mikhailovich's "secret prikaz," a seventeenth-century chancellery which Gurliand significantly interpreted as a legitimate instrument of the Muscovite ruler for the extension of his personal power through the use of loyal civil servants.[9] Gurliand's abilities and historical views attracted official notice, and he was invited to join Pleve's MVD staff. Here the ex-professor played an important role in the affairs of self-government, most notoriously in the unsuccessful attempt to suppress the Tver zemstvo. With Stolypin's arrival in Saint Petersburg, Gurliand was appointed editor of the semiofficial periodical *Russia,* but he remained directly involved in MVD legislative work. Men like these, both by service experience and by conviction, were strongly inclined to look to the statist assumptions of Pleve's ministry in their approach to the problems of administrative reform. One observer pejoratively but accurately characterized Gurliand as "absolutist, centralist, hostile to all societal creativity. Not for nothing is he a doctor of police law."[10] In their insistence upon a key role for the tsarist civil service, the MVD bureaucrats ultimately ratified the views of their new superior.

Although the essential outlook of 1903 was thus to reappear in the Ministry of Internal Affairs three years later, there existed in the wake of revolution new conditions that dictated extensive alterations in the old program. The revolution had placed a tremendous strain on the empire's administrative apparatus and fully revealed the depth of its shortcomings. Stolypin himself admitted somewhat later, "I became convinced of the inadequacy of governmental authority through personal experience as governor in Saratov during the disorders of 1905–1906. I doubt that anyone can in good conscience say that the existing district administration is not in need of change."[11]

In addition to exposing the weaknesses of the administrative apparatus, the revolution added the more ominous problem of the politicization of the civil service. On the one hand, many officials, especially of the judicial and finance ministries, had begun to express sympathy with the liberal opposition. On the other, individual governors and police persisted in encouraging monarchist organizations in counterrevolutionary violence directed primarily against the empire's Jewish population. Like Witte before him, Stolypin took measures to restore discipline. Several of the most flagrant violators of the law, such as the Suvalk governor held partially responsible for the 1906 Belostok pogrom, were dismissed. Circulars were issued forbidding civil servants to participate in various political parties and reminding them that "higher policy is decided by the government, and not subordinate administrative organs."[12] Still, the need for more permanent institutionalized means of central control over local officialdom was obvious.

The need to restore the administrative machinery to order and efficiency was therefore pressing in any case, but it was made even more urgent by the government's commitment to new tasks. The most important of these was land reform. During Witte's premiership the balance between supporters and opponents of communal agriculture had tipped in favor of the latter. By the time Stolypin arrived in the capital Gurko's Land Section was well on its way to completing the necessary legislation for freeing the peasants from the mir. Himself a long-time critic of the commune, the new minister had no intention of reversing the Land Section's work. On the contrary, he was to make the transformation of the Russian countryside from communal to private farming the cornerstone of his overall program. This decision to break up the mir in favor of individual holdings had a dual impact on local governance. First, much of the implementation of the reform would fall to the provincial and district organs, which therefore had to be in good working order.[13] Secondly, the disappearance of communal landholding logically implied the restructuring of village administration. The decision to remove the estate element from land ownership through the abolition of communal restrictions on the peasantry raised the issue of similarly removing the corporate principle from governance as well.

As if this were not enough, there was one final consideration that made a bolder approach to reform necessary. Bowing before overwhelming public demands for constitutionalism and law, the tsarist government had created a national parliament and granted basic civil rights to its citizens. Yet as critics like the Cadets and the more moderate Octobrists were quick to point out, these measures would be seriously flawed if not accompanied by steps to extend the rule of law beyond Saint Petersburg to govern the activity of local administrators. Even many officials who rejected liberal prescriptions for reform recognized the need for some cure of old ills. As the MVD formally admitted, the creation of the State Duma produced the need for "immediate concordance" of the principles of local governance with the new state structure.[14] And lest the authorities appear reluctant in this task, there was the constant pressure of public opinion to goad them on. Voices as dissonant as the Social Democrats and the Union of the Russian People continued to demand an end to the highhanded behavior of the civil service. Indeed, the gulf between state and society was broader than ever.

These, then, were the conditions born of revolutionary upheaval that necessitated fresh proposals and innovation in local reform. And the leaders of the Ministry of Internal Affairs, along with other pragmatic officials, were ready to make extensive concessions to the new state of affairs. Yet at the bottom of their response to social and political change lay old attitudes whose roots were in the work of Pleve and of Tolstoi before him.

The State Bureaucracy

With Stolypin's appointment as minister, work on local reform accelerated. Recognizing the pressing need for improvement in the "lamentable condition" of the administrative apparatus, the MVD staff pressed forward on proposals for a major restructuring of government in the provinces. Projects drafted by Gurliand and others were reviewed by a special ad hoc MVD committee chaired by Stolypin. Significantly, most members of the group had been outspoken critics of the policy followed by the ministry since Pleve's death. Gurko, Gerbel, and I. M. Strakhovskii, for example, had all been dissidents in the liberal Urusov Commission. And S. E. Kryzhanovskii, an MVD veteran who had drafted the legislation on establishing the Main Administration for Local Affairs and on reorganizing Saint Petersburg municipal government under Pleve, had been a bitter opponent of the weakness of Sviatopolk-Mirskii.[15] By late 1906 the committee had completed its deliberations. The ministry was prepared to present more than half a dozen bills touching on various parts of the tsarist local administrative system. Taken together the proposals represented the most comprehensive program for the reorganization of the provincial apparatus to come from the offices of the central government since the work of the Kakhanov Commission twenty years earlier.

What might best be called the Stolypin reform program, since it was he who sponsored it, covered a broad range of issues, but its main theme was simple—the reaffirmation of the central authorities' hegemony in local affairs. Where the Cadets championed the cause of self-government and the gentry right their estate institutions, Stolypin and the MVD characteristically rose to the defense of the local representatives of the state bureaucracy. Gurliand best articulated the dominant view somewhat later in *Russia*. Reviewing the history of administrative law, he commented, "The study of government is a broad science, and far from all its parts have been developed sufficiently. Nevertheless, one point is unconditionally firm: everything that this science builds, it builds on the principle of the state, not on anarchy."[16] Gurliand went on to identify the state directly with the activity of its own officials. In doing so he clearly rejected the liberal contention that the civil servants should be merely passive inspectors of local administration. Instead, he cast them as its directors and prime movers. At one point, for instance, the MVD spokesman ridiculed the Cadet proposals as creating "governors who above all must not govern, obligatory ordinances that above all must not be obligatory, and district authorities who above all must possess no authority."[17] In order to prevent this the MVD now proposed a restructuring of the local institutions of the state bureaucracy based on two principles drawn from the work of Pleve and Tolstoi, unity and decentralization.

The need for greater coordination in local governance was a leitmotif of all the MVD's work. As one of its draft projects read, it would be impossible to assure the "proper course" of state affairs if in the place of a unified local administration the central authorities encountered only "a conglomerate of variform institutions." While there existed many means of achieving the goal of unity, the MVD now resorted primarily to its traditional mechanism of "one-man rule." As the legislators explained, the government intended to provide itself with "special agents whose main duty is to realize in local life the principle of coherence in the state mechanism, unifying under their leadership and guidance the work of its separate elements."[18] The MVD planned to supply itself with a hierarchical chain of powerful subordinates reaching from Saint Petersburg down through the administrative apparatus to the village.

This certainly was the main theme of the draft bill for provincial reform, which was based upon a drastic increase in the governor's prerogatives both of supervision and direct administration. In the former area, for instance, the governor was given more specific authority to oversee tax collection and education. In the latter, he was assigned the role of head executor of Stolypin's massive agrarian reform. Similarly, his newly expanded authority was to be carried over to the provincial collegial institutions. Here most of the various boards and committees would be consolidated under a "provincial council" dominated by the governor.[19]

The task of unification was more difficult at the district level, for there existed no single official who could perform a function equivalent to that of the governor. The police chief was a possibility, but his association with the very unpopular law enforcement agencies deprived him of the requisite prestige in the eyes of inhabitants. The gentry marshal was a more likely candidate. He already presided over several district committees and certainly possessed dignity. But powerful factors also gravitated against his selection. For one thing, the past performance of the marshals had been spotty at best, marred by absenteeism and an unfortunate inclination for oppositional politics.[20] Moreover, as the representative only of the first estate, the marshal was closely identified with gentry privilege. Ultimately, however, it was neither historical shortcomings nor noble ties that ruled the marshal out, but the fact that he was chosen by public elements. Reflecting Tolstoi's earlier prejudice against the elective principle in administration, the MVD legislators insisted that the government "can not be restricted in its selection by the binding decision of any local corporation, whether estate or nonestate."[21] The reasoning behind this attitude was explained by Gurliand, who argued that "a local man, willingly or unwillingly, is a man of local interests, . . . always constrained by parochial sympathies, antipathies, calculations, and concerns."[22] In order to avoid reliance upon such a "local man," whether elected by gentry, zemstvo, or anyone else, the MVD proposed the creation of the office of "vice-governor." As the title indicated, the new dignitary would perform the same function in the district as his superior did in the province. All state servants would be under his supervision. He, too, would unify the local collegial institutions through chairmanship of a new body, in this case the "district council."[23]

Finally the reformers turned to the village. In the Urusov Commission Gurko and Strakhovskii had unsuccessfully championed the assignment of a civil servant to supervise administration at the grass roots. Now this idea was accepted. Stolypin's MVD recommended the creation of the post of "subdistrict commissar" (*uchastkovyi kommisar*), essentially a replacement of the land captain. Unlike his predecessor the commissar would be appointed by the MVD without the input of local gentry and would be fully responsible to the ministry through his superiors the vice-governor and governor.[24]

The ultimate goal of all these proposals to unify the state bureaucracy was decentralization. Once effective and responsible institutions had been created at all levels, it would be possible to transfer duties and obligations from any rung of the administrative ladder to another. The interior ministry's intentions in this regard were clearest in the district reform bill. In the explanatory note that accompanied the project, the MVD staff argued that the provincial organs had been "overloaded" for the simple reason that below that level there did not exist "an integrated administrative apparatus to which these duties could be assigned."[25] With the appointment of a vice-governor to head district affairs, the note concluded, operations could be decentralized from the provincial capital.

The MVD scheme thus included many elements drawn from the work of Tolstoi and his predecessors. These included reliance upon one-man administration, a preference for the appointive principle over the elective, and an emphasis on the central role of the MVD itself. At one point, for instance, the reformers made the forthright if impolitic contention that the ethnographic diversity, huge size, and social underdevelopment of the empire all necessitated "the concentration of general supervision and guidance" of local matters "in the hands of one department, which naturally can only be the Ministry of Internal Affairs."[26] In its essentials, however, the strategy of strengthening, or unifying, the state apparatus as a prerequisite for decentralization was developed by Pleve before the Revolution of 1905. The relationship between the two programs did not pass unnoticed. Strakhovskii, who participated in the drafting of both, commented that Stolypin's proposals "repeated not only the basic principles, but even the unfinished wording" of those of his former chief. The same point was made by observers outside the government, such as the astute scholar S. A. Korf.[27]

It would be unfair to Stolypin and his colleagues to ignore the real innovations included in the 1906 proposals. One that has already been mentioned was the shift in emphasis from the province to the district. Much more important was the attention devoted to the volatile issue of legality. Certainly under Pleve the interior ministry had not concerned itself deeply with this subject. And there were few clues in Stolypin's past to indicate anything much better. His choice of training in the natural sciences meant, as one friend put it, that he "had not imbibed as a dogma the principle of legality as the law faculties at the universities were teaching it with the passion of an unrequited love."[28] And there is little evidence that he was seized by this passion later in his service career. Upon his appointment as minister, one of his first acts was to ask a lawyer kinsman for a good introductory text on the subject.[29] Rather than concern himself with legal theory Stolypin repeatedly referred to himself as a man of deeds. Minister of Justice I. G. Shcheglovitov, certainly a qualified and well-informed observer, later wrote that Stolypin was "a very zealous man who gave juridical considerations the least significance, and who if he perceived a measure as necessary refused to admit to any obstacles."[30]

Nevertheless, the MVD program for administrative reform included a pronounced emphasis on such "juridical considerations." One expression of this was the care given to the question of administrative justice, of policing the state bureaucracy. The basic plan, apparently conceived by the former law professor Gurliand, who won over his superior Stolypin, was to improve the supervisory capabilities of the collegial institutions. Both the new provincial and the district councils were to meet in three capacities: executive, disciplinary, and administrative-judicial. It was in these last two that much of administrative justice would be performed. The composition of the councils would differ depending upon the capacity in which they were operating, but public representatives would always be present. Stolypin and Gurliand placed much store in this popular participation.[31]

An even clearer sign of the determination to impose a stricter watch on the civil service came from the unlikely source of the Department of Police. Traditionally its subordinates were among the most arbitrary and corrupt members of the state bureaucracy. One official observer characterized the prevailing ethic this way: "Wide use of the 'law of the fist,' harsh and petty exactions, disrespect for the public in general and the rights of individuals in particular, . . . indifference to and simple ignorance of the law, ill breeding, poor education, coarseness, improper use of coercive measures, etc., without end."[32] Now, however, working through a semiofficial weekly founded late in 1907, the *Police Messenger*, reformers in the department initiated a campaign for discipline and restraint among rank-and-file peace officers. As the editors argued at one point, popular hostility toward them would end only when the citizenry was shown that the term *police* was not "synonymous with abuse." The police force, they argued, could no longer remain "an institution paralyzing the free activity of our populace," and must become "a strict and law-abiding regulator." Or, as columnist L. Kosunovich put it, a "new era" was opening in which the police uniform would become "a symbol synonymous with the restoration of rights, justice, and respect for the individual."[33]

This concern for legality was in part an attempt to meet progressive demands for civil liberty. It would be incorrect, however, to interpret it as evidence of liberalism among the leadership of the interior ministry. The reorganization of the collegial bodies for purposes of administrative justice fell far short of the liberal ideal. Public participation was severely circumscribed. Sometimes when the district council met in its disciplinary capacity, for example, only the gentry marshal represented the citizenry. Moreover, the tsarist courts remained largely excluded. A rationale for this was offered in the MVD memorandum on provincial reform. After reviewing western European practice the authors argued that each nation must develop institutions appropriate to it. In Russia, they continued, "There are no grounds for placing administrative-judicial control outside the organs of active administration."[34] Transfer of supervision over the state bureaucracy to the courts would contradict the history and spirit of Russian law. As Stolypin frankly maintained in the Council of Ministers, the courts handled "private rights" of the citizen and not "public matters" relating to "state authority."[35]

The same held true of the campaign for a new style of law enforcement. In the same article in which they described the police function as that of "law-abiding regulator," the editors of the *Police Messenger* went on to insist, "True governmental wisdom does not disown this very essential instrument of coercion, but strengthens and develops it.... The more cultured and enlightened a nation, the stronger its police, the broader police authority and prerogatives."[36] The precise meaning of this call for a more powerful force was made explicit in the following issues. Here the editors admitted that tsarist patrolmen often violated the law and in so doing alienated the citizenry. However, they described the illegal acts as the result of a decline in police legal powers over the preceding century. The editors, therefore, proposed firm regulations that would give police expanded rights to arrest and fine. Much of what had previously been arbitrary behavior by individual police officers would now become lawful. Presumably, the rationalization of such behavior through its codification would lead to consistency in police operations, which in turn would make the expansion of police power more palatable to the citizenry. In any case, the editors concluded: "It is necessary to make the authorities even more energetic in order to raise the cultural level of the country."[37]

This last comment helps explain why Stolypin and his staff were so willing to concern themselves with the issue of law. Beyond serving as a concession to progressives, legality was a potential vehicle for the more effective exercise of state bureaucratic power. Strict legal norms, if applied primarily by the civil service itself without interference from the courts, could rationalize operations and heighten central control locally. In this sense, legality would complement the other elements of the government's program, unity and decentralization. This highly illiberal approach was apparent in the MVD plans for self-government.

Self-Government

Pleve and his staff had understood decentralization to be a dual process involving deconcentration of activity from the higher levels of the state bureaucracy to the lower and devolution of duties from the civil service to the organs of self-government. Therefore, their recommendations for enlarging the role of the provincial administrative apparatus were coupled with suggestions for expanding zemstvo and municipal competence. Stolypin shared this general understanding of decentralization. At a reception in Saint Petersburg for provincial officials and citizens involved in the implementation of land reform, he noted, "It is also necessary to interest local zemstvos in responsible governmental work." With developments like the electrification of Russian cities and the introduction of trolleys indicating the rapid pace of social change in the empire, he continued, centralized government had become an "obvious anachronism." Turning to the representatives of the various ministries present, one witness observed that Stolypin "clearly and definitely stated the necessity for immediate decentralization of authority."[38] Indeed, in the face of new conditions he proposed to go far beyond Pleve's halting initiatives of three years before.

The basic outline of Stolypin's program for the zemstvos and town councils was contained in an MVD working paper completed in February 1907. At the heart of the document was an extensive list of functions to be transferred to self-government. In the area of transport, for instance, these included responsibility for highways, ports, and river traffic. In the field of public health, the self-governing institutions were assigned not only such routine obligations as sanitation inspection and registration of illnesses but the weightier duties of supervising the empire's system of legalized prostitution and directing the nation's temperance societies in combating drunkenness. The former task had been performed previously by the local police, the latter by the Ministry of Finance. Although the MVD jealously reserved for itself the position of leadership in agrarian reform, wide scope was to be afforded the zemstvos in complementary activities like offering the peasantry agronomic aid and credit.[39]

Delegation of new duties to the institutions of self-government was an important step, but it would remain meaningless if they lacked the ability to perform them. Therefore, the MVD quite logically joined its recommendations for expanding the jurisdiction of the zemstvos and town councils with proposals to improve their capabilities. In order to guarantee that the local bodies possessed the wherewithal to fulfill their new tasks, an attempt was made to strengthen their finances. The MVD rapidly increased the size and number of its ad hoc subsidies to individual zemstvos and municipalities.[40] With an eye to the longer term, Stolypin and his staff proposed legislation to regularize and expand the flow of state funds still further. In particular, the Council on Local Affairs was to be given almost unlimited authority to issue grants whenever it deemed them "useful and necessary."[41]

Fiscal weakness was a serious obstacle to self-governmental activity, but hardly the only one. A lack of executive organs left the zemstvos and town councils dependent upon the tsarist police and the peasant estate institutions. As a remedy, Stolypin and his colleagues proposed two major steps. Although they found it "obviously impossible" to accept the liberal notion of transferring control over the state police to the public, they did resolve to establish special executive agencies for self-government. The zemstvos and towns were to be given the right to hire staffs to perform such functions as building and sanitation inspection, fire protection, and tax collection. Like the regular police, these personnel were to have the power to demand compliance with local ordinances and exact fines in case of refusal.[42]

While this extension of at least a small portion of police authority to self-government was a significant step, it was far overshadowed by the MVD's second recommendation. Acquiescing to a time-honored demand of the zemstvo movement, the ministry proposed the introduction of a local zemstvo. To be more precise, the MVD followed Witte's precedent in suggesting the creation of not one such unit, but two. The first was to be modelled after the district zemstvo and introduced in place of the peasant volost. The second, envisioned more as a hybrid between urban and rural forms of self-government, would be substituted for another existing estate institution of the peasantry, the village community.[43]

While the replacement of the peasant organizations with the new zemstvos was envisioned as a fairly simple process, there was one difficulty. Both the volost and village community had performed not only functions that were "self-governing," but also some not normally assigned to the zemstvos. Among these latter were maintenance of the village police and the handling of conscription. Lacking any alternative institutions that might assume these tasks, the MVD was forced to assign them to the local zemstvos.[44] Although this meant that the two would therefore serve both as organs of self-government and of the MVD, it was hoped that the combination could be managed without conflict.

In addition to addressing these major problems of the self-governing institutions, the MVD reformers also turned their attention to the difficult issue of popular participation and the franchise. Here they were driven by their own recognition of the need for broader involvement and by public pressure. The Cadet party, for one, had made the demand for universal suffrage a cardinal plank in its platform, and even the moderate Octobrists had attacked the preference given to the nobility by the existing property qualification and all-gentry first curia. For its part the MVD was quite willing to abandon the estate principle as a basis for zemstvo representation. As the ministry's working paper on self-government plainly stated, the estate idea "is not in accord with the character of the zemstvo institutions, which pursue not corporate but general socio-economic interests of a given locality."[45] In keeping with this view, the MVD proposed to restructure the old electoral system, abolishing both the gentry definition of the first curia and the peasant of the third.

While they were prepared and even anxious to go this far in the democratization of the zemstvo, Stolypin and his staff were not ready to accept universal suffrage. Their revision of the franchise for zemstvo and town council elections was intended to broaden participation beyond existing limits, but it was also structured to guarantee a leading role for men of means and moderation. Deputies would be, in the words of the MVD legislators, "individuals of a certain cultural level and sufficient means, and in social attitudes suitably stable."[46] In order to achieve this dual goal of reform and stability, the MVD proposed a new curial system for the district zemstvo based upon property ownership. The rather straightforward scheme grouped large landholders in a first curia, owners of urban real estate in a second, and participants in the new volost zemstvo in a third. This three-tiered system of curiae based on property served as a double-edged weapon. On one side, the introduction of only a minimal property requirement for participation in the volost assembly—and thus the possibility of election to the district zemstvo—allowed potential involvement by many small property holders. On the other, a proposed qualification of seventy-five hundred rubles of assessed property for full membership in the first and second curiae would reserve these electoral groupings for the wealthy.[47] Should this fail to insure adequate representation of large holders, the MVD included one final twist in its scheme, an idea suggested much earlier by Tolstoi. All property owners whose holdings exceeded one hundred fifty thousand rubles were to become zemstvo deputies directly without election.[48]

Stolypin's program for the reform of self-government might be interpreted as a liberalization of tsarist local administration. It is certainly true that the MVD made proposals that seemed to move in this direction. Wider jurisdiction for self-government, the local zemstvo, broader participation through electoral reform—these were all measures championed by zemstvo activists, including the Cadets. Nevertheless, this view of the Stolypin reform as a step toward liberalization overlooks one major element of the MVD's work which put it quite at odds with liberal values.

In their approach to the question of democracy Russian progressives had always coupled wider public participation with the idea of independence. Their concern had been not merely to increase the involvement of the citizenry in governmental affairs but to do so in a way that guaranteed to the populace freedom of action. This attitude reflected the basic liberal perception of the evolution of tsarist society, an evolution in which the steady maturation of the public justified the expansion of self-determination. Naturally, this view applied to local as well as national matters. Self-government was seen as the epitome of a free citizenry directing its own affairs. Consequently, it could be meaningful only if liberated from the tutelage (or "tyranny" as some liberals would call it) of the central authorities. Decentralization, in turn, was to be valued only if it broadened the autonomy as well as activity of self-government.

The approach of the Ministry of Internal Affairs to this issue was fundamentally different. Like the liberals, Stolypin and his subordinates were clearly aware of the value of public participation in administrative affairs. In their eyes, however, increased participation did not mean the central government need relinquish its directing role in social development. On the contrary, as the MVD proposals for restructuring the state bureaucracy indicated, the Stolypin program was founded precisely upon the assertion of "state" leadership. As one might expect, this different understanding of the place of the tsarist government gave Stolypin and his colleagues a different perception of local affairs. Self-government was seen neither as an independent entity nor an expression of popular sovereignty, but simply as another part of the state's administrative apparatus in which the public, almost as a privilege, had been invited to participate. In terms drawn directly from the work of Tolstoi and Pleve, the MVD in its working paper declared that the zemstvos and town councils were "administrative organs authorized by the state and elected by the populace" to handle tasks assigned to them by the central government. Their tasks were "in no way essentially different" from those performed by other administrative organs, and therefore the institutions of self-government were as far as possible to be placed in "identical conditions of accountability and responsibility" with these other bodies.[49] All of which was to affirm that as state institutions the zemstvos and town councils were primarily responsible not to their electorate but to the central authorities.

Stolypin's statist conception of local government also infused his understanding of decentralization. Where liberals interpreted the process as the expansion of public activity and autonomy, Stolypin viewed it solely in terms of the former. Actually, he followed his predecessor Pleve in maintaining that broader participation through decentralization would require more, not less, state supervision. The Council of Ministers ruled on the MVD program, "The example of other countries with highly developed self-government graphically demonstrates that insofar as the jurisdiction of self-government widens, so too are the means of state inspection strengthened. Precisely so with us should the forthcoming expansion of the competence of the zemstvo and municipal institutions ineluctably entail the establishment of more effective supervision over them."[50]

The continued, or rather heightened, emphasis on central guidance and control ran like a red thread through the MVD bills. Take, for instance, the question of oversight of the two new local zemstvos. During 1905, MVD liberals like Urusov had argued for the abolition of the only existing state bureaucratic institution that would perform this function, the land captaincy. This step was recommended specifically as an indication of the government's confidence in the public. Stolypin and his staff reversed this course. While agreeing that the gentry land captaincy had been a failure, they insisted upon replacing it with the office of commissar. In this way the presence of the state bureaucracy below the district level would be maintained.[51]

The fundamental gulf that separated liberals and Stolypin on the issue of state supervision was especially evident in their very different application of the concept of legality to self-government. For liberals the establishment of the rule of law would guarantee the liberty of individual citizens and their self-government. Legal norms defended by a fully independent judiciary were to serve as a shield protecting zemstvos and town councils from the arbitrary interference of the civil service. Thus, for example, liberals bitterly denounced that article of the 1890 zemstvo statute which allowed governors to challenge self-governmental measures not only on the grounds of their illegality but also their inexpediency.

Stolypin, too, wished to introduce stricter observance of juridical procedure into the relationship between civil service and self-government. The MVD bills were all full of references to the principle of legality as basic to local reform. In part, this reflected an astute politician's awareness of the positive sentiments these steps would evoke among the citizenry. Yet the espousal of the ideal of law was motivated by more than political considerations. As has been noted, Stolypin and his staff had come to understand how legality could serve an important centralizing function. Laws, like ministerial directives or instructions, could serve as a means of guiding activity, of setting standards to which the behavior of all administrative organs including the zemstvos and town councils had to conform. In this sense, legal norms would be not an obstacle to central involvement in local affairs, as liberals hoped, but an instrument for that involvement. Significantly, in Stolypin's descriptions of the reform program the idea of law was almost always mentioned in conjunction with the other tool of central control, unity through one-man supervision.

The use to which legality was put by the MVD was apparent in its working paper on self-government. The governor's power to rule on the expediency of zemstvo acts, the most flagrant violation of strict juridical norms in the existing statutes, was dropped. However, new provisions giving ample opportunity for administrative interference were added. Should a zemstvo or town council fail to carry out an obligation, the local representatives of the state bureaucracy were to be empowered to perform the duty at the expense of the defaulting organ of self-government. Indeed, a fixed amount was to be set aside in all zemstvo and municipal budgets for this purpose. Beyond this, the government was to have the right "in cases indicated by the law" to dissolve zemstvo assemblies and town councils and call new elections, a prerogative that the MVD described as analogous to the tsar's authority to dissolve the State Duma. Finally, in cases of prolonged failure by a unit of self-government to meet local needs or of "extended disorder" in its affairs, the Council of Ministers was to be able to suspend the guilty body for up to three years and substitute the activity of the state bureaucracy.[52] Although in their working paper the MVD staff indicated that this extraordinary measure was primarily intended to rectify administrative malfeasance, suspension for political reasons was not ruled out. Indeed, as a precedent for the measure the ministry pointed to Pleve's highly political attempt to suppress the zemstvo in Tver. The main difference was that where Pleve's action was seen as an exceptional—and, to many, an illegal—step, such behavior was now to be given a firm basis in law.[53]

Somewhat later in the debate over reform, Gurliand sent a letter to Stolypin denouncing certain opponents who saw in the MVD's concern for legality an attempt "to turn this fine principle into a weapon for the final enthralment of public activity." "In other words," he wrote, "they suspect that if administration now very often suffers from illegality in its forms . . . then with the approval of the project it will become irreproachable in form but all the more uncontrolled in content."[54] In a very important sense the critics were correct. Through their handling of the principle of law, and through their general understanding of decentralization as a combination of public activity and central control, Stolypin and his subordinates had developed a program for broadening popular participation without surrendering the guiding role of the state bureaucracy.

The Estates

Stolypin's approach to the estate principle as it applied to local administration was unambiguous. In what was definitely their most monumental departure from the work of Pleve, the minister and his staff concluded that the time had come to remove the corporate element from tsarist local governance. Among the reasons cited for the decision were many that had been voiced earlier. In reference to the peasant institutions, for example, the MVD legislators pointed out the numerous shortcomings of the existing volost and village community, including the "inertia" of village assemblies, the poor quality of peasant officials, and the institutions' overloading with general administrative tasks that should rightfully be borne by the entire population.[55] Stolypin and his staff also recognized that the advance of trade and industry in the countryside had brought into the village many nonpeasant merchants, artisans, and workers who ought to be included in local governance.[56] Moreover, in a correct assessment of the political situation within the country, they admitted that the estate principle "does not meet with public approval and evokes dissatisfaction everywhere."[57]

These long-standing considerations against the corporate institutions were important in MVD thinking, but government policy in 1905 had created new ones as well. The October Manifesto had included a promise of civil equality within the empire, a pledge that certainly implied a weakening of estate distinctions. This consequence of the regime's recent constitutionalism was made explicit in an imperial ukaz of 5 October 1906. Referring to the manifesto's guarantee of "civil freedom and the equality of all Russian citizens before the law," the government announced a "fundamental review" of the structure of local governance and of the courts. In anticipation of that review, however, the ukaz granted "all Russian citizens regardless of their origins . . . rights to state service identical to those of the gentry estate."[58]

This particular element of the October Manifesto suited the MVD perfectly. As has been noted, one prerequisite for the ministry's program of decentralization was the extension of its apparatus into the countryside. In the past such efforts at what might be called the bureaucratization of local affairs had often been at the expense of a corporate institution, usually of the gentry. In the 1860s for instance, the MVD penetrated to the district level by replacing the gentry-elected police chief with one appointed by the governor. Now this process would continue. In the district, the proposed vice-governor was to supplant the gentry marshal as titular head of administration. At the grass roots, the gentry land captaincy would be eliminated altogether, replaced by the MVD's new rural representative, the commissar. Stolypin and his staff took some pains to argue that they had other goals than a direct assault on the institutions of the first estate, but it was also an unavoidable result.[59]

The ideal of civil equality naturally gravitated against the retention of peasant corporate institutions, too. An even more powerful force in this direction was the government's agrarian reform. Since the program aimed at encouraging individual villagers to leave the commune and convert their land to private property, it struck at the heart of peasant self-government. With a large portion of the peasants living independently of the mir like other citizens, there seemed to be no further justification for the administrative isolation of the peasant estate. Therefore, the MVD reformers proposed the outright liquidation of the volost and village community in favor of two all-estate local zemstvos.

The abandonment of the estate idea as the fundamental mode of defining the relationship between the tsarist state and its citizenry logically entailed the substitution of another. The new principle espoused by Stolypin and his staff was that of property, of economic class as determined by ownership. Citizens would participate in local affairs on the basis not of corporate status but of the size and nature of their holdings. The application of this notion to the district zemstvo through an electoral system structured around curiae and a property qualification has already been discussed. It was equally apparent in the MVD bills for the two new zemstvos below the district. Both were to have property requirements, and special privileges were to be extended to wealthier proprietors. At the lowest level—that of the village zemstvo—owners of land assessed at more than seventy-five hundred rubles were to be given the extraordinary right to form separate administrative units of their own. They would also be entitled to sit in volost zemstvo assemblies without election.[60]

The handling of this question in the MVD bills indicated precisely who would be the main public constituencies of the Stolypin program. It told which groups among the citizenry were to join the state bureaucracy in real participation in the political process. First position was reserved for wealthy proprietors, especially rural proprietors. In the countryside, "cultured elements" would have the right to turn their estates into independent administrative units and to sit in volost and district zemstvo assemblies without election. In the cities, they would dominate town councils. Beyond the privileged groups, and in alliance with them, would come the new peasant private-holders created by agrarian reform. These "sober and strong" farmers, as Stolypin called them, would take their place as junior partners in a social coalition supporting the modernized tsarist regime.

Reform in Perspective

The main elements of the Stolypin reform program can be brought into relief in a number of ways, one of which is by raising the question of foreign models. In deriving their ideas on local affairs, Russian public figures very consciously looked to the experience of western Europe. Cadets, for example, drew their recommendations directly from English liberalism, while many Octobrists admired Imperial Germany. Even gentry rightists, who followed the Slavophil tradition of stressing the Russian essence of their position, were attracted by Western examples, including the English and Prussian, and by Western thinkers like Tocqueville. Similarly, Stolypin and his staff were also concerned with the ideas and practices of foreigners. The MVD bills on local reform were replete with dozens of references to outside precedent.

The interior ministry was not very selective in its borrowing. Allusions to others ranged from great states like France down to Switzerland and even the German free cities. Some models, however, were especially influential. In the past, writers on this subject have emphasized one of two sources of inspiration for Stolypin and his colleagues. Some, like his kinsman A. Meyendorf, have pointed to the primacy of England in his thinking.[61] They have described Stolypin's agrarian and constitutional measures as ultimately aimed at the inculcation of English parliamentarianism and individualism on Russian soil. Others have taken a different tack, inspired largely by another more famous contemporary of Stolypin, Lenin. Basing his argument on a class analysis of the tsarist agrarian and electoral reforms, Lenin characterized Stolypin as attempting to put the empire on a Prussian path dominated by the landed aristocracy.[62]

It cannot be denied that both the English and Prussian examples had attractions for the Russian statesman. Britain was to be admired for its relative domestic tranquility, its combination of growth and order. Prussia, too, was to be envied for its strength and stability, particularly in the countryside where nobles and peasant smallholders coexisted peacefully and where agricultural productivity far surpassed that of Tsarist Russia.[63] Yet in reference to his administrative reforms at least, it is arguable that Stolypin was equally inspired by a third model, France. MVD working papers and explanatory notes made constant reference to French bureaucratic practice, such as drawing repeated analogies between the Russian governor and the prefect or between the proposed vice-governor and subprefect.[64] This comparison was logical. France had been the birthplace of the idea that lay at the heart of Stolypin's agrarian reform, the notion that the best way to guarantee the conservatism of the peasant was to grant him land of his own. Moreover, in more directly administrative matters France had pioneered in the development of decentralization as a tool of bureaucratic control both under the Second Republic and in the final decade of the nineteenth century.[65] Witte and Pleve were both aware of this precedent, and it should be no surprise that their successor Stolypin was as well.[66]

If the admiration for France in the MVD work was not illogical, it was indicative. For over half a century France had been associated in the minds of educated Russians with the power of the state administration and its hegemony over local affairs. As the liberal legal professor V. M. Gessen put it, France, after Russia, was the most bureaucratic state in contemporary Europe.[67] Stolypin's affinity for the French administrative model therefore underlined the fundamental gap that divided him from much of the public. His approach was based neither upon the individualism and democracy of England nor upon the landed aristocratic ideal of Prussia. Rather he looked to the French example of an effective and efficient state bureaucracy as the prime force guiding society.

Of course, reference to any foreign model can be carried too far. Though Stolypin and his staff approved of French organization of local affairs, for instance, other aspects of that nation's republican political system were anathema to most Russian bureaucrats. Certainly they had little interest in universal suffrage or responsible cabinets, or in the notion of a state ultimately bound by popular approval through parliament or plebiscite. As Gurko argued in reference to Pleve's interest in French administrative practice, the minister "failed to take into consideration that the French government was the outcome of public tendencies, and that it worked under the constant and vigilant supervision of an organized and well-developed public opinion."[68] The primary inspiration for the Stolypin program came not from outside precedent, but from within Tsarist Russia's own political and administrative heritage. Stolypin and his staff can best be seen as heirs to a tradition of state authority that stretched back into the Muscovite period and found its most recent expression in the work of ministers like Tolstoi and Pleve.

During the second half of the nineteenth century, rapid social change within the Tsarist Empire had posed a serious challenge to its administrative system. Minister of Internal Affairs Tolstoi attempted to meet that challenge locally by developing a new synthesis of the major elements of government. His efforts were based on two cardinal principles: the hegemony of the state as identified with its civil service, and reliance upon estate institutions as the primary vehicle for popular involvement in administrative affairs. Within a decade, however, it had become clear that the Tolstoi synthesis was unsuccessful. It suffered particularly from the deficiencies of excessive centralization and a corresponding failure to give adequate scope for public participation. In response to mounting difficulties, a second interior minister, Pleve, made yet another attempt at synthesis. Fully accepting the major premise of Tolstoi's approach—the predominance of the state bureaucracy—Pleve sought to correct the faults in his predecessor's work by carrying out a program of decentralization.

THE STOLYPIN REFORM PROGRAM, 1906–1907

Overloading of the upper levels of the administrative apparatus would be remedied by deconcentration to the lower. Failure to enlist the aid of the public would be resolved by devolution of various functions to the organs of self-government. Implicit in this program was movement away from the estate principle and toward the all-estate ideal of the zemstvos and town councils. Yet while Pleve did shift priorities from the corporate institutions to those of self-government, he wavered and ultimately drew back from a radical break with Tolstoi's estate orientation.

Stolypin's reform program was a logical culmination of this process. Like his predecessors, Stolypin undertook to develop administrative structures that would draw extensively upon the activity of the citizenry but would do so without sacrificing the leading position of the central authorities and their local agents. He sought to achieve participation without real democratization of popular sovereignty. At the basis of his program was the concept of decentralization articulated by Pleve. Deconcentration of authority within the civil service was to be joined with devolution of activity to self-government. Yet where Pleve was hesitant in his approach to the zemstvos and town councils, Stolypin was bold. More significantly, where Pleve ultimately accepted the estate principle, Stolypin rejected it. Instead, he proposed the substitution of the principle of property as the primary criterion for citizens' involvement in local governance. After all, inculcation of the concept of private property among the peasantry lay at the base of his agrarian reform. It was only logical that it be applied to the empire's system of governance as well. In sum then, through his program of decentralization and property Stolypin hoped to create at last a satisfactory synthesis of the elements of tsarist administration. He sought to reconcile tsarist tradition with the requirements of political modernity.

CHAPTER VI

THE DEBATE OVER REFORM, 1906–1908

The years 1906 and 1907 were uncertain ones for Tsarist Russia. Although revolutionary violence slowly receded, the struggle over the empire's future continued unabated. Attention centered on the twin issues of a constitution and land. These two questions dominated contemporary political discourse and have similarly shaped subsequent historical discussion. Yet in actuality both were settled very quickly. In November 1906 Stolypin employed the tsar's emergency powers to introduce his far-reaching agrarian reform. Seven months later, in what has come to be known as the 3 June coup, he used those same powers to prorogue the Second Duma and formally revise the national franchise. No further innovations were introduced in either area before the fall of the tsarist regime. The struggle for reform, therefore, shifted away from land and the constitution to other arenas, particularly local government.

By the time local administration emerged as a central issue, most segments of the educated public had formulated their views on the question. Some, like the Cadets and the Ministry of Internal Affairs, had made their proposals for reform quite explicit. Others, such as the Octobrists and the gentry right, had only articulated general attitudes. But in all cases convictions on the proper ordering of provincial governance were deeply held. Appropriately enough in the empire's new "constitutional" era, the liberal Cadet party took the lead in the struggle over local reform. However, in a closer reflection of the political realities of post-Revolutionary Russia, debate soon flowed back into more traditional channels. Liberal efforts were quickly blunted, and leadership in the renovation of the state apparatus was again assumed by the government itself.

The Liberal Initiative

The renewed debate over local government that accompanied the convocation of the First State Duma in April 1906 found the Cadets at center stage. By skillfully capitalizing on popular dissatisfaction with the old order, the party had won a stunning victory in the Duma elections. Approximately one-third of the newly elected deputies identified themselves as Cadets, making that faction the largest in the Duma. And a majority of the remaining delegates were willing to follow the Cadet lead.[1] Since the government, directed by the lethargic Goremykin, was uninterested in presenting the Duma with a serious program for consideration, the Cadets seized the legislative initiative. This was certainly in keeping with the party's conception of the role of the Duma majority. Closely following English precedent, as always, the Cadets rejected the government's interpretation of the October Manifesto in which ministers remained responsible to the tsar. Instead, they insisted that the cabinet, if one can call the loose Council of Ministers such, should be under control of the Duma. As Cadet spokesman V. D. Nabokov argued in a fiery speech attacking Goremykin, "The executive power must bow to the legislative!"[2] In this spirit the Duma almost immediately drafted an address to the throne summarizing its demands. Among them was a call for "the fundamental reorganization of local administration and self-government."[3]

The Cadet Duma faction set to work on local reform immediately. To guide their legislative activity in this area the Cadet delegates adopted six fundamental principles, all aimed at the development of self-government. They included universal suffrage, the termination of state tutelage over public activity, wider jurisdiction for self-government, the strengthening of local finances, introduction of a local zemstvo, and the extension of self-government to all provinces of the empire. Though the delegates considered each of these principles crucial, they recognized that not all could be implemented at once. The introduction of similar practices in western European states like England had required decades and could hardly be accomplished in Russia at the stroke of a pen. Instead, the Cadets decided to focus on three key issues: universal suffrage, ending central tutelage, and territorial extension of self-government.[4] Achievement of these three goals, particularly the first two, would all but guarantee the ascendancy of self-government. The granting of universal suffrage would herald the end of estate privileges and open the zemstvos and town councils to the entire citizenry. The limitation of the state's right to interfere with the work of these institutions would strike a blow at the predominance of the central authorities on the local scene. Viewed in terms of the basic elements of tsarist local administration, the estates would be on their way to destruction, the state bureaucracy bridled, and self-government left supreme.

From the start the Cadets recognized the need to act with dispatch, particularly given the ugly turn of events in recent zemstvo elections. Fearing a continued swing to the right, some Cadet delegates urged that the Duma vote to postpone further zemstvo balloting. The majority, however, rejected the notion, preferring instead to press forward with legislation to reform the zemstvo franchise.[5] The task of drafting legislation on this and other aspects of local reform was assigned to a committee under the chairmanship of I. I. Petrunkevich, the most venerable of zemstvo liberals and the party's Duma floor leader. Over fifty delegates responded to an invitation to join the committee, which was quickly divided into three subgroups. Of these the most important was that on the zemstvo, and its work was most clearly representative of the party's overall program.

Like the Cadet party, the zemstvo subcommittee affirmed the need to introduce reform piecemeal. Devoting all their spare time to the subcommittee's work, the members drafted two basic projects within a month.[6] The first entailed a full reorganization of the zemstvo electoral system based on the Cadet notion of a "four-tail" suffrage. Not only were all males over the age of twenty-one to be included, women were, too. All major voting restrictions, especially the gentry-dominated curial system, were to be completely abolished. Significantly, only two substantial groups were disenfranchised, convicted criminals and tsarist police. The barring of the latter reflected the general public disdain for local policemen and a more specific fear that they might use their authority to intimidate voters.[7]

The subcommittee's other project aimed at "the elimination of estate and bureaucratic elements from the organization of the zemstvo institutions." Since the proposed suffrage reform already dealt with the most important corporate element, the gentry electoral curia, this second project focused primarily on freeing the zemstvo of civil service control. Two features of the existing statutes drew particular attention. First, the subcommittee members proposed that the governor, and by implication his superiors in Saint Petersburg, be deprived of the power to usurp zemstvo functions. Perhaps with Pleve's 1904 "coup" against the Tver zemstvo in mind, they proposed repeal of all legal clauses allowing governors either to force zemstvos to take particular measures or to act in their stead. Secondly, the subcommittee insisted upon the traditional zemstvo demand that the government no longer be empowered to rule on the "expediency" of zemstvo measures. In the subcommittee's new project governors were given authority to protest zemstvo actions only if they violated the law. And even here gubernatorial action was to be subject to the decision of the courts, not the central ministries.[8]

Admittedly, the two projects did not embody the Cadet ideal. The state bureaucracy still, for example, retained an active role in local administration outside self-government. Nevertheless, through these partial measures the subcommittee believed it could create, in the words of Cadet delegate F. F. Kokoshkin, "a firm foundation for the emerging democratic structure."[9] Zemstvo reform would extend the principles of constitutionalism to the empire's provinces and districts. Unfortunately for the subcommittee, however, these same principles had yet to be firmly implanted on the national level. Before the full committee could review the work of Kokoshkin and his colleagues, the tsarist government had disbanded the very legislative body that was to bring it to fruition.

The dissolution of the First Duma was the result of a number of factors, one of the chief being ironically the Cadets' own campaign to implement another part of their local reform program. At the same time that the Duma committees were quietly drafting legislation to strengthen self-government, the party had been carrying out a vociferous attack on the government in the name of legality. As has been noted, the Cadets believed that all the gains of the October Manifesto would be meaningless if the tsarist civil service could not be made to obey the rule of law. This applied not only to the ministers in Saint Petersburg but to the provincial officials. In fact, as reports of arbitrary arrests, unlawful executions, and official connivance at pogroms mounted through the spring of 1906, the Cadets became increasingly desperate in their efforts to force the restraint of legality on the imperial government's local as well as national agents.

In a parliamentary regime of the English type, the Cadets would have been able to impose their views through legislative control of the ministries that directed the local bureaucrats. In the new Russian state structure, lacking as it did the notion of ministerial responsibility to the Duma, the Cadets did not possess this power. Instead, they were left only with the right to make interpellations, or inquiries, about individual official misdeeds. Of course, the task of controlling the entire tsarist administrative apparatus through the clumsy instrument of interpellation was enormous. Nevertheless, Cadets and other Duma delegates set to work with a determination born of indignation at the violence of governmental repression. In less than three months the Duma adopted well over three hundred such interpellations. Among the most frequent were attacks on the use of the death penalty and martial law against suspected subversives.[10]

A good sense of the tenor of the inquiries was conveyed at the Duma's 3 July session, when Assistant Minister of Internal Affairs Makarov reported on thirty-three of the delegates' interpellations. Makarov's attempts to defend the administration brought forth a torrent of derision from the deputies. One Cadet orator captured Duma opinion by decrying the acts in question as "not only an open affront to justice, to the most elementary demands of freedom, but also a violation of the most basic principles of our law." Yet another saw Makarov's remarks as proof of the "complete lawlessness" and "full caprice" of the tsarist civil service, both central and local.[11] A similar reception was accorded the minister of internal affairs himself when he appeared in the Duma to respond to an inquiry on police incitement of pogroms. Stolypin's admission of misdeeds that had occurred before he personally took office and his subsequent assurance that they would not be repeated were greeted by howls and catcalls from the delegate benches. His speech was punctuated with shouts for his resignation. Ignoring his promises, the Duma overwhelmingly resolved that "only the immediate resignation of the existing ministry and the transfer of authority to a cabinet enjoying the confidence of the State Duma can lead the country out of its great and rapidly growing difficulties."[12]

The successful operation of any parliament or representative assembly requires a minimal consensus on its legitimacy, a consensus normally reflected in a certain restraint and civility in its proceedings. The interpellation debates amply demonstrated that the new Duma lacked both this civility and the legitimacy that fosters it. The Cadets and their colleagues displayed a fundamental unwillingness to accept the regime's definition of the constitution created by the October Manifesto. The tsarist ministers, for their part, were no better; it is true that they refrained from indulging in the type of verbal abuse employed by their opponents, but they did so out of a deep-rooted contempt for the new legislative body, not respect.[13] As soon as they had assured themselves that the act would not precipitate another revolutionary outburst, the central authorities moved to dissolve the assembly.

The forced closing of the First Duma on 18 July brought a halt to the Cadet committee work on local governmental reform. It also heralded a major change in the empire's political situation. When the

Duma reconvened the following year, its deliberations were to be different in one essential respect. The draft projects under serious consideration were not those of the Cadets, or of any other popular party, but of the tsarist government. Although it was not clear at the time, by the summer of 1906 Russian liberals had lost the legislative and political initiative. They were not to regain it until the empire was shaken by world war.

The Stolypin Initiative

If the First Duma had been a fiasco for the Cadets, it was hardly more successful from the government's standpoint. An overwhelming majority of the delegates elected by the populace had been openly hostile to the regime, and no substantive legislation had been approved. Of course, this absence of constructive work was in no small part the direct result of the ministers' own refusal to cooperate with the newly established national assembly. When the Duma opened its deliberations, Goremykin and most of his colleagues declined to submit substantive projects for consideration, preferring to introduce insultingly trivial bills for the opening of a laundry and greenhouse at the University of Dorpat.[14]

The failure of this policy of essentially ignoring the legislature was clearly perceived by many leading figures in Saint Petersburg, including the tsar. On the very night that he approved the edict of dissolution, Nicholas II also removed Goremykin as chairman of the Council of Ministers. In his place he appointed the one minister who had been most dissatisfied with Goremykin's refusal to deal seriously with the Duma, Stolypin.[15] From the very start the new chairman made evident his intention of reversing his predecessor's approach. As Stolypin remarked to a colleague shortly after his promotion, "There are 180 days before the Second Duma assembles. We must make good use of them so that when the Duma meets we may appear before it with a series of reforms."[16] Among the most important of these reforms was to be the reorganization of local government.

Work on the MVD proposals in this area had continued throughout 1906 without interruption. Before the year's end the interior ministry staff had completed bills restructuring the village community, volost, land captaincy, district apparatus, and zemstvo electoral system. By February 1907 a project for improving provincial administration and a working paper on reforming self-government were added to the list. These measures did not represent the entire Stolypin program for local governance; work on plans for remodelling the imperial police force was still in progress, for example. Nevertheless, the materials that had been prepared by February were quite complete in one sense. They fully embodied all the major principles of the Stolypin approach to local affairs.

First, the MVD projects included major steps toward strengthening the state bureaucratic hierarchy and decentralizing activity within that hierarchy. Particularly important was the district reform bill, which created the new office of vice-governor and mandated the deconcentration of operations from the provincial to the district level. Equally well represented was the other element of the MVD program of decentralization, the transfer of various functions from the state's civil service to the institutions of self-government. The working paper on zemstvo and municipal affairs was naturally the key document in this regard. Finally, the ministry's drafts incorporated Stolypin's plans to redefine the nature of popular participation in local government. Unwilling to wait for the convocation of the Second Duma, Stolypin had used the government's emergency powers under Article 87 of the new Fundamental Laws to implement his own agrarian program. Through a number of acts, particularly an ukaz issued on 9 November 1906, the government adopted as its goal the transformation of village landholding from the communal form unique to the peasantry to private property. Having thus taken steps to remove the estate element from the sphere of landownership, it was only logical that the authorities would attempt to eliminate it from local administration as well. This the MVD now proposed to do. The principle of "all-estate" participation on the basis of property ownership, or of economic class, would be substituted for the corporate idea.

The MVD proposals on local governance naturally required passage by the State Duma and State Council in order to become law. Before they could be introduced in these assemblies, however, they had to be considered and approved by the Council of Ministers. Witte and his colleagues had substantially reorganized the council in 1906 with an eye to coordinating the activity of the government's diverse branches in the new constitutional era. Yet as Witte had painfully discovered, the task of unifying the central administration was far from complete. Beneath the veneer of harmony imposed by the council there remained the old tensions and conflicts of interest between the separate departments of the tsarist civil service. The continued existence of traditional rivalries was evident in the council's reception of the Stolypin proposals. When Pleve had presented his program of decentralization to his fellow ministers the reaction had been one of vigorous opposition, particularly to those provisions extending MVD influence locally. Stolypin's program, with its even more explicit emphasis on MVD hegemony, evoked a similar response.

One obvious target for complaint was the attempt to unify the provincial apparatus by enlarging the powers of the governor. Minister of Finance Kokovtsov summarized, arguing that while "in theory, of course, one can view the creation of such a unifying authority as desirable, . . . in practice the subordination of all branches of provincial administration to one person cannot be implemented." The reason, Kokovtsov frankly pointed out, was that in Stolypin's projects the governor remained the appointee of the minister of internal affairs alone.[17] Hence the Council of Ministers insisted upon watering down the governor's new powers. For instance, the governor was not to have the right to initiate on his own authority inspections of the local offices of ministries other than the MVD. Nor was he to have carte blanche in demanding information from others.[18]

The same criticisms that were levelled at the governorship naturally applied to the projected district vice-governor as well. Stolypin's colleagues did not object to the establishment of the post, but they refused to accept what they considered to be the MVD's inflated conception of its function. The need for a unifying authority in the district "cannot be doubted," read the minutes of the council's deliberations. "However the Council of Ministers cannot agree to those broad terms in which the right of the vice-governor to direct all district authorities is drawn." Acting accordingly, the group ruled that the new chief of district administration be titled not the "vice-governor," but more modestly the "district commander." More substantively, the ministers also mandated that his powers of direct command and supervision be limited strictly to the MVD staff.[19]

As already suggested, the leading role in the opposition to the various elements of the local reform program was taken by the traditional rival of the MVD, the minister of finance. Following the precedent set by Witte in his conflict with Pleve, Kokovtsov fought hard to protect his own jurisdiction from encroachment. One of the sharpest quarrels in the council centered around the interior ministry's proposal to allow its Council on Local Affairs to disburse state subsidies to zemstvos and municipalities without Ministry of Finance approval. Despite Stolypin's insistence upon the measure, Kokovtsov's opposition was unbending, even to the point of resignation. In the end it was Stolypin who compromised.[20] Although Kokovtsov was thus the most vocal and active critic of the MVD, his dedication to the interests of his own particular bureaucratic constituency was shared by his colleagues. At various times in the council deliberations representatives of the ministries of justice, communications, and even the army followed Kokovtsov's example in taking exception to individual parts of the Stolypin program.[21]

In addition to pressing for changes that were conservative in the sense of maintaining existing relationships among the various governmental branches, the council members also suggested amendments to the MVD plans that were conservative in the more political sense of the term. Some worried, for example, that replacement of the gentry marshal by the district commander would be "an expression of a lack of confidence in the gentry estate." Therefore, the council mandated that "where it is deemed possible" the marshal himself be appointed to the post.[22] In the same vein the ministers questioned a portion of the project for remodelling village governance. Here the MVD proposed the transformation of the existing peasant volost and village community into all-estate bodies. While the council members were willing to accept the idea of a "volost zemstvo," they disputed the need for a more local all-estate administrative unit. Most villages, they argued, were populated "exclusively by ordinary peasants" and had needs so simple as not to require a separate body of their own.[23] Only in special cases, such as villages near railways or large factories, were inhabitants to be allowed to establish "settlement self-government" (*poselkovoe samoupravlenie*) on the model of the town councils.

The MVD project on the zemstvo electoral law was also substantially altered. Again the change was in a conservative direction, as the ministers acted to set limits on the democratizing effects of reform. The MVD had accepted without question the need for a property qualification for suffrage. In order to bring more accuracy into the process of determining voting status, though, the ministry proposed that property be measured not in terms of the actual amount owned but according to its assessment. Where the existing full qualification was set between two hundred and eight hundred desiatina of land, depending upon location, the new requirement would be simply a valuation of seventy-five hundred rubles.[24] This innovation was not acceptable to the council. The opponents of the measure pointed out that the imperial system of property assessment was in chronic disorder, with some holdings evaluated on the basis of laws dating back to 1864. More important, some ministers noted that the MVD proposal would give the zemstvos the opportunity to expand the franchise at will simply by increasing the assessed value of local property. Under these conditions, they argued, there existed a danger that the new law might "mean in essence the establishment of universal suffrage."[25] Therefore, the council directed that the MVD develop an alternative, suggesting specifically that it investigate the possibility of a qualification based on the amount of taxes actually paid to the zemstvos. Admittedly, here too liberals might try to broaden the suffrage by raising local rates, but such maneuvers would have a natural limit in the populace's ability and willingness to pay.

Although a rate system offered substantial advantages, it also carried dangers. One of the most glaring inequities of zemstvo finance was the overtaxation of urban real estate. To cite one official report, in some districts commercial-industrial property was levied ten times more heavily than land, and a figure of five to six times was "quite common."[26] Conversely, landed nobility held over half the seats in district zemstvos and almost nine-tenths in provincial, though they paid a mere tenth of all zemstvo taxes.[27] Given this situation, introduction of a more equitable tax-based franchise immediately threatened the preponderance of landed interests. In order to guard against the eventuality that owners of large estates might be "pushed into the background," the council insisted that their first electoral curia be apportioned a minimum of one-quarter of the deputies in each district zemstvo. Since according to the MVD proposal at least another third would come from the rural volosts, country interests were guaranteed a safe majority in all district assemblies. Finally, in order to prevent "the predominance of capitalism" in rural self-government, the ministers struck out the idea that owners of property valued at more than one hundred fifty thousand rubles be seated directly without election; otherwise factory proprietors would be most likely to benefit.[28]

The council's reception of the MVD program has been interpreted as something of a defeat for Stolypin.[29] Certainly most of the ministers' recommendations were included in the legislation submitted subsequently to the State Duma. Nevertheless, it seems much more accurate to describe the council sessions as a victory for the MVD rather than a setback. For one thing, many of the amendments had limited impact and were easily circumvented. The loss of the all-estate village unit, for example, could be minimized by seeing that the "special" settlement administration was introduced in a large number of cases.[30] Even the adoption of the tax principle as the basis for zemstvo elections could be handled in such a way as to meet Stolypin's needs. It is no accident that the minister and his staff became active defenders of the idea once they had reworked the pertinent legislation as they pleased. Indeed, beyond these individual points, it can be argued that the deliberations of the Council of Ministers were significant not in what was rejected of the Stolypin program, but in what was approved. The principle of administrative decentralization, both in terms of deconcentration and devolution, was not challenged. Nor were the plans to abandon the estate principle. True, the ministers did attempt to salvage some remnants of noble privilege, particularly in the proposal to make gentry marshals also district commanders, but the basic cornerstones of estate administration, the all-peasant volost and the all-gentry first curia in zemstvo elections, were dropped without serious objection. The council's amendments definitely did not cause the MVD to hesitate in its sponsorship of the reform package, for within a month of its meetings the ministry staff had redrafted most of the bills and rushed them to the Duma.

At this point it is worth speculating why Stolypin encountered far less opposition to his proposals than had either Pleve or Witte before him. In part the answer is supplied by considering the resources at his disposal. Pleve had been minister of internal affairs and Witte chairman of the Council of Ministers, but Stolypin was the first (and only, for that matter) to combine both posts. He was thus guaranteed the aura of formal leadership in the government without sacrificing a firm base of ministerial support. Even more important than Stolypin's official position, however, was his informal standing in governing circles. Although the revolutionary wave that had swept the country in 1905 was definitely receding before he took office, the new appointee received the lion's share of the credit for restoring order. Stolypin himself reinforced his picture as savior of the regime through displays of personal courage and determination similar to those he had shown earlier in Saratov. In August of 1906, for instance, would-be assassins exploded a bomb in his villa on Aptekarsky Island, wrecking his office and injuring two of his children. Stolypin's self-control and dramatic refusal to abandon his duties in the face of the attack did much to erase his image in Saint Petersburg as a provincial, substituting instead that of a heroic fighter of revolutionary anarchy.[31]

At the same time that the new chairman of the Council of Ministers was acquiring the reputation of defender of the existing order, he was also assuming the role of builder of a new one. Both his public speeches and private comments to friends were full of references to the government's pressing need to take progressive measures. On the occasion of the explosion in his home on Aptekarsky Island, for instance, Stolypin dramatically announced to colleagues who had rushed to the scene, "This shall not alter our program. We shall continue to carry out our reforms. They are Russia's salvation."[32] In this he was as good as his word. Under his direction the MVD implemented an aggressive agrarian reform and initiated similar action in many other areas, not the least of which was local government. Given Stolypin's great institutional power and enormous personal prestige, it was difficult for his fellow ministers to resist his proposals, particularly when he attached special importance to a measure. Even the stubborn Kokovtsov admitted that once the chairman had let his colleagues know that he valued local reform as much as his land program it "was enough to make the ministers, including myself, tend to view the suggestion sympathetically."[33]

Finally, in addition to these considerations centering around the person of Stolypin, one must also give weight to the general political situation in the empire. The Revolution of 1905 had demonstrated violently that some ameliorative action would have to be taken to prevent the collapse of the regime. Throughout the months of unrest the tsar and his government had repeatedly promised concessions. In one sense, the replacement of Goremykin with Stolypin can be seen as an indication of the monarch's desire to fulfill at least some of these promises. The urgency of reform, if only to prevent more radical change from below, was keenly felt by many of Stolypin's fellow officials. Minister of Justice Shcheglovitov, for instance, would later prove to be an ardent foe of all innovation, but in 1906 he supervised plans to abolish the peasant volost courts and replace them with "all-estate" judicial organs.[34] Assistant Minister of Internal Affairs Makarov was later to help halt reforming tendencies within the MVD, but similarly spent much of 1906 drafting legislation on the right of habeas corpus. In short, at the time of the council's consideration of the Stolypin project, the consensus in official circles on the need for some adjustment in the old order was impressive, leading in part to overall acceptance of the local reform program.

Approval of the MVD's work by the Council of Ministers guaranteed that at least some legislation on local governance would be ready in time for the opening of the Second Duma. Indeed, on 20 February 1907, the very day that the representative assembly began its deliberations, the MVD introduced bills for the reorganization of district, volost, and village administration. Two weeks later, on 6 March, the minister himself appeared in the Duma to formally explain and defend the government's program. Unlike Goremykin, who had confronted the First Duma with empty hands, Stolypin expressed his hope for passage of a full slate of reforms including those "restructuring local life on new principles."[35]

There can be little doubt that Stolypin seriously intended to develop a working relationship with the Duma.[36] After all, the entire effort of the interior ministry had been to produce substantive legislative proposals that would help create such a relationship. It was true that Stolypin's sufferance of opposition was strictly limited and that he might quickly abandon the Duma experiment if it became clear that he and the bulk of the deputies were separated by irreconcilable differences, but at the outset, the differences between the two parties did not appear irreconcilable. On its side, the Duma majority seemed to share Stolypin's interest in constructive legislation. Although the body was again dominated by Cadets, their approach to legislative work was quite different than it had been the preceding year. Rather than hoping to bring the government to its knees by refusing to cooperate, the liberals now adopted a policy of "saving the Duma" from abrogation through positive activity. In January 1907, for example, the Cadet Central Committee approved a motion by P. B. Struve that the party's Duma actions take "the form of amendments to the government's legislative proposals."[37] And among the proposals in which the Cadets were most interested were those relating to local administration. As the electoral platform drafted at the party conference of 28–30 October 1906 pledged, "It is necessary to give top priority to Duma passage of a reform of local self-government based on broad democratic principles."[38] Given the new attitudes of the government and the Cadets there seemed to be at least some small chance for compromise.

The possibility of cooperation between Stolypin and the liberal Duma in far-reaching reform was certainly taken seriously by rightists. Their response was one of real alarm, particularly over the MVD bills on local governance. Just as the Kutler land scheme had momentarily sparked fears that the central authorities might help the First Duma enact radical agrarian reform, so the Stolypin administrative projects now raised the specter of such collaboration with the second. Indeed, the speed with which the MVD was pressing forward with its program in this area indicated that the bills might well pass the Duma before the zemstvos and gentry assemblies could even voice an opinion on the matter. In order to forestall this very possibility, the Permanent Council of the United Nobility, for example, resolved to draft a petition asking the government to submit the projects to the self-governing and gentry institutions for preliminary consideration.[39] Meanwhile, others were taking action. Members of the rightist group in the State Council, the upper house of the tsarist legislature, had already composed a note opposing local reform. On 25 February A. A. Naryshkin and A. S. Stishinskii met with Stolypin to convey the group's reservations personally. The two dignitaries told the minister that his measures might weaken the standing of the entire gentry estate and strengthen the subversive third element. They too asked that the government allow preliminary debate by the zemstvos and gentry assemblies. Stolypin, however, dismissed the objections to his program and reiterated his plan of moving ahead with the reforms. Review by the local bodies was fruitless, he argued, capable only of producing "a mass of the most varied written materials" lacking any general significance.[40]

Stolypin's statement of intent, which was underlined publicly by his Duma speech of 6 March, called forth a flurry of conservative agitation. The Permanent Council of the United Nobility formally presented the government with its petition calling for local discussion of the Stolypin projects, and individual members of the council, including such influential notables as Naryshkin and Count A. A. Bobrinskii, began to lobby vigorously against the measures. Shortly after, on 27 March, the matter was submitted to the annual congress of the entire United Nobility, which not surprisingly reiterated its council's insistence on the need for local examination of the projects.[41] Parallel to these activities of the national gentry organization, plans were also pressed forward for an "all-zemstvo" congress to review the government's program. After a number of preliminary discussions, ninety-two zemstvo representatives met on 31 March to elect a committee to make arrangements for the convocation of the zemstvo body. They, too, joined in petitioning the government to submit its reforms to the self-governing institutions for examination.[42]

The energy of the gentry and zemstvo leadership in the capital was matched locally. In early March, on the initiative of Counts D. A. Olsuf'ev and A. A. Uvarov, the Saratov provincial assembly resolved that "all official legislation touching upon the future structure of zemstvo institutions" be submitted to the zemstvos themselves for consideration before introduction in the Duma.[43] This vote was particularly significant as an indication of the depth of discontent with the government's plans. Not only did the Saratov zemstvo assembly include many friends and relatives of former Governor Stolypin, but it was also heavily influenced by moderate Octobrist opinion. Although Olsuf'ev, for example, was a self-declared "rightist," Uvarov considered himself to be a Progressist and K. N. Grimm, the board chairman, an Octobrist.[44] The feelings of the Saratov notables were shared by many others. By May 1907 almost all provincial zemstvos and some gentry assemblies had managed to vote similar resolutions.

The results of all this petitioning, resolving, and organizing were rather modest. Under conservative pressure Stolypin did agree to allow local discussion of his ministry's proposals, and he also gave rather grudging consent to the convocation of the national zemstvo congress.[45] But he did not withdraw the local reform projects from the Duma. As it happened, Stolypin's opponents were saved from their primary fear—rapid passage of the bills—by events that had little to do with their own efforts. Quite independently of gentry and zemstvo agitation, the possibility of cooperation between the government and the Second Duma disappeared.[46]

Despite the mutual interest of Stolypin and the Cadets in constructive legislation, the two parties remained unable to find workable compromises on almost all major issues. In relation to local government, the Duma delegates formed two subcommittees to review the MVD projects for provincial, district, and village reform. Though the groups barely had time to meet before the Duma was dissolved, they managed to reject flatly the Stolypin proposals. Cadet V. M. Gessen, who had been a major figure in the articulation of the liberal zemstvo outlook of the 1890s, chaired one subcommittee. Under his influence the body denounced the provincial bill for its "centralization of all local governance in the hands of the governor" and the district project for imposing the authority of the new district commander on the institutions of self-government.[47] The same kind of fundamental disagreement in outlook between Stolypin and the Cadets extended to other areas, including agrarian reform and the use of repression to halt terrorism. Failing to find common ground with the Duma majority, on 3 June 1907 the government again dissolved the national assembly and moved ahead with a conservative revision of Duma suffrage. Speedy consideration of the local reforms was out of the question.

The Zemstvo Congresses

Safe from the threat of immediate passage of the government's projects, the public could now wholeheartedly debate the content of the Stolypin administrative reform. In provincial zemstvo assemblies especially, arguments were already raging over such issues as suffrage and the all-estate volost. This active discussion culminated in the deliberations of two national zemstvo congresses held in June and August. Their stenographic reports reveal better than any other record the sentiment of self-government on the Stolypin proposals.

THE DEBATE OVER REFORM, 1906–1908

Before analyzing the substance of debate at the zemstvo congresses, it is important to note that their composition differed sharply from that of the radical self-governmental assemblies of 1905. The earlier meetings had been dominated by future Cadets and their sympathizers. The new were controlled by the former zemstvo minority, now a majority of Octobrists and rightists. The preponderance of moderates and conservatives at the June 1907 congress was amply demonstrated by the elections to the chair. Octobrist M. V. Rodzianko received seventy-nine votes to a mere twenty-eight for the more liberal Count P. A. Geiden and seven for fellow Octobrist A. I. Guchkov. Guchkov defeated Geiden for election as a vice-chairman.[48] The make-up of the August gathering differed in that it was more conservative. A liberal boycott removed much of what had been the left wing at the first congress, and more rightists were in attendance. Octobrism was again strongly represented.

The shift to the center in zemstvo circles was evident throughout the deliberations of both congresses. Three distinct views on the question of reform emerged from the start of debate, which centered around the specific issue of electoral reform. One small group of delegates led by long-time progressive M. A. Stakhovich argued for a complete reorganization of the zemstvo on the basis of universal suffrage. Echoing the Cadet party platform, Stakhovich and his supporters insisted that the success of the empire's new civil order depended upon wide popular involvement in self-government. As one delegate from Smolensk maintained, the broad democratization of the zemstvo was absolutely necessary, for "no matter what constitution you write, until society itself is called upon to participate in self-government, none of the political rights of the citizen will be guaranteed."[49]

In opposition to those who saw fundamental reform as a prerequisite for progress stood a second group who considered it unthinkable. Led by the delegation from Kursk, the right wing of the congress argued against any "radical change" (*korennaia lomka*) in the zemstvo structure. N. E. Markov, for example, admitted the need for some minor adjustments but maintained that "there is not the slightest ground in fact for a basic alteration of the zemstvo institutions." Though he accepted some easing of electoral qualifications in response to the flight of gentry from the countryside, he insisted that the peasantry was "as a whole incapable of directing zemstvo affairs." Markov's Kursk compatriot Kasatkin-Rostovskii rejected reform more categorically in a speech that denounced the third element as revolutionaries, criticized the industrial bourgeoisie, and staunchly defended the gentry estate. Aptly summarizing the right wing's skepticism over the timeliness of reform, he argued, "It is impossible to renovate a house when it is aflame."[50]

The congress majority, however, chose neither of these views. As the Octobrist Golitsyn explained, his preference was for a middle course between those of Stakhovich and Markov. To the former he pointed out that the constitution could exist without universal suffrage in the zemstvo. To the latter he suggested that democratization need not mean the transfer of power from the gentry to the peasantry, but simply the broadening of popular involvement. He personally recommended some expansion of peasant participation from a "pedagogical viewpoint." The zemstvo would serve as a "school" where peasants "utterly incapable of [taking part in] state life" would be turned into "conscious citizens."[51] The essence of this moderate reformism was captured by the Simbirsk delegation in its formal report to the congress. The main theme of the document was the idea that "the law of life is the law of movement, silence and a full halt are signs of death." The Simbirsk zemstvo majority, it ended, "protests only against disorganized movement, which quickly becomes a whirlwind flinging into the abyss not only men, but also institutions."[52]

The Octobrist path between a "full halt" and "disorganized movement" was mapped out in the course of balloting on zemstvo suffrage. On the side of motion the congress overruled the defenders of the existing system, with its reliance upon the estate principle as a basis for electoral curiae. Only eight delegates objected as the assembly ruled that the future zemstvo should be totally "estateless."[53] In the same vein the delegates passed by an overwhelming majority A. A. Uvarov's motion that "reform of the zemstvo franchise unconditionally include a significant reduction of the property qualification."[54] Finally, in an impressive indication of the sincerity of its interest in change the congress took the unprecedented step of recommending that women be given the vote.[55]

While thus opting for reform, the zemstvo members were careful to hold it within conservative limits. Universal suffrage was ruled out when the delegates voted eighty-nine to eight in favor of the principle of a property restriction on electoral rights. Furthermore, by a ballot of sixty to thirty-seven, the congress rejected the government's proposal for a tax qualification in favor of the existing land criterion.[56] Among the minority defending the government's project were not only prominent left Octobrists like Uvarov, Golitsyn, and Iu. N. Glebov, but also the congress executive committee. The reasons for the tax principle's defeat were significant. Fear that landowners might be underrepresented relative to the more highly assessed commercial and industrial classes was a factor in the decision, but not the key one. Far more important was concern that the tax principle might be manipulated to democratize the suffrage radically. In particular, some delegates feared that a nominal levy on apartment rents might be used to include the politically dangerous free professions in the electorate.[57]

Having excluded undesirables by means of a property qualification, the congress moved to protect further the interests of "cultured elements"—a euphemism for the wealthy—through a system of voting curiae. Led by Uvarov and Glebov, some Octobrists and Cadets argued for a simple two-curia structure combining all landowners in one group and the urban propertied in a second. They based their proposal on the assumption that all agriculturalists shared a common interest and should therefore be encouraged to work together. As Uvarov explained, "All proprietors would be united in the defense of the principle of landed property." Capturing the spirit of the Stolypin program, he contended that the peasant smallholders created by agrarian reform would be "completely harmless to the large owners" since they would form a new "conservative element" that could be counted upon to defend its few acres much more energetically than the gentry its thousands. The majority of delegates were unpersuaded. After defeating Uvarov's scheme, the congress voted to impose a complicated system of five curiae that guaranteed the "adequate" representation of urban and rural magnates by grouping them separately from the less well-to-do.[58]

In essence the congress had resolved to create a new zemstvo. By rejecting the curial system of 1890 and deciding to broaden the suffrage, the delegates had explicitly abandoned Tolstoi's estate self-government. Yet in place of the corporate ideal they did not substitute full civil equality based upon universal suffrage. Rather, they introduced the new discriminatory principle of class based upon property. It was property ownership, synonymous with "culture" in the minds of the majority of delegates, that justified a curial system guaranteeing the predominance of the wealthy. And it was ownership of property, if only in limited quantities, that legitimized the somewhat broader participation to be offered Stolypin's peasant farmers. Through the principle of property, the Octobrist majority maintained, the zemstvo could be renovated without being ruined. Property insured movement without risking the whirlwind.

The spirit of conservative reform also characterized the deliberations of the two congresses on the issue of the local, or volost, zemstvo. Although time limitations shortened debate, the first congress ruled for the local zemstvo and, over the strident objections of twenty-seven rightists, voted in favor of its immediate introduction.[59] This decision was confirmed two months later at the second congress. Moreover, the majority mandated explicitly that the new unit be "all-estate," "self-governing," and "self-taxing."[60] In a more conservative vein, the second assembly followed its predecessor in recommending a property qualification for suffrage and a curial system of elections for the new unit of self-government. Rightists were able to win one concession when the congress voted to make introduction of the volost zemstvo facultative, that is, dependent upon petition from the separate provincial zemstvos. They were aided in this victory by some firm advocates of the reform, who felt that the measure should not be implemented immediately in areas where it might fail.[61]

In addition to reflecting the essential moderation of the Octobrists, the debate on the volost zemstvo revealed another deeply ingrained attitude of the zemstvo majority—mistrust of the state bureaucracy. Although the 1907 national zemstvo congresses were quite different from those held during the Revolution of 1905, most of the delegates present were still veterans of self-government and, like their more liberal colleagues, resented the intrusion of civil servants into local affairs. Hence they took care to protect their new volost zemstvo from undue interference. In the MVD conception, the reformed volost was to be both a zemstvo and an organ of the state bureaucracy, performing simultaneously both self-governing and state administrative functions. After all, the existing peasant volost performed many important administrative duties, and it was reasonable, in the MVD view, to expect its replacement to do the same. This approach was not shared by the congress. The delegates rejected the MVD's project, with no votes for it, though the executive committee's spokesman, M. D. Ershov, and eight others abstained. Moreover, by the overwhelming margin of fifty-one to eleven the congress explicitly ruled that the volost zemstvo could not be considered an administrative organ. As a concession to the government the zemstvo members did agree that the new body might aid the state bureaucracy in some limited duties, but only in areas precisely circumscribed by law and at the expense of the tsarist treasury. All police functions were to be excluded.[62]

Hostility to the civil service went beyond the question of the volost. Many of those in attendance, for example, urged a resolution that central supervision over all institutions of self-government be limited strictly to the legality and not the expediency of local actions.[63] A shortage of time prevented this issue from coming to a ballot, however. Pressing outside concerns including the fall harvest and upcoming elections to the Third Duma brought the second congress to a premature close. Therefore, the full depth of feeling on the issue of supervision and on the broader question of the state bureaucracy's role remained unsounded. The zemstvo representatives had ruled for the reorganization of rural self-government on the new principle of economic class. And they had spoken for the extension of self-government to the volost level. Other questions were left to the future.

Though the June and August congresses developed out of the campaign to slow consideration of the Stolypin program in the Second Duma, and despite the fact that both were characterized by a significant undercurrent of antibureaucratic sentiment, the government did not necessarily view them with hostility. In fact, there is considerable evidence that precisely the opposite was the case. As difficulties with the Duma mounted through the spring of 1907, Stolypin's interest in finding less radical allies than the Cadets grew proportionately. Even before the zemstvo gatherings there was indication that the central authorities were drastically altering their initially cool attitude toward the moderate zemstvo members. The most profound expression of this new approach was the 3 June coup. Provoked by the oppositional tenor of the Second Duma, Stolypin again resorted to dissolution, but this time the step was accompanied by the promulgation of a new electoral law.[64] According to the revised franchise, the representation of peasants, workers, and all non-Russians was drastically curtailed. Instead, preponderance in Duma elections was guaranteed to the rural elite, to precisely those elements who were so well represented at the zemstvo congresses. As Kryzhanovskii, the MVD bureaucrat who drafted the legislation, noted, the electoral measure was a retreat from a broad, democratic suffrage to "the constitutional idea which has its roots in the zemstvo world."[65] Through this device the government hoped to create a more conservative Third Duma with which to cooperate. A coalition between reforming bureaucrats, like Stolypin, and moderate reformers in the public, like the Octobrists, was to form the basis of what has been dubbed the "3 June system."

Stolypin certainly could find encouragement for his new approach in the debates of the zemstvo congresses, especially the first. True, the MVD's projects had been voted down, but the setback was not clear-cut. In the case of the zemstvo electoral bill, for instance, the congress had adopted a curial system that was admittedly similar to the government's. Although the proposed tax qualification, inserted in the MVD program at the initiative of the Council of Ministers, had been rejected, the margin of defeat had not been wide. Many of the leading figures at the congresses, including their executive committees, had championed the government viewpoint. Of course, the delegates' attitudes on the nature of the volost zemstvo were more at variance with the MVD's, but even here the gulf was hardly unbridgeable. The essential fact remained that the congresses had spoken not for radical reform but for conservative change, for reform without disorder.

Concrete evidence of Stolypin's willingness to cooperate with the zemstvos came later in the fall when the government made known its intention to submit the MVD projects to its Council on Local Affairs. The minister announced in a circular issued 14 October 1907 that proposals relating to the zemstvo would be reviewed by the council before their introduction in the Duma. Such a procedure, he noted, was "from the pragmatic viewpoint preferable to the submission of legislative proposals directly to the zemstvo assemblies for their conclusions."[66] The council had been created in 1903 by Pleve as a means of bringing together MVD bureaucrats and local leaders for cooperative work, but it had not convened before his assassination. Now the body was to perform for Stolypin precisely the same function of rapprochement between the government and moderate leaders from the zemstvos and town councils.

This demonstration of official interest in cooperation evoked a quick response from the zemstvos. Despite some dissent, as in Kazan where the provincial assembly refused to defer its debate of the MVD projects, the vast majority accepted the council as the proper forum for the review of Stolypin's proposals.[67] Agitation for the submission of the projects directly to the zemstvos ended. It appeared that the government had indeed found a more trustworthy ally than the Cadets in the business of local reform.

The Aristocratic Critique

The Octobrist majority had dominated the 1907 national zemstvo congresses, but at both gatherings there was also a vocal and active minority defending the old order against all but the slightest change. Though badly outvoted in the assembly proceedings, this small group represented a broad and growing movement among the empire's first estate that rejected even the Octobrists' gradualism. This sentiment found some expression in individual zemstvo assemblies, like that of Kursk, the home of Markov and Prince Kasatkin-Rostovskii. Yet as the two congresses demonstrated, self-government by and large remained true to its tradition of moderate reformism and "progress." The primary rallying points for the gentry right were not so much the all-estate zemstvos as the nobility's own corporate assemblies. It was here during the summer and fall of 1907 that an aristocratic critique of the Stolypin proposals, and of the idea of reform in general, was articulated.

The most active corporate body was that of Moscow, a long-time leader of noble opinion. On 7 April, less than a week after the third congress of the United Nobility had disbanded, Moscow Marshal P. A. Bazilevskii called a meeting of provincial leaders for the purpose of expediting the discussion of local reform.[68] The group that assembled elected a special commission to draft a report on the MVD proposals for consideration by the entire Muscovite gentry.

Although the commission was chaired by Bazilevskii himself and included eighteen members, its report was authored primarily by Feodr D. Samarin, probably with the aid of his brother Aleksandr.[69] The two were admirably suited for the task. The sons of a substantial magnate, both were men of considerable means vested with the social status that accompanies landed property.[70] Each also apparently possessed a temperament equal to his wealth. The normally critical observer Gurko, for example, described the pair as "of fine character" and Aleksandr as being surrounded by a "halo of integrity."[71] Both had long been active in the politics of Moscow's Bogorodsk district, where they were zemstvo deputies and where Aleksandr had been gentry marshal since 1899. To this familiarity with local conditions they added important connections in Saint Petersburg. Feodr, for instance, had been a member of the official commission that drafted the Bulygin project for a consultative Duma in 1905. Later he had been suggested by Witte and approved by the tsar as a possible successor to Kutler as minister of agriculture, though he ultimately declined to accept appointment.[72] Finally, as if these qualifications of wealth, character, and service were not enough, the two held important intellectual credentials. Nephews of the nineteenth-century Slavophil Iurii Samarin, the brothers were well versed in that particular school of romantic conservatism. In short, the Samarins were from among the wealthy gentry but were well able to claim the role of spokesmen for their entire estate. They possessed important influence in the capital but were free of the moral blemishes that often accompany its acquisition. They not only understood the gentry's material interests but also knew how to clothe those interests in attractive political theory.[73]

The Samarin Report, approved enthusiastically by the Moscow gentry assembly on 8 October 1907, was a frontal assault on the government program. The document is of particular interest, for it contained most of the logic and rhetoric that was to characterize the rightist critique of Stolypin's plans for the next four years. The heart of the report was a fundamental distinction between two forms of social change. The first, vigorously defended by the aristocratic authors, was organic and evolutionary growth, the notion of progress through incremental innovations based upon years of practical experience. Such change was rooted in a close knowledge of the land and its people. Juxtaposed to this, in the Samarins' view, was the path of radical reform. Here innovation was not measured, nor was it drawn from direct experience of social realities. Rather, proposals were deduced from theoretical constructs, products of a cold rationalism blind to local conditions. Measures introduced in this second way typically caused sharp discontinuity and threatened disorder, particularly in times of revolutionary stress. As the authors observed, "Considerations of principle and practice indicate that all institutional reform must be introduced gradually; legislation should take the form of partial corrections and improvements, without being carried away by alluring abstractions."[74] Hence the Stolypin program stood under threefold condemnation as excessively radical, overly theoretical, and dangerously timed.

To support their contentions, the report's authors turned to the experience of western Europe. As a model of healthy development they pointed to England. Like the Cadets, the conservative gentry were enthralled by the English mystique of a peaceful, well-ordered nation characterized by social harmony. Yet where liberals ascribed this imagined absence of social strife to Britain's parliamentary system, the conservative gentry emphasized the step-by-step evolution of that system over centuries. Improvement of local government in England, the report stated, "almost always takes the character of partial corrections to existing laws." As a contrary example of the chaos that would result from a failure to observe the injunctions of organic development, the authors turned readily to France, where, they argued, the rapid and violent overturn of traditional institutions after 1789 had led to a century of conflict. Now, Stolypin intended the same for Tsarist Russia. "Nowhere else has the government embarked upon such an indiscriminate break with all existing institutions," they wrote, "except in France at the time of the revolution."[75]

The Samarins' approach was hardly original. The two were clearly inspired by foreign thinkers, especially Alexis de Tocqueville. They shared his reservations about the Revolution of 1789. And, even more to the point for the Muscovites, they valued his critique of the centralizing reforms of the Bourbon royal bureaucracy, which Tocqueville maintained disrupted the organic harmony of the *ancien régime*. The Samarins also borrowed heavily from domestic political theory, particularly the nineteenth-century Slavophil critique of political rationality. More likely than not, however, the single most important source for the gentry ideologists was a polemical one, the defense of the Russian estates articulated by Pazukhin some twenty years earlier. Under much more difficult circumstances, they echoed Pazukhin's vision of a tsarist corporate order.

The commitment to the estate system was made explicit in the second half of the report, a detailed analysis of the MVD projects on village and district reform. The crucial issue for the authors was the replacement of the gentry marshal as titular head of district administration by a bureaucrat, the proposed commander. The Samarins supported the marshal passionately. They vehemently denied that he was merely a spokesman for gentry interests. On the contrary, they argued, the marshal's selection by the first estate alone was a guarantee of his impartiality. Not chosen by the broad masses, he was free from popular pressure. Not appointed by the central government, he was outside bureaucratic control. "In the eyes of generations," the report read, "the district marshal has evolved from the representative of one estate into the first citizen of the rural community [*zemshchina*]."[76]

Actually, one can argue that the marshaldom itself was not crucial to the gentry right. Before 1905 it had been primarily a post of honor, with performance being characterized as much by absenteeism as assiduity. Similarly, the marshal's significance in 1907 lay not in any particular administrative function but primarily in the fact that the post had become a symbol representing the totality of gentry hegemony in the countryside. The role of the district marshal, the Samarins contended, "corresponds precisely to the activity of the gentry generally, insofar as they participate in local self-government."[77] And it was the overall position of the first estate locally that was threatened both by Stolypin's legislation and by the class-oriented proposals of the Octobrists.

Of course, the defense of gentry interests was not put in terms of privilege or economics. Again the authors followed Pazukhin's example by focusing on the gentry's service to the state. "It is true that there have been in Russian society groups that have aspired to impose upon the gentry the alien role of a landed aristocracy," they wrote. "But these attempts have issued from a small group of large proprietors and never have had success among the mass of middle gentry, who have always envisioned their purpose primarily in service to the Tsar and to the Land."[78] The gentry were not an economic class but a group of notables distinguished by their self-sacrificing devotion to ruler and people. E. N. Markov had expressed himself similarly at the June national zemstvo congress in pleading that the first estate not be deprived of the right to sacrifice for the rest of the populace.[79] As examples of gentry altruism, Markov, the Samarins, and others repeatedly pointed to the philanthropic work of progressive marshals and zemstvo activists in the decade before 1905.[80] True, at the same time that they were extolling the work of their liberal brethren, the conservative gentry were driving them from public life. Markov was already notorious for his denunciation of the pre-Revolutionary marshals for "treason to Tsar, homeland and fellow nobles."[81] Yet this particular hypocrisy, masking as it did the solid bedrock of self-interest that lay under the surface of the appeal to the service tradition, was not noted by the rightist spokesmen.

The Moscow report, with its themes of duty, honor, and patriotism, was certain to find a broad response among other gentry. The extent of that response was evident at the fourth congress of the United Nobility, held in Saint Petersburg from 9 to 16 March 1908. The gathering was not scheduled by chance. In keeping with his announced intentions, Stolypin had pressed forward with plans for discussion of the MVD program by the Council on Local Affairs. After receiving approval from the Council of Ministers, the MVD had withdrawn its projects from the Duma and made arrangements for the body to open deliberations on 11 March. The United Nobility, by convening their own congress only two days earlier, guaranteed that their debate would have the maximum impact, at least from the standpoint of timing.

Discussion at the gentry congress followed the lines of the Moscow document rather closely, which was not surprising since the official reporter on local reform was none other than Feodr Samarin. As in the report to the gentry of his home province, Samarin began by arguing against any radical alteration of existing institutions. Again the contrast was between healthy evolutionary growth and destructive

[172]

revolutionary change, between what one noble described as the "organic theory of society" and a "mechanistic view" stemming from the French Enlightenment.[82] After a short debate the congress approved this viewpoint, rejecting the government's program as a "drastic restructuring of the entire system of local institutions" and, therefore, "in all respects undesirable and inexpedient."[83]

Most speeches at the session were devoted to the defense of the corporate principle, again primarily in terms of duty. For instance, the delegates took particular pains to distinguish Russia's estates from western European classes. The European social formations, V. N. Oznobishin explained, were formed for the purpose of economically exploiting others. In contrast, he continued, tsarist estates had developed out of the shared obligation of service.[84] The gentry right saw its privileged position, its "opportunity to serve," threatened from two directions. The first adversary was the empire's middle classes, who, through the establishment of a democratized, all-estate volost zemstvo, might usurp leadership in local affairs. Although an occasional orator at the congress criticized the peasants for a lack of patriotism and good sense, it was not so much their "little brothers" whom the United Nobility feared. Perhaps a combination of wishful thinking and guilt caused the notables to shrink from the possibility that the village masses—the other major estate—owed them implacable hostility. Rather, the gentry emphasized the rural intelligentsia. Anyone familiar with the history of the French Revolution, D. N. Kovan'ko maintained, could see that the government's reform would transfer power in Russia into the hands of the "very same third element" that seized power in France in 1789. Choosing a more contemporary referent, Prince Kasatkin-Rostovskii pointed to the experience of the first two State Dumas. Both had fallen under the control not of the gentry, merchants, or peasants, he argued, but under the influence of the third element, aided by subsidies from "Agences Israelites [sic]" and the propaganda of the Jewish press.[85]

The second enemy of gentry interests, and one no less dangerous in the eyes of some, was the state bureaucracy. Although all members of the United Nobility retained their traditional devotion to the tsar and to the state as an abstract entity, many viewed the officials who staffed the state apparatus with real hostility. A few gentry leaders, including those with important connections in Saint Petersburg like Count Bobrinskii, Naryshkin, and Samarin himself, sought to moderate the tone of criticism of the government.[86] Most, however, followed diehards like Prince Kasatkin-Rostovskii and Snezhkov in accusing the administration of having treacherously abandoned them. The bitterest attacks were directed against MVD bureaucrats. Gurliand's Jewish background and university professorship made him a prime target, but others fared little better. Kryzhanovskii, for instance, was accused of an "inborn unscrupulousness, which has carried him from the ranks of the radical revolutionaries in his youth to the very heights of formal service to the Tsar."[87]

The immediate cause of the attack on officialdom, and on the MVD staff in particular, was of course its authorship of the local reform. During 1905 and 1906 gentry wrath against the Witte administration had been stirred above all by Kutler's proposal, with its possibility of expropriation of noble lands. Now the gentry saw themselves as battling yet another "expropriation," this time of their hegemony in local administration through the full bureaucratization of the land captaincy and the replacement of their marshal as head of district affairs. Hence the delegates at the congress came to the defense of their estate representatives with all their energy. The government's plans, Oznobishin contended, involved the "clash of two world views." In place of the gentry's "service from a sense of duty," the MVD intended to substitute the bureaucrat's "service for pay." The hired official, Oznobishin continued, lacked the noble's devotion to the country and familiarity with local conditions and was indeed little better than that other hired employee, the member of the third element. Both were viewed as alien to the soil, motivated by a cold and abstract rationality. Many delegates agreed fully with Oznobishin's conclusion: "I see no difference in principle between the banner under which the bureaucracy marches and that other well-known one: 'workers, i.e., employees, of the world unite.'"[88]

The vitriolic indictment by the United Nobility of both the rural intelligentsia and the civil service demonstrated the determination of the gentry majority to oppose all administrative reform. There were voices at the congress in favor of drafting some constructive suggestions for the improvement of government in the provinces as an alternative to the MVD's program. Gurko, who had been forced from office in December 1906 by an embezzlement scandal and now joined the gentry activists, argued, "It is impossible to limit oneself to negation alone; the rejection of a project is essentially a defensive form of action; to win any position it is necessary to go over to the attack, i.e., to clearly and definitely state what the Gentry in this respect desires."[89] But such views were ignored. For most delegates the Slavophil's "organic" evolution meant, in reality, no change in local administration at all.

The debates at the assembly highlighted the sharp difference be tween the government, as represented by Stolypin, and the bulk of the Russian gentry. The nobles had at first warmly welcomed both Stolypin's 3 June coup against the Duma and his land program, but their motives were quite unlike his. To Stolypin, constitutional "adjustment" and agrarian reform were the first steps in a broad plan for conservative modernization of the empire. Land consolidation in particular would create a new class of peasant farmers who would serve both as a bulwark against revolution and as a source of material progress for the country. The reorganization of local governance, in this view, was merely another logical step forward. Aptly described as the political side of the Stolypin land reform, it would consolidate tsarism's new conservative social base by uniting the most able gentry with the most successful of the peasant smallholders in rural self-government. A much larger segment of the populace would now be able to participate actively in the strengthened administrative system. To the United Nobility, however, the Stolypin land program was something quite different. It was not a tool of moderate social change but a weapon against such change. Destruction of the commune and the inculcation of a sense of private property among the peasants would extinguish their revolutionary potential and obviate the need for further tampering with the existing order. The basic social structure of the empire, particularly as represented by the gentry's leading role in the provinces, would remain essentially unaltered. The reform of local governance was not merely unnecessary, but pernicious.

The proceedings of the Fourth Congress of the United Nobility demonstrated the profound effect of the Revolution of 1905 on the Russian gentry. Previously the first estate had been an ineffectual opponent of progress, often playing the role of its almost helpless victim. In the 1860s the government had successfully emancipated the serfs despite widespread gentry misgivings.[90] In the closing decades of the nineteenth century the state bureaucracy had initiated a major program of industrialization at the direct sacrifice of agrarian and, therefore, gentry well-being. The shock of 1905 changed all this. For the first time in decades the bulk of the first estate felt the need to organize to protect their interests, and they defined these interests in a stubbornly defensive, even reactionary, fashion. The forces arrayed against reform in the Russian Empire, often described only in terms of the tsar and court circles, had a powerful aristocratic base.

CHAPTER VII

THE DEBATE OVER REFORM, 1908–1914

The initial stages of the debate over local administration indicated the extent of polarization within the tsarist empire and the ways in which social change and revolution had mobilized even the educated citizenry in a dangerous fashion. In the years between 1908 and 1914, when the outbreak of war transformed the situation, tsarist statesmen struggled with the task of overcoming this polarization, or at least developing the minimum cooperation necessary for effective functioning of the political system. Historians traditionally divide this period into halves, with Stolypin's death as a watershed. Before his assassination in 1911, it is argued, the government sought to cooperate with the public and the Duma in fundamental reform, but thereafter the central authorities became increasingly rigid, even reactionary. It is certainly true that Stolypin was far more interested than his successors in major innovation on issues like landholding or popular participation. Those officials who followed him focused in a severely limited way on more immediate problems, like the shortcomings of the regular police system, but throughout these six years there was at least one element of continuity. Government leaders persisted in the attempt to improve the administrative machinery of the empire through decentralization, without sacrificing the essential hegemony of the state bureaucracy.

The Search for a Constituency

The Council on Local Affairs is undoubtedly one of the least studied institutions of the tsarist government. Yet during the Stolypin ministry it performed a crucial function. Created by Pleve in 1903 as part of the MVD's Main Administration for Local Affairs, the council did not meet before its sponsor's death. Nor did it convene during the revolution which followed. Only in 1908, in circumstances quite different from those in which Pleve established the body, did Stolypin revive and actually implement the idea. Ostensibly, the council was to be merely a legislative workshop, a place where civil servants and local citizens could fine-tune draft projects before their submission to the State Duma. As Stolypin put it in his inaugural address at the body's first session, here public representatives who were aware of the particular needs of their home provinces could "enliven" the "theoretical work" of the MVD staff. The institution, or "pre-Duma" as he called it, would operate "without any political coloration, on a strictly businesslike basis."[1]

Though the council would indeed perform the practical function outlined by Stolypin, the minister's emphasis on its nonpartisan nature was disingenuous. There can be little doubt that the motivation behind the sessions was highly political. While the Second Duma was in session Stolypin had not been concerned that MVD legislative projects lacked outside scrutiny. The dissolution of the Duma and the collapse of the government's attempt to cooperate with the Cadets, however, changed the situation. The authorities now pushed through the 3 June 1907 electoral law to end liberal predominance in the national assembly, and Stolypin turned to the recruitment of new allies from among more "moderate" elements. The Council on Local Affairs was a vehicle perfectly suited for this undertaking. Meetings were held behind closed doors, safe from the glare of the generally radical periodical press. And only a few of the participants were from the political left, either liberal or socialist. Membership was divided between delegates invited directly by the MVD and those elected by the newly conservatized zemstvos and town councils. Those attending the spring 1908 sessions, for example, included the chairmen, Stolypin and Kryzhanovskii, twenty other Saint Petersburg officials, two governors, and forty-seven delegates from self-government. Of the latter, all but a dozen were zemstvo men, an overrepresentation of the landed that gave the body a distinctly antiurban bias.[2] Politically speaking, sentiment among the public figures was primarily Octobrist, though rightists were also numerous. Thus, the council's private representatives were drawn from precisely those groups most favored by the 3 June electoral law. The pre-Duma, therefore, was not simply a workshop but a forum in which the government could establish and cement a cooperative relationship with the moderate citizenry, an arena in which Stolypin could begin to develop a more amenable constituency for his reform. In this sense, the body was a microcosm of the "3 June monarchy" as a whole.

As with the Second Duma, Stolypin initiated serious legislative work in the council immediately. On 11 March the MVD opened deliberations by presenting its projects on village governance, zemstvo elections, the land captaincy, and the administrative separation of large cities from their zemstvos. Although many individual points were involved in the proposals, the key question was that of representation, of determining which social groups would participate in local self-government and on what terms. Significantly, debate in the council did not revolve around the abandonment of the estate principle. Voices were raised in defense of the status quo; delegates from ultra-rightist Kursk especially denounced in familiar terms any "radical break with the existing estate-corporate order" in the countryside.[3] Yet the overwhelming majority of those present disagreed. The council's subcommittee on the volost, for instance, ruled unanimously in favor of an all-estate village unit, a view that was upheld in the body as a whole by a vote of thirty-two to one.[4] The same held for district and provincial zemstvo elections. What was at issue, therefore, was not whether a new participatory principle for tsarist governance was necessary but what form it would take.

The MVD had proposed in the legislation sent to the Second Duma a zemstvo electoral system based simply on the principle of representation in proportion to the amount of taxes paid. The ministerial projects now before the council were somewhat more complex.[5] The heart of the existing zemstvo franchise, beyond limitations of estate, was a full property qualification, or census (*tsenz*), of either a specific amount of land ranging from two hundred to eight hundred desiatina depending upon location or real estate other than land with an assessed valuation of over fifteen thousand rubles. The MVD now took this qualification, halved it, and placed it at the basis of zemstvo elections. District zemstvo electors were to be divided among three curiae. The first would be composed of landowners with holdings the size of the new full census. The second would include both owners of fixed property other than land assessed at more than seventy-five hundred rubles and representatives of owners whose real estate was valued down to a tenth of that sum. The third curia would be made up of the members of the district's volost assemblies. In regard to the first two curia, therefore, the MVD was willing to accept a liberalized variant of past practice. Yet at the same time important concessions to the innovative tax principle remained. Distribution of assembly seats among the three curiae would be on the basis of taxes paid. Moreover, the qualification for participation in volost elections, and hence indirectly in zemstvo balloting, was payment of a mere two rubles in zemstvo levies.

The revised electoral project was less democratic than its predecessor, which after all had been intended for the Cadet-dominated Second Duma, but it did represent a significant broadening of the local electorate. Even liberal critics of the bill admitted, for example, that considerable opportunity was opened to peasant smallholders, Stolypin's "sober and strong." Indeed, MVD concern that the project might be too radical had led to the inclusion of special restrictive provisions. For district elections it was mandated that the first curia would never fill fewer than one-third of all assembly seats. The last, essentially peasant, curia was to receive only half of the seats to which it was entitled by the tax principle. Through such steps the MVD staff hoped to protect what Stolypin himself described as "the influence and significance of that element which is more cultured, more educated, more experienced in zemstvo work, namely—the class of estate owners."[6] As one delegate frankly put it in reviewing the entire electoral system, "The zemstvo, in place of its estate character, acquires a class nature."[7]

Not all of the MVD program was readily accepted in the council. The retreat from the strict application of the tax principle was a source of special contention. The Octobrist party, as part of its electoral platform for the Third Duma, had drafted its own plan for zemstvo electoral reform based exclusively on local rates.[8] Not surprisingly, therefore, individual Octobrists in the pre-Duma decried any deviation from the tax ideal. Particularly forward in this regard were spokesmen of zemstvos in heavily industrial areas, like Golitsyn of Kharkov or Rikhter of Moscow. They were naturally supported by the delegates from town councils, the representatives of urban finance. The reasoning behind their stand was straightforward. As Golitsyn had written earlier in a special thesis on the subject, taxes were the "alpha and omega" of self-government. It was just that voting operate accordingly.[9] Moreover, taxation was seen by some as a means of democratizing the electorate without resorting to the radical step of universal suffrage. Rikhter was even so bold as to suggest the future possibility of using an income tax as an empire-wide qualification, should such a tax ever be introduced in Russia.

Defenders of the mixed land-valuation system were equally forceful in their views. Stolypin, in explaining the MVD reversal on the issue, insisted that the confused state of zemstvo levies and assessment made the tax rule impractical. Others maintained that taxation would give an unfair advantage to commercial-industrial interests who normally paid levies far in excess of those on land. Above all, however, many feared that the new approach might open the doors of participation too widely, including in the electorate "people little tied to local life" or "coincidentally residing in a given locale."[10] Less euphemistically, there was concern that a levy on rents or income might extend the franchise to members of the free professions or, worse yet, to the third element. The issue was decided at a joint meeting of the zemstvo, volost, and settlement subcommittees held on 19 March. The tax principle was defeated by a vote of twenty-two to sixteen though for reasons which are unclear, its two foremost defenders, Golitsyn and Rikhter, were unable to attend.[11]

The council's sensitivity to any possibility of democratization was evident in other amendments to the MVD work. Residence requirements were raised from one to three years and the minimum voting age from twenty-one to twenty-five. Although there was some sentiment for a more elaborate six-tiered curial system, the council essentially accepted the MVD tripartite division. In a striking display of rural bias, however, the second, urban, curia was limited to no more than one-sixth of the available seats regardless of taxes paid, and the first was guaranteed not one-third but a full half. For volost elections the two-ruble minimum was replaced by a qualification of one-twentieth of the traditional land census. Additionally, the council's volost and settlement subcommittees reversed the ruling of the Council of Ministers by voting to restore the MVD's original plan for direct participation of wealthy landowners in zemstvo assemblies without election.[12] Finally, the zemstvo electoral subcommittee rounded out the amending process with a long list of undesirables to be disenfranchised altogether. These included draft dodgers, professional criminals, tax defaulters, most Jews, and—in a remarkable show of hostility toward the third element—all zemstvo employees.[13]

Although participation was the most hotly contested question of the council session, Stolypin did not emphasize it in his opening remarks. Instead, he spoke at length not of elections but of the nature of the projected volost and settlement administrations. In the Second Duma Stolypin had specifically characterized the reformed volost as "an estateless, self-governing . . . local zemstvo."[14] Now, in addressing a generally more conservative audience, he described the future volost as a state bureaucratic institution. Explicitly reversing the MVD's earlier position, he maintained that the government "insists upon the necessity of a strong, well-ordered local administrative unit, though one based upon election."[15] As one official frankly admitted, the bills were not intended to introduce self-governing bodies at the grass roots but to "perfect the existing volost and village community."[16]

This characterization caused considerable unhappiness in the council. Though far less dogmatic than the Cadets, most delegates still considered themselves zemstvo men and viewed village reform in terms of the self-governmental principle. Hence, an overwhelming majority of the volost subcommittee ruled specifically that the future body be "a self-governing institution of the zemstvo type."[17] Simultaneously, there was strong sentiment against the assignment of any state bureaucratic tasks to the volost. Police functions drew special criticism. As influential a figure as the Octobrist Baron V. V. Meller-Zakomelskii, a man chosen by the council to chair its work on electoral reform, expressed categorical opposition to involving the volost in law enforcement. Some delegates were concerned that performing deeply unpopular police duties would put local officials "in a false relationship with the populace." Still more feared "an undesirable subordination of elected officials to the [state] police" which might undermine zemstvo autonomy. Only after detailed assurances from MVD representatives and the director of the Department of Police that any contact between volost functionaries and the police would be strictly defined in law did the pre-Duma majority accept the combination of state and self-governmental duties for the new rural unit.[18] Even so, the issue would later reemerge to plague the government.

The tensions in the council over village administration, taken together with the amendments to the MVD electoral project, have led some to interpret the spring pre-Duma session like the deliberations of the Council of Ministers in December 1906 and January 1907 as a setback for Stolypin, a retreat in the face of conservative pressure.[19] Certainly, business organizations and progressive politicians were upset with what they perceived as a capitulation to landed interests, particularly on the question of the tax principle. Such frustration may well have encouraged the subsequent leftward movement of those urbanites who managed to win election to zemstvo assemblies in 1909 and 1910.[20] Yet this hardly justifies a pessimistic reading of the council deliberations from the government's viewpoint. While municipal interests were poorly served, there is no compelling evidence that Stolypin was strongly committed to their satisfaction. Quite to the contrary, the 3 June Duma coup had weighted national elections strongly in favor of landed proprietors. Similarly, MVD work on local governmental reform had been overwhelmingly rural in its orientation, with urban improvements typically added almost as an afterthought. Indeed, in some ways the council actually restored ideas originally proposed by Stolypin and his staff. The practice of including wealthy owners directly in zemstvo assemblies without election, for instance, had been deleted from the MVD legislation by the Council of Ministers. Conversely, the now abandoned tax principle had first been suggested by Stolypin's fellow ministers, not Stolypin himself.

Rather than focus on differences, it is far more appropriate to stress the fundamental affinity among most pre-Duma delegates, whether civil servants or representatives of the public. There had been little difficulty in developing a strong majority against the estate principle of representation. And even on the hotly debated question of a new criterion for participation, supporters of the "liberal" tax and "conservative" land principles shared far more than not. Consider the views of Golitsyn, a "left" Octobrist and an ardent proponent of a rates-based franchise. Hardly a radical, he explicitly rejected any consideration of universal suffrage, given "the complete ignorance of the masses, their terrible lack of culture, and their recently incited immoral aspirations and instincts." Much like the defenders of the traditional zemstvo land qualification, he contrasted agrarians, who were "broad-minded as if in reflection of the power, strength, and energy of nature and the soil," to urbanites, who were "narrow, egoistic, involuntarily reflecting the ambience of city life."[21] In a similar vein, contemporary journalists commented not on the distinctions between the Octobrist tax-oriented electoral bill and that of the MVD, but on their likeness. Columnists of *New Times*, for example, argued that in opposition to the democratism of the Cadets and the immobilism of the gentry right, the guiding idea of both projects was "one and the same."[22]

Given this, it is fair to describe the council's maiden session not as divisive but as a first step toward the generation of some consensus on reform between progressive bureaucrats and moderates among the public. This unquestionably was the spirit in which the spring meetings closed. During a festive breakfast hosted by Stolypin at MVD headquarters, the Octobrist delegate Rikhter toasted the statesman as "our savior, our Minin." His confession that "there are no words in the entire range of the Russian vocabulary to express to you the full depth of the feelings you have aroused in our hearts" was followed by a hearty ovation. Stolypin responded shortly after at an evening banquet hosted by the delegates in a fashionable Saint Petersburg restaurant. Turning to the assembled dignitaries of zemstvo, town council, gentry, and civil service, he announced, "In the close alliance of these representatives I see the future of Russia."[23] Indeed, there are indications that Nicholas II, normally skeptical of proposed alterations in the existing order, was open to change. In March he wrote his mother, "Now, when it has become more tranquil, the gentry are beginning to complain about various innovations and reforms,—but one might ask how did they help the government during the terrible autumn of 1905. Not at all. They all hid silently, thinking the end had come."[24]

These were promising beginnings. General agreement had been reached between government and moderates on the zemstvo franchise and, through it, on the broader relationship that ought to exist among the empire's various social strata. Moreover, in another crucial area, there was unity on the question of land. Though debate was extended, most of Stolypin's agrarian legislation was to win easy approval in the Octobrist-dominated Third Duma. Yet the "close alliance" toasted so enthusiastically by Stolypin remained quite fragile. Firm partnership in the business of reform required consensus on the further issue of leadership. Which partner—the public or officialdom—would occupy the leading role in the Russian polity and thus ultimately direct the renovation of tsarist society? The potential for conflict here was enormous, particularly at a time when the basic framework of the 3 June system had yet to be determined. When the pre-Duma reconvened on 20 November 1908 to consider the MVD program reorganizing the local apparatus of the state bureaucracy, a confrontation was all but unavoidable.

The composition of the council at the winter session was roughly the same as before, though more governors were in attendance. Octobrists and rightists continued to predominate among the public representatives. Socialists were again totally excluded and Cadets nearly so, a fact reflected in vituperative attacks on the council by the liberal periodical press. With the work on village reform essentially completed, the delegates now turned their attention to the MVD bills on the land captaincy and on the provincial and district apparatus. Since these projects formed the heart of the ministry's program for strengthening the state bureaucracy through decentralization, Stolypin approached the debate with great vigor. On 5 December he appeared in the Third Duma to make a stirring defense of his agrarian legislation as a "wager on the sober and the strong, and not the drunken and the weak." In his opening speech to the Council on Local Affairs Stolypin was no less outspoken in presenting his similar wager on the civil servant. "I will not hide from you," he told the assembled delegates, "that I assign special significance to these measures." In the face of the rapid politicization of public life and growing complexity of local relations, he argued, the tsarist governmental system "cannot remain at the same level of efficiency as at the beginning of the last century. Nowhere in Europe, neither in Germany, Austria, nor

France, is there an administrative structure as weak as ours."[25] To resolve the discrepancy between escalating demands and present capabilities Stolypin offered the MVD reform package.

The activity of the United Nobility over the preceding two years made it a foregone conclusion that the government's projects would meet staunch opposition. The storm burst, so to speak, over the proposal to establish the office of district commander. In the council's district subcommittee MVD reporters Strakhovskii and Pestrzhetskii presented the plan in terms of solidifying the local bureaucratic hierarchy as a first step toward decentralization. Obviously aware of the strong antipathy of many delegates for the new institution, the two civil servants stressed the positive effect it would have on popular participation in government. Strakhovskii especially claimed that the appointment of a commander would free the gentry marshal, "whose stature one would call mythic if it were not so real," for a greater role in the zemstvo.[26] Despite this rather obsequious attempt to win over noble opponents, the MVD project came under immediate attack. After brushing aside Rikhter's idea that the commander be elected by the district zemstvo, the subcommittee majority voted to require the governor to consult with the provincial marshal and zemstvo chairman before making appointments. In order to guarantee the autonomy of self-government, the group stripped the commander of the right to inspect the executive organs of zemstvo and town council and to be present at sessions of the zemstvo assembly. Given the crucial place of agrarian reform in Stolypin's overall program, the MVD had assigned its new subordinate "special supervision" over farm consolidation. Now he was demoted to simple membership in the local land committee. Similarly, the proposal for "general guardianship" over education was replaced by a seat on the school council. This attempt to degrade the office of commander piecemeal, as Strakhovskii accurately described it, culminated in steps to retain district leadership for the gentry marshal. Most important, the subcommittee voted thirteen to nine to restore the noble functionary as chairman of the district council.[27]

These amendments obviously constituted a direct challenge to the MVD, and one that was taken up immediately. After guaranteeing by telephone that as many of his subordinates as possible would attend, Stolypin called a general session of the council to review the subcommittee report.[28] Chief on the agenda was the highly symbolic decision to transfer the chairmanship of the district council to the marshal. Supporters of the original legislation argued vigorously on behalf of the commander. Whereas Strakhovskii had earlier tried to avoid open criticism of the first estate, Stolypin and his staff now directly indicted the marshals on charges of malfeasance. Gurliand supported the accusation with secret reports from district police chiefs indicating widespread marshal absenteeism. Other MVD partisans pointed to the close identification of the noble officials with gentry interests. The local populace, argued N. F. Stradomskii, would be "offended and outraged that one estate is given such preference and privilege."[29] Defenders of the status quo responded with equal heat. A. N. Naumov dismissed the MVD data on absenteeism as biased and demanded a full investigation by the Senate.[30] Fellow nobles joined the attack by denouncing the civil service for incompetence in 1905 and malice in drafting the local reform.

The bitter arguments voiced in the pre-Duma went far beyond the individual issue of the district chairmanship in their implications. Underlying the entire debate was a fundamental difference in outlook on local governance and the general notion of reform through decentralization. The MVD position was best expressed by Kazan delegate S. A. Beketov:

One of the basic features of all the local reform projects is the principle of decentralization under firm supervision. The more widely administrative activity is decentralized with the establishment of new estateless zemstvos [volost and settlement], the more unified must be the state mechanism which performs the task of supervision over that activity.[31]

In other words, the opening of new avenues for public participation through decentralization would mean not the withdrawal of the state bureaucracy from local affairs but the reaffirmation of its guardianship.

The contrasting view was formulated most clearly by the aristocratic rightist Prince S. A. Panchulidze. He argued that centralization was a system in which the central authorities aspired "not merely to regulation of the general course of national development," but also to the direction of "all or, in any case, most sides of local life." Though willing to admit that the MVD proposals to widen the jurisdiction of zemstvo and town council showed some desire to move away from such centralization, Panchulidze insisted that the government's primary aim was to increase rather than decrease the influence of the civil servant. In the call for "unified authority" under the commander he saw reflected the old slogan, "Tout pour le peuple, rien par le peuple." Meaningful decentralization, he maintained, could only be achieved by strengthening social activity independent of state bureaucratic control. "Although decentralization is not identical with self-government, it is closely related to it," he concluded.[32]

Panchulidze's defense of the marshal on behalf of the zemstvo and the local citizenry was deceptive. Like other members of the United Nobility, he was undoubtedly interested above all in salvaging the traditional prerogatives of the first estate. Yet his arguments found considerable resonance among the pre-Duma membership as a whole. Stolypin prevailed in the crucial vote on the chairmanship of the district council by a tally of thirty-nine to thirty.[33] But the triumph was a formal one only. The margin of victory had been provided by the nine members of the MVD's Saint Petersburg staff, and nine more votes for the commander had been cast by governors. A further subtraction of the ballots of nine urban delegates reduces the government's support among the landed elite, supposedly the backbone of the 3 June system, to a mere dozen. Among the opposition were not only rightists like Panchulidze and A. D. Samarin but highly respected Octobrists and Progressists, including A. D. Golitsyn, V. V. Meller-Zakomelskii, and S. N. Maslov. Stolypin himself understood the reality of defeat. After the pre-Duma added further insult by overwhelmingly rejecting the conciliatory idea of encouraging marshals to serve as commanders, the minister quit the hall in fury. When Naumov and Samarin met with him later in the evening to persuade him to abandon "Gurliand's plan" for the district, Stolypin refused to listen, pounding his fist on the desk and shouting, "Either [accept] me and my reform, or I drop everything and leave you all with your opinions!"[34]

The debacle over the district apparatus indicated that the government faced serious obstacles in recruiting popular support for its program. The dynamics of public resistance were even more explicit in the pre-Duma review of the MVD's provincial reform. This project, which was debated at both the winter 1908 and spring 1909 council sessions, should have been far less controversial than the other MVD drafts. After all, the governorship already existed, and the proposed innovations were ostensibly technical and nonpolitical in nature. Certainly the bill involved no direct threat to the interests of gentry or self-government, since the MVD plans for the extension of gubernatorial control over zemstvos were being withheld for subsequent consideration. Nevertheless, the project encountered difficulty from the start.

In drafting the second article of the legislation, the MVD authors had described the governor as the provincial representative of "the

Central Government," rather than of the "Supreme Sovereign" as before. Although there was immediate reference to the tsar's role in the following articles, many pre-Duma delegates argued that the text implied a weakening of the emperor's authority. After a heated debate, the council majority voted to revise the project, leaving the governor as the agent of the central government but "by the supreme will of the sovereign." For some, even this was not enough. The ever vigilant Panchulidze, almost certainly seeing in the issue an opportunity to turn Nicholas II against the MVD and its renovation effort, demanded a formal guarantee that no slight to imperial prerogatives was intended. Stolypin and his staff were keenly aware of the monarch's jealous concern for the autocratic principle and understood the tentative nature of his commitment to progressive reform. They therefore apparently concluded that the least damaging course would be to duck the question altogether. Excuses were made to delay printing Panchulidze's dissenting report. When that obstreperous noble rose to raise the issue again at the pre-Duma's spring session, chairman Kryzhanovskii simply ruled him out of order.[35] Panchulidze was not to be daunted. After formally accusing the MVD official of lese majesty, he brought the matter to the annual congress of the United Nobility, which in turn appealed directly to the tsar. The sovereign's response was apparently sympathetic, for it was only with difficulty that Stolypin persuaded Nicholas II not to cashier Kryzhanovskii on the spot.[36]

This opposition to the bill in terms of autocracy was confined to rightists in the council. The plan to reorganize the provincial collegial institutions aroused much broader dissatisfaction. In his opening speech at the pre-Duma winter session, Stolypin had attached major importance to this aspect of the MVD work. He emphasized especially the creation of a provincial council made up of citizens and civil servants to handle discipline and administrative justice.[37] The new system, which had been designed by Gurliand, was characterized as an innovative way to limit bureaucratic caprice without a drastic break with existing practice. It represented an attempt to meet public concern for legality short of subjecting the civil service to the control of the courts. Despite Stolypin's obvious interest, the council barely approved the plan by a vote of thirty-three to twenty-eight. The margin of victory was again provided by MVD staffers.[38] The provincial bill as a whole received an equally unsubstantial mandate, passing thirty-five to thirty. Moreover, in both ballots the "nays" included not only public figures but eight governors as well. The cool reception for provincial reform was a bitter surprise for the project's sponsors. Gurliand, the primary author of the bill, responded by writing his chief Stolypin a ten-page memorandum in explanation of the measure's "very peculiar fate."[39] The document is one of the most revealing in the entire local reform debate and deserves detailed examination.

Most puzzling to Gurliand was the opposition of the MVD's traditionally loyal subordinates, the governors. He rejected out of hand the notion that any of the provincial chiefs, except perhaps one, were opposed to reform on principle. Instead, he simply ascribed their negativism to confusion and sheer misunderstanding of the ministry's intent.[40] In regard to the overall MVD program, it would be difficult to argue with this analysis. All the governors who voted had backed Stolypin on district reorganization, and those attending the spring 1908 session had favored an all-estate village administration as well.[41] But Gurliand's attempt to reduce gubernatorial misgivings over the provincial bill to sheer muddleheadedness is not convincing. Rather, one can speculate that the regional chiefs feared that even a slight broadening of public participation in the sensitive area of administrative justice through a revitalized collegial system might erode their own authority. For Stolypin and Gurliand, who were both forced to respond to the demands of national political parties for a limitation on bureaucratic abuse, some concession to the principle of legality appeared unavoidable. The governors, however, had been fully occupied with the struggle to hold the local administrative apparatus together under the stress of revolution. For them, a concession that drew the citizenry further into the administrative hierarchy in any way, much less in connection with the sensitive issue of discipline, was out of the question. Perhaps shaken by the liberalism of Sviatopolk-Mirskii, Witte, and Urusov, the provincial bureaucrats refused to accept their superiors' assurances that the reorganization was not radical.

Gurliand spoke with much greater assurance of the behavior of public delegates in the pre-Duma. The handful of Cadet sympathizers present, he argued accurately, found the reform unacceptable because of its failure to incorporate the long-standing liberal demand for judicial control over the civil service. On the right, he continued, opposition was equally deep-rooted, shared not only by diehards like Panchulidze but also by "relatively calmer gentry circles."[42] This he attributed to conservative misgivings on two counts. On the one hand, these nobles saw in the projects an attempt by the state bureaucracy to expand its power by coopting public leaders in the collegial institutions. In their view, Gurliand opined, the government was using the slogan of supremacy of the law "as an instrument for the final enslavement of the self-governing principle." On the other hand, there was also concern among rightists that subversives from the third element might use the collegial bodies to manipulate the authorities in the name of revolution. Though seemingly contradictory, the two views were current among sympathizers of the gentry right. Here fear of the liberal and socialist parties alternated with anxiety over the "centralizing radicalism" of reformist bureaucrats, with first the one and then the other predominating.

Finally, having explained the cooperation of pre-Duma liberals like G. F. Magnitskii with rightists like Samarin and Panchulidze, a case of strange bedfellows that provoked laughter on the council floor, Gurliand turned to the critical problem of the political center. After the vote on provincial reform, six delegates led by Octobrists Rikhter and N. P. Savitskii had drafted a dissenting opinion arguing that the bill failed to give the educated public adequate access to the colleges. Or, as they put it, the project "introduces nothing new, neither simplifies nor improves operations—essentially all remains as of old."[43] On the basis of this statement, Gurliand had to concede that these centrists at least were motivated by a desire for wider participation of zemstvo elements in administrative justice. Yet he went on to insist that other moderates like Princes A. D. Golitsyn and I. A. Kurakin had opposed the MVD merely out of confusion and a vague sense of solidarity with other nobles.[44] Certainly the Octobrists' earlier behavior gave no support for this interpretation. Indeed, the actions of these delegates throughout discussions of volost, settlement, district, and provincial administration all suggested a consistent reluctance to accept the main premise of the MVD work on decentralization, the primacy of the state bureaucracy in local affairs. Nevertheless, Gurliand ignored the warnings, assuming that uneasiness over reform was merely the product of miscommunication.

Stolypin himself apparently shared his subordinate's optimism. The pre-Duma deliberations had demonstrated the serious obstacles facing the minister in his search for popular approval. Both the political right and left had refused to compromise, and there were ominous signals from the court and the MVD's own provincial agents. Worst of all, potential had emerged for a serious rift between the government and the Octobrists over fundamental questions of policy. Still, Stolypin was determined to push ahead, hopeful that he could yet forge an alliance with the moderate public. His outlook was best expressed in a remarkable interview published in the newspaper *Volga* in the spring of 1909. Reviewing the progress of land consolidation, Stolypin drew a picture in which the government would find future support from its traditional partners, the landed gentry, and its newest clients, the peasant smallholders. Yet simultaneously he spoke of the need to combine the strength of the citizenry with that of the state officials, especially in the provinces. "It is the custom among us to blame them for all the evils of Russian life," Stolypin admitted. "But I am personally well acquainted with the Russian bureaucrat and can say that he is not at all so bad. Civil servants and landowners—they are often one and the same. Today an estate owner, tomorrow a civil servant."[45] Certainly it was with this affinity in mind, with confidence in the possibility of reconciling the state bureaucracy and landed interests, that Stolypin brought his reform program to the Duma.

Reform in the Duma: The 3 June System at Work

Like its two short-lived predecessors, the Third Duma embodied almost the full range of Russian political opinion. As a direct result of the 3 June electoral revision, however, the proportional weight of the various Duma factions was far more favorable to the government. Where the two initial assemblies had been dominated by Cadets, the third was primarily centrist in orientation. Octobrists and rightists held 273 seats, compared to 111 for the combined liberal and socialist left.[46] Stolypin's enemies admitted his success in creating a more conciliatory Duma. Lenin, for example, conceded, "The government is garnering the results of the infamous crime which it committed against the people on June 3. The grotesque electoral law which, for the benefit of a handful of landlords and capitalists, completely distorts the will not only of the nation as a whole, but even of the enfranchised minority, has yielded the fruits that tsarism hankered for."[47] On the opposite end of the ideological spectrum, the rightist Senator N. A. Khvostov privately expressed fear that the Third Duma would be more dangerous than the first, not in its radicalism but in its potential for implementing reform legislation. The latter might well include, he added anxiously, an electoral bill that would give his zemstvo seat to those who had burned his estate in 1905. "There is very little pleasing in the portfolio of the cadet bureaucrats," Khvostov pessimistically concluded.[48]

Stolypin clearly had high hopes. The government's land reform had been implemented in the fall of 1906 on the tsar's emergency authority, but the Cadet majority in the Second Duma had refused to accept the fait accompli. Indeed, the delegates' appeal to the peasantry to boycott the agrarian program had infuriated Stolypin and helped provoke the dissolution of the assembly. Now, by contrast, moderates in the Third Duma welcomed most of the agrarian legislation, approving it without great difficulty by the summer of 1910. There was similar progress in other areas, most notably elementary education. Yet the cooperation between the central authorities and the popular representatives remained tentative. Serious differences in outlook on the future evolution of Russian society emerged when debate shifted from landholding and schooling to the political issue of local administration. Central here was the MVD's bill on the volost.

Duma consideration of volost reorganization was agonizing. After being introduced in October 1908, the MVD project was referred first to the committee on self-government and then to a specially constituted subcommittee. The latter completed its work late in 1910, and it was February of the following year before the bill was returned to the house as a whole. Throughout, there was active disagreement not merely within each of the two committees but also between them. The ad hoc group, chaired by left Octobrist Iu. N. Glebov, tended to be relatively liberal in its approach. The parent body, conversely, was headed by the floor leader of the Duma's Nationalist group, P. N. Balashev, and generally moved in the opposite direction. The assembly majority wavered somewhere between. As a result, any narrative description of the parliamentary proceedings is doomed to be complex at best and tedious at worst. Instead, it is better to view the Duma work on volost reform thematically. The deliberations can be divided into two parallel but conceptually distinct debates, each revolving around an aspect of the overarching problem of political participation.

The first question to be resolved was essentially quantitative. How many citizens would be allowed to take part in voting for local self-government, and from which social strata would they come? What limits, if any, would there be to popular participation in the electoral process? Answers offered by the various Duma factions ran along a simple continuum. On the left the response was "most" or "all" of the empire's adults, and on the far right, "few." Faithful to their party programs, the Social Democrats, Trudoviks, and Cadets called for universal suffrage for the new volost. While the Cadets especially had been disillusioned by the failure of the masses to support them more actively in the period following the revolution, they continued to insist upon the equal involvement of all citizens in elections for self-government. Liberal A. I. Shingarev, for instance, opposed any estate or property restrictions. Zemstvo functions, he maintained, are "tasks of the entire populace, and those who do not possess property are no less, and perhaps more, interested in this work." Referring to the third element, he called upon his fellow delegates not to exclude those "upon whose backs zemstvo achievements had been built." Shingarev concluded by combining a statement of traditional liberal faith in the progressive movement of history with a warning. Should the obstructionism of the United Nobility somehow prevail, he predicted, "Tomorrow will bring the fiercest *pugachevshchina*. . . . Can one really alter history, can one actually turn back a great people that has started on the path to freedom, can one even dream of this?"[49]

In fact, that was precisely what many of the Duma right intended. Their stubbornly defensive sentiments were well captured by I. P. Sozonovich in his response to Shingarev. Any broadening of the village franchise was, to Sozonovich, a first step toward the introduction of radical constitutionalism among the peasantry. "I look upon the volost," he argued in a rather mixed metaphor, "as a state fortress at the very heart of the nation, and I should say that I am somewhat surprised at the weakness of the Government's defense of its last stronghold. Should the volost be surrendered to the zemstvo as the authors of this legislation wish, the doom of order and perhaps even of the state itself is guaranteed."[50] Duma rightists, if not the authorities, were determined to hold the estate volost against all comers. They denounced the third element as a subversive "pseudo-intelligentsia" and the peasantry as uncultured. Jews, whose future inclusion was barely suggested in the project, were characterized as "an infection," "predators," the empire's equivalent of blacks in America, Arabs in French Algeria, or the Irish in Great Britain. Women, enfranchised by the committee, were rejected as "long of hair but short on intelligence." The polemicist N. E. Markov summarized the feelings of his fellows when he insisted, "The volost should be as it is now—estate, peasant, unaffected by unnecessary new legislation."[51]

The strength of the Duma center guaranteed that neither of these two views would prevail. The bill submitted by the MVD was essentially identical to the one reviewed by the Council on Local Affairs in the spring of 1908, retaining a modest property requirement of one-fortieth of the existing zemstvo full qualification and a three-curia electoral system. It was not, however, left unaltered by the Duma. In both the subcommittee and its parent group, left Octobrists Glebov and Golitsyn successfully challenged a number of the bill's provisions, generally with the aim of broadening the electorate.[52] After considering at least ten alternatives, the committee members added a fourth curia, but they simultaneously reduced the criterion for participation in the first from half to one-fifth of a full zemstvo qualification. The government's minimum, which translated to a mere three to six de-siatina, was dropped on the grounds that any limitation beyond simple ownership of fixed property might exclude many peasants who were taking advantage of land consolidation to set up small farms. Further, committee members voted to include women and omit direct partici-pation of wealthy landowners without election. MVD spokesmen pro-tested the changes both in committee and on the Duma floor, but they were consistently overruled by a coalition of Octobrists and leftists.[53] Apparently Cadets, Progressists, and socialists reasoned that even lim-ited reform was preferable to none.

Despite official objections, the amendments approved by the as-sembly were not fundamental. In relation to curiae, for example, the MVD representative in the subcommittee had conceded, "The Gov-ernment does not insist unconditionally on its electoral system and does not see obstacles to acceptance of a different system."[54] And on the minimum qualification, Octobrists and the ministry were pursu-ing the same goal of including Stolypin's "sober and strong," disagree-ing only over the empirical question of whether the one-fortieth land requirement would close them out.[55] As before, on the issue of the quantity or limits of participation, bureaucratic reformers and mod-erates among the public shared common assumptions. Glebov, for one, had repeatedly maintained that the leading role in the reformed volost must be reserved for "cultured" elements, and he defined the term in a very specific way. Culture, in the delegate's view, was synonymous not with education but with lifestyle; more specifically, "Culture goes hand in hand with wealth." Enlightenment was under-stood in terms of fiscal responsibility, of respect for property. "It is impossible," Glebov argued in relation to universal suffrage, "to grant persons not contributing to the self-governmental treasury the right to dispose of the funds of others." These sentiments were echoed by MVD administrative expert A. I. Lykoshin. "The more property a man holds," he informed the committee, "the greater his interest in the welfare of a given locality."[56] Despite differences in detail, Stoly-pin and most Octobrists held a common vision of the social composi-tion of the future volost and of the future rural order generally. This vision rested upon the collaboration of the landed wealthy and con-servative peasant farmers.

Where the first debate in regard to the volost resolved the question of the extent of participation, the second centered on the nature or quality of that participation. Though differences in this area were perhaps less clearly articulated, they were substantive. In the view of the MVD reformers, public cooperation in administrative matters was to be encouraged. The government program, after all, aimed specifically at a mobilization of the citizenry for active involvement in local affairs. Yet this expansion of the popular role could occur only within a framework established by the central authorities and maintained by the state bureaucracy. Participation was to be guided, monitored, directed from above. This was certainly the heart of the MVD plan for decentralization, and it ran like a red thread through the entire volost bill. The institution, as Stolypin continued to insist despite the objections of the August 1907 zemstvo congress and opposition in the Council on Local Affairs, was first and foremost an "administrative" body, performing tasks of self-government only secondarily.

This perspective was not shared by the public, at least as represented in the Duma. For the majority of the delegates, citizen involvement in government was meaningful only if autonomous, or, to use the Russian term, "self-activating" (*samodeiatel'nyi*). In the countryside, popular participation essentially meant zemstvos. And it was in the very nature of the zemstvo that deputies defined the form and content of their activity in consultation with the local electorate. This basic orientation determined the response of the Duma majority to the volost legislation, and especially to the volost's designation as a state institution. On this important issue, one in which gentry interests were not directly threatened, rightists did largely support the government. Fear of anarchy lest the volost "fortress" be surrendered to progressives overcame resentment of the civil service. But the rest of the deputies felt differently.

The challenge to the MVD conception of the volost was best formulated in the subcommittee's official report, presented to the house by Glebov. After reiterating all the reasons for reform given in the MVD project, he went on to add, "It is necessary to bring zemstvo affairs closer to the populace, to interest the populace in improving local conditions, to stimulate that independent activity, the lack of which is the primary ill of the contemporary countryside." He continued, "Reform will not only have an impact locally, but will also sharply influence government policy generally, for only the strengthening and development of self-government can create a firm foundation for the . . . present representative system." And in his explanatory comments, he spoke approvingly of the old "societal" theory of self-government in which zemstvo and town council were defined as autonomous organs of "society itself." Though Glebov ultimately rejected this approach, partially because it narrowed the jurisdiction of self-government, the societal view was reflected in the subcommittee's characterization of the volost as "a small self-governing body—a volost zemstvo, closely tied to that of the district."[57] As it emerged from committee to the Duma floor the MVD bill bore the new title of legislation not for a state administrative unit but for a "volost zemstvo."

The determination to transform the volost was evident in a substantial list of committee amendments to the government project, all of them hotly contested by representatives of the interior ministry. One such case was the decision of the subcommittee members to make a substantive structural change in the volost executive. In place of the existing headman, they substituted a full board (*uprava*) modelled after those of the district and provincial zemstvos. As Glebov explained, the collegial body would be "more authoritative." Otherwise, he predicted, volost officials would fall into "the same servile state as at present, with every local bureaucrat from the police sergeant and constable up viewing them as subordinates." Responding for the government, MVD staffer Lykoshin presented a pragmatic defense of one-man leadership as less expensive, though he could not resist adding that a board would detract from the "intensity and effectiveness of [state] supervision."[58] The appeal to frugality struck a responsive chord initially. D. A. Leonov, an Octobrist normally much concerned for zemstvo independence, proposed an amendment making the board optional for volosts with a population under ten thousand. Rightist votes helped approve the measure by a ballot of 108 to 100.[59] However, when the amendment was reconsidered in connection with the bill's final reading, subcommittee spokesmen were able to place it in broader perspective. Glebov especially stressed that collegiality was "absolutely necessary . . . as a guarantee of the independence of the executive organ in its relations with the administration."[60] The appeal to zemstvo autonomy was successful as 135 delegates, including apparently some Octobrists who reversed themselves, voted to reinstate the subcommittee version over the objection of 96 others.

As Glebov's comments indicate, what was particularly at issue in relation to the volost was the location of supervisory authority. The MVD in its project firmly asserted state bureaucratic control, generally through what it envisioned as a reformed land captaincy. The land captain was to have extensive powers, including the right to confirm volost officials and conduct inspections, though all within the limits of legality. Significantly, Duma debate on this aspect of the volost legislation was most acrimonious. Delegates of the left launched a bitter attack on the land captaincy. Shingarev had to be reprimanded by the chairman for accusing the rural bureaucrats of base cowardice, and one Trudovik was temporarily expelled for denouncing them as "nonentities and reprobates unfit to feed pigs, much less govern the people."[61] Swayed by at least a moderate sympathy for these sentiments, the Duma majority sharply reduced the captain's prerogatives, removing for instance the right to review volost elections and to oversee tax collection. Indeed, a Cadet proposal to radically alter the structure of local administrative justice by transferring all supervision of the new self-governing unit to the courts was rejected by the surprisingly narrow margin of 124 to 110.[62]

This last Cadet defeat was softened considerably by one final amendment to the volost bill. Throughout their entire reform effort, Stolypin, Gurliand, and their colleagues in the MVD adamantly rejected the liberal equation of administrative justice with review by the independent judiciary. Instead they championed the idea of using an improved variant of the existing system of provincial and district boards, collegial bodies that included public representatives but were dominated by civil servants. The Duma subcommittee naturally did not deal with the entire collegial system, but it did revise the volost project in a provocative way. Arguing that oversight of the new zemstvo was a "purely judicial" matter, Glebov and his fellows altered the composition of the provincial board. The chairmanship was taken from the governor, who was disqualified by his lack of legal training and impartiality, and transferred to the head of the regional court. The new chairman was to be joined on the board by the chairman of the provincial zemstvo executive, the vice-governor, two additional jurists, and a permanent staff member. The supervisory body would be dominated not by MVD subordinates but by popular representatives and the judiciary. Naturally, government spokesmen bitterly opposed the revision and were initially able to reverse it. However, a group of delegates led by Octobrist Leonov and Progressist Efremov appealed the matter on the Duma floor. Here the defense of "strict legality" against the "overweening influence" of the governor prevailed. The liberalized subcommittee version was accepted.[63]

Final passage of the volost legislation on 13 May 1911 was a hollow victory for Stolypin. The vote came after an all but interminable delay. In January of 1909 the premier had informed committee chairman Balashev of his hope that both the volost and settlement bills would be implemented during the spring Duma session.[64] Two years later only the first had received full consideration in the assembly, and it still required submission to the upper house of the tsarist legislature, the State Council. Moreover, the Duma delegates had made very substantive amendments to the MVD plan. As Shingarev noted during the final debate on the volost measure, the project under consideration was no longer that of the MVD but an entirely new one.[65] In an important sense, it represented a different vision of the nature of the tsarist polity. This interpretation was confirmed by editorials in Gurliand's semiofficial *Russia* attacking the legislation for its liberalism.

Indeed, by the spring of 1911 Stolypin and his subordinates seemed to be retreating from reform altogether. During the Duma's volost discussions, for instance, MVD spokesman Lykoshin signalled a new attitude on district reorganization when he defended the gentry marshal from hostile attacks. In May the interior ministry confirmed the change by producing a new district bill that left the position of the marshal intact, something Stolypin had bitterly opposed two years before.[66] The turnabout on this and other related questions did not result from the Duma's volost debate alone. Equally if not even more important in a direct political sense was the constitutional crisis provoked by yet another MVD project on local administration, a plan to introduce rural self-government in the empire's western provinces. If the protracted volost deliberations showed the dynamics of Stolypin's failure in slow motion, then the "western zemstvo affair" demonstrated them dramatically.

The details of the western zemstvo episode have been discussed at great length and can be presented here in summary fashion.[67] Though advanced socio-economically, the European extreme of the Tsarist Empire remained ethnically something of a frontier for Great Russians. A distinct majority of the population consisted of Poles, Ukrainians, White Russians, Lithuanians, and Jews. Precisely for fear of these groups, particularly the rebellious Polish nobility, Alexander II had in the 1860s opposed the establishment of zemstvos in this region. By the turn of the century, however, strong sentiment was mounting for the reversal of this decision. In 1899 Minister of Internal Affairs Goremykin formally raised the issue by presenting a reform bill. Although Nicholas II was persuaded by Witte's *Autocracy and the Zemstvo* to reject the measure, within four years a hybrid form of appointive zemstvo was introduced in six of the provinces. The idea of fully elective self-government was taken up again by Sviatopolk-Mirskii and appeared in the platforms of several political parties, including the Cadets and Octobrists. By 1906 Stolypin, too, suggested the extension, but he apparently decided to postpone the step until a general reform of local government could be completed.[68] Three years later, however, the MVD staff returned to the question and produced a draft bill introducing elective zemstvos in nine western provinces.

Stolypin's reasons for moving ahead were undoubtedly mixed. In part, the Kovno native was inspired by concern for his home provinces, the region where he held estates and had effectively begun his service career. Simultaneously, he saw in the measure a vehicle for demonstrating the validity of the principles behind the stalled general zemstvo reform.[69] Above all, however, the action was motivated by considerations of political advantage. This was reflected in the circumstances under which the MVD bill was initiated. During the spring of 1909 Stolypin and the Octobrists had suffered a severe setback from the right over the issue of control over the naval general staff.[70] This, taken with the violent debates in the recent sessions of the Council on Local Affairs, made it clear that the task of uniting even prosperous landowners and businessmen behind the government's reform effort would be more formidable than Stolypin had anticipated. A new way of appealing to moderates of the center and right had to be found if the 3 June system was to operate. The vehicle chosen for this appeal was nationalism.

Nationalist sentiment was strong in the Duma, especially among rightists. During 1909, in fact, a number of conservative delegates primarily from the western provinces had organized a Nationalist group to press their views.[71] In May 1909, as part of this upsurge of nationalist opinion, some conservatives petitioned the government for a change in the State Council's electoral procedure for the western provinces, where the absence of zemstvos left the choice of councillors largely in the hands of the Polish nobility. Stolypin soon saw in the idea a way of winning broader political support. After some hesitation and consultation with the Octobrist Duma leadership, he announced plans to resolve the problem through territorial extension of the zemstvo.

The utility of the western zemstvo as a tool for a new "nationalist" reformism was evident in the legislation drafted by the MVD. The bill was based on the 1890 zemstvo statute, but with two significant innovations. First, the western zemstvos were to be all-estate, their electoral system not unlike that employed in the ministry's other local reform plans. Second, in an obvious attempt to appeal to rightist sentiment, the authors included special provisions to insure the predominance of ethnic Russians. Electors would be divided into two national curiae, one Russian and the other Polish. Distribution of seats would be based not on property, which would favor the Polish nobility, but on a mixed system of land and population. Moreover, the legislation reserved a majority of the key executive positions in the zemstvo for Russians. The numerous Jewish population would be excluded from participation altogether. In sum, the draft bill was a perfect blend of nationalism and moderate reform. An attack was made on gentry corporatism, but not in terms of democratization. Rather, reform aimed at bolstering the position of the peasantry in the name of the Russian state ideal.

Duma debate on the admittedly complex piece of legislation was extremely convoluted. The self-government committee at one point found itself in the embarrassing position of voting down its own amendments. The measure passed on the ballots of Octobrists and rightists, though not without change. For example, the delegates halved the proposed property qualification and increased the number of electoral curiae from two to three. The most substantial revisions, however, involved a weakening of the provisions for Great Russian hegemony. The Russian zemstvo chairmanship, for instance, was dropped.[72] Nevertheless, the legislation in its final form was acceptable to the government and was submitted to the State Council.

This second chamber of the tsarist legislature shared equal rights with the Duma, but its composition was drastically different. In order to provide a check on potential radicalism in the lower house, the drafters of the 1906 constitution had mandated that half the council membership be appointed by the monarch and the remainder elected by generally "safe" institutions like gentry assemblies, zemstvos, clergy, and business organizations. Consequently, the body included large numbers of nobles and bureaucrats, including state senators, jealous ex-ministers, and retired military men. Factions of the center and right predominated, with only token representation of Cadets and none of socialists.[73]

Despite this unpromising political complexion, Stolypin assumed that the western zemstvo bill would pass. He undoubtedly felt he could count on a number of centrist delegates, led by his brother-in-law A. B. Neidgart. And there was always the influence of Nicholas II. Given the council's make-up, the monarch's personal recommendation, to be prompted in this case by his chief minister, carried much weight. But Stolypin's confidence was ill placed. The western zemstvo measure provoked broad opposition in the council. Some delegates rejected the notion of separate national curiae as exacerbating ethnic animosities in the area. Others apparently feared the possible democratization of zemstvo affairs. Finally, individual delegates saw in the bill, regardless of its virtues or faults, a chance to assault the premier himself. As it turned out, intrigue determined the result of State Council deliberations in March 1911. Rightist leaders V. F. Trepov and P. N. Durnovo confidentially persuaded Nicholas II to allow deputies to vote their conscience, and the key provision of the project—national curiae—was voted down ninety-two to sixty-eight.[74]

The reversal stunned Stolypin. Overwhelmed by frustration, he determined to lash out at his enemies and break their resistance once and for all. By threatening resignation he coerced the reluctant tsar to close both houses of the legislature, implement the Duma bill under emergency authority, and banish the scheming Trepov and Durnovo from Saint Petersburg.[75] Stolypin thus turned the defeat into a formal victory, but from the political standpoint his behavior was, as Councillor Naumov put it, frankly suicidal.[76] Stolypin himself was aware that Nicholas II would probably never forgive the humiliation. Moreover, the act called down a storm of protest in both the State Council and Duma. Delegates of the lower house in particular denounced the violation of normal legislative procedure, even if intended to implement their own bill. Cadets attacked the government for its failure to rely upon the elected representatives of the populace, and rightists were equally strident in criticizing the head of the state bureaucracy for encroaching upon the monarch's authority. Even Octobrists, the government's supposed allies, went over to the opposition—a shift symbolized by Guchkov's enraged resignation as Duma president.[77] In April, delegates of all factions turned their backs upon Stolypin's plea for support, passing a formal vote of censure by the wide margin of 203 to 82. This crushing defeat marked the effective end of his ministry. Though still formally premier, his performance in office was listless and apathetic. English visitor Bernard Pares, for example, found Stolypin to be unusually lethargic in an interview given in this period, and there were rumors that he suffered from a progressive illness.[78] The final act, Stolypin's assassination in September 1911 at the Kiev Opera House, was, in fact, politically anticlimactic.

It is not surprising given the importance of the crisis in Stolypin's ultimate fall that many questions have been raised about the politics of the western zemstvo affair. What were the real motives of the measure's opponents? Were the rightist delegates of the State Council, for example, sincere in their concern over the bill's potential impact on ethnic rivalries within the empire? Was their opposition inspired instead by fear of democratization? Or were jealous former ministers like Durnovo simply taking advantage of an opportunity to make an essentially personal attack on a rival? Similarly, what was the basic motivation for Stolypin's aggressive action in the affair? Was his behavior part of a general if ill-conceived plan to cripple what he saw as conservative obstructionism, or was he simply acting out of personal pique and physical exhaustion with the burdens of government? Finally, there is the crucial issue of the essential nature of the crisis itself. Was the western zemstvo episode accidental, the product of individual circumstances that might well have been avoided? Or was it symptomatic of a broad malaise in the 3 June system?

These questions are more easily answered when the affair is placed within the context of Stolypin's struggle for local reform generally. Viewed from this perspective, for instance, sources of opposition in the State Council become clearer. While aspects of the Duma project may well have provoked particular hostility, the delegates' resistance to the bill is entirely consistent with the critique of reform developed by the gentry right, not during the deliberations over the western provinces, but five years earlier. Memoirs of individuals like Naumov demonstrate that the concerns of conservative councillors were very much in tune with those expressed, say, in 1908 during debate over the MVD plan for district reform.[79] The same can be said of Stolypin. Despite the obvious impact of personal factors, including ill health and anger at the rather duplicitous wavering of the tsar, the statesman's actions were also consistent with his general conception of the relationship between the central authorities and the public. In their legislative projects on local administration, MVD reformers had admitted the need for active participation by the citizenry, especially through the institutions of self-government. Yet the state bureaucracy was to retain ultimate supervision locally. The provincial governor, for example, would possess the right not only to veto measures of the zemstvos and town councils, but also to suspend them temporarily and act in their stead. Stolypin's approach to the national legislature was identical. He considered public participation through the Duma and State Council essential, but not to the point of blocking the effective operation of the state. In such cases the two houses could be treated as zemstvos writ large, temporarily bypassed in the name of the general good as defined by the leading spokesmen of the state bureaucracy.

This suggests a final conclusion on the 3 June system as a whole. Historians have differed radically in their assessments of tsarism's inability to produce effective reform beyond the Stolypin agrarian program. Some scholars, particularly in the West, have chosen to emphasize specific personal or political factors. Stolypin's death, the tsar's narrow conservatism, and the Octobrists' lack of cohesion are prominent examples.[80] Soviet scholars, conversely, have focused their analysis on deeper social antagonisms within the empire. Avrekh, in a somewhat idiosyncratic approach, has stressed the ongoing fear among ruling elites of what he sees as a "revolutionary" situation in

Russian society. Others have followed a more conventional Marxist-Leninist path, emphasizing the resistance of feudal elements to "objectively bourgeois" policies.[81]

All these interpretations accurately identify significant obstacles to reform, but at the same time they remain inadequate. In the case of the western zemstvos, for example, the tsar was apparently willing to guarantee passage of the rejected project should it be resubmitted to the State Council. And it is certainly possible to imagine a firm coalition between Stolypin and moderates like the Octobrists challenging and overcoming rightist opposition to this and other reforms. Yet it was precisely the inability of the chief parties involved to create such a coalition, to establish effective collaboration, that was at the root of the problem. Stolypin, like Pleve and even Witte before him, operated on the basis of a conception of government that was largely unacceptable not only to radicals of the left and right but to moderates among the educated public as well. The difference here was ultimately neither narrowly political nor broadly social in the Marxist sense, though these elements were present. Rather, it was ideological, relating to fundamental perceptions of the relationship between state authority and society. The gulf separating would-be reformers within and outside the government was evident as early as 1908 in the lack of response for the MVD local reform among the delegates of the supposedly well-inclined Council on Local Affairs. The Octobrist leader Guchkov was more accurate than he knew when he said, retrospectively, "In essence, Stolypin died politically long before his physical death."[82]

Police Reorganization: The Narrowing of Reform

Stolypin is traditionally described as tsarism's last great statesman, and certainly his immediate successors represent no challenge to this claim. Finance Minister Kokovtsov assumed the first and formally more elevated of Stolypin's posts, the chairmanship of the Council of Ministers. Kokovtsov had been appointed to head the Ministry of Finance twice, once in 1904 and again following the Revolution of 1905. He had guided his staff capably and had shown at least some awareness of the need for reform within the empire. Yet his outlook was a narrow one in which innovations were measured almost solely in terms of cost to the treasury. As one colleague put it, he was "moderate, exact, and conscientious," but also "pettifogging" and "without initiative."[83] Moreover, although he was adept at defending the interests of the Ministry of Finance against the claims of other branches of government, the new chairman lacked the political acumen to dominate or even coordinate his own cabinet. Kokovtsov himself later conceded that the behavior of his fellow ministers "clearly demonstrated my isolation and indeed full helplessness."[84]

The situation in regard to the second vacancy created by the assassination was somewhat different. Initially, the Ministry of Internal Affairs was left in the hands of Stolypin's assistant, A. A. Makarov. In December 1912, however, Nicholas II named Chernigov Governor N. A. Maklakov to replace the ineffectual Makarov. Like Stolypin, the new head of the MVD was young, a relative newcomer to the capital, and an activist—to the point even of visiting Saint Petersburg police stations at night to inspect conditions directly. Unlike Stolypin, he was little interested in broad political reform. An avowed sympathizer of the monarchist Union of the Russian People, Maklakov adamantly opposed any concession which might increase popular participation or further weaken autocratic authority. He encouraged Nicholas II in his not too secret desire to dissolve the Duma and replace it with a merely consultative body.[85]

The drastic contrast between Stolypin and Maklakov was naturally reflected in MVD policy in the area of local administration. The work of the Council on Local Affairs had continued uninterrupted since 1908, but it now effectively ground to a halt as officials with even the slightest inclinations toward liberalism were purged from their posts. Particularly debilitating was the replacement of the council's well-respected executive, M. V. Islavin, by Maklakov's Chernigov subordinate, P. V. Skarzhinskii.[86] Simultaneously, the ministry quickened its retreat from its earlier reform initiative. In March 1913, for example, the settlement bill was withdrawn from the Duma, and the provincial reform project was, in the words of one informed observer, left "in blissful repose."[87] Perhaps most striking of all, however, was the MVD's treatment of the legislation on the volost.

In accord with normal procedure, the volost reform approved by the Duma was passed on to the State Council for consideration. Here the bill remained in committee almost three years. It reached the floor for full debate only in May 1914 and then in seriously amended form.[88] Despite the delay, supporters of the measure in the council presented a vigorous argument on behalf of their version of the new volost, "a quiet, conservative local unit." Count D. A. Olsuf'ev, a rightist with no liberal sympathies, put the matter in its broadest terms. Distinguishing between "open-eyed" and "blind" conservatism, the speaker argued that the traditional patriarchal order in the countryside was dead and gone. In the present conjuncture, as he put it, well-considered reform was the only "escape from our political dead-alley." "It seems to me," he concluded, "that our new state structure... can function only under conditions of mutual concession, mutual agreement, for otherwise the machine will grind to a halt."[89]

Despite the pleas of Olsuf'ev and others, the council refused by a vote of seventy-seven to seventy-two so much as to discuss the bill. Even a suggestion that the government be asked to draft a new project was withdrawn after short debate. In part the defeat of volost reform reflected the fundamental conservatism of the upper house. Though opponents of the measure pointed to a number of technical problems in the proposal, these objections were, in Olsuf'ev's words, merely "window dressing." At root was a fear that reform might shift predominance in the countryside away from the first estate and at the same time open the gates to further liberal legislation. Council leader Durnovo for one insisted that the bill would give power to "those very peasants who but eight years ago pillaged and burned estates," and rightist A. A. Arsen'ev denounced the "assault under the cover of the zemstvo on the estate nature of our government."[90] The corporatist sentiments of the rightist nobility were no weaker when challenged in 1914 than they had been in the wake of revolution in 1905.

Yet as the closeness of the ballot suggests, the volost project might well have been approved had it not been for the MVD's attitude. Initially, while Makarov held office, ministry spokesmen showed continued interest in the measure. This ceased with Maklakov's appointment. When the amended bill was debated by the full State Council, no MVD representative appeared to defend it. Instead, Maklakov chose to communicate informally his opposition in principle to volost reform and thus, in the opinion of State Councillor Gurko at least, seal its fate. Goremykin, who in 1914 had replaced Kokovtsov as chairman of the Council of Ministers, was apparently indifferent to the entire affair.[91]

The abandonment of the volost bill indicated unequivocally that the interior ministry had moved away from any attempt to redefine the nature of popular participation in local administration. The process of questioning the existing estate system, which had begun under Pleve and accelerated in 1905, was brought to an end. This did not mean, however, that the MVD assumed a passive stance in regard to the shortcomings of the local apparatus. Instead, Maklakov turned his staff's attention to an area closer to his own personal concern as an ex-governor charged with the task of combating rebellion directly—the reorganization of the tsarist police.

THE DEBATE OVER REFORM, 1908-1914

Efforts to improve the empire's law enforcement agencies had started a full decade earlier. In 1903 the government had adopted Pleve's plan of abandoning the traditional reliance upon elected village patrolmen in the countryside in favor of the creation of a state police force, the guard. Yet before the new body could be fully deployed this modest start at reorganization was overwhelmed by revolution. In the face of massive popular hostility the tsarist police force all but collapsed, and only the military could restore order. Already in 1904 some 55,525 soldiers were used to assist in the task of containing unrest, and during the following year the total reached the equivalent of 3,398,361.[92] In searching for the causes of the catastrophe, the central authorities were quick to turn to police deficiencies. The dominant sentiments circulating in Saint Petersburg offices in this regard were best captured in the report of a "Special Conference" created to review the imperial system of emergency legislation.

Ever since Alexander II's assassination in 1881 the tsarist government had possessed "temporarily" the statutory power to declare any area in the empire under a variety of extraordinary regulations.[93] Depending upon the type of emergency, these gave local officials extensive authority for otherwise arbitrary acts, such as forbidding public or private gatherings, suspending periodicals, and making arrests without warrants. In his 12 December 1904 Manifesto the tsar had bowed to pressure and promised to establish a commission to carry out a review of the system. As a result of the government's unwillingness to allow any potential liberals to participate in this sensitive work touching upon state security, the composition of the group was conservative in the extreme. The chairman, Count A. P. Ignat'ev, was a former officer and governor general whose right-wing sympathies made him a focal point of opposition to Witte within the state bureaucracy and ultimately led to his assassination in 1906.[94] Despite the unquestioned loyalty of the conferees, however, their report was a scathing critique of the tsarist police. Arguing that the inadequacy of the administrative apparatus was a prime reason for the widespread abuse of official emergency powers, they presented an impressive list of police shortcomings. The force, they insisted, was too small, with recent additions like the guard "far from meeting pressing needs."[95] The average patrolman was characterized as miserably qualified as a result of poor pay and the nearly total absence of training. Overall efficient operation of the force was hampered both by severe friction between police and judicial officials and among the police themselves. Relations between the regular force and the separate political police made up of *okhrana* and gendarmes were described as particularly bad, often to the point of open hostility. Moreover, Ignat'ev and his colleagues argued that all police were seriously overburdened, a condition exacerbated by "an almost complete absence of properly organized social welfare" in the empire.[96]

Finally, in perhaps their most perceptive insight, the conferees noted that in their relationship with the populace the tsarist police were caught in what might best be called a vicious circle of lawlessness. Malfunctioning of the administrative system, they maintained, forced local civil servants to resort arbitrarily to emergency powers. The reckless use of this extralegal authority, while perhaps resolving immediate difficulties, in the long run undermined the citizenry's respect for law and engendered both oppositional sentiment and outright criminal activity. This in turn drove the embattled officials to impose more repressive and capricious regulations, thus repeating the cycle.[97]

This indictment was accurate, and it is not surprising that the government responded to it immediately. Throughout 1905 Witte and Durnovo struggled to implement measures that would at least hold law enforcement agencies together until the storm of unrest had subsided. At the time of the outbreak of revolution, for example, the state guard had only been introduced in eighteen of the intended forty-six provinces. Now the authorities rushed to complete the process, deploying the guardsmen in mounted squadrons to combat peasant rebellion. A parallel effort was made to beef up urban police complements, though on a largely ad hoc basis. Finally, in January 1906 the Council of Ministers approved legislation raising outdated police salaries by an average of 25 percent.[98]

Expensive though these steps may have been, they remained only stopgaps. In a sense, the tsarist ministers were battling the results of almost half a century of neglect. Basic pay scales and staff complements had been set in the 1860s, with only individual improvements thereafter. Moreover, the tasks assigned to the police in every area of administration had ballooned as the empire's socio-economic development quickened. The extremes to which difficulties could run were startling. In the case of the Estonian port of Revel, for example, a special effort was made initially to keep pace with change. But between 1881 and 1913 the municipal population expanded from fifty thousand to one hundred twenty-three thousand and prices rose rapidly. Apartment rents doubled between 1908 and 1913 alone. Yet after 1881 neither police pay nor staff in the city had increased substantially. In a situation in which the average patrolman received lower wages than an unskilled worker, the local governor was unable to fill vacancies in the force. He had to resort to the technically illegal transfer of guardsmen from surrounding rural areas in order to keep the peace.[99] Problems of this magnitude were not limited to large centers. Belaia Tserkov in Kiev Province had grown from a village to a booming town of forty-three thousand, yet its police force remained at twenty.[100] Even in the capital the outlook was not terribly promising. Despite a determination to bring the ratio of patrolmen to inhabitants up to an ideal level of one to four hundred, in 1906 there remained a shortfall of almost one thousand recruits.[101]

The general intensification of MVD reform activity that came with Stolypin's appointment extended to the area of law enforcement as well. For example, the MVD drafted legislation to introduce specialization into investigative work through the establishment of detective departments in eighty-nine major cities. The bill was approved by the Third Duma in July 1908. In a similar vein, the Department of Police initiated publication of its weekly journal, the *Police Messenger,* to encourage the exchange of useful information and the development of professionalism among Russian law enforcement agencies. On a more punitive note, the central government launched a number of inspections to examine the state of the police apparatus in the wake of revolution and to investigate charges of malfeasance. Several cases of glaring corruption and misuse of administrative authority were uncovered. Most notoriously, Senator N. P. Garin discovered abuses in the Moscow force ranging from systematic extortion of local residents to a misappropriation of funds that caused a 476-man shortfall in the complement of patrolmen.[102] Taken together with the experience of 1905, the inspections spurred the MVD to attempt a full reorganization of the police. Stolypin assigned this task in 1906 to a special commission under the chairmanship of his assistant minister and Saratov colleague, Makarov. The group began work under the assumption, as Makarov himself put it, that the need for reform "is so obvious as not to require proof."[103]

The consensus that the tsarist law enforcement system suffered from severe deficiencies did not mean there was any agreement on methods for improvement. In fact, given the central role of the police in the governmental apparatus, it is not surprising that the sharp differences in perspective that characterized the debate over local reform generally would apply here as well. The liberal outlook was best expressed in a striking thesis written, ironically, by Lopukhin, the man who had headed the police under Pleve. The ex-chief depicted the force as a composite of confusion, corruption, incompetence, and despotism. At the root of these evils, in his estimation, was a fundamental misconception of the nature of the state—the central government was perceived to be independent of the rest of society, standing over and above the interests of the populace. In this vision, Lopukhin argued, the police ultimately were reduced to the role of defending the autocracy against any social organization that might threaten its freedom of action. Consequently, the force had to be structured to avoid the slightest hint of responsibility to the citizenry. Inspection and supervision were left entirely in the hands of the central authorities, with no real input by the courts or public. The institutions of self-government were denied the right to establish their own enforcement agencies, thus maintaining the state's monopoly over effective executive power. The result, Lopukhin argued, was to alienate the populace not merely from police institutions themselves but from the very notion of respect for law. As he concluded, "The contemporary anarchy ruling in Russia is the direct consequence of that role played by the police in national life."[104]

This analysis, with its notion of a dichotomy between state and society and its critique of centralization, was drawn directly from the zemstvo movement's ideology. So, too, were Lopukhin's recommendations. If the basic ill was the irresponsibility of the force, the cure was to transfer law enforcement to "society itself." The bulk of police functions were to be performed by zemstvos and town councils under judicial supervision.[105] This demand for the democratization of the police through their subordination to self-government and the courts was shared by others, including not only liberal and socialist politicians but also most publicists. In its review of newspaper commentary for 1908 and 1909, the Department of Police itself was forced to admit overwhelming opinion favoring a reform that would inculcate in the police a stronger sense of legality and responsibility to the citizenry.[106] As the editors of the *Contemporary Word* put it, the tsarist police system would be properly organized "only when there ... [existed] within the country a legal, and not police, order."[107]

The Makarov Commission was drawn very heavily from among the security agencies themselves. Consequently, the approach taken by the renegade Lopukhin had very little appeal. The Department of Police had been a stronghold of monarchism in 1905 and remained so thereafter. Sentiments in support of the Union of the Russian People and by implication its pogrom activities continued despite efforts by Stolypin himself to restrain them.[108] Indeed, his control over the police bureaucracy was questionable at best. Consider the case of P. G. Kurlov, who figured prominently in the Makarov group's deliberations. This right-winger had been appointed as MVD assistant minister in charge of police over Stolypin's strenuous objections. And in 1911 he was to be implicated in his superior's assassination.[109] Not surprisingly, therefore, Makarov and his fellows completely ignored the possibility of any liberalization of police affairs. Instead they turned to the competing reform idea pioneered by Pleve and revived by Stolypin, administrative decentralization.

The possibility of applying the idea of decentralization to the police had been suggested earlier. In 1905 the Ignat'ev Commission had sent MVD staffer V. E. Frish abroad to study police affairs elsewhere in Europe. Great Britain, the nation whose system of law enforcement Lopukhin most admired, was not included on the itinerary. The new police expert summarized results of his tour in several reports, one of them a comprehensive scheme for the reorganization of the tsarist police. Frish began rather unoriginally by calling for a substantial increase in the numbers and pay of police. To this understandable concern for quantitative improvement he added recommendations relating to the quality of the force—for example, he suggested that specialization be encouraged through the creation of a cadre of judicial police, or "police commissars," who would be responsible only for investigating crimes. These new agents were to be given special "punitive" (*karatel'nyi*) authority to impose fines and make short-term arrests for petty deviance. Elsewhere, he pressed for steps to militarize the regular police both in training and deployment. He suggested, for instance, that the rank and file might be drilled and inspected by regular army officers or formed into "brigades" and "detachments."[110] Indeed, in order to weaken ingrained hostility among the public, the reformer went so far as to insist on completely new uniforms for patrolmen. "The less the new organization resembles the old," he noted, "the more sympathy it will evoke among the populace."[111]

Substantial though these recommendations were, Frish did not consider them the heart of the matter. The basic difficulty facing the police system, he argued, was the mass of duties performed by the force. As his report read, "In the last analysis acting on everything and for everyone, they are unable to perform their central function—defending public security and tranquility. Here is the primary reason why police in Russia do not possess the respect and popularity present in other western European states, and especially England."[112] What the author had in mind was what might be called the "service functions" of the police. These included unpopular tasks such as tax collection, enforcement of the peasants' corvée-like duty to repair roads, and supervision of the carting of sewage.

To deal with this problem Frish proposed that police activities in socio-economic fields be transferred to other institutions. He called for the establishment of new executive organs under self-government—a zemstvo and a municipal police force—to carry these burdens. Frish's plan was in no sense the equivalent of Lopukhin's. The self-governmental enforcement agencies projected by the loyal bureaucrat were to be under the strict inspection of the state police, not independent. In fact, Frish predicted that devolution of service tasks to the new bodies would strengthen rather than weaken the position of the central authorities by improving the supervisory capabilities of the tsarist police. "The goal of the transfer of a significant number of contemporary police functions to the public institutions," he maintained, "is to heighten the authority and prestige of the state organs."[113]

The program outlined by Frish, then, was essentially the same as that being applied by Stolypin and the MVD to the entire administrative apparatus. Indeed, it included not only the fundamental concept of decentralization, but also the ministry's prerequisite of "unity." Whereas in regard to the province and district this had meant the concentration of power in the hands of the governor or commander, in relation to the police it translated into subordination of all law enforcement agencies to gubernatorial control. Frish urged that such bodies as the river and port police or detective departments be placed under the governor. Much more important, he extended the demand for unification to the hitherto autonomous gendarmes and *okhrana*. Though theoretically under the direction of the Department of Police, both had operated largely at will in the provinces. The gendarmes especially, with their own general staff and tradition of personal loyalty to the monarch, had pursued their tasks with scant regard for local authorities.[114] This was now to end. Molding police into a single hierarchical body would open the door for decentralization here too.

Although the Frish project was originally intended for the Ignat'ev Commission, Makarov and his colleagues appear to have used the document as a starting point for their own work. Given the ambitious, not to say utopian, tone of the scheme to totally remake the image and reality of the tsarist police, it is not surprising that many of its individual provisions were altered or abandoned by the Makarov group, even though Frish himself took an active part in the deliberations. In the case of recruiting, for instance, Frish had argued that candidates should meet stiff educational requirements. The commissioners, however, gave up any insistence upon formal schooling as hopeless, settling instead on simple literacy as adequate for patrolmen.[115] Similarly, proposals for a separate corps of specialized judicial police or for new uniforms were rejected as too costly.

Nevertheless, most of the major recommendations presented by Frish found their way into the commission's final plan for police reorganization. The call for a larger and better paid force certainly struck a responsive chord. In regard to numbers, the commissioners envisioned a five-thousand-man increase in the rural guard, strenuous efforts to bring urban complements up to the ideal ratio of one patrolman for every four hundred inhabitants, and substantial increments in the police officer corps. Roughly speaking, the staff of constables, assistant constables, and inspectors would be doubled and the staff of patrolmen increased by one-quarter. Suggested salary hikes were equally ambitious. Average pay for patrolmen and guardsmen was projected at more than double existing rates in most cases, and some constables and sergeants stood to gain considerably more.[116] At the same time that the force was to be strengthened materially, it was also to receive additional legal authority. Specifically, the commission recommended the introduction of "punitive orders," or the right of patrolmen to impose fines or short-term arrest for petty violations without recourse to the courts.[117] This notion, championed by the Ignat'ev Commission, Frish, and the Department of Police through the *Police Messenger,* was intended to rationalize and legitimize police operations by giving legal sanction to the hitherto arbitrary and often illegal application of coercive measures by officers. It was hoped that the formal regulation of what had been personal discretion through specific rules would help reconcile the populace to the police without sacrificing the power of the state bureaucracy.

Though these individual steps were important, Makarov and his colleagues also followed Frish in placing their primary hopes on the beneficial effect of yet another step, the devolution of police service activities. Numerous police functions were now to be transferred to other administrative bodies. A random but by no means exhaustive sample of duties included by the commission would include delivery of subpoenas and other legal documents, participation in tax collection, enforcement of sanitation and building codes, supervision of burials and cemeteries, prevention of epidemics and control of harmful insects (especially locusts), supervision of trade and verification of weights and measures, care of abandoned children and drunkards, fire prevention, inspection of roads and bridges, maintaining vital statistics (births, deaths, marriages) for Old Believers, and supervision of the imperial system of legalized prostitution. Indeed, the entire list would provide, as one police chief later put it, "the text for an interesting cultural-historical monograph."[118]

The massive devolution of service tasks was a simple enough remedy, but it embodied a significant redefinition of the police concept. Tsarist peace officers had been viewed previously as general administrators, an anachronistic characterization that had its roots in seventeenth-century Europe. Now the authorities were adopting a new, essentially modern definition of police as primarily crime fighters. The turn to specialization through drastic reduction of police jurisdiction also involved another basic change in policy. A good many of the duties to be removed from the police could be transferred to the other branches of the state bureaucracy or dropped altogether. Yet a substantial portion would have to be performed by the institutions of self-government, which in turn would necessarily require executive organs of their own. The Makarov commissioners accepted the inevitability of this step, but they vehemently rejected the slightest implication of public control over the police function. Police Director M. I. Trusevich, for example, in a 1908 report to the commission, vetoed the creation in Russia of independent municipal forces on the Western model. In his view, the immaturity of the citizenry, or "insufficiency of cultured elements" within the empire, ruled out popular direction of law enforcement. Subordination of the police to self-government, he insisted, would introduce into their activity "not only party politics in the broad sense, but also all kinds of currents in local life which create discord and petty squabbles."[119] The commission's final provisions for zemstvo and municipal executive agencies reflected this thinking. The new staffs were to be under the constant supervision of the state police, who retained the right to give directions and if necessary act in their stead. Indeed, the self-governmental employees were explicitly not to be called "police" and were not to wear uniforms resembling those of patrolmen.[120]

Despite extensive safeguards, there was concern in the commission that reform might imply a dangerous widening of popular influence and a converse weakening of the state. One participant, for example, suggested that the reorganization might have the "secret goal" of providing a concession to the liberation movement. Trusevich's response was indicative. The commission's task, he argued, was "not at all to adapt the organization of the police to various types of freedom or to create anything resembling western municipal police," but "to create a strong and well-organized state police loyal to the Throne and free from existing shortcomings."[121] In this, the police reformers were acting within the same framework as Stolypin and the rest of the

MVD staff. Though more defensive in approach—no surprise, given their goal of internal security and their rightist sentiments—they worked toward a decentralization of administrative activity that would enhance the authority of the state bureaucracy.

Given the congruence of the Makarov project with other MVD local reform legislation already approved by the Council of Ministers, Stolypin clearly expected the report to move rapidly to the State Duma for consideration.[122] In actuality, dissension over two crucial issues drastically slowed progress. As with provincial and district reform, police reorganization was predicated upon the unification of the force locally under one-man control. Early in the Makarov Commission work, a subcommittee chaired by Trusevich proposed the establishment of an assistant governorship for police affairs to perform this role. The idea provoked violent opposition, for it involved subordination of the local gendarmes to the new functionary. The gendarmes had previously operated autonomously under their own provincial commander. Corps commandant Major General F. F. von Traube was particularly outspoken in denouncing this "radical break" with tradition, which he believed would "completely destroy the corps." Harkening back to the era of Nicholas I, when the gendarmes had been established as a personal instrument of the tsar, Traube and others insisted that independence was essential as a guarantee of both the corps' loyalty and its effectiveness as a watchdog over the regular administration.[123] Representatives of the Ministry of Justice, on the other side, were equally strident in demanding that the capricious gendarmes be bridled lest, as Senator A. A. Glishinskii put it, the entire reform "come to nothing."[124] Admitting that combining the regular and political police was something like mixing butter and water, Trusevich's group tried to find an acceptable compromise. The original plan was retained over the objections of Traube, but as a concession to the gendarmes the new assistant governor was made subordinate to the corps in matters under its jurisdiction.[125]

Ironically, this assertion of unified control over the gendarmes was hotly contested by its intended benefactors, the governors. In a special session held in December 1908 to review the Trusevich recommendations, a large number of provincial chiefs spoke out against the idea of an assistant governor. Fearing a case of the tail wagging the dog, they contended that the partial subordination of the new dignitary to the gendarmes would turn him into a tool for subverting the governor's authority.[126] As it turned out, these objections were ultimately ignored by the Makarov Commission, which left Trusevich's plan intact. Serious reservations about the issue remained, however.

When the Council of Ministers convened to review the entire reform in 1911, Minister of Finance Kokovtsov tried again to remove gendarmes influence over the assistancy.[127] Although this attempt at change also failed, many officials within the state bureaucracy continued to press for revision.

The difficulty over the gendarmes stemmed from the irreconcilability of two fixed preconditions of any police reform. The corps was to be retained as an essentially autonomous entity, yet simultaneously the entire local police force was to be unified under a single commander. A similar conflict of imperatives applied to another crucial aspect of reorganization. Revolution and social change within the empire had made a drastic improvement of the police system a necessity but at the same time had placed a tremendous burden upon the imperial treasury that was to support it. The first objections to the Makarov project on the grounds of expense, interestingly enough, came from within the MVD. Under existing law, Russian municipalities bore a substantial financial burden in regard to police, providing local forces with offices, housing, supplies, and arms. For large cities like Moscow and Saint Petersburg the cost was generally an irritating but manageable 4 or 5 percent of the municipal budget, but for smaller centers it could be much greater. According to MVD statistics, 123 town councils devoted between 10 and 21 percent of their revenues to the police; 63 others devoted over 22 percent to that purpose.[128]

Now the Makarov group proposed an increase in the urban contribution from some four million rubles to as much as nineteen million, though with a 15 percent limit for any individual municipal budget.[129] The plan drew vocal opposition from the staff of the Main Administration for Local Affairs. Noting that the empire's cities were already collectively in arrears for some nine million rubles—none of which the government expected to recover—spokesmen for this MVD department insisted that at a minimum the municipalities be provided with a new tax on real estate to defray the added expense. The commissioners refused to become involved in such a complication, however, and rejected any amendments of a financial nature. Although the administration's chief Gerbel himself wrote a personal appeal to Makarov on the matter in April 1909, it was to no avail.[130]

A second budgetary critique of reform was not so easily overridden. After assuming office in the wake of revolution, Minister of Finance Kokovtsov had adopted a conservative fiscal policy aimed at avoiding deficits and borrowing by cutting waste. He was appalled at the enormity of the bill for the Makarov reorganization. The battle between the finance and interior ministries, traditional rivals, began on a sour note for the MVD. Makarov's staff had estimated that the proposed reform would raise total outlay for the police from a present 35 million rubles to 58 million, with most of the increase borne by self-government. A closer analysis by Ministry of Finance experts placed the cost of the plan at almost 113 million rubles, not less than 92 million of which would be at state expense.[131] Angered at what appeared to be a colossal attempt at deception by police authorities, Kokovtsov and his subordinates attacked almost every provision of the Makarov report that entailed an expenditure, and indeed a number that did not. As a result of selective leaking by officials on both sides, the controversy spilled over into the press. The editors of the *Russian Word*, for example, admitted that the Makarov error was "pathetic," yet insisted that Kokovtsov's frugality threatened to wreck the state. Writers of the rightist *Citizen* went even further, accusing the finance staff of behaving "like yids [*zhidy*] at the Alexandrovskii market." On the other side, moderate and leftist journals applauded the finance critique, lauding what appeared to be the "complete collapse" of the project.[132]

As it turned out, the Makarov plan was far from dead. With Stolypin's firm support, the proponents of reform won most of their major points in a Council of Ministers session held 12 July 1911.[133] Adroitly parrying the council decision, Kokovtsov was able to carry the dispute into a special commission charged with working out final financial details. So successful were the finance ministry's representatives in slowing the progress of reform in this arena that by the spring of 1912 Makarov—now minister in place of the fallen Stolypin—was forced to accept sharply reduced police salaries in order to break the deadlock.[134] Worse yet, by year's end the project still was not ready for submission to the Duma.

It was in this situation that the tsar named Maklakov to head the MVD. The new minister demonstrated a pronounced interest in police reform from the start. Within two days of his appointment he began a thorough examination of the Makarov Commission's materials and soon initiated an effort to resolve outstanding difficulties. For example, in February 1913 the MVD convened a conference of senior police officials and governors to review the proposed legislation. The group made a number of minor amendments but focused its attention primarily on the gendarmes. Maklakov was no sympathizer of the corps, and in fact had already named V. F. Dzhunkovskii as assistant minister with the specific task of reducing gendarmes participation in political investigation.[135] He now responded favorably to gubernatorial misgivings about the plan to make the new assistant governor a subordinate of both his provincial chief and the gendarmes staff in Saint Petersburg. Fearing that the assistancy opened the door to gendarmes interference in regular police matters, Maklakov and the other participants in the February conference voted unanimously to drop the office altogether.[136] This essentially cleared the way for forward movement of the legislation. After a final unsuccessful attempt to wring financial concessions from the stingy Kokovtsov in May 1913, the project was ready for the Duma.

Once the 3 June 1907 electoral revision had sharply reduced oppositional representation, the Duma had been receptive to plans for improving tsarist law enforcement. Between 1907 and 1912 the assembly had approved over forty-five hundred new positions, with thirty-seven hundred of these in urban centers.[137] This reflected a broad concern among the educated public over the growth of criminality in the empire. This worry initially centered around revolutionary violence, but gradually shifted to petty deviance, or "hooliganism" (khuliganstvo).[138] In response to a 1912 government inquiry on crime in the countryside, for example, a large majority of district zemstvos and governors described the situation as serious and called for both repressive and ameliorative measures to restore order.[139] Gentry circles were most outspoken, with delegates at the 1912 Congress of the United Nobility characterizing hooliganism as "paralyzing the proper course of village life" and threatening the very existence of noble landholding.[140] Even some liberals and socialists, though more restrained in their views, were willing to admit the problem. The depth of concern was obvious in Duma proceedings. In the spring of 1913, to cite one case, an Octobrist motion to battle hooliganism by increasing punishments for petty offenses and by giving land captains greater punitive authority was referred to the government by a three-to-one margin.[141]

Despite these positive signs, the police legislation was likely to provoke opposition in the Duma. From a fiscal standpoint, it is important to note that many of the assembly's earlier increases in police complements were to be supported by special state subsidies, not by funds from self-government. The Makarov proposals meant an increase of at least six million rubles in annual municipal expenditures for the police, something urban representatives would never accept willingly.[142] Much more troubling was the evolution of popular attitudes on the related issues of police authority and civil rights. As early as 1908 the Department of Police had expressed concern over press reaction to the government's reform plan, and the reception of the Makarov project after its publication in 1911 was not encouraging.[143] The editors of the *Russian News,* for example, argued that the proposals left the basic structural shortcomings of the force intact. They particularly denounced the provisions for punitive orders, the continuation of the gendarmes, the absence of effective judicial supervision, and the expense of reorganization. These sentiments were echoed in most other periodicals. Columnists of *Siberian Life* worried that the roots of police caprice were left untouched, insisting that until the principle of personal inviolability was firmly established citizens would not be protected from official abuse.[144] The general attitude of journalists was best summarized by one "Talinskii" in a 1913 column for *Urban Affairs.* The Makarov plan, he maintained, "contains no essential changes in the existing police system.... In order to improve the quality of the police, in our opinion, it will be necessary to establish the responsibility of officers to the courts without the approval of their superiors." Given the commissioners' failure to address the fundamental issue of civil freedom, he concluded, it would be up to the Duma to bring police reform into line with the empire's new constitutional order.[145]

It was not surprising that the generally liberal press would criticize the government bill for violating legal principles, but there was ample evidence to expect the same in the Duma. Delegates to the Third Duma had shown a strong inclination to link the issues of police reform and civil liberties. Discussion of the MVD budget had routinely provided an occasion for socialists, liberals, and even Octobrists to criticize administration violation of civil rights and to call for an end to emergency regulations and police caprice. Periodic scandals among the political police, such as the unmasking of the notorious double agent Azev in 1909, had also provoked calls for the imposition of controls on all law enforcement agencies. The Fourth Duma was somewhat more conservative in composition than its predecessor, but the majority of representatives demonstrated real sensitivity on the particular point of the limits of administrative authority.[146] Duma President M. V. Rodzianko, for example, provoked a rightist walkout by opening the session with a strong attack on the arbitrary behavior of the civil service. Similarly, in the debate over hooliganism there was violent criticism of the government's flagrant use of emergency regulations. Cadet V. A. Maklakov, brother of the new interior minister, attacked the central authorities for abandoning Stolypin's "platonic invitation to legality" in favor of "a cynical call to lawlessness." And he was supported by Octobrist spokesmen. Indeed, Count D. P. Kapnist, a man later to be the Duma committee's formal reporter on police reform, defended the Octobrist plan to give land captains increased punitive authority over hooligans specifically as a way of preventing this power from being assigned to the state's policemen.[147]

One of the most impressive displays of Duma hostility, though, came in connection with the 1913 debate over the MVD budget. The deputies passed the measure with a moderate cut of two hundred thousand rubles but also appended a highly critical resolution denouncing the ministry for a use of emergency regulations that "arouses in the people general dissatisfaction and a legitimate feeling of rebellion against unnecessary restrictions." And they attacked the MVD for its failure to introduce either legislation on civil rights or a major reform of local self-government.[148] Minister Maklakov was apparently relieved at the budget's approval, but the expression of oppositional sentiment only strengthened his desire to persuade Nicholas II to dissolve the Duma and reduce its legislative role.[149] The political atmosphere, on the sides of both the assembly and the government, was hardly propitious for police reform. Indeed, the head of the Saint Petersburg *okhrana* warned in October 1913 that the reopening of Duma deliberations with the introduction of government bills on police and on the press might provoke a general strike in the capital.[150]

The make-up of the committee created to review the police project precisely reflected the composition of the Duma as a whole. The right and left held eight seats each and various centrist factions that had earlier been united in the Octobrist party held seven.[151] Octobrist N. A. Khomiakov occupied the chair. Given the continued hostility of liberals and socialists, government hopes for passage clearly rested upon the possibility of persuading the centrist delegates to collaborate with the right. On some points such cooperation was achieved. In regard to the size of urban complements, rightists actively defended the Makarov goal of one patrolman for every four hundred inhabitants. They argued that the lack of "culture" among the Russian populace and the possibility of renewed unrest necessitated a strong force. Most Octobrists agreed, though usually for more pragmatic reasons. Kapnist, for instance, emphasized conditions like the severe cold (which kept patrolmen from remaining at their posts for long stretches), the large expanse of many Russian cities, and poor municipal lighting. Similarly, rightists and centrists united to approve provisions for the establishment of police positions at private expense, a conservative measure normally employed by estate owners and industrialists.[152]

Still, the committee deliberations indicated that police reorganization would not pass the Duma without a struggle. Liberals and socialists were outspokenly opposed. The comments of Cadet sympathizer P. P. Gronskii were typical. Claiming that the MVD "continues to take the viewpoint of a police government, and not a legal and constitutional one," he called for the outright rejection of the project in favor of municipalization of the police. Alexander F. Kerensky, the young Trudovik who in 1917 was to find the task of maintaining order in revolutionary times overwhelming, joined Gronskii in the demand for self-governmental control. The MVD legislation, he concluded, "even worsens the existing situation, strengthening the irresponsibility of the police and concentrating all direction in the hands of the governor."[153]

Much more ominous were reservations among the Octobrists. Kapnist, in reporting on the draft legislation, accepted many of the government's basic premises but added that "colossal work" was needed to resolve several open questions. Among these were the difficult issues of the gendarmes, gubernatorial supervision, and punitive orders. Though he congratulated the Makarov Commission for the "rich material" it had produced, Kapnist noted, "Much in the projects for the reorganization of the police requires development, much exclusion."[154]

Consistent with this approach, delegates of the center treated the Makarov proposals with reserve, as in the case of the gendarmes. Here, Octobrists and the left called for a drastic reduction of activity, and perhaps outright abolition. Maklakov himself appeared before the committee to defend the corps.[155] After making several flattering remarks on the gendarmes' performance, the interior minister tried to minimize the question by shifting attention to reinforcement of the regular police force. The ploy failed. Progressist N. N. L'vov, for one, continued to insist that the goal of reform should be not simply numerical strengthening of law enforcement agencies but creation of a "lawful police system." On the request of Assistant Minister Dzhunkovskii, resolution of the gendarmes problem was postponed, but sharp differences of opinion remained.[156]

The MVD suffered simple defeat in other areas. Patrolmen lost the right to administer fines for certain types of petty violations. Gubernatorial supervision of police officers was weakened in favor of the authority of provincial boards. The post of rural police sergeant was abolished altogether, to be replaced by an expanded staff of senior guardsmen. In a gesture of considerable symbolic significance, the government bill was edited to delete reference to the role of the minister of internal affairs and of governors as direct commanders of the police. These last two steps evoked particular though futile objection from MVD representatives.[157] Apparently differences among delegates over issues like these were severe enough to become personal. At one point rightists objected so strenuously to Khomiakov's procedure that the chairman resigned and stalked out of the meeting room; it required several days of negotiation to iron out the dispute.[158]

The Duma committee was unable to complete its work before the outbreak of war in the summer of 1914. As a result, any conclusion on the fate of police reorganization can only be speculative. It is useful, however, to view the issue within the context of MVD work on local government generally. Certainly Maklakov's decision to focus almost exclusively on the police represented a significant narrowing of the reform effort. As Department of Police Director S. P. Beletskii informed the committee on 20 November 1913, "Originally police reorganization was part of a broad plan for the reform of state administration outlined by former Minister of Internal Affairs P. A. Stolypin, which projected extensive decentralization under the political direction of the central authorities. Minister A. A. Makarov had the same idea in mind. However the ministry must take into account the changing conjuncture and now rejects the plan for broad reform."[159] Nevertheless, the central notion of Stolypin, the goal of decentralization, remained at the heart of MVD plans. In like fashion, the differences of outlook that characterized the early debate on local reform continued. Polarization between representatives of the right and left did not decrease, and moderates' reservations about collaborating with the leaders of the state bureaucracy remained. Even in regard to the basic questions of police and order centrists continued to be worried by a reform program that applied the ideas of decentralization and legality to increase rather than truly circumscribe state bureaucratic power. Whether these divisions could have been overcome had Russia been left in peace is an open question. What is certain is that the tsarist order could not stand the strains of war. Military defeat, when superimposed on existing social and political tensions, eventually plunged the empire into a period of revolution, civil war, and chaos unequalled since the Time of Troubles three hundred years before.

CONCLUSION

Tsarist local administration in the nineteenth century was a hybrid composed of three elements: state bureaucracy, self-government, and estates. Above all, the system, like the society it served, was traditional, attuned to the moderate demands of a relatively stable, agrarian world. In the face of rapid social change the governing apparatus of the Russian state was placed under increasing strain, which gave rise to a violent debate over the question of reform and the empire's future. In response to the pressing problems of the administrative system, and indeed of tsarist society generally, three views emerged, each in effect representing one of the basic elements of the administrative structure.

Perhaps the most straightforward attitude on reform was that of Russian liberals. Progressives like the members of the Cadet party sought to resolve the difficulties of local administration through drastic democratization. Decentralization, defined by liberals as the transfer of responsibility and, simultaneously, of authority to zemstvos and town councils, would open the doors to almost unlimited popular participation. Society itself would meet its own administrative needs locally and nationally. In direct opposition to this approach, though not entirely divorced from it in basic assumptions, was the program of the gentry right. Despite the propensity of historians to focus their attention when discussing resistance to reform in the old regime on the machinations of figures in the court of Nicholas II, this period saw the emergence of a broadly based, rigid conservatism among the Russian landed nobility. Like the liberals, gentry activists saw the need for a public role in administration, yet they differed dramatically in their understanding of the nature of the social order. Rather than turn to notions of civil equality, or even of property, they championed the traditional idea of estate as the basic component of society. In regard to local administration especially, they stubbornly defended "organic" corporate institutions against "rationalization" as represented either by democracy or state bureaucracy.

Where the first two perspectives revolving around self-government and estate are easily, if not perfectly, characterized as "liberal" and "conservative," the program of reformers within the state bureaucracy is much more difficult to categorize. Soviet historians have demonstrated the difficulty by their prolonged and rather inconclusive attempts to assign figures like Witte or Stolypin to bourgeois or feudal camps or alternately to develop the anomalous Marxist category of Bonapartism. The primary difficulty is that while bureaucratic reformers clearly stood for movement in Russian society, they did so in a fashion quite distinct from liberal or socialist progressives. They sought to expand participation in local government through decentralization as a means both of improving the capabilities of the imperial administrative apparatus and of integrating newly mobilized groups into the polity. Yet they insisted that decentralization should not undermine the state bureaucracy's overall ability to supervise and ultimately to direct the evolution of tsarist society. In their hands, administrative reform became a tool for the continuation of essentially centralizing patterns of control into the era of mass politics.

It must be emphasized that none of these perspectives on reform was accidental. Each was rooted in Russian political culture and in major social developments of the day. The liberal outlook, for example, was drawn from the experience of the zemstvo movement and from perception of the seemingly progressive evolution of western European history. Both suggested that monarchic and, by extension, royal bureaucratic rule was an anachronism that should and would be swept away by the maturation of the public, as would estate and other restrictions on civil equality. Compromise with the representatives of the state bureaucracy or with more conservative elements among the citizenry ultimately was neither advisable nor necessary. As Boris Chicherin wrote in concluding an otherwise sober and cautious assessment of the potential for constitutionalism at the turn of the century, "Sooner or later, one way or another this will come to pass . . . for it is in the nature of things. The force of events ineluctably produces this outcome."[1] This fundamental optimism, this confidence in the potential for democracy within the empire, was confirmed for many by the events of 1905 in which the Russian public had, or so it appeared, risen in support of liberal demands for the limitation of autocracy. Although shaken by the setbacks that followed the convocation of the First Duma, the basic assumptions of the liberal world view remained intact.

If confidence, or at least hope, contributed strongly to Russian liberalism, then alarm and pessimism inspired gentry conservatism. Two developments in particular fueled the mobilization of noble opinion. The first estate found itself increasingly threatened by the emergence of new groups demanding larger political and social roles.

CONCLUSION

These included the industrial bourgeoisie and middle-class professionals, who rivalled the landed gentry by virtue of their wealth and education, and the rapidly expanding proletariat and peasant masses, who were less qualified from the standpoint of "culture" but were willing to press their claims violently. Simultaneously, the nobility itself seemed to be losing influence in Saint Petersburg. The tsarist government, hitherto generally solicitous of gentry interests, had launched a program of state-sponsored industrialization at agrarian expense. And even the supposedly conservative Pleve had initiated plans for a bureaucratization of administration that threatened the corporate institutions of the nobility. Both developments were confirmed by the Revolution of 1905. The challenge of competing social groups was starkly evident in shrill cries for democratization and in the burning of manors, and the central authorities moved toward a radical attack on gentry and peasant corporate organs. The essentially defensive, uncompromising attitude of the landed gentry was the direct result. Rather than reach out to other potentially conservative strata, including, for example, urban proprietors, the inclination was to turn back to the ideas which had justified noble privilege for centuries, the interlocking notions of service and estate.

Reformers in the state bureaucracy were equally convinced by their perception of history and contemporary events of the rectitude of their position. Witte, Pleve, and Stolypin all looked to a tradition of state innovation stretching back to the reign of Peter the Great and beyond. They understood the functional role of the civil service as the defender of domestic tranquility and as the chief vehicle of imperial power internationally. And they believed, however accurately, that the tsar and his bureaucratic agents had historically acted as the primary guarantors of Russian culture and popular well-being. These themes of internal order, external prestige, and general prosperity were interwoven as motivations for most major governmental acts. Witte's industrialization, for instance, would keep the empire competitive with its European neighbors and simultaneously benefit the citizenry through the expansion of commerce and manufacture. Stolypin's agrarian reform would establish a stratum of peasant smallholders who would be a force for both conservative stability and agricultural productivity. Given the self-perceived importance of the state bureaucracy, how could its most forceful leaders be willing to relinquish their authority?

Of course, as prescriptions for the proper ordering of Russian society, all these views involved fundamental value judgments on the nature of a just social order. A full evaluation of the programs, especially in regard to their moral bases, is beyond the scope of this work. As a historical matter, however, it is appropriate to consider their practical implications in order to assess the viability of each approach under the conditions existing in pre-Revolutionary Russia. From this standpoint, the program of the landed gentry is certainly most vulnerable. In regard to local government specifically, the rightist view was predicated upon the revitalization of estate institutions that had not recently played an effective role in tsarist administration. More broadly, the gentry outlook was based on a steadily more anachronistic analysis of the structure of Russian society. Developments like industrialization, urbanization, and increased mobility were undermining the old corporate divisions, creating a new and more fluid milieu in which the estate ideal was out of place. Even where the concepts had some continuing relevance, as in the countryside, relations among various groups fell far short of the noble vision of organic harmony. Peasant rebellion demonstrated most dramatically the collapse of traditional restraints on conflict among estates.

Gentry ideologues were to some degree aware of these difficulties. F. D. Samarin, for example, admitted at one point that social development was making old corporate distinctions artificial by realigning the empire's social strata. "No one really believes that the estates are something eternally unchanging," he argued. Yet Samarin insisted that all new groups, save possibly the commercial-industrial class, were as yet social entities "in becoming" (*im werden*). Only in the distant future, when they had proven their service capacity and their ties to "our historically given state structure," could they stand together with the traditional estates.[2] In regard to the peasantry, noble spokesmen tried to avoid the obvious implications of rural rebellion. In many cases an attempt was made to shift blame from the allegedly naive and innocent muzhiks to outside agitators, alien elements like the intelligentsia who malevolently aroused the peasants' primitive instincts. But such rationalizations are hardly persuasive. Certainly they found little contemporary response outside the ranks of the landed gentry.

Russian liberalism did not suffer from a lack of support among the educated public. The initial electoral success of the Cadets and even the responsiveness to their program of some Octobrists serve as ample testimony of this. Yet outside the middle and upper classes liberalism faced severe difficulties. A full consideration of the overall receptivity of the masses to constitutional principles requires separate study. But one can doubt that progressives like the Cadets would have been easily able to bridge the gap between themselves and the workers and peasants had they succeeded in their democratization of self-government. In a sense, the Western-oriented reformers were trapped in a vicious circle. Aware of the lack of "culture" among the general populace, they believed that the incorporation of the masses in central and local governance through universal suffrage would be a vehicle for the inculcation of liberal ideas. As Peter Struve, editor of *Liberation*, wrote in a piece published in 1905, "The only way to direct the enormous social movement presently stirring Russia's urban and rural working population into the channel of lawful struggle for their interest is to invite the entire population, on equal rights, to share in the political life—that is, to institute universal franchise.... Under the universal franchise the masses, having become responsible managers of their own destiny, will learn and understand what is possible and what is not."[3] Yet it can be argued that successful operation of representative democracy presupposed the very restraint and "responsibility" it aimed at instilling. Political equality alone might well fail to resolve the basic social and economic grievances that contributed to violence in 1905 and later.

On the other end of the social ladder is the experience of Russian liberals with the tsarist ruling strata. Certainly only limited gains were made in the struggle to dislodge traditional, nonliberal elites from their dominant positions, especially after 1906. The speed with which the Cadets were relegated to a peripheral role in local reform and were forced to take a back seat to state-sponsored legislative initiatives suggests a severe underestimation on their part of the power of the autocracy and its officialdom. The violence and effectiveness of gentry reaction to progressive reform once the nobility had been mobilized for political action (a process in which liberals themselves participated through the zemstvo movement) indicates a similar misperception of the influence and inflexibility of the landed elite.

No less formidable were the obstacles facing the proponents of the state bureaucratic approach to reform. Most immediately, there was the task of turning the civil service itself into a more coherent and effective administrative instrument. The magnitude of this problem was well illustrated by efforts to improve the quality of the regular police force. Finance officials estimated that achievement of what the interior ministry deemed minimally adequate pay and staff levels would require a tripling of state expenditures. And this was but a partial step toward the creation of truly modern, professional law enforcement agencies. There remained the more difficult issue of developing a police ethic more attuned to the requirements of bureaucratic rationality and the rule of law. The leadership of the interior ministry, working particularly through the *Police Messenger,* made an attempt to instill new values, but with limited success. Reviewing the progress of reform in 1910, one official correspondent was forced to admit that the large majority of the tsarist police either "still slept like hibernating bears unaware of the changes around them" or surreptitiously resisted change in favor of the old ways.[4]

The problem of molding the civil service into a more efficient body was magnified by the politicization of officialdom in the wake of the Revolution of 1905. The judicial bureaucracy, characterized by one rightist journalist as "nine-tenths Cadet," demonstrated a troubling affinity for the liberal opposition.[5] Even more worrisome was the participation of MVD subordinates, from governors to patrolmen, in unauthorized counterrevolutionary violence. Stolypin certainly was forced to devote much effort to combating this evil, and he was far from completely victorious. In the case of the notorious Odessa City Chief, I. N. Tolmachov, for example, Nicholas II's attitude prevented Stolypin from either limiting his subordinate's support for the Union of the Russian People's illegal acts or replacing him. Less striking but equally significant were the misgivings of some MVD local agents over government agrarian reform. Though hostility to land consolidation was hardly universal among provincial bureaucrats, many did drag their feet in implementing the program. Their lack of energy was especially damaging given the emphatic nature of Stolypin's commitment to the plan.[6] Both in responsiveness to central authority and in sensitivity to the new constitutional era, the civil service left much to be desired. As one police official lamented, "To be a civilizer, first you must be civilized."[7]

Beyond severe internal difficulties, the leaders of the state bureaucracy faced the even more fundamental issue of popular participation. Perhaps the most salient feature of late tsarist politics was the mobilization of the public around demands not merely for involvement in government but for participation on terms of autonomy and self-determination. And it was this demand for an effective sharing of real power that tsarist officials found impossible to meet. The inability of Witte, Pleve, and Stolypin to retain the confidence of the traditional social elite, the Russian gentry, was one aspect of this problem. Their matching failure in winning over progressives and moderates among the citizenry was another. Rightist opposition to evolutionary change might well have been overcome had reformers, official and public, been able to cooperate effectively, but the insistence of state bureaucrats on retaining ultimate guardianship over the empire's future undermined any possibility for such cooperation.

CONCLUSION

It might be argued that the success of the Communists in developing an effective though highly centralized administrative system after 1917 indicates the viability of a similar approach by state bureaucrats in the tsarist era. One scholar, for example, has implied that official plans of the 1860s for popular participation through centrally supervised zemstvos parallel Lenin's notion of local soviets as "transmission belts" between rulers and people.[8] Yet the two cases differ fundamentally. Pre-Revolutionary statesmen sought to integrate traditional and newly emergent elite groups—nobility, industrialists, professionals—into the existing political system. And they hoped to open participatory channels for the masses that would reconcile them to the established order. The Communists, conversely, created a new order. Unlike their predecessors, Lenin and his colleagues could appeal directly to workers and peasants by claiming to rule on their behalf against elite groups of the educated public, who were simply excluded from the political process or, at best, included under party domination guaranteed by force. In this the Soviets were aided by the violence of the revolutionary process between 1917 and 1921, which uprooted the gentry and severely shook the middle classes. This effect was reinforced by the upheaval of the "Stalin revolution" of the 1930s, which through forced industrialization and terror created a new elite quite unlike the tsarist elite. In a sense, the Communists produced a tabula rasa upon which to work by destroying those public elements which had been such an obstacle to the tsarist ministers' reform plans. Only in the last few decades, with the very tentative maturation of interest groups among the populace, have the rulers of the USSR really begun again to grapple with the issues of decentralization and participation.

In conclusion, then, it is best to return to the issue with which this study began, the capacity of the tsarist political system for reform. Scholars of modernization have argued persuasively that economic and social change can easily outpace the development of effective political institutions. Although the problem of political innovation is multifaceted, at its heart is the challenge of integrating newly active groups into the existing polity. The case of local administration indicates that both the tsarist government and the public were grappling with precisely this issue in the last decades of the regime. Consensus existed on the need for greater popular involvement in the political process, for at least some effort to transform the empire's inhabitants from subjects into participating citizens. Yet the programs for change produced by tsarist statesmen and by various leaders among the educated classes differed fundamentally in their basic assumptions. No compromise could be found on ways to create institutions better able to broaden participation and meet the pressing need for more effective administration in the provinces. This failure to overcome the fragmentation of the political system and renovate local government was crucial. As a result, the central authorities were denied administrative organs that might have helped implement ameliorative measures like agrarian reform. A valuable opportunity to bridge the sharp divisions in Russian society among government, the educated classes, and the masses through cooperation in local affairs was missed. Moreover, the lack of success in this area involved a general loss of legitimacy by the existing order. All these factors contributed substantially to the ultimate result when the strains of war brought the tsarist system to its final crisis in 1917.

ABBREVIATIONS

Abbreviations have been used for archives and several frequently cited official publications and institutions:

GBL   Otdel Rukopisei Gosudarstvennoi Biblioteki im. Lenina v Moskve

GDSO   Gosudarstvennaia duma. *Stenograficheskie otchety*

GSSO   Gosudarstvennyi sovet. *Stenograficheskie otchety*

KA   *Krasnyi arkhiv*

MVD   Ministerstvo vnutrennikh del

SZ   *Svod zakonov Rossiiskoi Imperii.* Saint Petersburg, 1912 ed.

TsGAOR   Tsentral'nyi Gosudarstvennyi Arkhiv Oktiabr'skoi Revoliutsii

TsGIA   Tsentral'nyi Gosudarstvennyi Istoricheskii Arkhiv SSSR

Archival citations are generally given in the following order: abbreviation of archive, *fond* number, *opis'* number, year (where indicated on document), *delo* number, and page number.

NOTES

INTRODUCTION

1. For the Soviet debate on absolutism, see Akademiia Nauk SSSR, *Absoliutizm v Rossii (XVII–XVIIIvv.): Sbornik statei* (Moscow, 1964); A. Ia. Avrekh, "Russkii absoliutizm i ego rol' v utverzhdenii kapitalizma v Rossii," pp. 82–104, and "K diskussii ob absoliutizme v Rossii," *Istoriia SSSR* 4 (1972): 65–88; Alexander Gerschenkron's critical review, "Soviet Marxism and Absolutism," pp. 853–869; and A. M. Davidovich's restatement of the traditional Soviet view, *Samoderzhavie v epokhu imperializma*.
2. See Arthur Mendel's "On Interpreting the Fate of Imperial Russia," in *Russia under the Last Tsar,* ed. Theofanis George Stavrou, pp. 13–41, for a discussion of the two opposing standpoints.
3. Sergei Iu. Witte, *Samoderzhavie i zemstvo,* p. 212.
4. See in particular *Tsarizm i tret'eiiunskaia sistema* and *Stolypin i tret'ia duma;* and V. S. Diakin's *Samoderzhavie, burzhuaziia, i dvorianstvo v 1907–1911gg.*
5. The view is most clearly stated in George L. Yaney, *The Systematization of Russian Government.* See also the critical comments of John Keep, "Programming the Past," pp. 569–580. For general summaries of Western scholarship on tsarist bureaucracy, see Daniel T. Orlovsky, "Recent Studies on the Russian Bureaucracy," pp. 448–467; and Marc Raeff, "The Bureaucratic Phenomena of Imperial Russia, 1700–1905," pp. 399–411.

CHAPTER I

1. M. V. Islavin, *Obzor trudov vysochaishe utverzhdennoi pod predsedatel'stvom stats'-sekretaria Kakhanova osoboi kommisii,* 1: 121. The modern Russian term *komissiia* appears variously in tsarist documents. This work will generally follow the specific tsarist usage in each case, rather than uniformly impose the modern spelling.
2. For a brief summary of the legal situation in this regard see Marc Szeftel, "The Form of Government of the Russian Empire prior to the Constitutional Reforms of 1905-6," in *Essays in Russian and Soviet History in Honor of Geroid Tanquary Robinson,* ed. John S. Curtiss (New York: Columbia University Press, 1963), pp. 105–119.
3. Anatole Leroy-Beaulieu, *The Empire of the Tsars and the Russians,* 2:91.

4. A. D. Gradovskii, "Sistemy mestnago upravleniia na zapade Evropy i v Rossii," 5:74-75.

5. The term *state bureaucracy* requires some definition. Formally, the tsarist civil service was composed of many types of officials, including, for example, those of the empire's self-governing bodies. For our purposes, however, *state bureaucracy* will be limited to the officials of the ministries and departments in the capital and their direct subordinates on the local level. It should be noted that on occasion these officials are referred to simply as *the bureaucracy.* While other institutions, like self-government, were bureaucracies too, the restricted use of the term in reference only to the administrative apparatus of the central authorities will avoid confusion and be more in keeping with tsarist usage.

6. Theda Skocpol, *States and Social Revolutions*, p. 27.

7. A. P. Korelin, "Dvorianstvo v poreformennoi Rossii (1861-1904gg.)," p. 163. See also Walter M. Pintner, "The Social Characteristics of the Early-Nineteenth Century Russian Bureaucracy," pp. 429-443; Don Karl Rowney, "Higher Civil Servants in the Russian Ministry of Internal Affairs," pp. 101-110; P. A. Zaionchkovskii, *Pravitel'stvennyi apparat samoderzhavnoi Rossii v XIXv.*, pp. 90-105; and Pintner and Rowney, eds., *Russian Officialdom*, chapters 8-11.

8. Sergei Iu. Witte, *Samoderzhavie i zemstvo.* For other examples of this viewpoint, see Vladimir I. Gurko, *Features and Figures of the Past;* and S. E. Kryzhanovskii, *Vospominaniia.*

9. Witte, *Samoderzhavie*, pp. 45f. See also Witte's defense of autocracy as described in Iu. B. Solov'ev, *Samoderzhavie i dvorianstvo v kontse XIX veka*, pp. 283-289.

10. Witte, *Samoderzhavie*, pp. 203-207. The analogy was borrowed from the English visitor Donald Mackenzie Wallace.

11. S. K. Gogel, *Die Ursachen der russischen Revolution vom Jahre 1917*, p. 115.

12. For descriptions of the administrative system, see the useful summary in N. P. Eroshkin, *Istoriia gosudarstvennykh uchrezhdenii dorevoliutsionnoi Rossii;* N. M. Korkunov's classic *Russkoe gosudarstvennoe pravo;* and Yaney, *Systematization*, chapters 6 and 8-10.

13. Korkunov, *Russkoe gosudarstvennoe pravo*, 2:405.

14. On the governor's duties, see ibid., pp. 440-464; and "Obshchee uchrezhdenie gubernskoe," *SZ*, 2, articles 201f.

15. References to duties of the police force are scattered unsystematically throughout tsarist law codes. For the most thorough compilation, see N. Volkov, ed., *Zakony o politsii.*

16. *Istoricheskii ocherk organizatsii i deiatel'nosti departamenta politsii*, TsGAOR, f. DP, op. 302, d. 707, ch. 2, pp. 112-113.

17. N. A. Rubakin, *Rossiia v tsifrakh*, p. 62.

18. P. Sheimin, "Politsiia," *Entsiklopedicheskii slovar Brokgauz-Efron*, 24:337.

19. On Russia's estates, see Korkunov, *Russkoe gosudarstvennoe pravo*, 1:274f; and Gradovskii, "Sistemy upravleniia," 6:92-101 and 145-160.

20. A. D. Pazukhin, "Sovremennoe sostoianie Rossii i soslovnyi vopros," pp. 5-58.
21. Ibid., p. 41.
22. Ibid., p. 54.
23. There are a number of usages in the Russian context for the term *gentry* (*dvorianstvo*). Unless otherwise indicated, *gentry* here denotes landed gentry, particularly those entitled to participate in the first estate's corporate assemblies. On the definition of *gentry*, see Korelin, "Dvorianstvo," pp. 91-115.
24. Pazukhin, "Sovremennoe sostoianie," pp. 28-29 and 31.
25. Ibid., p. 37.
26. On the gentry estate in the period after the emancipation, see Korelin, "Dvorianstvo"; and Jerome Blum's excellent essay, "Russia," pp. 68-97.
27. Peasant law and administration are detailed in A. A. Leont'ev, *Krest'ianskoe pravo;* and I. M. Strakhovskii, *Krest'ianskiia prava i uchrezhdeniia.*
28. The term *samoupravlenie* has been defined variously, as will be shown. Though "self-administration" is the most literal translation, the more common "self-government" will be used here. The best recent works on the introduction of self-government and the administrative reforms of the 1860s generally are S. Frederick Starr, *Decentralization and Self-Government in Russia, 1830-1870;* and Terence Emmons, *The Russian Landed Gentry and the Peasant Emancipation of 1861.*
29. On the various theories of self-government, see P. P. Gronskii, "Teorii samoupravleniia v russkoi nauke," in *Iubileinyi zemskii sbornik,* ed. B. B. Veselovskii and Z. G. Frenkel, pp. 76-85; N. I. Lazarevskii, "Samoupravlenie," in *Melkaia zemskaia edinitsa,* 1:1-61; and Korkunov, *Russkoe gosudarstvennoe pravo,* 2:488-501.
30. Lazarevskii, "Samoupravlenie," pp. 39 and 51.
31. In the mid-1880s, for example, almost 82 percent of provincial zemstvo delegates were gentry, and in the following decade the figure was 90 percent. B. B. Veselovskii, *Istoriia zemstva za sorok let,* 3:680-681. See also Veselovskii, *K voprosu o klassovykh interesakh v zemstve.*
32. Lazarevskii, "Samoupravlenie," p. 51.
33. Witte, *Samoderzhavie,* p. 76.
34. Korkunov, *Russkoe gosudarstvennoe pravo,* 2:540.
35. Islavin, *Obzor trudov,* 1:3-4. On the commission and its work see Islavin; also P. A. Zaionchkovskii, *Rossiiskoe samoderzhavie v kontse XIX stoletiia,* pp. 217-233; and L. G. Zakharova, *Zemskaia kontrreforma 1890g.*
36. A. A. Polovtsov quoted in Solov'ev, *Samoderzhavie,* p. 106.
37. See, for instance, the views presented in MVD, *Ministerstvo vnutrennikh del: Istoricheskii ocherk, 1802-1902,* pp. 172-173.
38. Ibid., p. 194.
39. Ibid., p. 173. See also B. B. Glinskii, "Period tverdoi vlasti," 127:690.

40. For a review of Tolstoi's "counterreforms," as they were known, see Zaionchkovskii, *Rossiiskoe samoderzhavie*, pp. 366-428; and James I. Mandel, "Paternalistic Authority in the Russian Countryside, 1856-1906," chapters 3-4.

41. In his draft report on the measure, Tolstoi insisted that the land captain must be connected "through the intermediary of provincial institutions to the central governmental authorities." Zaionchkovskii, *Rossiiskoe samoderzhavie*, p. 370.

42. MVD, *Ministerstvo*, p. 193; and Glinskii, "Period tverdoi vlasti," 128:564.

43. *SZ*, 2, p. 222, article 87.

44. On the new electoral law see N. I. Lazarevskii, "Zemskoe izbiratel'noe pravo," in Veselovskii and Frenkel, *Iubileinyi sbornik*, pp. 50-75.

45. Zaionchkovskii, *Rossiiskoe samoderzhavie*, p. 10. Zakharova, in *Zemskaia kontrreforma*, describes Tolstoi's appointment as "an open turn to feudal reaction," p. 72.

46. On land captain activity see, for instance, the data in N. P. Nikol'skaia, "Zakon o zemskikh nachal'nikakh"; or Mandel's discussion in "Paternalistic Authority," chapter 5.

47. A. A. Kireev quoted in Solov'ev, *Samoderzhavie*, p. 270.

48. Ibid., pp. 193-194.

49. Quoted in Blum, "Russia," p. 70.

50. See Theodore H. Von Laue, *Sergei Witte and the Industrialization of Russia;* or, for a Soviet view, P. A. Khromov, *Ekonomicheskoe razvitie Rossii*, pp. 277-394.

51. Data on population growth is given in W. W. Eason, "Population Changes," in *The Transformation of Russian Society*, ed. Cyril E. Black, pp. 72-90. On the urbanization process in the empire's two capitals, see the interesting James H. Bater, *St. Petersburg;* and Robert E. Johnson, *Peasant and Proletarian.*

52. V. R. Leikina-Svirskaia, *Intelligentsiia v Rossii vo vtoroi polovine XIX veka*, pp. 58-59.

53. R. A. Lewis and R. H. Rowland, "Urbanization in Russia and the USSR," in *The City in Russian History*, ed. Michael Hamm, p. 213.

54. TsGIA, f. 1284, op. 185, d. 5a, ch. 1, pp. 53-54.

55. The sharpest exchange on this issue is James Y. Simms, Jr., "The Crisis in Russian Agriculture at the End of the Nineteenth Century," pp. 377-398; G. M. Hamburg, "The Crisis in Russian Agriculture: A Comment" and Simms, "On Missing the Point: A Rejoinder," *Slavic Review* 37, no. 3 (September 1978): 481-490.

56. The figure for urbanites is much higher if the few provinces where the more rural Polish gentry predominated are excluded. Korelin, "Dvorianstvo," pp. 169-170. It should be noted that by the end of the century some nobles were returning to the land in an attempt to make their estates viable. Many of these became active in provincial affairs.

See Roberta Thompson Manning, "Zemstvo and Revolution," in *The Politics of Rural Russia*, ed. Leopold H. Haimson, pp. 36-37.

57. See Richard G. Robbins, Jr., *Famine in Russia, 1891-1892*.

58. Islavin, *Obzor trudov*, 1:303 and 163-164.

59. *Novoe vremia*, no. 9,484 (31 July 1902), p. 1.

60. Ibid., no. 9,457 (4 July 1902), pp. 1-2.

61. *Vestnik politsii*, no. 18 (23 March 1908), p. 17.

62. Ibid., p. 18. See also A. Novikov, *Zapiski zemskago nachal'nika*, pp. 116-118.

63. See MVD, Departament politsii, *Istoricheskii ocherk obrazovaniia i razvitiia politseiskikh uchrezhdenii v Rossii*, pp. 33-35.

64. *Zhurnal vysochaishe uchrezhdennago osobago soveshchaniia po peresmotru iskliuchitel'nyh zakonopolozhenii* (Saint Petersburg, n.d.), pp. 14-17.

65. MVD, Departament politsii, *Istoricheskii ocherk politseiskikh uchrezhdenii*, p. 35. The Council of Ministers gave the minister of internal affairs authority to approve such petitions unilaterally. During the Revolution of 1905 the government went further, extending this authority to all provincial governors.

66. On the multiplicity of tasks facing land captains see V. V. Tenishev, *Administrativnoe polozhenie russkago krest'ianina*, pp. 59-91; Novikov, *Zapiski;* A. A. Rittikh, ed., *Krest'ianskii pravoporiadok*, pp. 293f; and Mandel, "Paternalistic Authority," chapter 6.

67. *Novoe vremia*, no. 9,475 (22 July 1902), pp. 1-2.

68. See, for instance, L. Kosunovich, "Kulachnoe pravo," *Vestnik politsii*, no. 26 (1909), pp. 543-546.

69. *KA*, 3, p. 136.

70. Leroy-Beaulieu, *Empire of the Tsars*, 2:95.

71. *Vestnik politsii*, no. 28 (1909), p. 592.

72. The most thorough study of this question is S. A. Korf, *Administrativnaia iustitsiia v Rossii*.

73. I. M. Strakhovskii, *Gubernskoe ustroistvo*, p. 119.

74. Islavin, *Obzor trudov*, 1:162.

75. *Novoe vremia*, no. 9,475 (22 July 1902), pp. 1-2.

76. Leikina-Svirskaia, *Intelligentsiia*, p. 72.

77. S. D. Urusov, *Zapiski gubernatora*, pp. 59 and 231f.

78. On this subject see the entirety of Strakhovskii, *Gubernskoe ustroistvo*; V. M. Gessen, *Voprosy mestnago upravleniia*, pp. 27-66; I. Blinov, *Gubernatory*, pp. 310-321; and E. N. Berendts, *O proshlom i nastoiashchem russkoi administratsii*, p. 267.

79. Cited in Mandel, "Paternalistic Authority," p. 302. The first comprehensive code regulating land captain activity was published in Saint Petersburg by the MVD only in 1905. See *Nakaz zemskim nachal'nikam*.

80. Gurko, *Features and Figures*, p. 147.

81. Witte, *Samoderzhavie*, p. 184.

82. S. A. Korf, "Predvoditel' dvorianstva kak organ soslovnago i zemskago samoupravleniia," pp. 115-116.

83. Ibid., p. 116. See also Novikov, *Zapiski*, p. 134; and Gurko, *Features and Figures*, p. 147.
84. Gurko, *Features and Figures*, p. 146.
85. Data from Gosudarstvennyi sovet, *Otchet po deloproizvodstvu gosudarstvennago soveta za sessiiu 1903–1904gg.* (Saint Petersburg, 1905), p. 124.
86. A. V. Bondarevskii, "Volostnoe upravlenie i polozhenie krest'ian v tsarskoi Rossii (1861–1917gg.)" (dissertation, Kiev, 1950), p. 173; Mandel, "Paternalistic Authority," chapter 6; and Strakhovskii, *Krest'ianskiia prava*, pp. 123–129.
87. Mandel, "Paternalistic Authority," pp. 220–221 and 266–268.
88. TsGIA, f. 1284, op. 185 (1907), d. 5a, ch. 1, pp. 68–69.
89. Ibid., p. 68.
90. G. G. Savich, *K voprosu o melkoi zemskoi edinitse*, pp. 10–17.
91. Tenishev, *Administrativnoe polozhenie*, pp. 47–52. See also Strakhovskii, *Krest'ianskiia prava*, pp. 26f; and Rittikh, *Krest'ianskii pravoporiadok*, pp. 144–157 and 403–408.
92. On village police see Tenishev, *Administrativnoe polozhenie*, pp. 44f; Rittikh, *Krest'ianskii pravoporiadok*, pp. 396–403; Novikov, *Zapiski*, pp. 117–118; and the interesting reports on rural law enforcement in D. S. Fleksor, *Okhrana sel'skokhoziaistvennoi sobstvennosti*, pp. 53–58.
93. See Strakhovskii, *Krest'ianskiia prava*, pp. 26f; S. T. Semenov, *Dvadtsat' piat let v derevne*, pp. 93 and 158–161; and Rittikh, *Krest'ianskii pravoporiadok*, pp. 129–143. Complaints of the growing influence of the clerk were universal in this period. See, for example, Tenishev, *Administrativnoe polozhenie*, pp. 44–50.
94. Gosudarstvennyi sovet, *Otchet po deloproizvodstvu gosudarstvennago soveta za sessiiu 1902–1903gg.* (Saint Petersburg, 1904), pp. 207–208.
95. One Soviet scholar has noted that of 201 zemstvo delegates identifiably associated with the progressive movement in the decade before 1902, some 21 were marshals. N. M. Pirumova, *Zemskoe liberal'noe dvizhenie*, p. 90.
96. B. B. Veselovskii, *Krest'ianskii vopros i krest'ianskoe dvizhenie v Rossii*, is the basic work on this subject.
97. Leroy-Beaulieu, *Empire of the Tsars*, 2:67–68.
98. Veselovskii, *Istoriia zemstva*, 1:15.
99. Ibid., 2:476, 138–139, and 394–395.
100. On the development of the liberal movement in this period see Pirumova, *Zemskoe dvizhenie*; S. Galai, *The Liberation Movement in Russia, 1900–1905*; E. D. Chermenskii, *Burzhuaziia i tsarizm v pervoi russkoi revoliutsii*; Richard Pipes, *Struve: Liberal on the Left*, chapters 12–15; and Terence Emmons, "Russia's Banquet Campaign," pp. 45–86.
101. Yaney, *Systematization*, p. 355.
102. V. V. Ivanovskii, "Biurokratiia, kak samostoiatel'nyi obshchestvennyi klass," pp. 1–23.
103. Ibid., p. 23.

104. Gessen, *Voprosy*, p. 15.
105. Boris Chicherin, *Rossiia nakanune dvadtsatago stoletiia*, p. 93.
106. Gessen, *Voprosy*, p. 15.
107. D. N. Shipov, *Vospominaniia i dumy o perezhitom*, p. 150.
108. Pirumova, *Zemskoe dvizhenie*, p. 206.
109. Witte, *Samoderzhavie*, p. 23.
110. Lazarevskii, "Samoupravlenie," pp. 45-46.
111. *Pravo*, no. 22 (25 May 1903), pp. 2391-2392.
112. It is difficult to determine precisely how many times the governor's power was used. The Ministry of Internal Affairs itself later set the figure at "over 50 times" for the period between 1891 and 1907, but the estimate may well have been low. Moreover, no comment was made on how often the threat of veto was employed to deter zemstvo action. MVD, Glavnoe upravlenie po delam mestnago khoziaistva, *Ob ustanovleniia glavnykh osnovanii preobrazovaniia zemskikh i gorodskikh uchrezhdenii* (Saint Petersburg, 1907), p. 18. In any case, there is no doubt that the possibility of a gubernatorial veto was galling to zemstvo activists. See, for example, Shipov, *Vospominaniia*, pp. 100f.
113. See particularly *Melkaia zemskaia edinitsa*, 1 and 2.
114. Many of these are recorded in various sections of Veselovskii, *Istoriia zemstva*. See, for example, 3:402-406; and Pirumova, *Zemskoe dvizhenie*, pp. 178-180.
115. On the conference see S. I. Shidlovskii, *Obshchii obzor trudov mestnykh komitetov;* M. S. Simonova's "Bor'ba techenii v pravitel'stvennom lagare po voprosam agrarnoi politiki v kontse XIX veka," pp. 65-82, and "Politika tsarizma v krest'ianskom voprose nakanune revoliutsii 1905-1907gg.," pp. 217-242; and David A. Macey, "The Russian Bureaucracy and the 'Peasant Problem,'" pp. 177-187.
116. Of the members of the provincial committees in European Russia, 29 percent were civil servants, 37 percent large landowners, and 23 percent zemstvo participants. For district committees the figures were: 26 percent civil servants, 26 percent large landowners, and 22 percent zemstvo men. Many of the zemstvo participants, it should be noted, were also landed and gentry. Shidlovskii, *Obzor trudov*, pp. 4-10.
117. Ibid., pp. 226-232.
118. *Pravo*, no. 21 (11 May 1903), pp. 1468-1469.
119. Quoted in Witte, *Samoderzhavie*, p. 47.
120. See Emmons, *The Russian Landed Gentry;* and Daniel Field, *The End of Serfdom*.
121. See Solov'ev, *Samoderzhavie*, chapters 3 and 4.
122. *KA*, 3:95-96 and 161.
123. Pirumova, *Zemskoe dvizhenie*, p. 123.
124. Shipov, *Vospominaniia*, p. 152.
125. Ibid., pp. 152-154.
126. *Novoe vremia*, no. 9,094 (1 March 1903), p. 3.

CHAPTER II

1. S. Galai, *The Liberation Movement in Russia, 1900–1905*, p. 137. George Fischer, for example, dismisses Pleve as simply "generally unpopular and archconservative" (*Russian Liberalism*, p. 167). Galai and Fischer, like most historians, have based their views on the testimony of Pleve's liberal opponents. See particularly D. N. Shipov, *Vospominaniia i dumy o perezhitom*, pp. 174–176, 207n, and 237–238. For a similar view by a Soviet historian see M. S. Simonova's articles, "Zemsko-liberal'naia fronda," pp. 150–216, and "Politika tsarizma v krest'ianskom voprose nakanune revoliutsii 1905–1907gg.," pp. 217–242.

2. "Pis'mo V. K. Pleve k A. A. Kireevu," *KA*, 18:202.

3. Loris-Melikov wrote in recommendation of Pleve, "The official and moral qualities of Pleve are a sufficient guarantee that in the new sphere of activity he will apply the same energy and intelligent attitude to business which constantly distinguished his service in the judicial bureaucracy." Cited in P. A. Zaionchkovskii, *Rossiiskoe samoderzhavie v kontse XIX stoletiia*, pp. 341–342.

4. Vladimir I. Gurko, *Features and Figures of the Past*, p. 108.

5. Iu. B. Solov'ev, *Samoderzhavie i dvorianstvo v kontse XIX veka*, p. 65.

6. *Novoe vremia*, no. 9,371 (6 April 1902), p. 2.

7. Solov'ev, *Samoderzhavie*, p. 322.

8. D. N. Liubimov, *Russkaia smuta nachala deviatisotykh godov, 1902–1906*, p. 52. This part of Liubimov's memoir is reproduced with some changes in *Istoricheskii arkhiv* 8, no. 6 (November–December 1962): 69–84. According to this text Pleve spoke even more enthusiastically of the state bureaucracy, quoting Pushkin: "In Russia the government has always been in advance of the people."

9. Gurko, *Features and Figures*, p. 109.

10. *Osvobozhdenie*, no. 14 (2 January 1903), p. 245.

11. S. I. Kryzhanovskii in *Padenie tsarskogo rezhima*, 5:383.

12. M. V. Islavin, *Obzor trudov vysochaishe utverzhdennoi pod predsedatel'stvom stats'-sekretaria Kakhanova osoboi kommisii*, 1:121.

13. On the interior ministry-finance ministry conflict see George L. Yaney, "Some Aspects of the Imperial Russian Government on the Eve of the First World War," pp. 68–90, and *The Systematization of Russian Government*, pp. 305–318.

14. For a list of just a few of the mass of minor decisions that required central approval see TsGIA, f. 1284, op. 194, d. 150, pp. 242f.

15. I. M. Strakhovskii, *Gubernskoe ustroistvo*, p. 108.

16. It is worth noting that when conservatives pointed to zemstvo-governor friction as grounds for abolishing the zemstvos, the liberal publicists were quick to deny that the conflict had reached crisis proportions. See, for example, *Vestnik Evropy*, no. 5 (October 1903), p. 789.

17. On the collegial structure see N. M. Korkunov, *Russkoe gosudarstvennoe pravo*, 2:684–690; N. I. Lazarevskii, "Gubernskiie prisutstviia smeshan-

nago sostava," *Pravo*, no. 23 (1 June 1903), pp. 1567–1573; and finally the most extensive history of the system, S. A. Korf's *Administrativnaia iustitsiia v Rossii.*

18. *SZ*, 2, p. 49, article 436.

19. S. D. Urusov, *Zapiski gubernatora*, p. 63. One high-ranking official of the MVD commented, "If in Russia in general the letter of the law is in contradiction with reality, then this is particularly the case in relation to the Provincial Board." Strakhovskii, *Gubernskoe ustroistvo*, pp. 271–272.

20. Liubimov, *Russkaia smuta*, p. 15. The first memorandum is summarized at length in Korf, *Administrativnaia iustitsiia*, 1:423f. Korf dates the memorandum 20 May 1901, yet this is hardly consistent with his reference to Minister of Internal Affairs Pleve as its author.

21. TsGIA, f. 1284, op. 194, d. 150, p. 150; and Korf, *Administrativnaia iustitsiia*, 1:429–430.

22. "Zapiska departamenta obshchikh del po peresmotru zakonopolozhenii o gubernskikh uchrezhdenii," TsGIA, f. 1284, op. 194, d. 150, pp. 150–182.

23. Korf, *Administrativnaia iustitsiia*, 1:423–427. Even Korf, an outspoken critic of the ministry's program, admitted that the authors of the memorandum "very accurately" described the shortcomings of the colleges.

24. Ibid., p. 428.

25. On the term *khoziain* see in particular the special note added to the journal of the ministry's commission on provincial administration, TsGIA, f. 1284, op. 194, d. 150, p. 187.

26. Previously the governor could block an appointment only within a two-week period and only on grounds of political unreliability. *SZ*, 2, pp. 26–27, article 286.

27. TsGIA, f. 1284, op. 194, d. 150, pp. 164–165 and 173–174.

28. Ibid., pp. 177–179.

29. Ibid., p. 171.

30. In the original MVD memorandum of 20 May 1902, the council was to have nine divisions. Later the number was increased to twelve. TsGIA, f. 1284, op. 194, d. 150, pp. 153–157; and Korf, *Administrativnaia iustitsiia*, 1:428–429.

31. Strakhovskii, *Gubernskoe ustroistvo*, p. 81.

32. The text of the manifesto is reproduced in G. G. Savich, *Novyi gosudarstvennyi stroi Rossii*, pp. 3–5. On its drafting see Gurko, *Features and Figures*, pp. 217–220; and Liubimov, *Russkaia smuta*, pp. 38–39.

33. The commission held two sessions, one from 27 February to 5 March and the second from 6 June to 10 June 1903. Three governors, Prince I. M. Obolenskii, Prince B. A. Vasil'chikov, and N. M. Klingenberg, attended only the first session; two others, F. E. Keller and E. A. Vatatsi, attended only the second.

34. *Zhurnal vysochaishe uchrezhdennoi kommisii po preobrazovaniiu gubernskago upravleniia*, TsGIA, f. 1284, op. 194, d. 150, pp. 188–189.

35. Liubimov claims Governors Vatatsi of Kovno and Obolenskii of Kharkov supported Vasil'chikov. Liubimov, *Russkaia smuta*, p. 32. However, Obolenskii's comments as recorded in the commission's journal and his later reply to the MVD circular on provincial administration (see note 39) suggest he opposed Vasil'chikov. TsGIA, f. 1284, op. 194, d. 150, pp. 93-95 and 192.

36. Liubimov, *Russkaia smuta*, pp. 31-32.

37. One critic has suggested that the decision to keep the old board alongside the new council was caused by a combination of timidity and error on the part of the ministry. Korf, *Administrativnaia iustitsiia*, 1:450-451. Although concern for continuity and fear of too drastic a change may have had some role, it is unlikely the commission would have planned the structure of the colleges by mistake. See in particular Strakhovskii, *Gubernskoe ustroistvo*, pp. 81f.

38. Gurko, *Features and Figures*, p. 123n.

39. The replies are summarized in *Svod mnenii gubernatorov po voprosu o preobrazovanii gubernskago upravleniia*, TsGIA, f. 1284, op. 194, d. 150. There were no answers from four of the fifty provinces: two because the governorship was vacant; one because Governor Urusov was newly appointed; and one because Vatatsi chose not to reply, as he had participated in the MVD commission.

40. Ibid., pp. 75 and 91-93.

41. Specifically, the MVD commission planned to increase the governor's control of tax collection by convening provincial congresses of tax inspectors and improving the system of reporting on revenue to the governor. Many governors approved of these measures and argued for more. For example, the Tula governor insisted that the inspectors be made his direct subordinate, and his Riazan colleague recommended that tax collection be transferred to the land captains. Ibid., pp. 82-83.

42. Ibid., p. 72.

43. S. Iu. Witte, *Vospominaniia*, 2: 206-223; Gurko, *Features and Figures*, pp. 203-205; Liubimov, *Russkaia smuta*, pp. 55-56; and *KA*, 3:135-136.

44. See W. G. Wagner, "Tsarist Legal Policies at the End of the Nineteenth Century," pp. 371-394.

45. Gurko, *Features and Figures*, p. 19.

46. See the 20 August 1903 letter of the director of the MVD Department of General Affairs, TsGIA, f. 1284, op. 194, d. 150, ch. 2, pp. 16-17.

47. *Osvobozhdenie*, no. 1/25 (18 June 1903), p. 12.

48. Ibid., pp. 11-12.

49. On Pleve's role in Witte's downfall see Witte, *Vospominaniia*, 2:247; "Dnevnik A. N. Kuropatkina," *KA*, 2:59-60; and Gurko, *Features and Figures*, pp. 221-226. Significantly, Witte's removal did not end finance ministry opposition to Pleve's program. See V. N. Kokovtsov, *Out of My Past*, pp. 27-28.

50. The commission's recommendations are presented in Gosudarstvennyi sovet, *Otchet po deloproizvodstvu gosudarstvennago soveta za sessiiu 1903–*

1904gg. (Saint Petersburg, 1905), pp. 47-61. The list is a testimony to the centralization of Russian administration. Among the most important matters to be decentralized are the approval of lectures and exhibitions (unless covered by special regulation) and of private donations for charitable purposes. The list was approved by the council with few changes and enacted by the tsar on 19 April 1904.

51. TsGIA, f. 1284, op. 194, d. 150, pp. 242f.
52. *Iskra,* no. 35 (1 March 1903).
53. *Osvobozhdenie,* no. 19 (19 March 1903), p. 321.
54. *Vestnik Evropy,* no. 2 (April 1903), p. 761.
55. Ibid., no. 6 (December 1903), pp. 804-805.
56. The editors also refused to consider a provincial council unless the representatives of self-government held a clear majority. Ibid., no. 2 (April 1903), p. 766.
57. *Novoe vremia,* no. 9,693 (28 February 1903), p. 3.
58. Ibid., no. 9,695 (2 March 1903), p. 3.
59. Ibid., p. 3.
60. Ibid., no. 9,702 (9 March 1903), p. 3.
61. As quoted in *Novoe vremia,* no. 9,695 (2 March 1903), p. 4.
62. Ibid., no. 9,703 (10 March 1903), p. 2. Golovin maintained that in England the justice of the peace and in Prussia the *Landrat* represented the elective principle.
63. The editors admitted that "the present situation in which the leading role in district administration belongs to a person elected by one estate cannot be considered fully normal—of this there is no doubt." However, they contended that until a "fundamental change for the better" in domestic politics occurred, "the most proper resolution of this question is in our eyes the retention of the *status quo*" (*Vestnik Evropy,* no. 5 [October 1903], p. 782).
64. An 1899 finance-interior presentation on factory police, for instance, contained the admission that the only important change in the "district" (or rural) police had been the introduction of the sergeants in 1878 and that the effect of this reform had been "insignificant" (*nishtozhnyi*). Gosudarstvennyi sovet, *Otchet po deloproizvodstvu gosudarstvennago soveta za sessiiu 1899-1900gg.,* (Saint Petersburg, 1901), p. 662. A relatively complete compilation of imperial legislation on police force increases between 1881 and 1900 is presented in *Istoricheskii ocherk organizatsii i deiatel'nosti departamenta politsii,* TsGAOR, f. DP, op. 302, d. 707, ch. 2, pp. 36-81.
65. Gosudarstvennyi sovet, *Otchet za 1899-1900gg.,* p. 662.
66. Ibid., pp. 661f, and *Istoricheskii ocherk organizatsii i deiatel'nosti departamenta politsii,* TsGAOR, f. DP, op. 302, d. 707, ch. 2, p. 79.
67. This is reflected in the data on cases handled under Article 34 of the *Polozhenie o gosudarstvennoi okhrane,* the empire's special code for political crimes. Between 1895 and 1900, for example, cases of factory disorder, essentially urban in nature, numbered 268 and involved 1,745 arrests.

Agrarian disorders totalled 127, with only 347 people prosecuted. *Istoricheskii ocherk organizatsii i deiatel'nosti departamenta politsii,* TsGAOR, f. DP, op. 302, d. 707, ch. 2, pp. 158–159.

68. See, for instance, the data presented by S. S. Ostroumov, *Prestupnost' i ee prichiny v dorevoliutsionnoi Rossii,* p. 105. Many of the muzhik criminals, it should be noted, must have been "peasants" who had in actuality joined the factory labor force.

69. D. S. Fleksor, *Okhrana sel'skokhoziaistvennoi sobstvennosti,* p. 53.

70. *Svod vysochaishikh otmetok po vsepoddanneishim otchetom general-gubernatorov za 1900g.* (Saint Petersburg, 1901), pp. 8–9.

71. Many of the sergeants, including 572 maintained at the expense of industrialists, confined their attention to the factories. This was compensated in part by aid the urban police occasionally rendered to the rural police. The rural force also included 506 district police chiefs and their assistants. They usually resided in the district city, however, and their effect on the villages was very limited. *Istoricheskii ocherk organizatsii i deiatel'nosti departamenta politsii,* TsGAOR, f. DP, op. 302, d. 707, ch. 2, pp. 112–113.

72. TsGAOR, f. 102, op. 2 (1907g.), d. 14, ch. 4a, p. 2.

73. V. V. Tenishev, *Administrativnoe polozhenie russkago krest'ianina,* pp. 54–55.

74. Fleksor, *Okhrana,* pp. 54–56.

75. Gosudarstvennyi sovet, *Otchet po deloproizvodstvu gosudarstvennago soveta za sessiiu 1902–1903gg.* (Saint Petersburg, 1904), pp. 206f.

76. Ibid., pp. 206–207 and 215.

77. Ibid., pp. 207–208.

78. Ibid., pp. 210–213.

79. Ibid., pp. 214–216.

80. Ibid., p. 207.

81. A. A. Lopukhin, *Iz itogov sluzhebnago opyta,* p. 4.

82. See Fleksor, *Okhrana,* pp. 56–57 and 75–76.

CHAPTER III

1. Vladimir I. Gurko, *Features and Figures of the Past,* p. 237.

2. Ibid., p. 6.

3. *Trudy redaktsionnoi kommisii po peresmotru zakonopolozhenii o krest'ianakh* (Saint Petersburg, 1903), 1:8; and Gurko, *Features and Figures,* p. 131.

4. Polovtsov, for example, recorded in his diary on 1 May 1902 that Pleve had expressed his willingness to cooperate with Witte's conference toward reform. *KA,* 3:142–144. See also Gurko, *Features and Figures,* p. 112.

5. Gurko, *Features and Figures,* p. 157, and *KA,* 3:144. Pleve had earlier been a spokesman for the government policy of maintaining communal landholding, but by the time of his appointment as minister his views

had changed. See David A. Macey, "The Russian Bureaucracy and the 'Peasant Problem,'" pp. 102–103 and 107–109.

6. Gurko, *Features and Figures*, p. 157. Hereafter the MVD body will be referred to simply as the Stishinskii Commission.

7. *Pravo*, no. 1 (1903), p. 807.

8. G. G. Savich, *Novyi gosudarstvennyi stroi Rossii*, pp. 3–4.

9. The Soviet historian M. S. Simonova has noted this ambivalence, arguing that it represented a conflict between feudal and bourgeois capitalist directions. She writes, "The attempt to reconcile a reactionary political course in relation to the peasantry with the demands of capitalist development and at the same time to preserve the feudal foundations of the traditional agrarian policy caused a profoundly contradictory and eclectic government project for agrarian reform" ("Politika tsarizma v krest'ianskom voprose nakanune revoliutsii 1905–1907gg.," p. 218). See also Macey's "Russian Bureaucracy," pp. 244f. The findings of the Stishinskii Commission are presented in *Trudy redaktsionnoi kommisii*.

10. D. N. Liubimov, *Russkaia smuta nachala deviatisotykh godov*, p. 38.

11. Gurko, *Features and Figures*, p. 197.

12. See Liubimov, *Russkaia smuta*, pp. 37–38; and S. E. Kryzhanovskii, *Vospominaniia*, pp. 12–14 and 210.

13. See Gosudarstvennyi sovet, *Otchet po deloproizvodstvu gosudarstvennago soveta za sessiiu 1902–1903gg.* (Saint Petersburg, 1904), pp. 645–655, and *KA*, 3:141.

14. *KA*, 3:141–142. Pleve did urge that the reform not be extended to five districts where agrarian disorders had taken place, but this proposal was rejected.

15. Gosudarstvennyi sovet, *Otchet za 1902–1903gg.*, p. 215.

16. For details on this incident see Gurko, *Features and Figures*, pp. 133–141.

17. Savich, *Novyi stroi*, pp. 4–5.

18. Commenting on the reference to the parish in the manifesto, the editors wrote, "It is difficult not to see this as an undoubted success for the idea expressed in the now universal rumors of a local zemstvo." *Navoe vremia*, no. 9,692 (27 February 1903), p. 3. Witte also took this view, as in his *Zapiska po krest'ianskomu delu*, pp. 62–64.

19. Gurko, *Features and Figures*, p. 218.

20. *Trudy redaktsionnoi kommisii*, 1:10.

21. Liubimov, *Russkaia smuta*, pp. 37–38.

22. D. N. Shipov, *Vospominanii i dumy o perezhitom*, p. 184. See also Gurko, *Features and Figures*, pp. 234–237; I. P. Belokonskii, "Zemskoe dvizhenie do obrazovaniia partii narodnoi svobody," no. 8/20 (August 1907), pp. 253f; and B. B. Veselovskii, *Istoriia zemstva za sorok let*, 3:545–546.

23. *Trudy redaktsionnoi kommisii*, 1:12.

24. Ibid., 1:39–44. The communes were to be called "land societies" (*zemel'nye obshchestva*). The village communities would retain their old name.

25. Gurko, *Features and Figures*, p. 160. For Gurko's view of the commission's work see ibid., pp. 134–140 and 156–166.
26. *Trudy redaktsionnoi kommisii*, 1:13.
27. G. A. Evreinov, *Krest'ianskii vopros v trudakh obrazovannoi v sostave ministerstva vnutrennikh del kommisii po peresmotru zakonopolozhenii o krest'ianakh*, p. 5.
28. A. D. Golitsyn, *Vospominaniia Kniazia A. D. Golitsyna*, p. 75; and A. N. Naumov, *Iz utselevshikh vospominanii, 1868–1917*, 1:187.
29. Gosudarstvennyi sovet, *Otchet po deloproizvodstvu gosudarstvennago soveta za sessiiu 1903–1904gg.* (Saint Petersburg, 1905), pp. 121–146. The MVD also asked for authority to issue "a special code, defining in detail the procedure by which land captains execute their duties."
30. V. A. Maklakov, *Vlast' i obshchestvennost' no zakate staroi Rossii*.
31. On the need to win over the public in this way see Polovtsov, *KA*, 3:139; Murav'ev as quoted in "Dnevnik A. N. Kuropatkina," *KA*, 2:11; and Witte as quoted in Liubimov, *Russkaia smuta*, pp. 48–50.
32. Shipov, *Vospominaniia*, pp. 174–175.
33. N. M. Pirumova, *Zemskoe liberal'noe dvizhenie*, p. 202.
34. *Osvobozhdenie*, no. 12 (2 December 1902), pp. 197–198; and Gurko, *Features and Figures*, p. 228.
35. *Osvobozhdenie*, no. 14 (2 January 1903), pp. 245–246.
36. *Pravo*, no. 10 (2 March 1903), p. 722.
37. TsGIA, f. 1284, op. 194, d. 150, p. 172.
38. Gurko, *Features and Figures*, p. 112. See also the private correspondence of A. I. Antonov with Pleve, TsGAOR, f. 586, op. 1, d. 320.
39. Gurko, *Features and Figures*, p. 228.
40. *Osvobozhdenie*, no. 14 (2 January 1903), p. 245.
41. Ibid., no. 22 (8 May 1903), p. 387.
42. Quoted in Pirumova, *Zemskoe dvizhenie*, p. 203.
43. For a thorough, if hostile, commentary on Witte's measures, see *Osvobozhdenie*'s preface to the published version of *Samoderzhavie i zemstvo*.
44. Veselovskii, *Istoriia zemstva*, 1:15; and Gurko, *Features and Figures*, pp. 234–237.
45. On the 1902 law and reaction to it see Veselovskii, *Istoriia zemstva*, 2:441–442; and Gosudarstvennyi sovet, *Otchet po deloproizvodstvu gosudarstvennago soveta za sessiiu 1901–1902gg.* (Saint Petersburg, 1903), pp. 437–447.
46. Gosudarstvennyi sovet, *Otchet za 1902–1903gg.*, pp. 717–733; Veselovskii, *Istoriia zemstva*, 2:442–443; and Shipov, *Vospominaniia*, pp. 199–203.
47. Veselovskii, *Istoriia zemstva*, 2:341, and 3:578; Shipov, *Vospominaniia*, p. 216; and Belokonskii, "Zemskoe dvizhenie," no. 9/21 (September 1907), p. 233.
48. Veselovskii, *Istoriia zemstva*, 2:635–636; and Shipov, *Vospominaniia*, p. 215.

49. This particular conference was convened on the initiative of Witte's Special Conference on the Needs of Agriculture, but Pleve took an active part. Veselovskii, *Istoriia zemstva*, 2:650, and 3:578; Shipov, *Vospominaniia*, p. 221; and MVD, Glavnoe upravlenie po delam mestnago khoziaistva, *Ob ustanovleniia glavnykh osnovanii preobrazovaniia zemskikh i gorodskikh uchrezhdenii* (Saint Petersburg, 1907), p. 14.

50. Shipov, *Vospominaniia*, p. 220.

51. Gosudarstvennyi sovet, *Otchet za 1902–1903gg.*, pp. 72–73.

52. Even Veselovskii, a firm critic of government policy, approved of the measure. Veselovskii, *Istoriia zemstva*, 1:191–192.

53. On Gerbel see Golitsyn, *Vospominaniia*, p. 72. Pleve even considered Shipov for the position. Shipov, *Vospominaniia*, p. 184.

54. Gurko, *Features and Figures*, pp. 184–185n.

55. Gosudarstvennyi sovet, *Otchet za 1902–1903gg.*, pp. 333–338.

56. Significantly, even the State Council majority had reservations about the extent of the proposed MVD supervisory powers. Ibid., pp. 336 and 392–395.

57. Gurko, *Features and Figures*, p. 227.

58. Liubimov, *Russkaia smuta*, p. 53.

59. *Osvobozhdenie*, no. 14 (2 January 1903), p. 245.

60. Ibid., no. 22 (8 May 1903), p. 387.

61. Gurko, *Features and Figures*, pp. 234–237; Belokonskii, "Zemskoe dvizhenie," no. 8/20 (August 1907), pp. 253–255; Veselovskii, *Istoriia zemstva*, 3:545–546; and Maureen Perrie, *The Agrarian Policy of the Russian Socialist-Revolutionary Party from its Origins through the Revolution of 1905–1907*, pp. 39–40 and 82–88.

62. Shipov, *Vospominaniia*, pp. 169–170.

63. Initially, Pleve intended to force Evreinov to resign as district marshal, but he settled for a reprimand. Dolgorukov was later forced out of office in the district zemstvo and forbidden to serve in public institutions for five years. On the repression of the Sudzha and Voronezh committees see Belokonskii, "Zemskoe dvizhenie," no. 7/19 (July 1907), pp. 233–240, and no. 8/20 (August 1907), pp. 241–247; *Osvobozhdenie*, nos. 10–13 (2 November–19 December 1902); and Simonova, "Zemsko-liberal'naia fronda," pp. 170–179. Liubimov maintains that governors unable or unwilling to take active measures against the local committees, like those of Kursk and Voronezh, resigned. Liubimov, *Russkaia smuta*, p. 44.

64. *Osvobozhdenie*, no. 19 (19 March 1903), pp. 321–323.

65. Shipov, *Vospominaniia*, p. 207n.

66. Belokonskii, "Zemskoe dvizhenie," no. 9/21 (September 1907), pp. 242–243; and Shipov, *Vospominaniia*, p. 220.

67. Veselovskii, *Istoriia zemstva*, 3:576–577; Shipov, *Vospominaniia*, pp. 215–218; Belokonskii, "Zemskoe dvizhenie," no. 9/21 (September 1907), pp. 232–242; and S. Galai, *The Liberation Movement in Russia, 1900–1905*, pp. 170–171.

68. Evreinov, *Krest'ianskii vopros*, pp. 3-4; and Naumov, *Iz utselevshikh vospominanii*, 1:335.

69. Liubimov, *Russkaia smuta*, pp. 19-23.

70. Ibid., p. 21n. Liubimov claims that only a warm reception by the tsar for the Kursk provincial marshal resolved the issue.

71. *Osvobozhdenie*, no. 10 (2 November 1902), pp. 146-147.

72. Nicholas II passed over A. A. Mukhanov in favor of the gentry's second candidate. Gurko, who points to this incident as one of the most important in alienating the gentry from Pleve, claims the decision was the tsar's own and that Pleve only took responsibility for it to protect the ruler's prestige. Gurko, *Features and Figures,* pp. 233-234. It should be noted, however, that Mukhanov had been active in the Chernigov zemstvo, and earlier that same year Pleve had forced from office another leader of the zemstvo, A. A. Rusov. Veselovskii, *Istoriia zemstva,* 3:547, and 4:307-309.

73. *Novoe vremia*, no. 9,701 (8 March 1903), pp. 2-3; no. 9,703 (10 March 1903), p. 2; and no. 9,725 (1 April 1903), p. 2. At the very time that the MVD was struggling to strengthen its powers of appointment over the land captains, Golovin proposed they be elected.

74. The address is reproduced in *Osvobozhdenie*, no. 15-16/39-40 (19 January 1904), pp. 290-291. On the Smolensk gentry see Veselovskii, *Istoriia zemstva,* 2:514-519, and 3:685.

75. Gurko, *Features and Figures,* pp. 123-124.

76. On the Union of Liberation and the liberal movement generally see Belokonskii, "Zemskoe dvizhenie," no. 9/21 (September 1907), pp. 257-259; Chermenskii, *Burzhuaziia,* pp. 30-35; Galai, *Liberation Movement,* pp. 177f; George Fischer, *Russian Liberalism,* pp. 139-152; Richard Pipes, *Struve: Liberal on the Left,* pp. 332-358; and K. F. Shatsillo, "Formirovanie programmy zemskogo liberalizma i ee bankrotstvo nakanune pervoi russkoi revoliutsii," pp. 75-95.

77. Veselovskii, *Istoriia zemstva,* 3: 576-580; and Belokonskii, "Zemskoe dvizhenie," no. 9/21 (September 1907), p. 243 and pp. 260-267.

78. Veselovskii, *Istoriia zemstva,* 3: 577-578; and *Osvobozhdenie,* no. 15-16/39-40 (19 January 1904), p. 289.

79. Belokonskii, "Zemskoe dvizhenie," no. 10/22 (October 1907), pp. 254-258; Gurko, *Features and Figures,* pp. 239-241; and Naumov, *Iz utselevshikh vospominanii,* 1:361.

80. See Chermenskii, *Burzhuaziia,* pp. 32f; and S. Galai, "The Impact of War on the Russian Liberals in 1904-5," pp. 85-109.

81. "25 let nazad (Iz dnevnikov L. Tikhomirova)," *KA*, 38:59.

CHAPTER IV

1. For these programs and several dozen others, see V. V. Vodovozov, ed., *Sbornik programm politicheskikh partii v Rossii;* and *Polnyi sbornik platform vsekh russkikh politicheskikh partii.*

2. On the liberal movement in 1904-1906, see E. D. Chermenskii, *Burzhuaziia i tsarizm v pervoi russkoi revoliutsii*, pp. 12-127; George Fischer, *Russian Liberalism*, chapter 5; Richard Pipes, *Struve: Liberal on the Left*, pp. 359-390; Terence Emmons, "Russia's Banquet Campaign"; and K. F. Shatsillo, "Formirovanie programmy zemskogo liberalizma i ee bankrotstvo nakanune pervoi russkoi revoliutsii," pp. 75-95.

3. N. I. Lazarevskii, "Biurokratiia i obshchestvo," *Pravo*, no. 4 (30 January 1905), pp. 205-214.

4. Ibid., pp. 207-209.

5. Pipes, *Struve: Liberal on the Left*, p. 366; and D. N. Liubimov, *Russkaia smuta nachala deviatisotykh godov*, p. 145.

6. An analysis of the petition campaign is given in Roberta Thompson Manning, "The Russian Provincial Gentry in Revolution and Counterrevolution," pp. 108-133.

7. On Sviatopolk-Mirskii and his appointment, see "Dnevnik kn. Ekateriny Alekseevny Sviatopolk Mirskoi za 1904-1905gg.," *Istoricheskie zapiski* 77 (1965): 236-241; Vladimir I. Gurko, *Features and Figures of the Past*, pp. 293-296; and S. Iu. Witte, *Vospominaniia*, 2:321-323.

8. "Dnevnik kn. Ekateriny Alekseevny Sviatopolk Mirskoi za 1904-1905gg.," pp. 241-242.

9. A. A. Lopukhin, *Otryvki iz vospominanii*, pp. 44-45; Gurko, *Features and Figures*, pp. 300-302; Witte, *Vospominaniia*, 2:328-329; and S. E. Kryzhanovskii, *Vospominaniia*, pp. 16-18.

10. Vysochaishe uchrezhdennoe osoboe soveshchanie o nuzhdakh sel'skokhoziaistvennoi promyshlennosti, *Protokoly po krest'ianskomu delu* 3 (15 December 1904): 20-25.

11. Ibid., p. 25.

12. Lopukhin, *Otryvki iz vospominanii*, p. 45.

13. Liubimov, *Russkaia smuta*, pp. 145-146; Gurko, *Features and Figures*, pp. 304-309; "Dnevnik kn. Ekateriny Alekseevny Sviatopolk Mirskoi za 1904-1905gg.," pp. 249-252; and Shatsillo, "Formirovanie," pp. 83-91.

14. "Dnevnik kn. Ekateriny Alekseevny Sviatopolk Mirskoi za 1904-1905gg.," p. 266.

15. For details on the conference see Liubimov, *Russkaia smuta*, pp. 156-157; Lopukhin, *Otryvki iz vospominanii*, pp. 46-58; Gurko, *Features and Figures*, pp. 300-304; "Dnevnik kn. Ekateriny Alekseevny Sviatopolk Mirskoi za 1904-1905gg.," pp. 260-266.

16. Gurko, *Features and Figures*, p. 304.

17. Nicholas II accepted the resignation but asked the minister to stay on for one month until a successor could be found. The text of the 12 December Ukaz is reproduced in Sidney Harcave, *First Blood*, pp. 282-285.

18. Komitet ministrov, *Zhurnaly komiteta ministrov po ispolneniiu Ukaza 12 Dekabria 1904g.*

19. Harcave, *First Blood*, pp. 142-143; and Chermenskii, *Burzhuaziia*, p. 164.

20. "Dnevnik kn. Ekateriny Alekseevny Sviatopolk Mirskoi za 1904-1905gg.," p. 259. The voluminous material on the decision to issue the

October Manifesto is ably summarized by Howard D. Mehlinger and John M. Thompson, *Count Witte and the Tsarist Government in the 1905 Revolution*, pp. 29–46. On the Witte cabinet see also Theodore H. Von Laue, "Count Witte and the 1905 Revolution," pp. 25–46.

21. V. P. Semennikov, ed., *Revoliutsiia 1905 goda i samoderzhavie*, pp. 54–55.

22. The manifesto and Witte's report are translated in Mehlinger and Thompson, *Count Witte*, pp. 331–335. For the original text of the report see Witte, *Vospominaniia*, 3:4–7.

23. Witte, *Vospominaniia*, 3:526.

24. S. Iu. Witte, *Zapiska po krest'ianskomu delu*. On the authorship of the memorandum see David A. Macey, "The Russian Bureaucracy and the 'Peasant Problem,'" p. 317; and Gurko, *Features and Figures*, p. 326.

25. Witte, *Vospominaniia*, 3:77. On the Durnovo appointment see this source, pp. 68–77; Gurko, *Features and Figures*, pp. 403–410; Shipov, *Vospominaniia i dumy o perezhitom*, pp. 339–345; and Mehlinger and Thompson, *Count Witte*, pp. 78–80.

26. For the dynamics of Urusov's promotion see Gurko, *Features and Figures*, p. 404. Witte in his memoirs distances himself from Urusov, but it is more than likely that his recollections were colored by Urusov's later disgrace. Witte, *Vospominaniia*, 3:71–72.

27. The commission and its work are described in "Zhurnal kommissii po razrabotke proekta preobrazovaniia mestnago upravleniia," TsGIA, f. 1288, op. 1, d. 3 (1906).

28. Ibid., pp. 4–7.

29. Ibid., pp. 19–25 and 30.

30. The board was to have six members: two zemstvo representatives, the highest ranking local judicial official, the tax inspector, and the commander and his assistant. Ibid., p. 28.

31. Ibid., p. 27.

32. Witte denies responsibility for the Kutler plan in *Vospominaniia*, 3:195–204. His testimony is challenged, however, by Gurko, *Features and Figures*, p. 325, and Vladimir N. Kokovtsov, *Out of My Past*, p. 100. On the Witte cabinet's land policy see B. B. Veselovskii, ed., *Agrarnyi vopros v sovete ministrov (1906g.)*; M. S. Simonova, "Agrarnaia politika samoderzhaviia v 1905g.," pp. 199–215; Mehlinger and Thompson, *Count Witte*, pp. 178–208; Macey, "The Russian Bureaucracy," chapter 6; and Richard Hennessey, *The Agrarian Question in Russia, 1905–1907*.

33. A copy of the draft bill is available in the Witte Papers, Columbia University Archive of Russian and East European History and Culture, box 7, folder 14, document 1.

34. Kokovtsov, *My Past*, p. 124.

35. S. E. Kryzhanovskii in *Padenie tsarskogo rezhima*, 5:395–396.

36. Edward J. Bing, ed., *The Secret Letters of the Last Tsar*, p. 211.

37. Gurko, *Features and Figures*, p. 709.

38. Bernard Pares, *The Fall of the Russian Monarchy*, p. 86.

39. *Polnyi sbornik platform vsekh russkikh politicheskikh partii*, pp. 11–28.

40. See Oskar Anweiler, *Die Ratebewegung in Russland 1905-1921* (Leiden: E. J. Brill, 1958).

41. Of the many sources on the peasantry see S. M. Dubrovskii, *Krest'ianskoe dvizhenie v revoliutsii 1905-1907gg.*; P. N. Pershin, *Agrarnaia revoliutsiia v Rossii*; and Maureen Perrie, *The Agrarian Policy of the Russian Socialist-Revolutionary Party*, pp. 118-139. Peasants did occasionally express formal opinions on these issues. The All-Russian Peasant Union, for instance, passed resolutions against all existing officials from governor to village policeman and in favor of estate equality and the election of new officials through universal suffrage. It is unclear, however, to what degree the resolutions accurately reflected peasant opinion rather than that of the liberal and socialist intelligentsia advising the union. Vodovozov, *Sbornik programm*, 3:42-44.

42. P. N. Miliukov in Vodovozov, *Sbornik programm*, 1:35-36.

43. Chermenskii, *Burzhuaziia*, p. 162.

44. For the initial program of the Cadet Party see N. I. Astrov et al., eds., *Zakonodatel'nye proekty i predpolozheniia partii narodnoi svobody, 1905-1907gg.*, pp. xi-xix. On the agrarian question in particular see the same source, pp. 301-325; and D. I. Pestrzhetskii, *Obzor agrarnago proekta konstitutsionno-demokraticheskoi partii.*

45. The following analysis of the Cadet viewpoint on local administration is drawn from a number of programs, draft bills, and policy statements developed by the party in the period between its founding and the dissolution of the Second Duma. The basic principles of the party in this area were stated as early as September 1905 and underwent remarkably little change over the next two years, a fact that reflects the real unanimity within the organization on this question. See *Doklad organizatsionnago biuro s'ezdu zemskikh i gorodskikh deiatelei 12-15 sentiabria 1905g.*; Astrov et al., *Zakonodatel'nye proekty*; A. A. Mukhanov and V. D. Nabokov, *Pervaia gosudarstvennaia duma*; the materials published in *Vestnik partii narodnoi svobody*, nos. 21-22 (1906) and no. 10 (1907); and *Samoupravlenie*, nos. 5, 13-16, and 20-23 (1907).

46. Astrov et al., *Zakonodatel'nye proekty*, p. xi.

47. In place of the existing volost the Cadets proposed a new subdistrict (*uchastkovoe*) zemstvo that would include the entire local population and would work closely with the district zemstvo, after which it was modelled. Where the population of a village was large enough to warrant it the old village community was to be replaced with a settlement (*poselkovoe*) organization that was also to be all-estate in nature. Ibid., pp. 201-221.

48. Ibid., p. 149.

49. Ibid., p. 36.

50. Ibid., p. 39.

51. On the field courts-martial and the Cadet attitude see Alfred Levin, *The Second Duma*, pp. 259-270; and V. A. Maklakov, *Vtoraia gosudarstvennaia duma*, pp. 40f. The Cadets brought forward a number of bills

protecting citizens' rights, including particularly a "legislative project on habeas corpus, the home, and private correspondence" (Astrov et al., *Zakonodatel'nye proekty*, pp. 69-73).

52. Astrov et al., *Zakonodatel'nye proekty*, p. 39.

53. Ibid., p. 147. For the Cadet view of the zemstvo see also I. P. Belokonskii, *Shto takoe zemstvo, shto ono sdelalo dlia naroda i kakim dolzhno byt'* (Moscow, 1906).

54. Astrov et al., *Zakonodatel'nye proekty*, p. xiv.

55. Ibid., pp. 135-137 and 150-152.

56. A. A. Lopukhin, *Iz itogov sluzhebnago opyta*, pp. 2-3.

57. For official reports on the destruction of estates see *KA*, 9:70-93, and 11-12:182-192.

58. Samarin Papers, GBL, f. 265, k. 208, ed. 25.

59. Witte Papers, Columbia University Archive, box 8, folder 19, document 1.

60. Among the zemstvo's employees was I. P. Belokonskii, a statistician later distinguished for his history of the zemstvo movement. Raevskii had encouraged the zemstvo to sponsor the 1902 all-Russian conference on popular education. On the Kursk zemstvo see Veselovskii, *Istoriia zemstva za sorok let*, 4:332f.

61. Ibid., pp. 58 and 384f.

62. On the formation of the congress see *Trudy I-go s'ezda upolnomochennykh dvorianskikh obshchestv 32 gubernii*, pp. 138, 142, and 178; I. D. Vaisberg, "Sovet ob'edinennogo dvorianstva i ego vliianie na politiku samoderzhaviia," pp. 87-88; A. N. Naumov, *Iz utselevshikh vospominanii*, 2:45-46; and Geoffrey A. Hosking and Roberta Thompson Manning, "What was the United Nobility?," in *The Politics of Rural Russia*, ed. Leopold H. Haimson, pp. 150-154. The organization will be referred to as the United Nobility for short.

63. *Trudy I-go s'ezda*, pp. 178-180. In a similar vein the commission rejected Saint Petersburg Marshal V. V. Gudovich's proposal that the provincial marshals be given an automatic vote. Vaisberg, "Sovet ob'edinennogo dvorianstva," pp. 87-88.

64. *Trudy I-go s'ezda*, pp. 17, 39, and 149. Leaders of the congress did try to restore unity by persuading the most vituperative critics, S. S. Bekhteev and Kursk's N. E. Markov, to apologize for the sharpness of their remarks. Trubetskoi did not return.

65. Veselovskii, *Istoriia zemstva*, 4:54-55 and 61.

66. Ibid., pp. 68 and 387, and V. S. Golubev, *Po zemskim voprosam*, 2:39-42.

67. Veselovskii, *Istoriia zemstva*, 4:54-64.

68. Vaisberg, "Sovet ob'edinennogo dvorianstva," p. 194.

69. There exists a wide range of sources on both the "coup" of 3 June and the Stolypin agrarian reform. For a basic discussion of the former, see A. Ia. Avrekh, *Tsarizm i tret'eiiunskaia sistema*, and "Tret'eiiunskaia monarkhiia i obrazovanie tret'edumskogo pomeshchich'e-burzhuaznogo bloka,"

pp. 3–70; and Geoffrey A. Hosking, *The Russian Constitutional Experiment*, pp. 28–45. On the Stolypin agrarian reform, see S. M. Dubrovskii, *Stolypinskaia zemel'naia reforma;* George L. Yaney, "The Concept of the Stolypin Land Reform," pp. 275–293, and "The Imperial Russian Government and the Stolypin Land Reform"; Hosking, *Russian Experiment*, pp. 56–73; Macey, "The Russian Bureaucracy"; and the documents in S. M. Sidel'nikov, ed., *Agrarnaia reforma Stolypina*.

70. For example, V. Levitskii, "Pravye partii," in *Obshchestvennoe dvizhenie v Rossii v nachale XX-go veka*, ed. L. Martov et al., 3:347f; Vaisberg, "Sovet ob'edinennogo dvorianstva," pp. 218f; and Hosking and Manning, "United Nobility," pp. 159–160 and 169.

71. Stolypin expressed his ideas many times, most succinctly in his gubernatorial report of 1904. *KA*, 17:84–87. Gurko's views have already been analyzed.

72. TsGAOR, f. 434, d. 30, p. 16; and N. M. Pirumova, *Zemskoe liberal'noe dvizhenie*, p. 123.

73. *Pravo*, no. 4 (29 January 1906), p. 331.

74. *Trudy III-go s'ezda upolnomochennykh dvorianskikh obshchestv 32 gubernii, s 27 marta po 2 aprelia 1907g.*, p. 42.

75. Ibid., pp. 110–111.

76. *Trudy IV-go s'ezda upolnomochennykh dvorianskikh obshchestv 32 gubernii, s 9 po 16 marta 1908g.*, pp. 255–259. See also the speeches of Ia. N. Ofrosimov, Iu. V. Arsen'ev, and Prince N. B. Shcherbatov, pp. 74–84 and 240.

77. *Trudy I-go s'ezda*, pp. 167–168.

78. F. Dan and N. Cherevanin, "Soiuz 17 Oktiabria," in *Obshchestvennoe dvizhenie v Rossii v nachale XX-go veka*, 3:174. On the origins of Octobrism see Chermenskii, *Burzhuaziia*, pp. 197f; Shipov, *Vospominaniia*, pp. 391–422; Dan and Cherevanin, "Soiuz 17 Oktiabria"; and Michael C. Brainerd, "The Octobrists and the Gentry, 1905–1907," in Haimson, *The Politics of Rural Russia*, pp. 67–93.

79. Other signers included A. A. Stolypin, brother of the future minister, A. N. Nikitin, deputy chairman of the Saint Petersburg town council, and N. P. Perepelkin of the Moscow council.

80. The diversity of the party is indicated by the composition of its provincial branches. Of the 145 members in early 1906 for whom information is available, 41 were listed as businessmen, 33 as officials, 20 as members of the free professions, 15 as large landowners (*pomeshchiki*), 10 as "employees" (*sluzhashchie*), 8 as teachers, 8 as petty bourgeois (*meshchane*), and 5 as clergy; there were only 3 peasants and 2 workers. A more accurate picture of the party's complexion, however, is provided by its central committee. Eleven members represented trade and industry, 6 were large landowners, and 5 were from the free professions. Chermenskii, *Burzhuaziia*, p. 207.

81. Veselovskii, *Istoriia zemstva*, 4:58; and Brainerd, "Octobrists and Gen-

try," pp. 64-66 and 78-79. Sixty-six of the Octobrist delegates to the Third Duma had experience in zemstvo work. See Robert Edelman, *Gentry Politics on the Eve of the Russian Revolution*, p. 42.

82. Shipov, *Vospominaniia*, pp. 529-534; and Dan and Cherevanin, "Soiuz 17 Oktiabria," pp. 188-190.
83. Shipov, *Vospominaniia*, pp. 530-531.
84. See A. D. Golitsyn, *Vospominaniia Kniazia A. D. Golitsyna*, pp. 126-143 and 194; and Veselovskii, *Istoriia zemstva*, 4:319-321.
85. *Polnyi sbornik platform vsekh russkikh politicheskikh partii*, p. 99.
86. Ibid., p. 101.
87. Ibid., p. 98.
88. Dan and Cherevanin, "Soiuz 17 Oktiabria," p. 172.
89. *Polnyi sbornik platform vsekh russkikh politicheskikh partii*, pp. 94-95.
90. Golitsyn, *Vospominaniia*, pp. 168f.
91. Shipov, *Vospominaniia*, pp. 536-537.
92. Von Laue, "Count Witte," p. 32.

CHAPTER V

1. See, for example, K. K. Troitskii, *Iz vospominanii chinovnika osobykh poruchenii*, Columbia University Archive of Russian and East European History and Culture, 2:1.
2. Maria P. Bock, *Reminiscences of My Father, Peter A. Stolypin*, pp. 3-5; A. Meyendorf, "A brief appreciation of P. Stolypin's tenure of office" and note of 6 February 1938, pp. 4-8, Columbia University Archive; and Mary Schaeffer Conroy, *Peter Arkad'evich Stolypin*.
3. Stolypin was not entirely without influential relations at the court, including his brothers-in-law A. B. and D. B. Neidgart. Credit for recommending Stolypin to Nicholas II has been assigned variously to them and to Prince A. D. Obolenskii, Goremykin, and Gurko. Nevertheless, the key element in his selection was his reputation for courageously battling revolution in Saratov. Vladimir I. Gurko, *Features and Figures of the Past*, pp. 460-461; and S. E. Kryzhanovskii, *Vospominaniia*, p. 211.
4. Kryzhanovskii, *Vospominaniia*, p. 209.
5. The single incident which contributed most to Stolypin's fame was one in which he alone quieted a crowd of monarchists trying to inflict mob violence on third-element workers in the town of Balmashev. Stolypin's daughter describes the event in detail, although interestingly enough fails to mention that the crowd represented the right and not the left of the political spectrum. Maria P. Bock, "Stolypin in Saratov," pp. 187-193.
6. *KA*, 17:86.
7. Bock, *Reminiscences*, p. 125.
8. Stolypin did bring to the ministry several former associates, including A. A. Makarov, a Saratov judicial official who became assistant minister,

and I. G. Knoll, Saratov's vice-governor now named head of Stolypin's chancellery. There was, however, no major reworking of the staff as under Pleve.

9. I. Ia. Gurliand, *Prikaz velikago gosudaria tainykh del* (Iaroslavl, 1902).

10. "Iz dnevnika L'va Tikhomirova," *KA*, 73:174.

11. E. Verkhopatskii, *Gosudarstvennaia deiatel'nost' predsedatelia soveta ministrov stats-sekretaria Petra Arkad'evicha Stolypina*, 2:6.

12. *KA*, 32: 181-182. See also Stolypin's circular of 14 September 1906 in TsGAOR, f. DP II (1905), no. 13, ch. 1, pp. 109-110; and Alfred Levin, "P. A. Stolypin," p. 452.

13. In a circular dated 15 September 1906 Stolypin characterized the new responsibilities connected with the reform this way: "Swiftness in the designated land operations is one of the most positive and effective means of pacifying the village populace, this . . . lays upon its executors an obligation of extraordinary state importance." *KA*, 32:163.

14. S. A. Korf, *Administrativnaia iustitsiia v Rossii*, 1:455-456.

15. Kryzhanovskii, *Vospominaniia*, p. 18. Strakhovskii was Gurko's assistant in the MVD Land Section and had participated as an adviser in the Urusov group. Also on Stolypin's committee were the minister's Saratov comrades Knoll and Makarov, Director of the MVD's Department of General Affairs A. D. Arbuzov, and Saint Petersburg Governor A. D. Zinov'ev. I. M. Strakhovskii, *Gubernskoe ustroistvo*, p. 74n.

16. *Rossiia*, no. 925 (26 November 1908), p. 1.

17. Ibid., no. 941 (14 December 1908), p. 1.

18. MVD, "Po proektam polozhenii: 1) O poselkovom upravlenii, 2) o volostnom upravlenii, i 3) o pravitel'stvennykh uchastkovykh kommisarakh," TsGIA, f. 1284, op. 185 (1907), d. 5a, ch. 1, p. 49.

19. MVD, *Polozhenie o gubernskom upravlenii. Proekt* (Saint Petersburg, 1907), pp. 4-14. The project is analyzed in detail in Korf, *Administrativnaia iustitsiia*, 1:455f.

20. In a note accompanying its projects the MVD presented detailed information on absenteeism. Between 1905 and 1908, for example, district marshals had missed over half of the administrative sessions of the conference of land captains and more than 90 percent of the judicial sessions, a very poor record when it is remembered that the marshals chaired the bodies. For this and other data see "Spravka," TsGIA, f. 1284, op. 185 (1907), d. 5a, ch. 1, pp. 153-156. The MVD staff obviously reworked the *spravka* later in the debate over reform, since it includes data for the two years following the initial presentation of the MVD projects.

21. "Proekt ob izmenenii i dopolnenii deistvuiushchii uzakonenii ob uezdnykh ustanovleniiakh," TsGIA, f. 1284, op. 185, d. 5a, ch. 1, p. 36.

22. *Rossiia*, no. 940 (13 December 1908), p. 2.

23. "Proekt ob izmenenii," TsGIA, f. 1284, op. 185, d. 5a, ch. 1, pp. 36-43.

24. "Po proektam polozhenii," TsGIA, f. 1284, op. 185 (1907), d. 5a, ch. 1, pp. 77-81; and MVD, *Polozhenie o pravitel'stvennykh uchastkovykh kom-*

misarakh (Saint Petersburg, 1907). The office was originally referred to as "subdistrict commander" (*nachal'nik*) but was renamed, presumably after the district vice-governor was given the title *commander* instead.

25. "Proekt ob izmenenii," TsGIA, f. 1284, op. 185, d. 5a, ch. 1, p. 36.
26. Quoted in Korf, *Administrativnaia iustitsiia*, 1:458.
27. Strakhovskii, *Gubernskoe ustroistvo*, p. 75; and Korf, *Administrativnaia iustitsiia*, 1:455f.
28. Meyendorf, note of 6 February 1938, p. 4, Columbia University Archive.
29. The relative was Meyendorf, who recommended N. M. Korkunov's standard text *Russkoe gosudarstvennoe pravo*. Ibid., note of May 1938, p. 5.
30. *Padenie tsarskogo rezhima*, 2:439.
31. For details see MVD, *Polozhenie o gubernskom upravlenii*; and "Proekt ob izmenenii," TsGIA, f. 1284, op. 185, d. 5a, ch. 1. The Ministry of Justice developed separate draft legislation on the related but independent question of officials' responsibility for personal crimes. This bill was submitted to the Second Duma but never enacted.
32. *Vestnik politsii*, no. 38 (1910), p. 846.
33. Ibid., no. 32 (1908), p. 4, and no. 20 (1908), p. 408. Robert W. Thurston has described interestingly a similar campaign on the local level by Moscow City Chief A. A. Adrianov ("Police and People in Moscow, 1906–1914," pp. 332–338). It should be emphasized that Adrianov's appointment in the wake of a nationally reported corruption scandal among Moscow police made this a rather special case. Moreover, the frequency with which Adrianov was forced to take disciplinary action can be seen as much as a testimony to the deep-rooted nature of police malfeasance as to the success of his efforts.
34. Korf, *Administrativnaia iustitsiia*, 1:476–478.
35. "Proekt ob izmenenii," TsGIA, f. 1284, op. 185, d. 5a, ch. 1, pp. 41–43.
36. *Vestnik politsii*, no. 32 (1908), p. 4.
37. Ibid., no. 33 (1908), p. 4.
38. Troitskii, *Iz vospominanii*, 2:7–8.
39. MVD, Glavnoe upravlenie po delam mestnago khoziaistva, *Ob ustanovleniia glavnykh osnovanii preobrazovaniia zemskikh i gorodskikh uchrezhdenii* (Saint Petersburg, 1907), pp. 24f and 129–132. Like Pleve, Stolypin had requested the various ministries to draft lists of matters that could be decentralized. Troitskii, *Iz vospominanii*, 2:8–9.
40. On the ministry's attitude toward subsidies see A. V. Zenkovskii, *Pravda o Stolypine*, pp. 200f.
41. Vladimir N. Kokovtsov, *Out of My Past*, pp. 168–169.
42. MVD, *Ob ustanovleniia glavnykh osnovanii*, pp. 73–75 and 136–137.
43. *Osobyi zhurnal soveta ministrov* 1, no. 7 (1907): 1–4.
44. On the volost, for instance, see "Po proektam polozhenii," TsGIA, f. 1284, op. 185 (1907), d. 5a, ch. 1, pp. 75–76.
45. MVD, *Ob ustanovleniia glavnykh osnovanii*, p. 76.
46. Ibid., p. 90.
47. Following the precise nature of the proposed curial system, landowners

whose property was assessed at a value of 7,500 rubles or more were to form the first curia; urban property holders with an assessment of 7,500 rubles or more plus representatives from a preliminary electoral congress of urban holders with property assessed at between 750 and 7,500 rubles would form the second; and all other participants in volost assemblies would form a third. The MVD proposal for reform of the town council electoral system was much simpler. Here the existing property qualification was to be halved. Ibid., pp. 75–94 and 137–139; and *Osobyi zhurnal soveta ministrov* 1, no. 7 (1907): 24–25, and no. 43 (1907): 75–77.

48. *Osobyi zhurnal soveta ministrov* 1, no. 7 (1907): 4–5.

49. MVD, *Ob ustanovleniia glavnykh osnovanii*, pp. 1 and 6.

50. *Osobyi zhurnal soveta ministrov* 3, no. 356 (1907): 5–6. Any other approach to decentralization, such as that of the Cadets, was explicitly rejected by the MVD as a "violation of the unity of the state" (MVD, *Ob ustanovleniia glavnykh osnovanii*, p. 8).

51. The MVD staff noted that some supported the abolition of the land captaincy without replacement, but the ministry insisted that the introduction of the new local zemstvos would create the need for even more supervision on the village level. "Po proektam polozhenii," TsGIA, f. 1284, op. 185 (1907), d. 5a, ch. 1, pp. 78–79.

52. MVD, *Ob ustanovleniia glavnykh osnovanii*, pp. 18–20.

53. Ibid., p. 20. The MVD staff rejected the old method of handling such cases through individual legislative acts for each case as "extraordinarily complicated and slow." Liberals might well have preferred the status quo, but it clearly did not satisfy Stolypin and his staff.

54. "Po voprosu o gubernskoi reforme," TsGIA, f. 1284, op. 185, d. 73, ch. 7, p. 179.

55. The MVD staff argued that the volost had long ago ceased to be an organ of peasant self-government and had become merely an executive arm of the state bureaucracy and district zemstvo. This de facto assignment of general administrative tasks to the peasant institutions was described as a "clear injustice," and one of which the peasantry was well aware. "Po proektam polozhenii," TsGIA, f. 1284, op. 185 (1907), d. 5a, ch. 1, pp. 66–69.

56. As Stolypin's subordinates put it, the "patriarchal character" of rural existence had waned in the face of the influx of "alien" elements. Ibid., pp. 53–54.

57. MVD, *Ob ustanovleniia glavnykh osnovanii*, p. 86.

58. The text of the ukaz is reproduced in S. M. Sidel'nikov, ed., *Agrarnaia reforma Stolypina*, pp. 95–97.

59. In his comments on district reform, for example, Gurliand stressed that it was not the gentry character of the district marshal that ruled him out as supervisor of local affairs, but the more general issue that he was elected at all. *Rossiia*, no. 940 (13 December 1908), p. 2.

60. *Osobyi zhurnal soveta ministrov* 1, no. 7 (1907): 2–4.

61. See Meyendorf, "A brief appreciation," p. 11, Columbia University Arc-

hive; or Bernard Pares' remarks on a "yeoman" class in Launcelot A. Owen, *The Russian Peasant Movement, 1906-1917*, p. vi.

62. Lenin outlined two possible paths of agrarian development for the empire, the Prussian and the American. The former was a strategy of reform based upon domination by a landed, Junker-like aristocracy supported by a stratum of wealthy peasants (*Grossbauern*). Lenin, *Collected Works* (Moscow: Foreign Language Publishing House, 1962), 13:238-242. For a critique of this view in favor of the American perspective, see Donald W. Treadgold, "Was Stolypin in Favor of Kulaks?," pp. 1-14.

63. Germany, especially Prussia, played an important role in Stolypin's life from his birth, when his father had taken his expecting mother to Dresden to have German physicians deliver the child. The family's estate, Kolnoberzhe, was located near East Prussia, and apparently Stolypin made many trips there. On Stolypin's admiration for the Prussian rural order, see Bock, *Reminiscences*, p. 22; and Meyendorf, note of 21 May 1938, p. 2, Columbia University Archive.

64. See, for example, TsGIA, f. 1284, op. 185 (1907), d. 5a, ch. 1, pp. 174-175. Sometimes French references were coupled with mention of the Prussian office of *Landrat,* a post that had its roots in the statist reforms of Stein and Hardenberg at the beginning of the nineteenth century.

65. For a Russian view on this, see Z. Avalov, *Detsentralizatsiia i samoupravlenie vo Frantsii.*

66. S. Iu. Witte, *Samoderzhavie i zemstvo,* p. 23; and Gurko, *Features and Figures,* p. 123n.

67. V. M. Gessen, *Voprosy mestnago upravleniia,* pp. 11-12.

68. Gurko, *Features and Figures,* p. 123n. This, it might be added, suggests a severe weakness in the recent attempt by Soviet scholars like Avrekh and Diakin to characterize Stolypin as a "Bonapartist" maneuvering between competing classes. The line of argument is fruitful within the context of earlier Soviet historiography in that it allows room for a certain independence on the part of the tsarist state, which is not seen as fully dependent on feudal forces. Nevertheless, the Bonapartist approach ultimately remains bound to the notion that the views of Stolypin and other state leaders are reducible to feudal or bourgeois components, rather than representing a separate perspective essentially hostile to real dependence on any social group. Hence it will be argued here, for example, that strains between Stolypin and moderates like the Octobrists have more to do with the minister's conception of the relationship between state and public than with any feudal restraints on his thinking.

CHAPTER VI

1. Estimates of Cadet party strength in the First Duma at various dates range from 34 to 40 percent. In addition, the Cadets could count on

considerable support from among the large block of "nonparty" deputies, the Trudovik group, and the national minority factions. For the party breakdown of the First Duma see N. Borodin in A. A. Mukhanov and V. D. Nabokov, eds., *Pervaia gosudarstvennaia duma*, 1:23–27; P. N. Miliukov, *Vospominaniia*, 1:363; and S. M. Sidel'nikov, *Obrazovanie i deiatel'nost' pervoi gosudarstvennoi dumy*, pp. 192–196.

2. *GDSO*, 1 (13 May 1906), p. 325.
3. Ibid. (5 May 1906), p. 241.
4. Mukhanov and Nabokov, *Pervaia duma*, 2:24–25.
5. Ibid., p. 26.
6. The projects were published in *Vestnik partii narodnoi svobody*, nos. 21–22 (1906); and Mukhanov and Nabokov, *Pervaia duma*, 2.
7. Mukhanov and Nabokov, *Pervaia duma*, 2:41.
8. Ibid., pp. 29–65.
9. Ibid., p. 66.
10. V. A. Maklakov, *The First State Duma*, p. 150. For a catalogue of most of the interpellations see the index to *GDSO*, 1.
11. *GDSO*, 1 (3 July 1906), pp. 1,928–1,930.
12. Ibid. (8 June 1906), p. 1,043.
13. Vladimir N. Kokovtsov, *Out of My Past*, pp. 135f; and Vladimir I. Gurko, *Features and Figures of the Past*, pp. 459f.
14. Gurko and others have argued that the government lacked time to prepare proposals, but even he admits that Goremykin had "decided to ignore the Duma's very existence" (Gurko, *Features and Figures*, p. 468).
15. Goremykin apparently characteristically retired to his bedroom, locking its door and that of the adjacent sitting room to avoid being bothered by callers. Ibid., p. 485.
16. Ibid., p. 494. In a letter to Shipov Stolypin repeated the point, writing, "I find that real action is needed, real reforms, and that in the period of 200 days separating us from the new Duma we should devote ourselves fully to the preparation of such [reforms] and to their implementation" (D. N. Shipov, *Vospominaniia i dumy o perezhitom*, p. 470).
17. *Osobyi zhurnal soveta ministrov* 1, no. 43 (1907): 7.
18. Ibid., pp. 10–13 and 21.
19. Ibid., no. 7 (1907): 17–20.
20. Kokovtsov, *My Past*, pp. 168–169.
21. In reference to the MVD proposals on self-government, for instance, it was necessary to convene a special conference of representatives of the various ministries to work out the details of reform. See *Osobyi zhurnal soveta ministrov* 3, no. 356 (1907).
22. Ibid. 1, no. 7 (1907): 21–23.
23. Ibid., pp. 22f.
24. On the old system, see B. B. Veselovskii, *Istoriia zemstva*, 3:10f. For the MVD proposal, see *Osobyi zhurnal soveta ministrov* 1, no. 7 (1907): 24–25, and no. 43 (1907): 75–77.
25. *Osobyi zhurnal soveta ministrov* 1, no. 7 (1907): 23–24.

26. Quoted in N. F. Ditmar, *O zemskom oblozhenii promyshlennykh i torgovykh predpriatii i o predstavitelstve torgovopromyshlennago klassa v zemskikh uchrezhdeniiakh*, p. 36.
27. The figures are N. I. Lazarevskii's, quoted by Ruth Delia MacNaughton and Roberta Thompson Manning, "Zemstvo and Revolution: The Onset of the Gentry Reaction, 1905–1907," in *The Politics of Rural Russia*, ed. Leopold H. Haimson, p. 216, n. 75.
28. *Osobyi zhurnal soveta ministrov* 1, no. 7 (1907): 27–28.
29. See, for example, V. S. Diakin's "Stolypin i dvorianstvo," pp. 244–246; and *Samoderzhavie, burzhuaziia, i dvorianstvo v 1907–1911gg.*, pp. 41–42.
30. In its project on the settlement, drafted shortly after the council's deliberations, the MVD proposed introduction in all villages where more than 10 percent of the population was nonpeasant and in some with even less than that proportion. MVD, *Polozhenie o poselkovom upravlenii* (Saint Petersburg, 1907), p. 1, article 3.
31. See, for example, the testimony of Kokovtsov, *My Past*, pp. 163–165.
32. Gurko, *Features and Figures*, p. 498.
33. Kokovtsov, *My Past*, p. 168.
34. For Shcheglovitov's own description of his views at this time see his testimony in *Padenie tsarskogo rezhima*, 2:337f.
35. *GDSO*, 2 (6 March 1907), pp. 107–110.
36. On Stolypin's attitude see Gurko, *Features and Figures*, pp. 494f; Kokovtsov, *My Past*, pp. 170–186; and V. A. Maklakov, *Vtoraia gosudarstvennaia duma*, p. 86.
37. Richard Pipes, *Struve: Liberal on the Right*, p. 47. See also Alfred Levin, *The Second Duma*, pp. 31–34.
38. N. I. Astrov et al., eds., *Zakonodatel'nye proekty i predpolozheniia partii narodnoi svobody, 1905–1907gg.*, p. 131.
39. TsGAOR, f. 434, op. 1, d. 76, p. 79.
40. On the meeting see Naryshkin's report to the Permanent Council two days later. Ibid., p. 90. The right group's note is discussed in Diakin, "Stolypin," p. 246.
41. Some delegates insisted that the United Nobility directly petition the tsar to withdraw the projects, but this idea was rejected. *Trudy III s'ezda upolnomochennykh dvorianskikh obshchestv 32 gubernii, s 27 marta po 2 aprelia 1907g.*, pp. 13–34 and 127–133.
42. *Stenograficheskie otchety 1-go vserossiiskago s'ezda zemskikh deiatelei v Moskve*, p. 1 (hereafter cited as *SO 1-go s'ezda*).
43. Veselovskii, *Istoriia zemstva*, 4:80.
44. Ibid., pp. 58 and 385–387.
45. TsGAOR, f. 434, op. 1, d. 76, p. 104; *Trudy III s'ezda*, pp. 15 and 25; and *SO 1-go s'ezda*, pp. 1–2.
46. There is a large literature on the dissolution of the Second Duma. Of contemporary accounts Maklakov's *Vtoraia duma* is best. For more recent work see Levin, *Second Duma;* and George Tokmakoff, "P. A. Stolypin and the Second Duma," pp. 49–62. It has been argued that the cam-

paign against local reform was in reality directed against the Duma itself and was central in the government's decision to resort to abrogation again. See I. D. Vaisberg, "Sovet ob'edinennogo dvorianstva i ego vliianie na politiku samoderzhaviia," or the much more convincing comments by Geoffrey A. Hosking and Roberta Thompson Manning, "What Was the United Nobility?," in Haimson, *The Politics of Rural Russia*, pp. 161-163. Although pressure from the right, particularly in the imperial court, may have contributed to the decision to dissolve, the basic cause was definitely the unbridgeable gulf between the government and the Duma majority.

47. Gosudarstvennaia duma, Vtoroi sozyv, *Obzor komissii i otdelov* (Saint Petersburg, 1907), pp. 147-150.

48. *SO 1-go s'ezda*, pp. 1-5.

49. Ibid., p. 14. It should be noted that Stakhovich was not a Cadet but a member of the Party of Peaceful Renewal, which stood between the Cadets on the left and the Octobrists on the right.

50. Ibid., pp. 17-18 and 27-29. Markov's speech was also noteworthy in a minor way for his remark that those gentry remaining in the countryside were becoming as rare as wild oxen (*zubry*). Markov's reference to the wild ox, or urus, an extinct animal thought to have inhabited the Germanic forest, attracted considerable notoriety. The term *zubr* came to be applied to extreme rightists who fought all reform, thus acquiring a second meaning of die-hard.

51. Ibid., pp. 36-37.

52. Ibid., p. 30.

53. Ibid., p. 211.

54. Ibid., pp. 116 and 135.

55. Ibid., p. 235. Women were not, however, to be given the right to serve as delegates in zemstvo assemblies.

56. Ibid., pp. 89 and 115.

57. One delegate termed the tax principle a "transitional step" toward universal suffrage. Markov denounced it as giving too much scope to individuals "living by mental office labor." See ibid., pp. 91-115 for the full debate on the tax principle.

58. Ibid., pp. 155-157. The five curiae were: estate owners whose holdings equalled or exceeded the full property qualification; urban proprietors fulfilling the qualification; other private landowners; other urban proprietors; and, finally, members of peasant communes.

59. Ibid., p. 278.

60. For the debate on this issue see *Stenograficheskie otchety 2-go vserossiiskago s'ezda zemskikh deiatelei*, pp. 13-106 (hereafter cited as *SO 2-go s'ezda*). The executive committee report on the question written by M. D. Ershov was also published under the title *Doklad po proektam "Polozhenii o volostnom i poselkovom upravleniiakh," sostavlennyi po porucheniiu soveta obshchezemskago s'ezda 1907g.*

61. *SO 2-go s'ezda*, pp. 139-150 and 201-213.

62. Ibid., pp. 89–90 and 107–126.

63. Ibid., pp. 126–134.

64. The text of the law is given in *SZ*, 1, part 2, pp. 48–99. For an analysis of its content see Haimson, "Introduction: The Russian Landed Nobility and the System of the Third of June," in *The Politics of Rural Russia*, pp. 1–29. It is significant that the curial system upon which the law was based did not differ drastically from that recommended by the first 1907 zemstvo congress for district zemstvo elections.

65. S. E. Kryzhanovskii, *Vospominaniia*, pp. 106–120.

66. Veselovskii, *Istoriia zemstva*, 4:169. The Ministry of Internal Affairs formally notified the Duma and State Council of its decision on 16 November. *Osobyi zhurnal soveta ministrov* 3, no. 356 (1907).

67. Veselovskii, *Istoriia zemstva*, 4:169.

68. "Doklad sobraniia predvoditelei i deputatov dvorianstva chrezvychainomu moskovskomu sobraniiu 8 Oktiabria 1907g.," in *Trudy IV-go s'ezda upolnomochennykh dvorianskikh obshchestv 32 gubernii*, pp. 474–475.

69. As it turned out only ten of the commission's members signed the report. The moderate Count F. A. Uvarov resigned from the group, probably as a result of its rightist sympathies, but the reasons for the absence of the other seven signatures are unknown. Ibid., pp. 396, 427, 460, and 475–476. On Samarin's leading role see GBL, f. 265, p. 1.

70. Their father owned at least three estates totaling 67,000 desiatina of land. A. M. Anfimov, *Krupnoe pomeshchich'e khoziaistvo evropeiskoi Rossii (konets XIX–nachalo XX veka)*, p. 385.

71. Gurko, *Features and Figures*, p. 357.

72. S. Iu. Witte, *Vospominaniia*, 2:204–213.

73. On the political views of F. D. Samarin see Shipov, *Vospominaniia*, pp. 152–154. It is worth noting that other members of the Moscow commission also had imposing credentials. Count P. S. Sheremetev, for example, was of a gentry family even more influential than the Samarins. As the leader of the Podolsk district zemstvo he had cooperated with the Samarins in battling liberal influence within the province, and he was also a close associate of Baron N. G. Cherkasov, a prominent conservative delegate to the Duma. On Sheremetev see Veselovskii, *Istoriia zemstva*, 4:534–535 and 542, and his own letters to the Samarins in GBL, f. 265.

74. "Obshchiia zamechaniia na proekte reformy mestnago upravleniia," *Trudy IV-go s'ezda*, p. 382.

75. Ibid., pp. 383–384.

76. "Uezdnyia ustanovleniia," *Trudy IV-go s'ezda*, p. 441. The term *zemshchina* is difficult to translate directly. To Slavophils of the nineteenth and early twentieth centuries it signified an organic union of all rural inhabitants who worked the land. The term also retained an earlier connotation of distinction from and even hostility to the central government. In the mid-sixteenth century it had referred to that part of

Muscovy administered by noble and peasant institutions, as opposed to the *oprichnina,* or the segment ruled by Ivan the Terrible directly through royal servitors.

77. Ibid., p. 442.
78. Ibid.
79. *SO 1-go s'ezda,* p. 100.
80. See as examples *Trudy IV-go s'ezda,* p. 442; and *SO 1-go s'ezda,* pp. 99-100, 159-162, and 207-208.
81. A. N. Naumov, *Iz utselevshikh vospominanii, 1868-1917,* 2:77-78.
82. *Trudy IV-go s'ezda,* pp. 236-237.
83. Ibid., p. 68. The resolutions passed by the congress were published separately by the editors of the newspaper *Volga* under the title *Zakliuchenie s'ezda upolnomochennykh ob'edinennykh dvorianskikh obshchestv po voprosu o mestnoi reforme.*
84. *Trudy IV-go s'ezda,* pp. 105-107.
85. Ibid., pp. 80-81 and 141-142. Snezhkov made the same point in a report to the congress entitled "The Proletarian Zemstvo" [Proletarskoe zemstvo]. The MVD's liberalization of the zemstvo suffrage would lead, he argued, to the election not of honest, conservative peasants, but statisticians, teachers, and other such radicals. TsGAOR, f. 434, d. 30, pp. 105-106.
86. Samarin, for instance, felt compelled to note that however wrong its proposals were, the government was acting "sincerely, with a full desire for the good of the people—of this there can be no doubt" (*Trudy IV-go s'ezda,* p. 94). On Naryshkin's sentiments see TsGAOR, f. 434, op. 1, d. 76.
87. Naumov, *Iz utselevshikh vospominanii,* 2:79; and *Trudy IV-go s'ezda,* p. 259.
88. *Trudy IV-go s'ezda,* pp. 78-80.
89. Ibid., p. 219. The suggestion that Gurko and Olsuf'ev be assigned to present alternative proposals on the question of volost reform received no positive response from the congress.
90. See especially Daniel Field's definitive *The End of Serfdom.*

CHAPTER VII

1. *Novoe vremia,* no. 11,494 (12 March 1908), p. 3.
2. N. M. Perepelkin, *Doklad o rabotakh vesennei sessii soveta po delam mestnago khoziaistva,* pp. 9-10; and TsGAOR, f. 826, op. 1, d. 47, p. 481.
3. See in particular the dissenting opinion against volost reform written by three rightists on behalf of the Kursk and Tula provincial zemstvos. TsGIA, f. 1288, op. 1, d. 14 (1908g.), no. 10, pp. 4-5.
4. Ibid., no. 9, p. 1; and TsGIA, f. 1288, op. 1, d. 2 (1908g.), "Zhurnal kommisii po volostnomu upravleniiu," p. 3. There were several abstentions in both votes.
5. The project is summarized by P. Koropachinskii, *Reforma mestnago*

samoupravleniia po rabotam soveta po delam mestnago khoziaistva, pp. 12-14.
See also TsGIA, f. 1288, op. 1, d. 2 (1908g.), "Zhurnal kommisii po
zemskoi izbiratel'noi reforme."

6. *Novoe vremia*, no. 11,494 (12 March 1908), p. 3.
7. Koropachinskii, *Reforma*, p. 14.
8. The plan is analyzed in *Pravo*, no. 11 (November 1908), pp. 621-628.
9. A. D. Golitsyn, *Zapiska k proektu zemskago izbiratel'nago zakona*, p. 1.
10. Koropachinskii, *Reforma*, p. 15.
11. *Novoe vremia*, no. 11,502 (20 March 1908), p. 3.
12. Koropachinskii, *Reforma*, pp. 16-18.
13. TsGIA, f. 1288, op. 1, d. 2 (1908g.), p. 59.
14. *GDSO*, 2, 5 (6 March 1907), p. 111.
15. *Novoe vremia*, no. 11,494 (12 March 1908), p. 3.
16. TsGIA, f. 1288, op. 1, d. 2 (1908g.), p. 4.
17. *Novoe vremia*, no. 11,496 (14 March 1908), p. 2.
18. V. S. Golubev, *Po zemskim voprosam, 1901-1911*, 2:91.
19. See particularly V. S. Diakin, "Stolypin i dvorianstvo," pp. 255-261.
20. On urban activity in zemstvo elections see Ruth Delia MacNaughton
    and Roberta Thompson Manning, "The Crisis of the Third of June
    System and Political Trends in the Zemstvos, 1907-14," in *The Politics
    of Rural Russia*, ed. Leopold H. Haimson, pp. 201-202.
21. Golitsyn, *Zapiska*, pp. 2-3 and 6.
22. *Novoe vremia*, no. 11,496 (14 March 1908), p. 3.
23. Ibid., no. 11,520 (7 April 1908), p. 3; and E. Verkhopatskii,
    *Gosudarstvennaia deiatel'nost' predsedatelia soveta ministrov stats-sekretaria
    Petra Arkad'evicha Stolypina*, 1:138-139.
24. *KA*, 1-2/50-51:184. Also cited in V. S. Diakin, *Samoderzhavie, bur-
    zhuaziia, i dvorianstvo v 1907-1911gg.*, p. 104.
25. TsGAOR, f. 826, op. 1, d. 49 (1909-1910gg.), p. 479.
26. TsGIA, f. 1284, op. 185, d. 5a (1907g.), "Po proektu uezdnoi reformy,"
    pp. 193-195.
27. Ibid., pp. 173f.
28. A. N. Naumov, *Iz utselevshikh vospominanii, 1868-1917*, 2:137.
29. TsGIA, f. 1284, op. 185, d. 5a (1907g.), p. 217.
30. Naumov, *Iz utselevshikh vospominanii*, 2:136-137.
31. TsGIA, f. 1284, op. 185, d. 5a (1907g.), p. 218.
32. Ibid., p. 257.
33. Ibid., pp. 220-221; and TsGIA, f. 1282, op. 2, d. 29, pp. 135-136.
34. Naumov, *Iz utselevshikh vospominanii*, 2:137-138.
35. Sovet s'ezda upolnomochennykh dvorianskikh obshchestv, *Doklad
    soveta po voprosu ob izmenenii polozheniia gubernatorov soglasno proekta
    pravitelstva o preobrazovanii obshchago uchrezhdeniia gubernskago* (1910), pp.
    4-7.
36. P. N. Zyrianov, "Krakh vnutrennei politiki tret'eiiunskoi monarkhii v
    oblasti mestnogo upravleniia (1907-1914gg.)," pp. 377-380.
37. TsGAOR, f. 826, op. 1, d. 49 (1909-1910gg.), pp. 379-380.

38. *Zhurnal obshchago prisutstviia soveta po delam mestnago khoziaistva*, no. 5 (19 March 1909).
39. TsGIA, f. 1284, op. 185, d. 73, ch. 7, "Po voprosu o gubernskoi reforme," pp. 178-188.
40. Ibid., p. 181.
41. TsGIA, f. 1282, op. 2, d. 29, pp. 135-136.
42. TsGIA, f. 1284, op. 185, d. 73, ch. 7, p. 179.
43. Quoted in Sovet s'ezda upolnomochennykh dvorianskikh obshchestv, *Doklad*, pp. 18-19.
44. TsGIA, f. 1284, op. 185, d. 73, ch. 7, pp. 180-181.
45. Verkhopatskii, *Gosudarstvennaia deiatel'nost'*, 2:1-6.
46. Geoffrey A. Hosking, *The Russian Constitutional Experiment*, p. 46.
47. V. I. Lenin, *Collected Works* (Moscow: Foreign Language Publishing House, 1962), 13:123.
48. *KA*, 28:205-206.
49. *GDSO*, 3, 4 (14 February 1911), pp. 1982-1987.
50. Ibid. (16 February 1911), pp. 2131-2134.
51. Ibid. (26 March 1911), p. 1754. See also pp. 1646-1679.
52. See the stenographic reports of the Duma committees in *Izvestiia po delam zemskago i gorodskogo khoziaistva*, no. 8 (August 1909), and no. 9 (September 1910).
53. In fact, the minimum requirement for participation in the second curia was reduced from one-fifteenth to a mere twenty-fifth of the full qualification. See *GDSO*, 3, 4 (26 March 1911), pp. 1702-1806, for the full debate on the electoral provisions.
54. *Izvestiia po delam zemskago i gorodskogo khoziaistva*, no. 8 (August 1909), p. 20.
55. Ibid., no. 3 (March 1910), pp. 16-18.
56. Ibid., no. 10 (October 1910), pp. 10-14.
57. Ibid., no. 1 (January 1911), pp. 36-37. See also *GDSO*, 3, 4 (14 February 1911), pp. 1952-1968.
58. *Izvestiia po delam zemskago i gorodskogo khoziaistva*, no. 11 (November 1910), pp. 20-21.
59. *GDSO*, 3, 4 (30 March 1911), pp. 1941-1971.
60. Ibid. (9 May 1911), pp. 3696-3701.
61. Ibid. (28 April 1911), p. 2541.
62. On the captaincy see ibid. (23 March 1911), p. 1528; (28 April 1911), pp. 2557-2563; and (9 May 1911), pp. 3673-3676.
63. Ibid. (9 May 1911), pp. 3756-3759. The dissenting opinion to the commission report written by Leonov and Efremov is reproduced in *Izvestiia po delam zemskago i gorodskogo khoziaistva*, no. 2 (February 1911), p. 42.
64. Diakin, "Stolypin," p. 266.
65. *GDSO*, 3, 4 (14 February 1911), p. 1977.
66. TsGIA, f. 1284, op. 185, d. 5a (1907g.), pp. 3-31.
67. For a full treatment of the crisis see Hosking, *Russian Experiment*, pp. 106-149; Edward Chmielewski, "Stolypin's Last Crisis," pp. 95-126;

A. Ia. Avrekh, *Stolypin i tret'ia duma;* Robert Edelman, *Gentry Politics on the Eve of the Russian Revolution,* pp. 106-127; and Diakin, *Samoderzhavie,* pp. 212-227.

68. Hosking, *Russian Experiment,* p. 118.

69. In the Council on Local Affairs, for example, Stolypin emphasized the nonstate nature of the project, though he was also careful to justify this in terms of nationality. Verkhopatskii, *Gosudarstvennaia deiatel'nost',* 2:17.

70. See Hosking, *Russian Experiment,* pp. 74-105.

71. See Edelman, *Gentry Politics,* chapter 3.

72. *GDSO,* 3, 3 (29 May 1910), pp. 2838-2839.

73. On the council see Howard D. Mehlinger and John M. Thompson, *Count Witte and the Tsarist Government in the 1905 Revolution,* pp. 291-298; Marc Szeftel, *The Russian Constitution of April 23, 1906,* pp. 275-281; and Alexandra Shecket Korros, "The Landed Nobility, the State Council, and P. A. Stolypin," in Haimson, *The Politics of Rural Russia,* pp. 123-141.

74. *GSSO,* 6 (4 March 1911), p. 1256.

75. Vladimir N. Kokovtsov, *Out of My Past,* pp. 452-455.

76. Naumov, *Iz utselevshikh vospominanii,* 2:177-178.

77. Party spokesmen presented the Octobrist position in *GDSO,* 3, 4 (27 April 1911), pp. 2864-2868.

78. Bernard Pares, "Conversations with Mr. Stolypin," *Russian Review* 2, no. 1 (February 1913): 109-110; and S. E. Kryzhanovskii, *Vospominaniia,* pp. 211-214. Robert Edelman has argued provocatively that Stolypin continued to look forward with anticipation to the elections to the Fourth Duma, hoping that a Nationalist electoral victory would restore his political position. It should be noted, however, that evidence in support of this view is drawn largely from the testimony of Nationalists, whose fortunes rested heavily upon Stolypin's willingness to carry on the political struggle. See *Gentry Politics,* pp. 130 and 139-140.

79. Naumov, *Iz utselevshikh vospominanii,* 2:134-151 and 170-171.

80. See, for example, Hosking, *Russian Experiment,* pp. 243-246; Szeftel, *Russian Constitution,* pp. 341f; and P. N. Zyrianov's review "Tret'eiiunskaia monarkhiia v sovremennoi amerikanskoi istoriografii," pp. 188-204.

81. See Avrekh, *Stolypin i tret'ia duma;* A. M. Davidovich's restatement of the traditional view in *Samoderzhavie v epokhu imperializma;* and Diakin's *Samoderzhavie,* which begins with a fruitful reworking of the old approach, but ultimately describes Stolypin solely as retreating in the face of feudal ("legitimist") opposition.

82. *Padenie tsarskogo rezhima,* 6:252.

83. Vladimir I. Gurko, *Features and Figures of the Past,* pp. 464-465.

84. Hosking, *Russian Experiment,* pp. 198-199. See also the testimony of V. F. Dzhunkovskii, "Vospominaniia, za 1914g.," TsGAOR, f. 826, op. 1, d. 54, pp. 38-39.

85. *Padenie tsarskogo rezhima*, 5:191–200. See also E. D. Chermenskii, *Chetvertaia gosudarstvennaia duma i sverzhenie tsarizma v Rossii*, pp. 38–43.
86. Naumov, *Iz utselevshikh vospominanii*, 2:139.
87. TsGIA, f. 1291, op. 50, d. 1, ch. 3, p. 243. In the winter of 1913–1914 the MVD chancellery, directed by N. V. Pleve, son of the former minister, developed a new project for district reform again based on the idea of a district vice-governor. On the project and its debate among the MVD staff in the autumn of 1914 see TsGIA, f. 1282, op. 2, d. 29.
88. For example, the State Council's committee imposed a relatively stiff minimum voting requirement of one-twentieth of a full zemstvo qualification. *GSSO*, 9, 40 (12 May 1914), p. 2157.
89. Ibid., 43 (19 May 1914), pp. 2291–2297.
90. Ibid., p. 2348.
91. Ibid., 40 (12 May 1914), p. 2156; and Gurko, *Features and Figures*, p. 533.
92. Figures calculated by Mehlinger and Thompson, *Count Witte*, p. 90. The 1905 figure includes multiple use of the same units to quell separate disorders.
93. For a review and critique of the system see V. M. Gessen, *Iskliuchitel'noe polozhenie*.
94. *KA*, 32:218n.; and Witte, *Vospominaniia*, 3:208–210.
95. Vysochaishe uchrezhdennoe osoboe soveshchanie po peresmotru ustanovlennykh dlia okhrany gosudarstvennago poriadka iskliuchitel'nykh zakonopolozhenii, *Zhurnal*, p. 14.
96. Ibid., p. 22.
97. Ibid., p. 13.
98. MVD, Departament politsii, *Istoricheskii ocherk obrazovaniia i razvitiia politseiskikh uchrezhdenii v Rossii*, p. 38.
99. TsGAOR, f. 102, op. 2, d. 14, ch. 4g, "Po komissii o reforme politsii," pp. 397–407.
100. MVD, Departament politsii, "Ob usilenii politsii v gor. Kurska i m. Beloi Tserkvi," 29 October 1908.
101. GBL, f. 358, Rubakin, box 148, no. 5, "O politsii."
102. *Pravitel'stvuiushchemu senatu, po pervomu departamentu, senatora, revizuiushchago po vysochaishemu poveleniiu Moskovskoe gradonachal'stvo, Doneshenie*, pp. 24–25.
103. TsGAOR, f. 102, op. 262, d. 28, "Protokoly zasedanii komissii po reforme politsii ot 11–13, 15 dekabria 1908g.," p. 1.
104. A. A. Lopukhin, *Iz itogov sluzhebnago opyta*, pp. 46–47.
105. Ibid., pp. 55–58.
106. TsGAOR, f. 102, op. 262, d. 60, "Obzor otzyvov periodicheskoi pechati," pp. 1–4.
107. *Sovremennoe Slovo* (1 February 1909).
108. See, for example, *Vestnik politsii*, no. 20 (1908), pp. 6–7, and no. 23 (1908), p. 3.
109. Maria P. Bock, *Reminiscences of My Father, Peter A. Stolypin*, p. 242. On the assassination see Avrekh, *Stolypin i tret'ia duma*, pp. 367f.

110. V. E. Frish, *Proekt uchrezhdeniia gosudarstvennoi strazhi v Rossii*, pp. 35 and 45.
111. Ibid., p. 23.
112. Ibid., pp. 22-23.
113. Ibid., p. 26.
114. See, for example, Lopukhin, *Iz itogov sluzhebnago opyta*, pp. 11-34; and P. G. Kurlov, *Gibel' imperatorskoi Rossii*, pp. 101-106.
115. TsGAOR, f. 102, op. 262, d. 33, "Proekt osnovnykh polozhenii razrabotannykh podkomissiei Trusevicha," pp. 16-17.
116. Ibid., pp. 21-24. For a summary of existing salaries see TsGAOR, f. 102, op. 262, d. 52, pp. 13-16.
117. TsGAOR, f. 102, op. 262, d. 31, "Protokoly zasedanii podkomissii po reforme politsii ... ot 18, 21, 28 marta i 1 i 29 aprelia 1908g.," pp. 17-18.
118. *Vestnik politsii*, no. 45 (1913), p. 997.
119. TsGIA, f. 1217, op. 171 (1909g.), d. 1, ch. 1, pp. 3-6.
120. TsGAOR, f. 102, op. 262, d. 33, "Proekt osnovnykh polozhenii razrabotannykh podkomissiei Trusevicha," pp. 35-37.
121. TsGAOR, f. 102, op. 262, d. 31, p. 48.
122. See *GDSO*, 2 (6 March 1907), pp. 107-110.
123. TsGAOR, f. 102, op. 262, d. 31, pp. 40-48.
124. Ibid., p. 35.
125. TsGAOR, f. 102, op. 262, d. 28, p. 28.
126. Ibid., p. 9.
127. *Osobyi zhurnal soveta ministrov* 1, no. 6 (1912): 10 and 21-22.
128. Mezhduvedomstvennaia kommisiia po preobrazovaniia politsii v imperii, *Zhurnal*, 18 April 1909, pp. 8-9.
129. TsGAOR, f. 102, op. 2, d. 14, ch. 4g, p. 50.
130. Mezhduvedomstvennaia kommisiia po preobrazovaniia politsii v imperii, *Zhurnal*, 12 May 1909, pp. 19-23.
131. TsGAOR, f. 102, op. 2, d. 14, ch. 4g, pp. 48-53.
132. *Russkoe Slovo*, 22 July 1911; *Grazhdanin*, 13 May 1912; and *Ranee Utro*, 22 July 1911.
133. See *Osobyi zhurnal soveta ministrov* 1, no. 6 (1912), on the 12 July 1911 and 31 January 1912 sessions.
134. TsGAOR, f. 102, op. 2, d. 14, ch. 4g, pp. 264-269.
135. *Padenie tsarskogo rezhima*, 5:69.
136. TsGIA, f. 1276 (1911g.), "Po proektakh o preobrazovaniia politsii," op. 7, d. 12, pp. 1,314-1,315; Dzhunkovskii's commentary in TsGAOR, f. 826, op. 1, d. 52, "Vospominaniia, za 1913-1915gg.," pp. 24-25; and Kurlov, *Gibel' imperatorskoi Rossii*, p. 142.
137. N. A. Rubakin, *Rossiia v tsifrakh*, p. 65.
138. See Neil B. Weissman, "Rural Crime in Tsarist Russia," pp. 228-240. On crime generally the best summary is S. S. Ostroumov, *Prestupnost' i ee prichiny v dorevoliutsionnoi Rossii*.
139. See the materials of the Osoboe mezhduvedomstvennoe soveshchanie

po voprosu o merakh bor'by s khuliganstvom v sel'skikh mestnostiakh, TsGIA, f. 1276, op. 78, d. 116 (1913g.).

140. *Trudy VIII s'ezda upolnomochennykh dvorianskikh obshchestv 32 gubernii, 1912g.,* p. 63.

141. *GDSO,* 4, 38 (12 April 1913), pp. 640-669.

142. For estimates of increased expenditures see *Osobyi zhurnal soveta ministrov* 1, no. 6 (1912): 12-14.

143. See TsGAOR, f. 102, op. 262, d. 60, "Obzor otzyvov periodicheskoi pechati na zakonoproekt reforma politseiskikh uchrezhdenii"; and op. 2, d. 14, ch. 4g, "Po komissii o reforme politsii," pp. 257-271.

144. TsGAOR, f. 102, op. 262, d. 60, pp. 5-6.

145. *Gorodskoe Delo,* no. 23 (1913), pp. 1,577-1,582.

146. On the composition of the Fourth Duma and alterations in the party structure of the Octobrists see E. D. Chermenskii, "Vybory v chetvertuiu gosudarstvennuiu dumu," pp. 21-40; Hosking, *Russian Experiment,* pp. 182-184; and Edelman, *Gentry Politics,* pp. 167-169.

147. *GDSO,* 4, 1, 27 (8 March 1913), p. 1211-1213, and 38 (29 April 1913), pp. 640-641.

148. Quoted in *Russia under the Last Tsar,* ed. Theofanis G. Stavrou, p. 109.

149. See his comments in *Padenie tsarskogo rezhima,* 5:191-200.

150. *KA,* 18:223.

151. *GDSO,* 4, 2, 5 (25 October 1913), p. 278.

152. TsGIA, f. 1278, op. 5, d. 549 (1913g.), "Zhurnaly komissii o preobrazovanii politsii," pp. 182-187 and 205-207.

153. Ibid., pp. 5-6.

154. Ibid., p. 142.

155. Ibid., pp. 43-44.

156. TsGAOR, f. 826, op. 1, d. 52, p. 212.

157. TsGIA, f. 1278, op. 5, d. 549 (1913g.), pp. 59-67 and 145-148; and *Vestnik politsii,* no. 35 (1914), pp. 611-613.

158. TsGAOR, f. 826, op. 1, d. 54, pp. 56-57.

159. TsGIA, f. 1278, op. 5, d. 549 (1913g.), p. 10.

CONCLUSION

1. Boris Chicherin, *Rossiia nakanune dvadtsatago stoletiia,* p. 160.

2. *Trudy IV-go s'ezda upolnomochennykh dvorianskikh obshchestv 32 gubernii,* pp. 101-102.

3. Quoted in Richard Pipes, *Struve: Liberal on the Left,* p. 382. Significantly, Struve's later realization of some of the difficulties involved in this outlook helped make him a pariah in the liberal movement. See Pipes, *Struve: Liberal on the Right,* pp. 75-81.

4. Quoted in *Vestnik politsii,* no. 5 (1910), pp. 138-140.

5. Ibid., no. 26 (1908), p. 12.

6. See Stephen Sternheimer, "Administering Development and Developing Administration," pp. 277–301.
7. *Vestnik politsii*, no. 35 (1909), p. 742.
8. S. Frederick Starr, *Decentralization and Self-Government in Russia, 1830–1870*, p. 351.

BIBLIOGRAPHY

ARCHIVAL SOURCES

Tsentral'nyi Gosudarstvennyi Istoricheskii Arkhiv SSSR

Fond 1239 Vysochaishe uchrezhdennoe osoboe soveshchanie po peresmotru ustanovlennykh dlia okhrany gosudarstvennago poriadka iskliuchitel'nykh zakonopolozhenii
Fond 1276 Sovet ministrov
Fond 1278 Gosudarstvennaia duma
Fond 1282 Ministerstvo vnutrennikh del, Kantseliariia
Fond 1284 Ministerstvo vnutrennikh del, Departament obshchikh del
Fond 1288 Ministerstvo vnutrennikh del, Glavnoe upravlenie po delam mestnago khoziaistva

Tsentral'nyi Gosudarstvennyi Arkhiv Oktiabr'skoi Revoliutsii

Fond DP Departament politsii
Fond 102 Departament politsii
Fond 434 Sovet ob'edinennogo dvorianstva
Fond 586 V. K. Pleve
Fond 826 V. F. Dzhunkovskii

Otdel Rukopisei Gosudarstvennoi Biblioteki im. Lenina v Moskve

Fond 178 Departament politsii
Fond 265 Samarin
Fond 358 Rubakin
Fond 384 Bonch-Bruevich

Columbia University Archive of Russian and East European History and Culture

Golitsyn, A. D. *Vospominaniia Kniazia A. D. Golitsyna*
Liubimov, D. N. *Russkaia smuta nachala deviatisotykh godov, 1902–1906*
Mendeleev, P. P. *Vospominaniia*
Meyendorf, A. *A brief appreciation of P. Stolypin's tenure of office*
Troitskii, K. K. *Iz vospominanii chinovnika osobykh poruchenii.* 2 vols.
Witte papers

BIBLIOGRAPHY

PUBLISHED SOURCES AND DISSERTATIONS

Afanas'ev, N. I. *Sovremenniki: Al'bom biografii.* 2 vols. Saint Petersburg, 1909–1910.

Agrarnyi vopros v sovete ministrov (1906g.). Moscow-Leningrad, 1924.

Anfimov, A. M. *Krupnoe pomeshchich'e khoziaistvo evropeiskoi Rossii (konets XIX -nachalo XX veka).* Moscow, 1969.

Anweiler, Oskar. "Die russische Revolution von 1905." *Jahrbücher für Geschichte Osteuropas* 35 (1955):161–193.

Armstrong, John A. *The European Administrative Elite.* Princeton: Princeton University Press, 1973.

———. "Old Regime Governors: Bureaucratic and Patrimonial Attributes." *Comparative Studies in Society and History* 14 (1972):2–29.

Ashley, Percy W. *Local and Central Government: A Comparative Study of England, France, Prussia and the United States.* New York: E. P. Dutton, 1906.

Astrov, N. I. et al., eds. *Zakonodatel'nye proekty i predpolozheniia partii narodnoi svobody, 1905–1907gg.* Saint Petersburg, 1907.

Avalov, Z. *Detsentralizatsiia i samoupravlenie vo Frantsii.* Saint Petersburg, 1905.

Avinov, N. N., ed. *Mestnoe samoupravlenie.* Moscow, 1912.

Avrekh, A. Ia. "Russkii absoliutizm i ego rol' v utverzhdenii kapitalizma v Rossii." *Istoriia SSSR,* no. 2 (1968), pp. 82–104.

———. *Stolypin i tret'ia duma.* Moscow, 1968.

———. "Tret'eiiunskaia monarkhiia i obrazovanie tret'edumskogo pomeshchich'e-burzhuaznogo bloka." *Vestnik moskovskogo gosudarstvennogo universiteta (Istoriko-filologicheskaia seriia)* 1 (1956):3–70.

———. *Tsarizm i tret'eiiunskaia sistema.* Moscow, 1966.

———. "Utrachennoe 'ravnovesie'." *Istoriia SSSR,* no. 4 (1971), pp. 60–75.

Bater, James H. *St. Petersburg: Industrialization and Change.* Montreal: McGill-Queen's University Press, 1976.

Beliavskii, N. N. *Politseiskoe pravo.* Iur'ev, 1910.

Belokonskii, I. P. "Zemskoe dvizhenie do obrazovaniia partii narodnoi svobody." *Byloe,* no. 7/19 (July 1907), pp. 207–240; no. 8/20 (August 1907), pp. 241–274; no. 9/21 (September 1907), pp. 226–267; and no. 10/22 (October 1907), pp. 246–270.

Berendts, E. N. *Koe-shto o sovremennykh voprosakh.* Saint Petersburg, 1907.

———. *O proshlom i nastoiashchem russkoi administratsii.* Saint Petersburg, 1913.

Bing, Edward J., ed. *The Secret Letters of the Last Tsar.* New York: Longmans, Green, 1938.

Black, Cyril E., ed. *The Transformation of Russian Society.* Cambridge, Mass.: Harvard University Press, 1967.

Blinov, I. *Gubernatory: istoriko-iuridicheskii ocherk.* Saint Petersburg, 1905.

Blum, Jerome. *Lord and Peasant in Russia from the Ninth to the Nineteenth Century.* Princeton: Princeton University Press, 1961.

———. "Russia." In *European Landed Elites in the Nineteenth Century,* edited by David Spring. Baltimore: Johns Hopkins University Press, 1977.

BIBLIOGRAPHY

Bock, Maria P. *Reminiscences of My Father, Peter A. Stolypin.* Metuchen, N.J.: Scarecrow Press, 1970.
_____. "Stolypin in Saratov." *Russian Review* 12 (July 1953):187–193.
Bompard, Maurice. *Mon Ambassade en Russie, 1903–1908.* Paris: Plon, 1937.
Bordua, David J., ed. *The Police: Six Sociological Essays.* New York: Wiley, 1967.
Brinkman, A. "Nepolnomoshchnye zakony (k psikhologii russkoi ispolnitel'noi vlasti)." *Russkaia mysl'* 6 (1907):17–28.
Caiden, Gerald E. *Administrative Reform.* Chicago: Aldine, 1969.
Chermenskii, E. D. *Burzhuaziia i tsarizm v pervoi russkoi revoliutsii.* Moscow, 1970.
_____. *Chetvertaia gosudarstvennaia duma i sverzhenie tsarizma v Rossii.* Moscow, 1976.
_____. "Vybory v chetvertuiu gosudarstvennuiu dumu." *Voprosy istorii,* no. 4 (1947), pp. 21–40.
Chicherin, Boris. *Rossiia nakanune dvadtsatago stoletiia.* Berlin, 1901.
Chmielewski, Edward. "Stolypin's Last Crisis." *California Slavic Studies* 3 (1964):95–126.
Conroy, Mary Schaeffer. *Peter Arkad'evich Stolypin: Practical Politics in Late Tsarist Russia.* Boulder, Colo.: Westview Press, 1976.
_____. "Stolypin's Attitude Toward Local Self-Government." *Slavonic and East European Review* 46 (July 1968):446–461.
Crozier, Michel. *The Bureaucratic Phenomenon.* Chicago: University of Chicago Press, 1964.
D. G. *Nasha politsiia.* Moscow, 1906.
Dashkevich, L. "Sel'skaia politseiskaia strazha." *Vestnik Evropy,* no. 1 (January 1904), pp. 373–377.
Davidovich, A. M. *Samoderzhavie v epokhu imperializma (klassovaia sushchnost' i evoliutsiia absoliutizma v Rossii).* Moscow, 1975.
Deriuzhinskii, V. F. *Politseiskoe pravo: posobie dlia studentov.* Saint Petersburg, 1908.
Diakin, V. S. *Samoderzhavie, burzhuaziia, i dvorianstvo v 1907–1911 gg.* Leningrad, 1978.
_____. "Stolypin i dvorianstvo (Proval mestnoi reformy)." In *Problemy krest'ianskogo zemlevladeniia i vnutrennei politiki Rossii: Dooktiabr'skii period,* pp. 231–273. Leningrad, 1972.
Ditmar, N. F. *O zemskom oblozhenii promyshlennykh i torgovykh predpriatii i o predstavitel'stve torgovopromyshlennago klassa v zemskikh uchrezhdeniiakh.* Saint Petersburg, 1911.
Doklad organizatsionnago biuro s'ezdu zemskikh i gorodskikh deiatelei 12–15 sentiabria 1905 g. Saint Petersburg, 1905.
Dubrovskii, S. M. *Krest'ianskoe dvizhenie v revoliutsii 1905–1907 gg.* Moscow, 1956.
_____. *Stolypinskaia zemel'naia reforma.* Moscow, 1963.
Edelman, Robert. *Gentry Politics on the Eve of the Russian Revolution: The*

BIBLIOGRAPHY

Nationalist Party, 1907-1917. New Brunswick: Rutgers University Press, 1980.

Elistratov, A. I. *Osnovnyia nachala administrativnago prava.* Moscow, 1914.

Emmons, Terence. *The Russian Landed Gentry and the Peasant Emancipation of 1861.* Cambridge: Cambridge University Press, 1968.

────. "The Russian Landed Gentry and Politics." *Russian Review* 33 (July 1974):269-283.

────. "Russia's Banquet Campaign." *California Slavic Studies* 10 (1977): 45-86.

Erman, L. K. "Sostav intelligentsii v Rossii v kontse XIX i nachale XXv." *Istoriia SSSR* no. 1 (1963), pp. 161-177.

Eroshkin, N. P. *Istoriia gosudarstvennykh uchrezhdenii dorevoliutsionnoi Rossii.* Moscow, 1968.

Ershov, M. D. *Doklad po proektam "Polozhenii o volostnom i poselkovom upravleniiakh," sostavlennyi po porucheniiu soveta obshchezemskago s'ezda 1907g.* Moscow, 1907.

Evreinov, G. A. *Krest'ianskii vopros v trudakh obrazovannoi v sostave ministerstva vnutrennikh del kommisii po peresmotru zakonopolozhenii o krest'ianakh.*

Field, Daniel. *The End of Serfdom: Nobility and Bureaucracy in Russia, 1855-1861.* Cambridge, Mass.: Harvard University Press, 1976.

Fischer, George. *Russian Liberalism: From Gentry to Intelligentsia.* Cambridge, Mass.: Harvard University Press, 1958.

Fleksor, D. S. *Okhrana sel'skokhoziaistvennoi sobstvennosti.* Saint Petersburg, 1904.

Friedgut, Theodore H. *Political Participation in the USSR.* Princeton: Princeton University Press, 1979.

Frish, V. E. *Administrativnyia i politseiskiia uchrezhdeniia Frantsii, Avstrii i Prussii.* Saint Petersburg, 1905.

────. *Proekt uchrezhdeniia gosudarstvennoi strazhi v Rossii.* Saint Petersburg, 1908.

Galai, S. "The Impact of War on the Russian Liberals in 1904-5." *Government and Opposition* 1 (1965):85-109.

────. *The Liberation Movement in Russia, 1900-1905.* Cambridge: Cambridge University Press, 1973.

Gerschenkron, Alexander. "Soviet Marxism and Absolutism." *Slavic Review* 30 (December 1971):853-869.

Gessen, V. M. *Iskliuchitel'noe polozhenie.* Saint Petersburg, 1908.

────. *Lektsii po politseiskomu pravu.* Saint Petersburg, 1907-1908.

────. *Voprosy mestnago upravleniia.* Saint Petersburg, 1904.

Gillis, John R. "Political Decay and the European Revolution, 1789-1848." *World Politics* 22 (April 1970):344-370.

Glinskii, B. B. "Period tverdoi vlasti (Istoricheskie ocherki)." *Istoricheskii vestnik* 127 (February 1912):667-690; 128 (April 1912):219-239; and 129 (May 1912):564-588.

Gogel, S. K. *Die Ursachen der russischen Revolution vom Jahre 1917.* Berlin, 1926.

Golitsyn, A. D. *Zapiska k proektu zemskago izbiratel'nago zakona.* Kharkov, 1908.

BIBLIOGRAPHY

Golubev, V. S. *Po zemskim voprosam, 1901-1911.* 2 vols. Saint Petersburg, 1913.

Gorlin, R. H. "Problems of Tax Reform in Imperial Russia." *Journal of Modern History* 49 (June 1977):246-265.

Gosudarstvennaia duma. *Obzor deiatel'nosti komissii i otdelov.* Saint Petersburg, 1907, 1912, and 1915.

———. *Stenograficheskii otchet.* Saint Petersburg, 1906-1914.

Gosudarstvennyi sovet. *Otchet po deloproizvodstvu gosudarstvennago soveta za sessiiu 1899-1904gg.* Saint Petersburg, 1900-1905.

———. *Stenograficheskii otchet.* Saint Petersburg, 1906-1917.

Gradovskii, A. D. "Sistemy mestnago upravleniia na zapade Evropy i v Rossii." *Sbornik gosudarstvennykh znanii* 5:72-124; and 6:92-160. Saint Petersburg, 1878.

Gurko, Vladimir I. *Features and Figures of the Past: Government and Opinion in the Reign of Nicholas II.* Stanford: Stanford University Press, 1939.

Hagen, Manfred. "Der russische 'Bonapartismus' nach 1906." *Jahrbücher für Geschichte Osteuropas* 24 (1976):369-393.

Haimson, Leopold H., ed. *The Politics of Rural Russia.* Bloomington, Ind.: Indiana University Press, 1979.

———. "Social Stability in Urban Russia, 1905-1917." *Slavic Review* 23 (December 1964):619-642; and 24 (March 1965):1-25.

Hamburg, G. M. "The Crisis in Russian Agriculture: A Comment." *Slavic Review* 37 (September 1978):481-486.

———. "The Russian Nobility on the Eve of the 1905 Revolution." *Russian Review* 38 (July 1979):323-338.

Hamm, Michael F., ed. *The City in Russian History.* Lexington, Ky.: University of Kentucky Press, 1976.

Harcave, Sidney. *First Blood: The Russian Revolution of 1905.* New York: Macmillan, 1964.

Hennessey, Richard. *The Agrarian Question in Russia, 1905-1907: The Inception of the Stolypin Reform.* Giessen: Wilhelm Schmitz Verlag, 1977.

Hosking, Geoffrey A. "P. A. Stolypin and the Octobrist Party." *Slavonic and East European Review* 47 (January 1969):137-160.

———. *The Russian Constitutional Experiment: Government and Duma, 1907-1914.* Cambridge: Cambridge University Press, 1973.

Huntington, Samuel P. "Political Development and Political Decay." *World Politics* 17 (April 1965):386-429.

———. *Political Order in Changing Societies.* New Haven: Yale University Press, 1968.

Hutchinson, J. F. "The Octobrists and the Future of Imperial Russia as a Great Power." *Slavonic and East European Review* 50 (April 1972):220-237.

Iordanskii, N. K. "Gorodskoe samoupravlenie i obshchestvennaia bezopasnost'." *Obrazovanie,* no. 4 (1905), pp. 16-27.

Islavin, M. V. *Obzor trudov vysochaishe utverzhdennoi pod predsedatel'stvom stats'-sekretaria Kakhanova osoboi kommisii.* 2 vols. Saint Petersburg, 1908.

BIBLIOGRAPHY

Ivanovskii, V. V. "Biurokratiia, kak samostoiatel'nyi obshchestvennyi klass." *Russkaia mysl'*, no. 8 (1903), pp. 1–23.

Izgoev, A. P. A. *Stolypin: Ocherk zhizni i deiatel'nosti*. Moscow, 1912.

Johnson, Robert E. *Peasant and Proletarian: The Working Class of Moscow in the Late Nineteenth Century*. New Brunswick: Rutgers University Press, 1979.

Jozefi, V. *K voprosu o reorganizatsii politsii*. Kiev, 1905.

K voprosu o reforme politsii. Vitebsk, 1908.

Katkov, M. A. *Rol' uezdnykh predvoditelei dvorianstva v gosudarstvennom upravlenii Rossii: K voprosu o reforme uezdnago upravleniia*. Moscow, 1914.

Keep, John L. H. "Programming the Past: Imperial Russian Bureaucracy and Society under the Scrutiny of Mr. George Yaney." *Canadian-American Slavic Studies* 8 (Winter 1974):569–580.

Kennan, George F. "The Breakdown of the Tsarist Autocracy." In *Revolutionary Russia*, edited by Richard Pipes, pp. 1–32. Garden City, N.Y.: Doubleday, 1969.

Khodataistvo soveta s'ezda gornopromyshlennikov iuga Rossii po voprosu o predstavitel'stv v zemskikh uchrezhdeniiakh. Kharkov, 1908.

Khromov, P. A. *Ekonomicheskoe razvitie Rossii*. Moscow, 1967.

Kokovtsov, Vladimir N. *Out of My Past*. Stanford: Stanford University Press, 1935.

Kolychev, A. *Po gorodskim voprosam*. Saint Petersburg, 1908.

Komitet ministrov. *Zhurnaly komiteta ministrov po ispolneniiu Ukaza 12 Dekabria 1904g.* Saint Petersburg, 1905.

Korelin, A. P. "Dvorianstvo v poreformennoi Rossii (1861–1904gg.)." *Istoricheskie zapiski* 87 (1971):91–173.

———. "Institut predvoditelei dvorianstva, o sotsial'nom i politicheskom polozhenii dvorian." *Istoriia SSSR*, no. 3 (1978), pp. 31–48.

———. "Rossiskoe dvorianstvo i ego soslovnaia organizatsiia (1861–1904gg.)." *Istoriia SSSR*, no. 5 (1971).

Korf, S. A. *Administrativnaia iustitsiia v Rossii*. 2 vols. Saint Petersburg, 1910.

———. "Predvoditel' dvorianstva kak organ soslovnago i zemskago samoupravleniia." *Zhurnal ministerstva iustitsiia*, no. 3 (1902).

———. *Reforma senata*. Saint Petersburg, 1912.

Korkunov, N. M. *Russkoe gosudarstvennoe pravo*. 2 vols. Saint Petersburg, 1909.

Koropachinskii, P. *Reforma mestnago samoupravleniia po rabotam soveta po delam mestnago khoziaistva*. Ufa, 1908.

Korvin-Piotkovskii, L. V. *Sovremennyi chinovnik i ego sud'ba*. Saint Petersburg, 1905.

Koshko, I. F. *Vospominaniia gubernatora (1905–1914g.)*. Petrograd, 1916.

Krasnyi arkhiv. 106 vols. Moscow-Leningrad, 1922–1941.

Kratkie zhurnaly zasedanii obshche-zemskago s'ezda v moskve s 25–28 avgusta 1907 goda. Moscow, 1907.

Kryzhanovskii, S. E. *Vospominaniia*. Berlin: Speer and Schmidt.

Kulisher, E. M. *Gorodskaia i zemskaia politsiia v nekotorykh zapadnoevropeiskikh gosudarstvakh*. Saint Petersburg, 1909.

Kurlov, P. G. *Gibel' imperatorskoi Rossii*. Berlin, 1923.

BIBLIOGRAPHY

LaPalombara, Joseph G., ed. *Bureaucracy and Political Development*. Princeton: Princeton University Press, 1963.

Laverychev, V. Ia. *Tsarizm i rabochii vopros v Rossii, 1861–1917*. Moscow, 1972.

Leikina-Svirskaia, V. R. *Intelligentsiia v Rossii vo vtoroi polovine XIX veka*. Moscow, 1971.

Leont'ev, A. A. *Krest'ianskoe pravo*. Saint Petersburg, 1909.

Leontowitsch, Victor. *Geschichte des Liberalismus in Russland*. Frankfurt-am-Main: V. Klostermann, 1958.

Leroy-Beaulieu, Anatole. *The Empire of the Tsars and the Russians*. 2 vols. New York: AMS Press, 1969.

Levin, Alfred. "P. A. Stolypin: A Political Appraisal." *Journal of Modern History* 37 (December 1965):445–463.

———. "Russian Bureaucratic Opinion in the Wake of the 1905 Revolution." *Jahrbücher für Geschichte Osteuropas* 11 (1963):1–12.

———. *The Second Duma*. Hamden, Conn.: Archon Books, 1966.

Lopukhin, A. A. *Iz itogov sluzhebnago opyta: Nastoiashchee i budushchee russkoi politsii*. Moscow, 1907.

———. *Otryvki iz vospominanii*. Moscow, 1923.

Macey, David A. "The Russian Bureaucracy and the 'Peasant Problem': The Pre-History of the Stolypin Reforms, 1861–1907." Ph.D. dissertation, Columbia University, 1976.

Maklakov, V. A. *The First State Duma*. Bloomington, Ind.: Indiana University Press, 1964.

———. *Rechi i sudebnyia, dumskiia i publichnyia lektsii, 1904–1926*. Paris, 1949.

———. *Vlast' i obshchestvennost' na zakate staroi Rossii*. 3 vols. Paris, 1936.

———. *Vtoraia gosudarstvennaia duma*. Paris, 1948.

Mandel, James I. "Paternalistic Authority in the Russian Countryside, 1856–1906." Ph.D. dissertation, Columbia University, 1978.

Manning, Roberta Thompson. "The Russian Provincial Gentry in Revolution and Counterrevolution." Ph.D. dissertation, Columbia University, 1975.

Maslov, P. *Agrarnyi vopros v Rossii*. Moscow, 1926.

Mehlinger, Howard D., and Thompson, John M. *Count Witte and the Tsarist Government in the 1905 Revolution*. Bloomington, Ind.: Indiana University Press, 1972.

Melkaia zemskaia edinitsa. 2 vols. Saint Petersburg, 1903–1904.

Menashe, Louis. "Alexander Guchkov and the Origins of the Octobrist Party: The Russian Bourgeoisie in Politics." Ph.D. dissertation, New York University, 1966.

Mezhduvedomstvennaia kommisiia po preobrazovaniia politsii v imperii. *Trudy*. Saint Petersburg, 1911.

Miakotin, V. "Sovremennaia 'detsentralizatsiia'." *Russkoe bogatstvo*, no. 4 (April 1908), pp. 121–138.

Miliukov, P. N. *Vospominaniia (1859–1917)*. 2 vols. New York: Chekhov Publishing House, 1955.

Ministerstvo vnutrennikh del. *Ministerstvo vnutrennikh del: Istoricheskii ocherk, 1802–1902*. Saint Petersburg, 1902.

BIBLIOGRAPHY

_____. *Otchet po revizii zemskikh uchrezhdenii moskovskoi gubernii.* 3 vols. Saint Petersburg, 1904.

_____. *Trudy redaktsionnoi kommisii po peresmotru zakonopolozhenii o krest'ianakh.* 3 vols. Saint Petersburg, 1903.

_____. Departament politsii. *Istoricheskii ocherk obrazovaniia i razvitiia politseiskikh uchrezhdenii v Rossii.* Saint Petersburg, 1913.

_____. Glavnoe upravlenie po delam mestnago khoziaistva. *Obshchestvennoe i chastnoe prizrenie v Rossii.* Saint Petersburg, 1907.

Mogilianskii, M. M. *Pervaia gosudarstvennaia duma.* Saint Petersburg, 1907.

Monas, Sidney. *The Third Section: Police and Society under Nicholas I.* Cambridge, Mass.: Harvard University Press, 1961.

Mosolov, A. *Pri dvore imperatora.* Riga, 1937.

Mukhanov, A. A., and Nabokov, V. D., eds. *Pervaia gosudarstvennaia duma.* 3 vols. Saint Petersburg, 1907.

Mulukaev, R. S. *Politsiia i tiuremnye uchrezhdeniia dorevoliutsionnoi Rossii.* Moscow, 1964.

Naumov, A. N. *Iz utselevshikh vospominanii, 1868-1917.* 2 vols. New York, 1954.

Nikol'skaia, N. P. "Zakon o zemskikh nachal'nikakh." Dissertatsiia, Perm University, 1946.

Novikov, A. *Zapiski zemskago nachal'nika.* Saint Petersburg, 1899.

Obninskii, V. *Novyi stroi.* 2 vols. Moscow, 1909.

Obshchestvennoe dvizhenie v Rossii v nachale XX-go veka. eds. L. Martov, P. Maslov, and A. Potresov. 3 vols. Saint Petersburg, 1909-1911.

Ol'minskii, M. *Gosudarstvo, biurokratiia i absoliutizm v istorii Rossii.* Saint Petersburg, 1910.

Olsufev, D. A. *Ob uchastii zemstv v obsuzhdenii zemskoi reformy.* Saint Petersburg, 1907.

Orlovsky, Daniel T. "Recent Studies on the Russian Bureaucracy." *Russian Review* 34 (October 1976):448-467.

Ostroumov, S. S. *Prestupnost' i ee prichiny v dorevoliutsionnoi Rossii.* Moscow, 1960.

Owen, Launcelot A. *The Russian Peasant Movement, 1906-1917.* New York: Russell and Russell, 1963.

Padenie tsarskogo rezhima: Stenograficheskie otchety doprosov i pokazanii, dannykh v 1917g. v chrezvychainoi sledstvennoi komissii vremennogo pravitel'stva. 7 vols. Moscow, 1925.

Pares, Bernard. *The Fall of the Russian Monarchy.* New York: Knopf, 1939.

Pazukhin, A. D. "Sovremennoe sostoianie Rossii i soslovnyi vopros." *Russkii vestnik* 175 (January 1885):5-58.

Perepelkin, N. M. *Doklad o rabotakh vesennei sessii soveta po delam mestnago khoziaistva.* Moscow, 1908.

Perrie, Maureen. *The Agrarian Policy of the Russian Socialist-Revolutionary Party from its Origins through the Revolution of 1905-1907.* Cambridge: Cambridge University Press, 1976.

Pershin, P. N. *Agrarnaia revoliutsiia v Rossii.* Moscow, 1966.

BIBLIOGRAPHY

Pestrzhetskii, D. I. *Obzor agrarnago proekta konstitutsionno-demokraticheskoi partii.* Saint Petersburg, 1906.

Pinchuk, Ben-Cion. *The Octobrists in the Third Duma.* Seattle: University of Washington Press, 1974.

Pintner, Walter M. "The Russian Higher Civil Service on the Eve of the 'Great Reforms'." *Journal of Social History* 8 (Spring 1975):55–68.

————. "The Social Characteristics of the Early Nineteenth-Century Russian Bureaucracy." *Slavic Review* 29 (September 1970):429–443.

Pintner, Walter M., and Rowney, Don Karl, eds. *Russian Officialdom: The Bureaucratization of Russian Society from the Seventeenth to the Twentieth Century.* Chapel Hill: University of North Carolina Press, 1980.

Pipes, Richard. "Russian Conservatism in the Second Half of the Nineteenth Century." *Slavic Review* 30 (March 1971):121–128.

————. *Struve: Liberal on the Left, 1870–1905.* Cambridge, Mass.: Harvard University Press, 1970.

————. *Struve: Liberal on the Right, 1905–1944.* Cambridge, Mass.: Harvard University Press, 1980.

Pirumova, N. M. *Zemskoe liberal'noe dvizhenie.* Moscow, 1977.

Polner, T. I. *Zhiznennyi put' kniazia Georgiia Evgeneivicha L'vova.* Paris, 1932.

Polnyi sbornik platform vsekh russkikh politicheskikh partii. Saint Petersburg, 1906.

Pravitel'stvuiushchemu senatu, po pervomu departamentu, senatora, revizuiushchago po vysochaishemu poveleniiu Moskovskoe gradonachal'stvo, Doneshenie. Saint Petersburg.

Pravitel'stvuiushchii senat. *Istoriia pravitel'stvuiushchago senata za dvesti let, 1711–1911gg.* Saint Petersburg, 1911.

Pskovskoe gubernskoe soveshchanie po peresmotru zakonopolozhenii o krest'ianakh. *Protokoly.* Pskov, 1904.

Raeff, Marc. "The Bureaucratic Phenomena of Imperial Russia, 1700–1905." *American Historical Review* 84 (April 1979):399–411.

————. *Origins of the Russian Intelligentsia: The Eighteenth-Century Nobility.* New York: Harcourt, Brace and World, 1966.

————. "The Russian Autocracy and Its Officials." *Harvard Slavic Studies* 4 (1957):77–91.

Rakhmatullin, M. A. "K diskussii ob absoliutizme v Rossii." *Istoriia SSSR,* no. 4 (1972), pp. 65–88.

Reingardt, N. V. *Sudebnaia politsiia.* Kazan, 1900.

Revoliutsiia 1905–1907gg. v Rossii: Dokumenty i materialy. Moscow, from 1955.

Rieber, Alfred J. "Bureaucratic Politics in Imperial Russia." *Social Science History* 2 (Summer 1978):399–413.

Rittikh, A. A., ed. *Krest'ianskii pravoporiadok.* Saint Petersburg, 1904.

Robbins, Richard G., Jr. *Famine in Russia, 1891–1892.* New York: Columbia University Press, 1975.

Robinson, Geroid Tanquary. *Rural Russia under the Old Regime.* New York: Macmillan, 1949.

Rogger, Hans. "The Formation of the Russian Right, 1900–1906." *California Slavic Studies* 3 (1964):66–94.

BIBLIOGRAPHY

_____. "Was There a Russian Fascism? The Union of Russian People." *Journal of Modern History* 36 (December 1964):398–415.

Rowney, Don Karl. "Higher Civil Servants in the Russian Ministry of Internal Affairs: Some Demographic and Career Characteristics, 1905–1916." *Slavic Review* 21 (March 1972):101–110.

Rubakin, N. A. *Rossiia v tsifrakh.* Saint Petersburg, 1912.

_____. *Vory i razboiniki na kazennoi sluzhbe.* London, 1903.

Savich, G. G. *K voprosu o melkoi zemskoi edinitse: selo Pavlovo i ego obshchestvennoe ustroistvo.* Saint Petersburg, 1906.

_____. *Novyi gosudarstvennyi stroi Rossii.* Saint Petersburg, 1907.

Sbornik zakliuchenii gubernskikh soveshchanii po proektu nakaza zemskim uchastkovym nachal'nikam. Saint Petersburg, 1899.

Semennikov, V. P., ed. *Revoliutsiia 1905 goda i samoderzhavie.* Moscow-Leningrad, 1928.

Semenov, S. T. *Dvadtsat' piat let v derevne.* Petrograd, 1915.

Seton-Watson, Hugh. *The Russian Empire, 1801–1917.* Oxford: Oxford University Press, 1967.

Shatsillo, K. F. "Formirovanie programmy zemskogo liberalizma i ee bankrotstvo nakanune pervoi russkoi revoliutsii (1901–1904gg.)." *Istoricheskie zapiski* 97 (1976):50–98.

Shidlovskii, S. I. *Obshchii obzor trudov mestnykh komitetov.* Saint Petersburg, 1905.

_____. *Vospominaniia.* 2 vols. Berlin, 1923.

Shingarev, A. I. *Melkaia zemskaia edinitse.* Moscow, 1917.

Shipov, D. N. *Vospominaniia i dumy o perezhitom.* Moscow, 1918.

Sidel'nikov, S. M. *Obrazovanie i deiatel'nost' pervoi gosudarstvennoi dumy.* Moscow, 1962.

Sidel'nikov, S. M., ed. *Agrarnaia reforma Stolypina.* Moscow, 1973.

Simmonds, George W. "The Congress of Representatives of the Nobles' Associations, 1906–1916: A Case Study of Russian Conservatism." Ph.D. dissertation, Columbia University, 1964.

Simms, James Y., Jr. "The Crisis in Russian Agriculture at the End of the Nineteenth Century: A Different View." *Slavic Review* 36 (September 1977):377–398.

Simonova, M. S. "Agrarnaia politika samoderzhaviia v 1905g." *Istoricheskie zapiski* 81 (1968):199–215.

_____. "Bor'ba techenii v pravitel'stvennom lagare po voprosam agrarnoi politiki v kontse XIX veka." *Istoriia SSSR*, no. 1 (1963), pp. 65–82.

_____. "Politika tsarizma v krest'ianskom voprose nakanune revoliutsii 1905–1907gg." *Istoricheskie zapiski* 75 (1965):217–242.

_____. "Zemsko-liberal'naia fronda (1902–1903gg.)." *Istoricheskie zapiski* 91 (1973):150–216.

Skocpol, Theda. *States and Social Revolutions: A Comparative Analysis of France, Russia, and China.* Cambridge: Cambridge University Press, 1979.

Sliozberg, G. B. *Dorevoliutsionnyi stroi Rossii.* Paris, 1933.

Solov'ev, Iu. B. *Samoderzhavie i dvorianstvo v kontse XIX veka.* Leningrad, 1973.

BIBLIOGRAPHY

Soveshchanie po voprosu o reforme politsii. Vitebsk, 1908.

Sovet ministrov. *Osobyi zhurnal soveta ministrov.* Saint Petersburg.

Starr, S. Frederick. *Decentralization and Self-Government in Russia, 1830–1870.* Princeton: Princeton University Press, 1972.

Stavrou, Theofanis George, ed. *Russia under the Last Tsar.* Minneapolis: University of Minnesota Press, 1969.

Stenograficheskie otchety 1-go i 2-go vserossiiskago s'ezda zemskikh deiatelei v Moskve. Moscow, 1907.

Sternheimer, Stephen. "Administering Development and Developing Administration: Organizational Conflict in the Tsarist Bureaucracy, 1906–1914." *Canadian-American Slavic Studies* 9 (Fall 1975):277–301.

Strakhovskii, I. M. *Gubernskoe ustroistvo.* Saint Petersburg, 1913.

――――. *Krest'ianskiia prava i uchrezhdeniia.* Saint Petersburg, 1903.

Strakhovsky, L. I. "The Statesmanship of Peter Stolypin: A Reappraisal." *Slavonic and East European Review* 37 (June 1959):348–370.

――――. "Stolypin and the Second Duma." *Canadian Slavonic Papers* 6 (1964):3–18.

Svod postanovlenii I-X s'ezdov upolnomochennykh ob'edinennykh dvorianskikh obshchestv, 1906–1914gg. Petrograd, 1915.

Svod vysochaishe otmetok po vsepoddanneishim otchetam gubernatorov za 1897–1902gg. Saint Petersburg, 1898–1907.

Svod zakonov Rossiiskoi Imperii. Saint Petersburg, 1912.

Szeftel, Marc. *The Russian Constitution of April 23, 1906.* Brussels, 1976.

Tarasov, I. T. *Lektsii po politseiskomu (administrativnomu) pravu.* 3 vols. Moscow, 1908.

Tenishev, V. V. *Administrativnoe polozhenie russkago krest'ianina.* Saint Petersburg, 1908.

Thurston, Robert W. "Police and People in Moscow, 1906–1914." *Russian Review* 39 (July 1980):320–338.

Tilly, Charles. "Does Modernization Breed Revolution?" *Comparative Politics* 5 (April 1973):425–447.

Timberlake, Charles E., ed. *Essays on Russian Liberalism.* Columbia, Mo.: University of Missouri Press, 1972.

Tokmakoff, George. "P. A. Stolypin and the Second Duma." *Slavonic and East European Review* 50 (January 1972):49–62.

Treadgold, Donald W. "Was Stolypin in Favor of Kulaks?" *Slavic Review* 14 (February 1955):1–14.

Trudy I-IV s'ezda upolnomochennykh dvorianskikh obshchestv 32 gubernii. Saint Petersburg, 1906–1909.

Turkin, V. *Biurokratiia.* Moscow, 1906.

Urusov, S. D. *Zapiski gubernatora: Kishinev 1903–1904g.* Moscow, 1907.

Ustoev, S. *Mestnoe samoupravlenie: kritika proekta P. A. Stolypina ob unishtozhenii obshchiny.* Saint Petersburg, 1908.

Uvarov, A. A. *Doklad grafa A. A. Uvarova po proektu reformy zemskago izbiratel'nago zakona.* Saratov, 1907.

Vaisberg, I. D. "Sovet ob'edinennogo dvorianstva i ego vliianie na politiku

BIBLIOGRAPHY

samoderzhaviia (1906–1914gg.)." Kandidatskaia dissertatsiia, Moscow University, 1956.

Verkhopatskii, E. *Gosudarstvennaia deiatel'nost' predsedatelia soveta ministrov stats-sekretaria Petra Arkad'evicha Stolypina.* 3 vols. Saint Petersburg, 1911.

Veselovskii, B. B. *Istoriia zemstva za sorok let.* 4 vols. Saint Petersburg, 1911.

————. *K voprosu o klassovykh interesakh v zemstve.* Saint Petersburg, 1905.

————. *Krest'ianskii vopros i krest'ianskoe dvizhenie v Rossii (1902–1906gg.).* Saint Petersburg, 1907.

Veselovskii, B. B., and Frenkel, Z. G., eds. *Iubileinyi zemskii sbornik.* Saint Petersburg, 1914.

Vodovozov, V. V., ed. *Sbornik programm politicheskikh partii v Rossii.* 6 vols. Saint Petersburg, 1905–1906.

Volkov, N., ed. *Zakony o politsii.* Moscow, 1910.

Vol'tke, G. *Osnovnyia cherty zhelatel'noi organizatsii uezdnago upravleniia v sviazi s ustroistvom melkoi zemskoi edinitsy.* Saint Petersburg, 1905.

Von Laue, Theodore H. "Count Witte and the 1905 Revolution." *Slavic Review* 17 (February 1958):25–46.

————. *Sergei Witte and the Industrialization of Russia.* New York: Columbia University Press, 1963.

Vserossiiskii s'ezd krest'ian-staroobriadtsev. *Materialy po voprosam zemel'nomu i krest'ianskomu.* Moscow, 1906.

Vysochaishe uchrezhdennaia kommisiia dlia peresmotra zakonopolozhenii po sudebnoi chasti. *Trudy.* Saint Petersburg, 1895.

Vysochaishe uchrezhdennoe osoboe soveshchanie po peresmotru ustanov-lennykh dlia okhrany gosudarstvennago poriadka iskliuchitel'nykh zakonopolozhenii. *Materialy.* Saint Petersburg.

————. *Zhurnal.* Saint Petersburg.

Wagner, W. G. "Tsarist Legal Policies at the End of the Nineteenth Century: A Study in Inconsistencies." *Slavonic and East European Review* 54 (July 1976):371–394.

Wallace, Donald Mackenzie. *Russia on the Eve of War and Revolution.* New York: Random House, 1961.

Weissman, Neil B. "Rural Crime in Tsarist Russia: The Question of Hooliganism, 1900–1914." *Slavic Review* 37 (June 1978):228–240.

Witte, Sergei Iu. *Samoderzhavie i zemstvo.* Stuttgart, 1903.

————. *Vospominaniia.* 3 vols. Moscow, 1960.

————. *Zapiska po krest'ianskomu delu.* Saint Petersburg, 1905.

Wortman, Richard. *The Development of a Russian Legal Consciousness.* Chicago: University of Chicago Press, 1976.

Yaney, George L. "The Concept of the Stolypin Land Reform." *Slavic Review* 23 (June 1964):275–293.

————. "The Imperial Russian Government and the Stolypin Land Reform." Ph.D. dissertation, Princeton University, 1961.

————. "Law, Society and the Domestic Regime in Russia in Historical Perspective." *American Political Science Review* 59 (June 1965):379–390.

BIBLIOGRAPHY

————. "Some Aspects of the Imperial Russian Government on the Eve of the First World War." *Slavonic and East European Review* 43 (December 1964):68–90.

————. *The Systematization of Russian Government: Social Evolution in the Domestic Administration of Imperial Russia, 1711–1905.* Urbana, Ill.: University of Illinois Press, 1973.

Zaionchkovskii, P. A. *Pravitel'stvennyi apparat samoderzhavnoi Rossii v XIXv.* Moscow, 1978.

————. *Rossiiskoe samoderzhavie v kontse XIX stoletiia (politicheskaia reaktsiia 80-kh—nachala 90-kh godov).* Moscow, 1970.

Zakharova, L. G. *Zemskaia kontrreforma 1890g.* Moscow, 1968.

Zakliuchenie s'ezda upolnomochennykh ob'edinennykh dvorianskikh obshchestv po voprosu o mestnoi reforme. Saratov, 1908.

Zenkovskii, A. V. *Pravda o Stolypine.* New York, 1956.

Zhurnaly i postanovleniia vserossiiskago s'ezda zemskikh deiatelei v Moskve s 10 po 15 iiunia 1907 goda. Moscow, 1907.

Zyrianov, P. N. "Krakh vnutrennei politiki tret'eiiunskoi monarkhii v oblasti mestnogo upravleniia (1907–1914gg.)." Kandidatskaia dissertatsiia, Moscow University, 1972.

————. "Tret'eiiunskaia monarkhiia v sovremennoi amerikanskoi istoriografii." *Istoriia SSSR,* no. 5 (1970), pp. 188–204.

————. "Tret'ia duma i vopros o reforme mestnogo suda i volostnogo upravleniia." *Istoriia SSSR,* no. 6 (1969), pp. 45–62.

INDEX

INDEX

Ershov, M. D., 166
estates, 17, 97, 103, 121, 178; Cadets on, 108, 150; gentry on, 117-118, 171-175, 178, 221, 223-224; Pleve and, 66-76, 87-88; role of, 7, 11-14, 18-20, 27-30; Stolypin and, 138, 142-144, 154, 158. *See also* gentry; peasantry
European Herald, 57, 59
Evreinov, A. V., 84, 86, 112, 245n63

F

field courts-martial, 109, 121, 249-250n51
France, 11, 145-146, 170-171, 173, 184
Frish, V. E., 209-211

G

Garin, N. P., 207
Geiden, P. A., 163
gendarmes, 48-49, 84, 205, 210, 213-214, 219
gentry, 64, 95, 144-145, 148; administrative role of, 12-14, 16, 22, 27-28; on bureaucracy, 36-38, 86-89, 115-117, 170-175, 184-189; Cadets and, 108; definition of, 13, 233n23, 234n56; hostility to reform, 5, 111-118, 160-164, 168-175, 178, 184-189, 191-192, 201, 221-224; Pleve and, 42, 49, 74-76, 86-89; Stolypin and, 127, 143-144, 160-162, 170-175, 184-189, 194, 226; Tolstoi and, 18-20, 30, 75. *See also* estates; gentry marshal
gentry marshal, 30, 89, 236n95; defense of, 88, 117, 171-172, 174, 184-186; and liberalism, 30, 114, 117, 172; Pleve and, 49, 75, 87-88; role of, 13, 16, 19, 27, 253n20; Stolypin and, 132, 143, 184-186, 197, 255n59

Gerbel, S. N., 82, 103, 128, 130, 214
Germany. *See* Prussia
Gessen, V. M., 33-34, 35, 162
Glebov, Iu. N., 164-165, 191-196
Glishinskii, A. A., 213
Golitsyn, A. D., 78, 120, 122, 164, 179-180, 182, 186, 189, 193
Golovin, F. A., 86, 119, 122
Golovin, K. F., 59, 88, 241n62, 246n73
Goremykin, I. L., 125, 149, 153, 159, 197, 204, 252n3, 257n14-257n15
governor, 13, 196, 219, 226; Cadets on, 110, 131, 150-151; debate over, 51-54, 57-59, 155, 183, 186-188; Pleve and, 48-52, 55, 75; and police, 213, 215-216; role of, 10, 19, 25-26, 44-46, 78-79; Stolypin and, 131-132, 186-187; views of, 51-54, 187-188, 213, 240n39-240n40. *See also* province
Govorukho-Otrok, M. Ia., 112-113
Gradovskii, A. D., 8
Great Reforms, 15, 17, 18, 43-44
Grimm, K. N., 113, 161
Gronskii, P. P., 219
Guchkov, A. I., 118-119, 121, 163, 200, 202
Gudovich, V. V., 30, 250n63
Gurko, V. I., 78, 128-130, 132, 146, 204, 246n72, 252n3, 257n14; on agrarian reform, 67, 69-70, 116, 129; appointment of, 71-72; on local government, 26-28, 70-72, 103-104, 174; and United Nobility, 174, 261n89
Gurliand, I. Ia., 103, 130, 174, 197; on provincial reform debate, 185-189; views of, 128, 131-132, 134, 196, 255n59

H

hundreder. *See* police, village

INDEX

INDEX

R

Raevskii, N. V., 113, 250n60
Reztsov, N. A., 119
Rikhter, N. F., 119-120, 122, 179-180, 182, 184, 189
Rittikh, A. A., 101
Rodzianko, M. V., 163, 217
Russia, 128, 131, 197
Russian Word, 215

S

Samarin, A. D., 117, 169-171, 186, 189
Samarin, F. D., 38, 169-172, 224, 261n86
Saratov Zemstvo Weekly, 113, 115
Savitskii, N. P., 189
school council, 49, 184
self-government, 13, 45; definition of, 15-17, 78-80, 136-142, 194-195, 233n28; establishment of, 14-15; liberals and, 32-36, 89, 108-110, 149-151; Octobrists on, 120-121, 163-168, 179-182, 194-195; Pleve and, 43, 67, 76-87, 147; Stolypin and, 136-142, 147, 153-154; Sviatopolk-Mirskii on, 96-97; Tolstoi and, 19-20, 87. *See also* decentralization; participation; town council; zemstvo
Senate, 56, 58, 96, 117, 185
sergeants, 10-11, 14, 23, 30, 62-63, 97, 101, 211, 219, 241n64, 242n7
settlement. *See* zemstvo, local
Shakhovskoi, D. I., 77
Shcheglovitov, I. G., 134, 159
Shcherbin, F. A., 85
Sheremetev, P. S., 260n73
Shingarev, A. I., 191-192, 195-197
Shipov, D. N., 32, 34, 38, 73, 81, 86, 90, 95, 106; and Octobrism, 118-119, 121-122; on Pleve, 77, 85
Siberian Life, 217

Simonova, M. S., 243n9
Sipiagin, D. S., 40, 41, 62, 68, 71, 72, 80, 91
Skarzhinskii, P. V., 203
Snezhkov, V. N., 116, 173, 261n85
Social Democrats, 94, 106-107, 130, 191
Socialist Revolutionaries, 69, 90, 105, 106-107
Sozonovich, I. P., 192
Special Conference on the Needs of Agriculture, 36, 97, 101, 245n49; on local reform, 36; organization of, 36, 68, 237n116; Pleve and, 68, 83, 85, 242n4; on police, 61-62
Stakhovich, M. A., 30, 34, 86-87, 114, 118, 121, 163-164, 259n49
state bureaucracy. *See* bureaucracy
State Council, 71, 75, 81, 86, 154; composition of, 199; on police reform, 62, 64-65; and Saint Petersburg urban reform, 82, 245n56; Sviatopolk-Mirskii and, 96, 98; on volost zemstvo, 203-204, 265n88; and western zemstvo, 199-202
State Duma. *See* Duma
Stishinskii, A. S., 69, 71, 96, 115, 160-161
Stishinskii Commission, 69, 71-75, 243n9
Stolypin, A. A., 251n79
Stolypin, P. A., 92, 129; and agrarian reform, 115-116, 126, 129, 143-144, 154, 175, 183, 190-191, 223, 226, 253n13; and bureaucracy, 131-136, 139-142, 145-147, 154, 183-190, 195, 202, 254n39; career of, 126-127, 158-159, 200, 256n63; and Council on Local Affairs, 168, 172, 176-190; and estates, 132, 142-144, 147, 154; and First Duma, 152; gentry and, 115-116, 132, 143, 160-162, 170, 175; on legality, 133-136, 140-142,

INDEX

INDEX